I received a ton of ...rds addressed to ...eireitei Bulletin ...as included in the ... material of *Color ...h+*, which went on sale last summer [in 2007]. The editorial office still gets them once in a while too. I don't know how or why they get delivered, but the Japanese postal service really is amazing.

-Tite Kubo

BLEACH is author Tite Kubo's second title. Kubo made his debut with *ZOMBIEPOWDER.*, a four-volume series for *WEEKLY SHONEN JUMP*. To date, *BLEACH* has been translated into numerous languages and has also inspired an animated TV series that began airing in the U.S. in 2006. Beginning its serialization in 2001, *BLEACH* is still a mainstay in the pages of *WEEKLY SHONEN JUMP*. In 2005, *BLEACH* was awarded the prestigious Shogakukan Manga Award in the *shonen* (boys) category.

BLEACH
Vol. 33: THE BAD JOKE
SHONEN JUMP Manga Edition
This volume contains material that was originally published in English
in SHONEN JUMP #92–95. Artwork in the magazine may have been
altered slightly from what is presented in this volume.

STORY AND ART BY
TITE KUBO

English Adaptation/Lance Caselman
Translation/Joe Yamazaki
Touch-up Art & Lettering/Mark McMurray
Design/Sean Lee
Editors/Pancha Diaz, Yuki Takagaki

Printed in the U.S.A.

Published by VIZ Media, LLC
P.O. Box 77010
San Francisco, CA 94107

10 9 8 7 6 5 4 3 2 1
First printing, December 2010

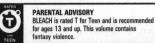

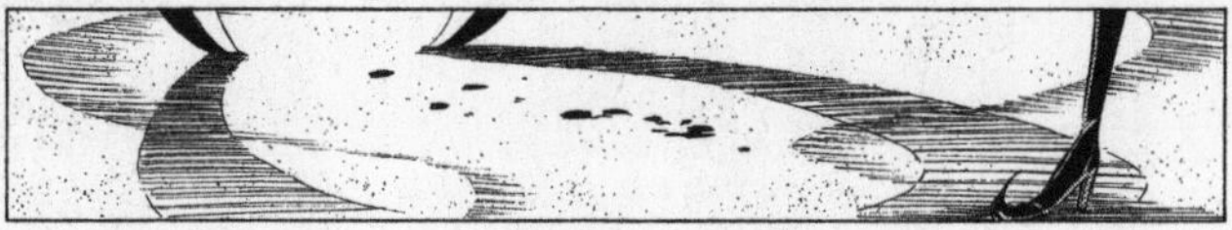

We are insects,

Parasitic worms writhing in
malicious constancy,

Soaring past the moon you
look up to

Until you pathetic creatures
are no longer visible.

BLEACH 33 THE BAD JOKE

Shonen Jump Manga

STARS AND

Nel

Nnoitora

Ichigo Kurosaki

plot

When high school student Ichigo Kurosaki meets Soul Reaper Rukia Kuchiki his life is changed forever. Soon Ichigo is a soul-cleansing Soul Reaper too, and he finds himself having adventures, as well as problems, that he never would have imagined. Now Ichigo and his friends must stop renegade Soul Reaper Aizen and his army of Arrancars from destroying the Soul Society and wiping out KarakuraTown as well.

Having penetrated the enemy's stronghold Las Noches to rescue Orihime, Ichigo and his allies face one defeat after another at the hands of the Espadas. Ichigo is fatally wounded but revived by Orihime's powers, and he prevails against the Espada Grimmjow. But soon afterward, a new enemy appears before him!

BLEACH ALL

ザエルアポロ
Szayelaporro

Renji Abarai

石田雨竜
Uryû Ishida

阿散井恋次

STORIES

BLEACH 33

THE BAD JOKE

Contents

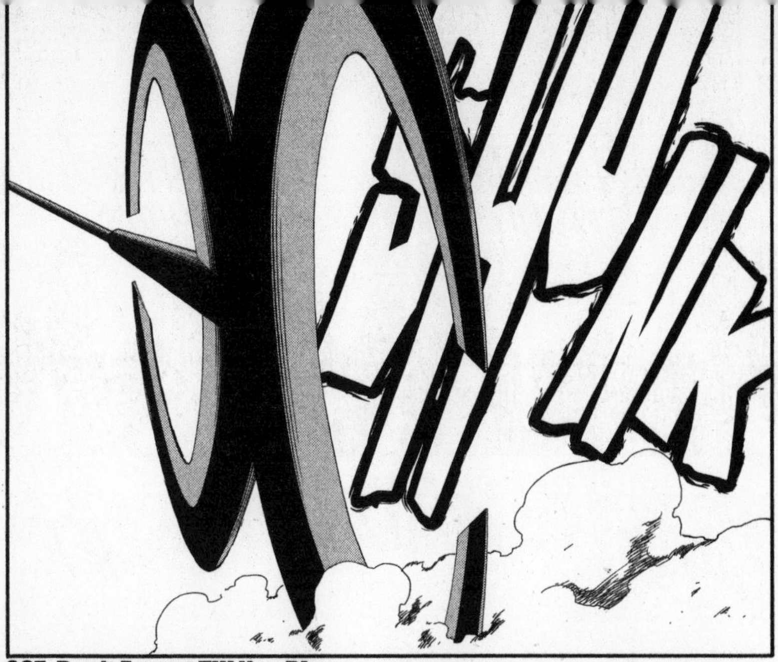
CHUNK

287. Don't Forget Till You Die

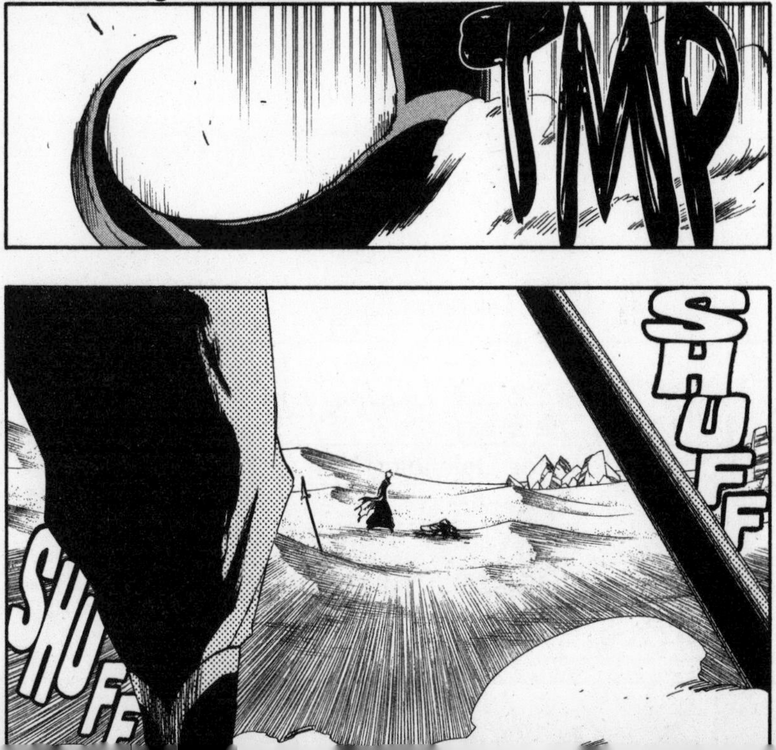
TMP
SHUFF
SHUFF

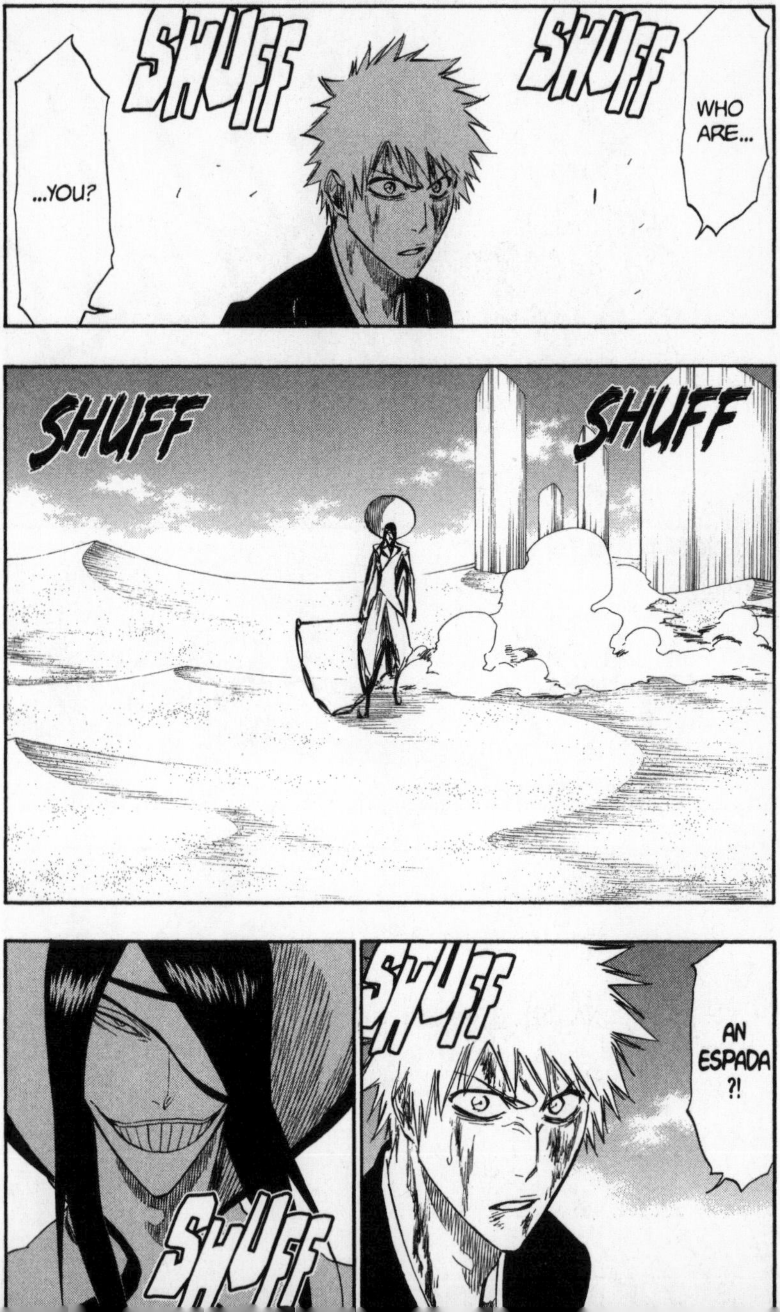
WHO ARE...
SHUFF
SHUFF
...YOU?
SHUFF
SHUFF
AN ESPADA ?!
SHUFF
SHUFF

READ THIS WAY

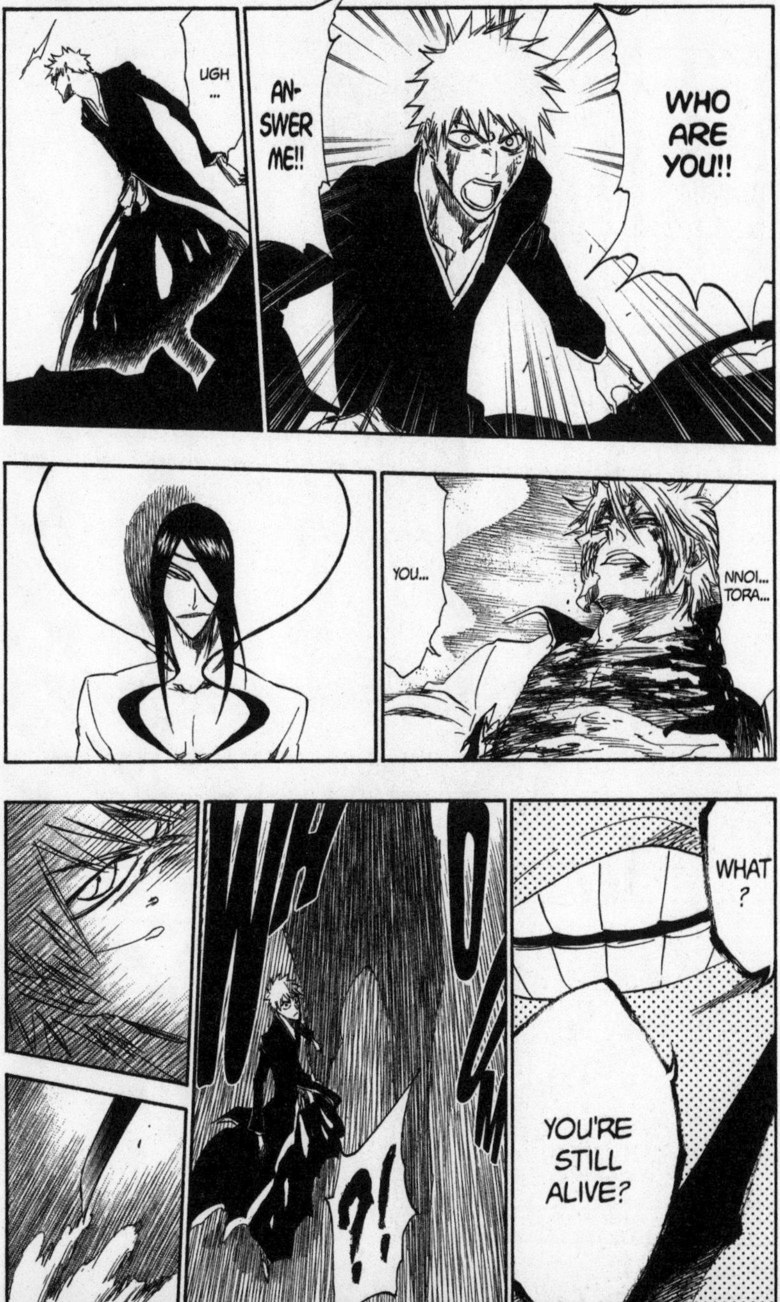
WHO ARE YOU!!
AN-SWER ME!!
UGH ...
NNOI... TORA...
YOU...
WHAT ?
YOU'RE STILL ALIVE?
?!

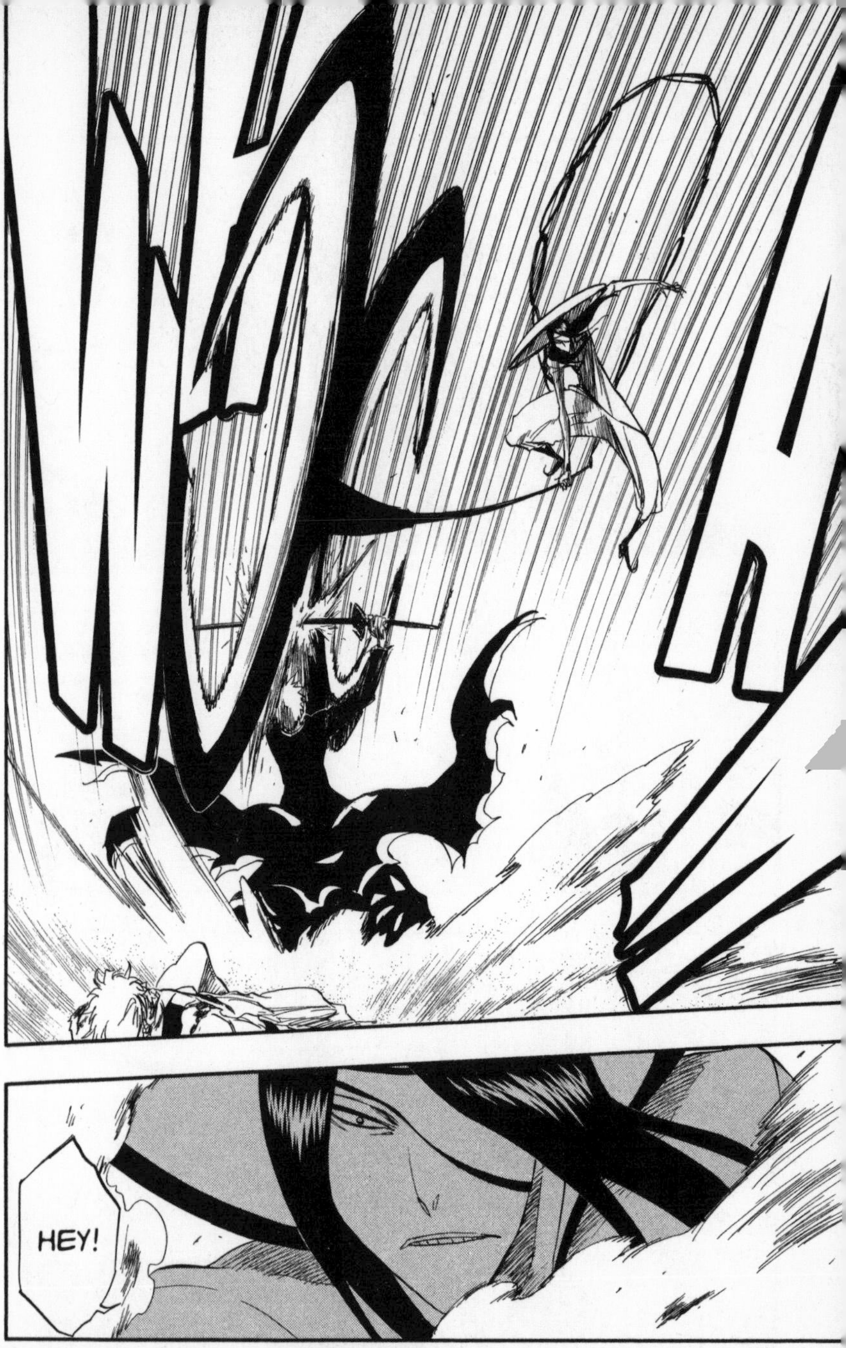
HEY!

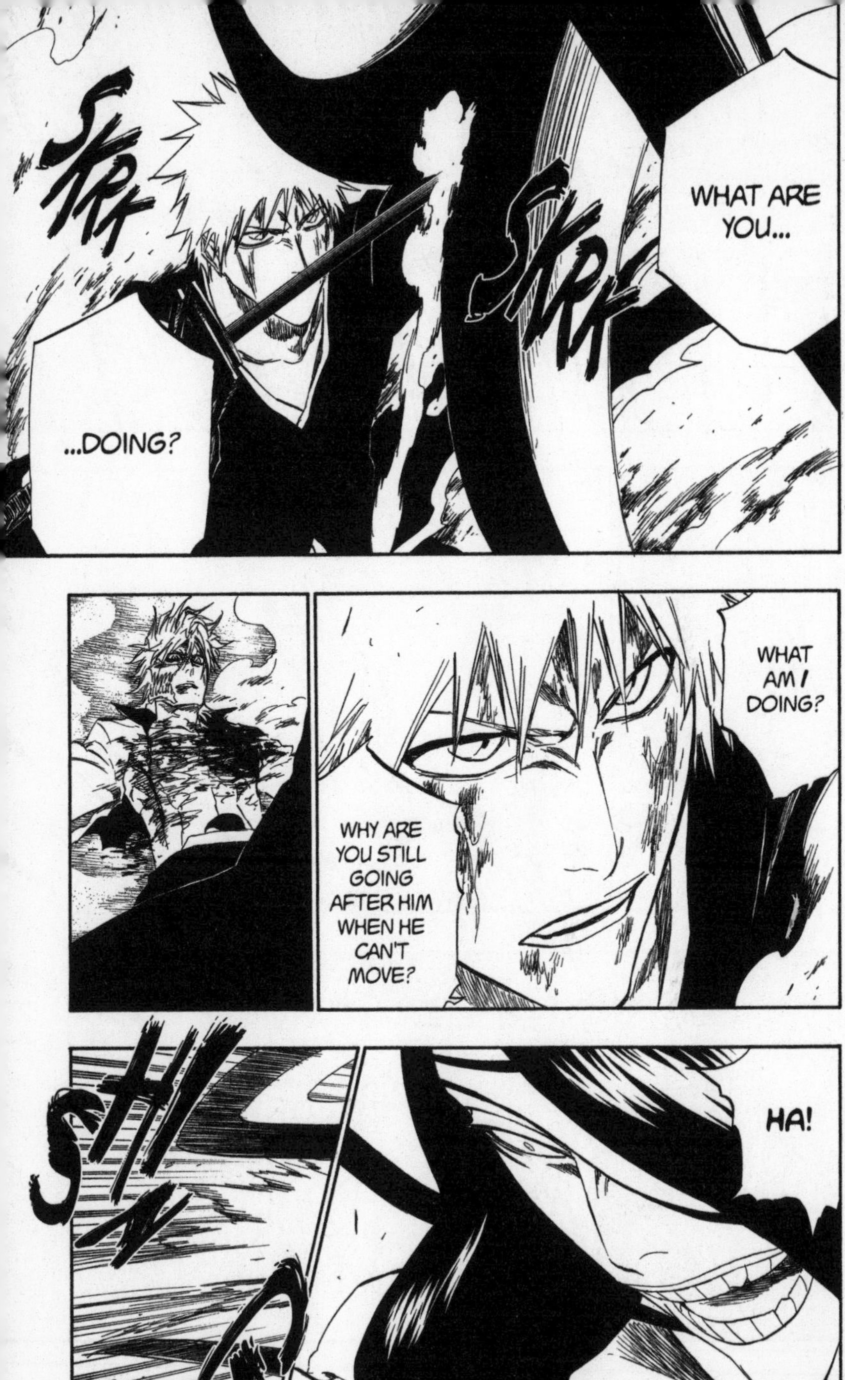
WHAT ARE YOU...
SKRK
SKRK
...DOING?
WHAT AM I DOING?
WHY ARE YOU STILL GOING AFTER HIM WHEN HE CAN'T MOVE?
HA!

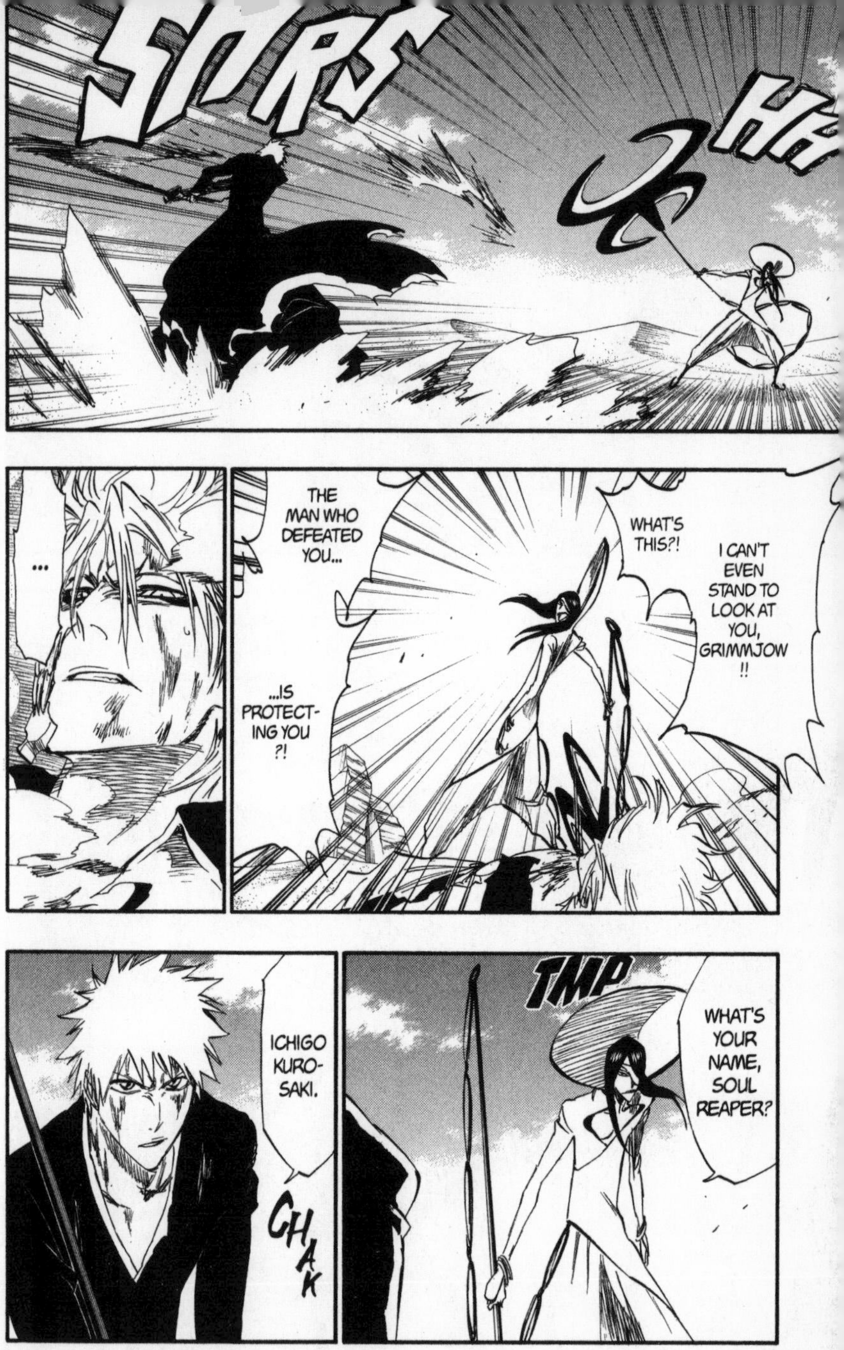
HA
I CAN'T EVEN STAND TO LOOK AT YOU, GRIMMJOW!!
WHAT'S THIS?!
THE MAN WHO DEFEATED YOU...
...IS PROTECTING YOU?!
...
TMP
WHAT'S YOUR NAME, SOUL REAPER?
ICHIGO KUROSAKI.
CHAK

READ THIS WAY

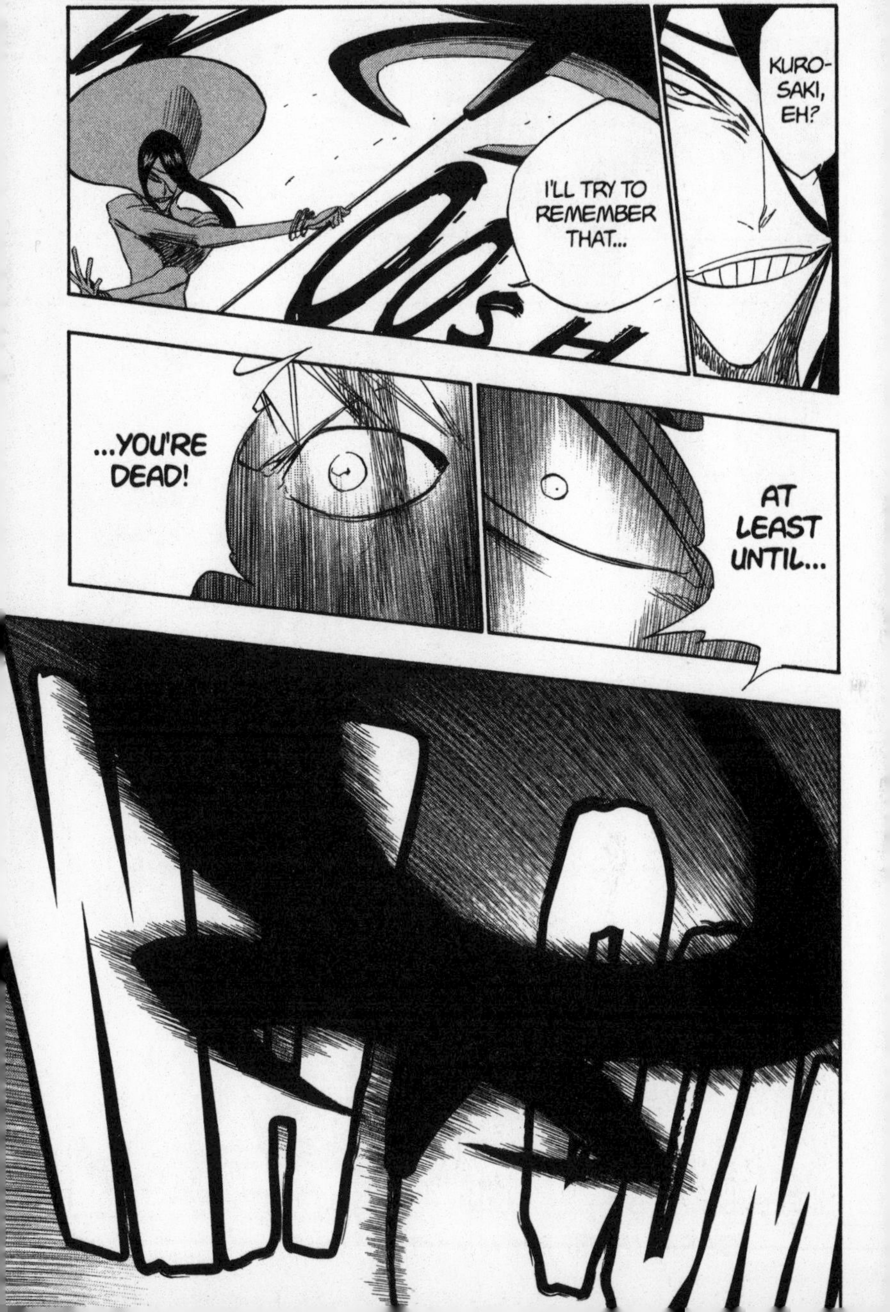
KURO-SAKI, EH?
I'LL TRY TO REMEMBER THAT...
WOOSH
AT LEAST UNTIL...
...YOU'RE DEAD!

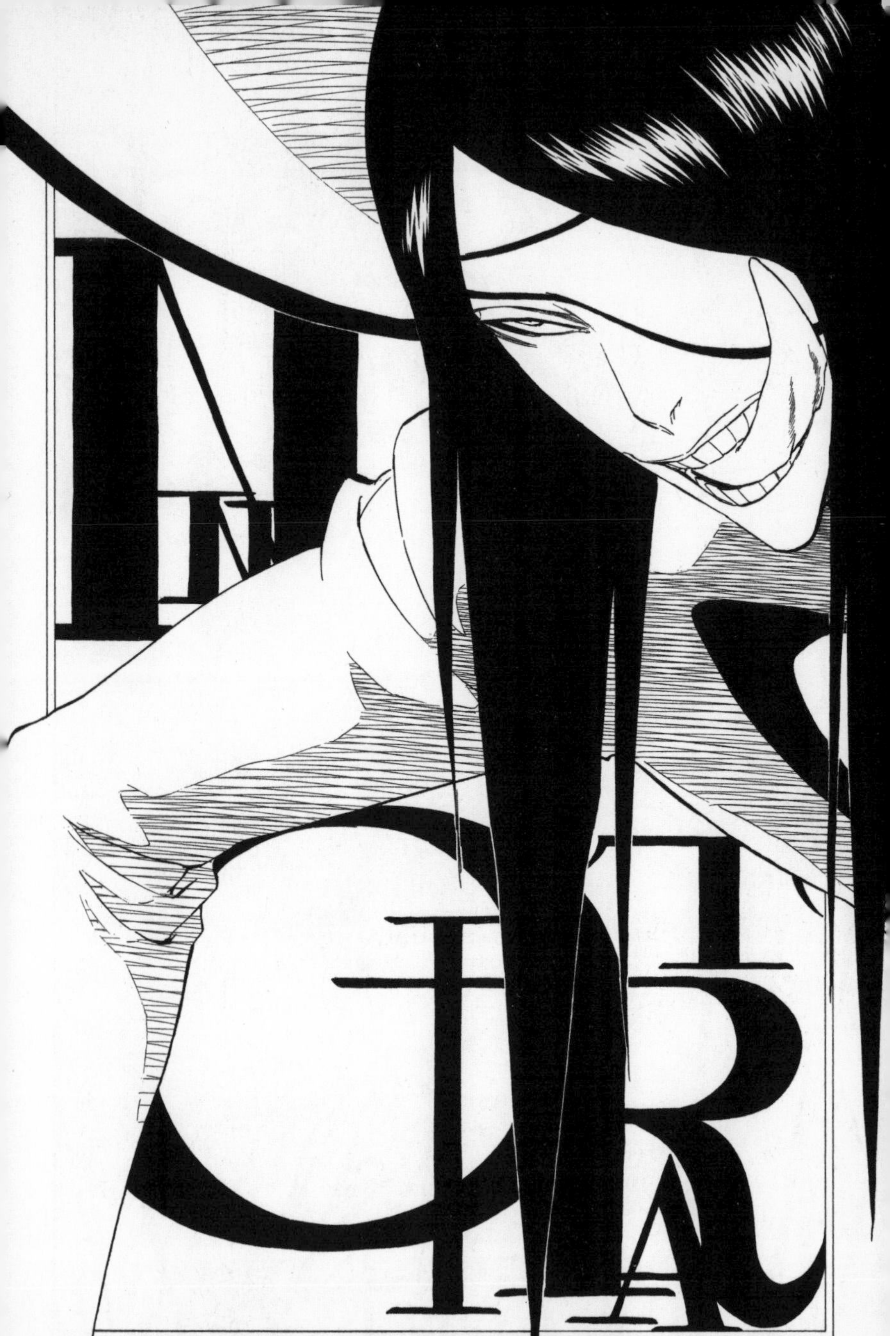

BLEACH 287. Don't Forget Till You Die

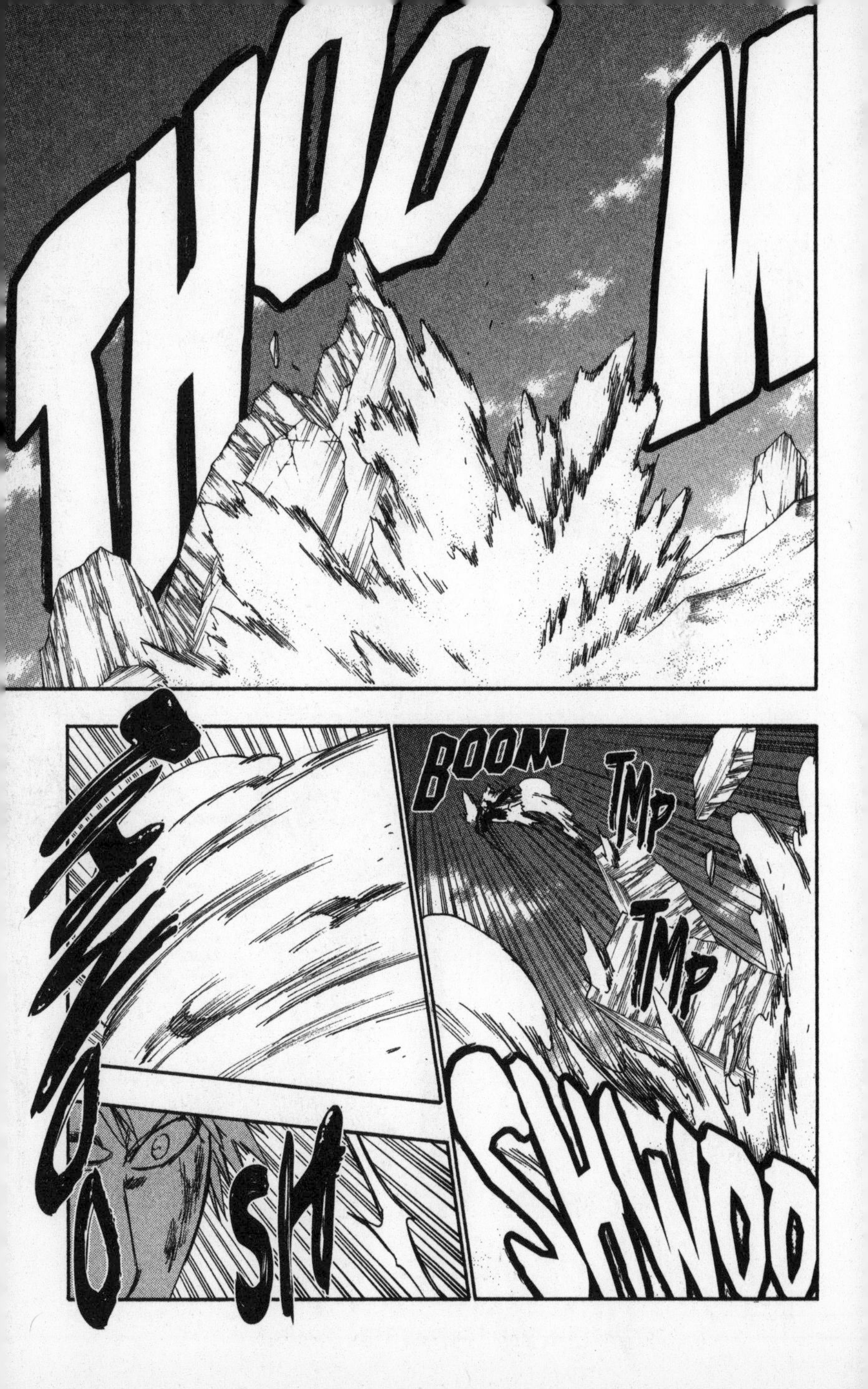
THOOM
BOOM
TMP
TMP
SHHOO

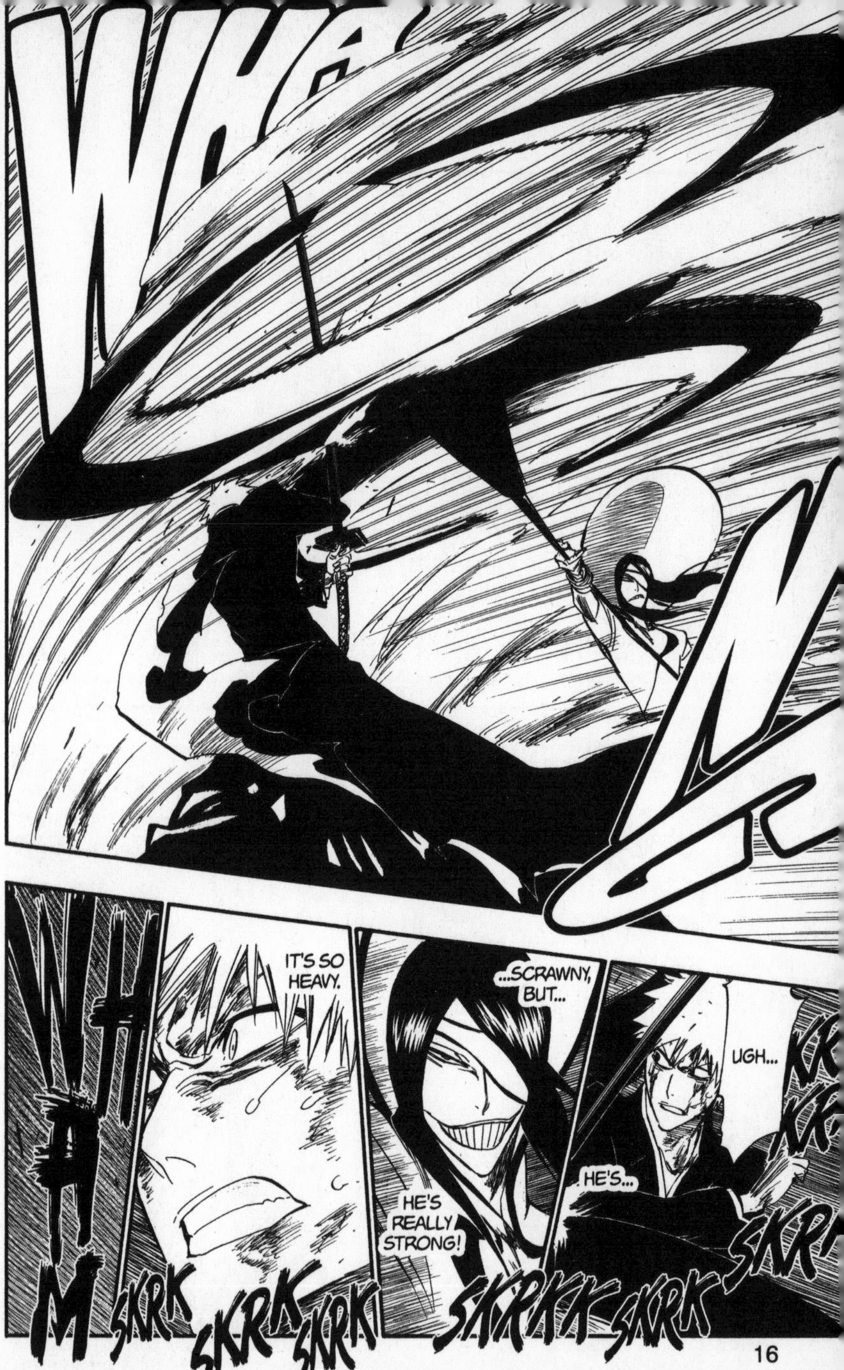
UGH...
HE'S...
SKRK
...SCRAWNY, BUT...
HE'S REALLY STRONG!
SKRKRK
IT'S SO HEAVY.
SKRK
SKRK
SKRK
WHAM

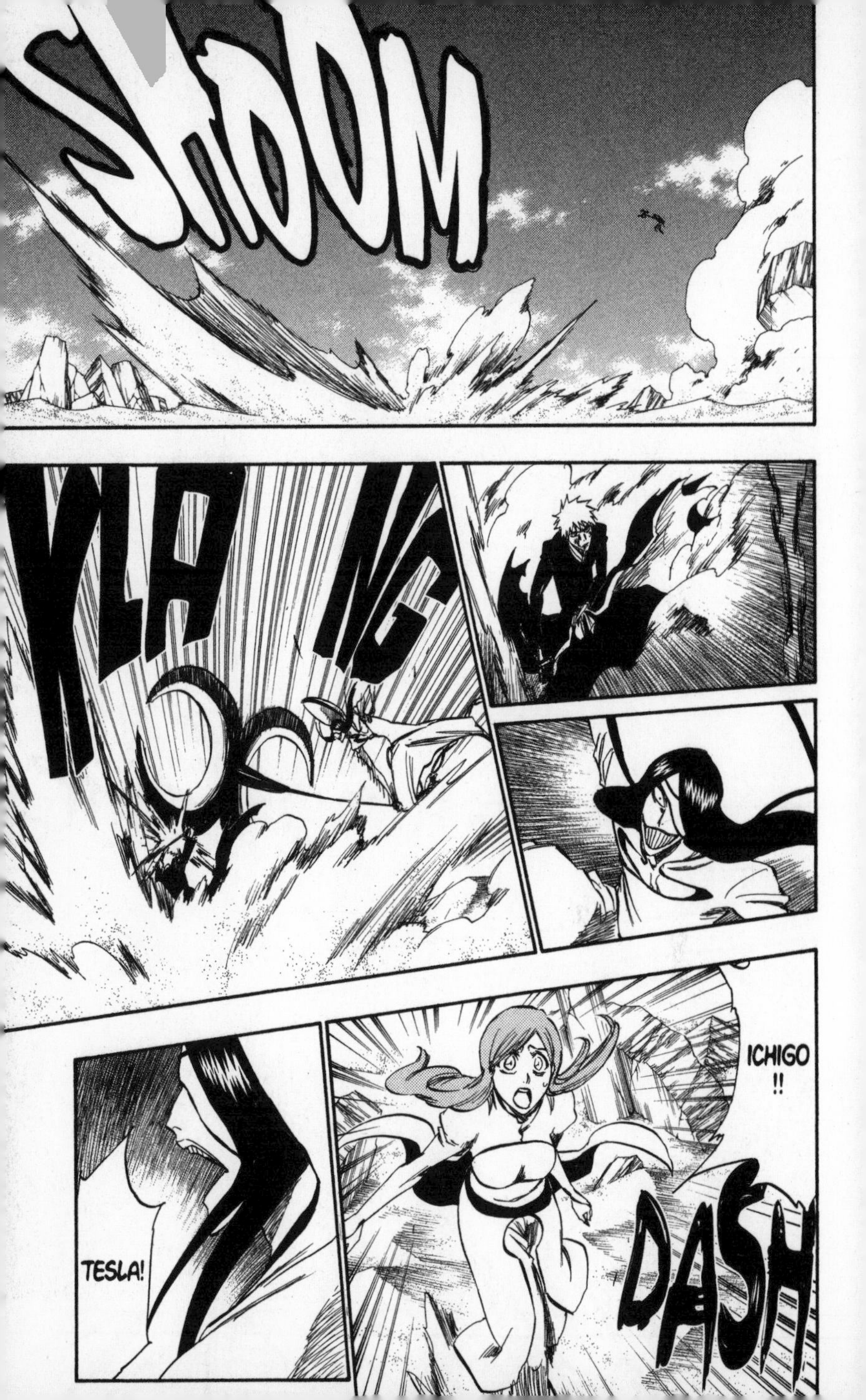
SHOOM
KLANG
ICHIGO !!
DASH
TESLA!

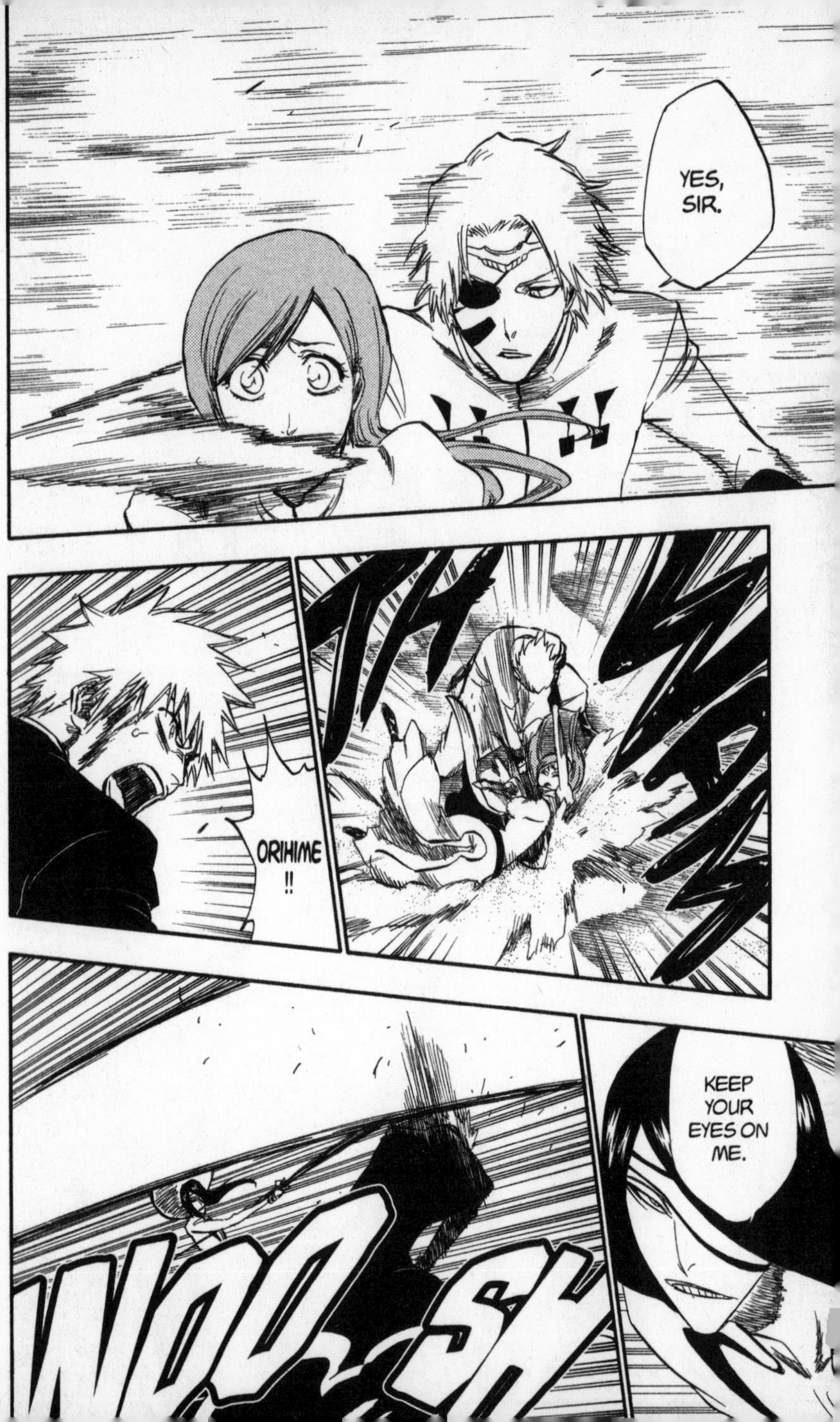
YES, SIR.
ORIHIME!!
KEEP YOUR EYES ON ME.

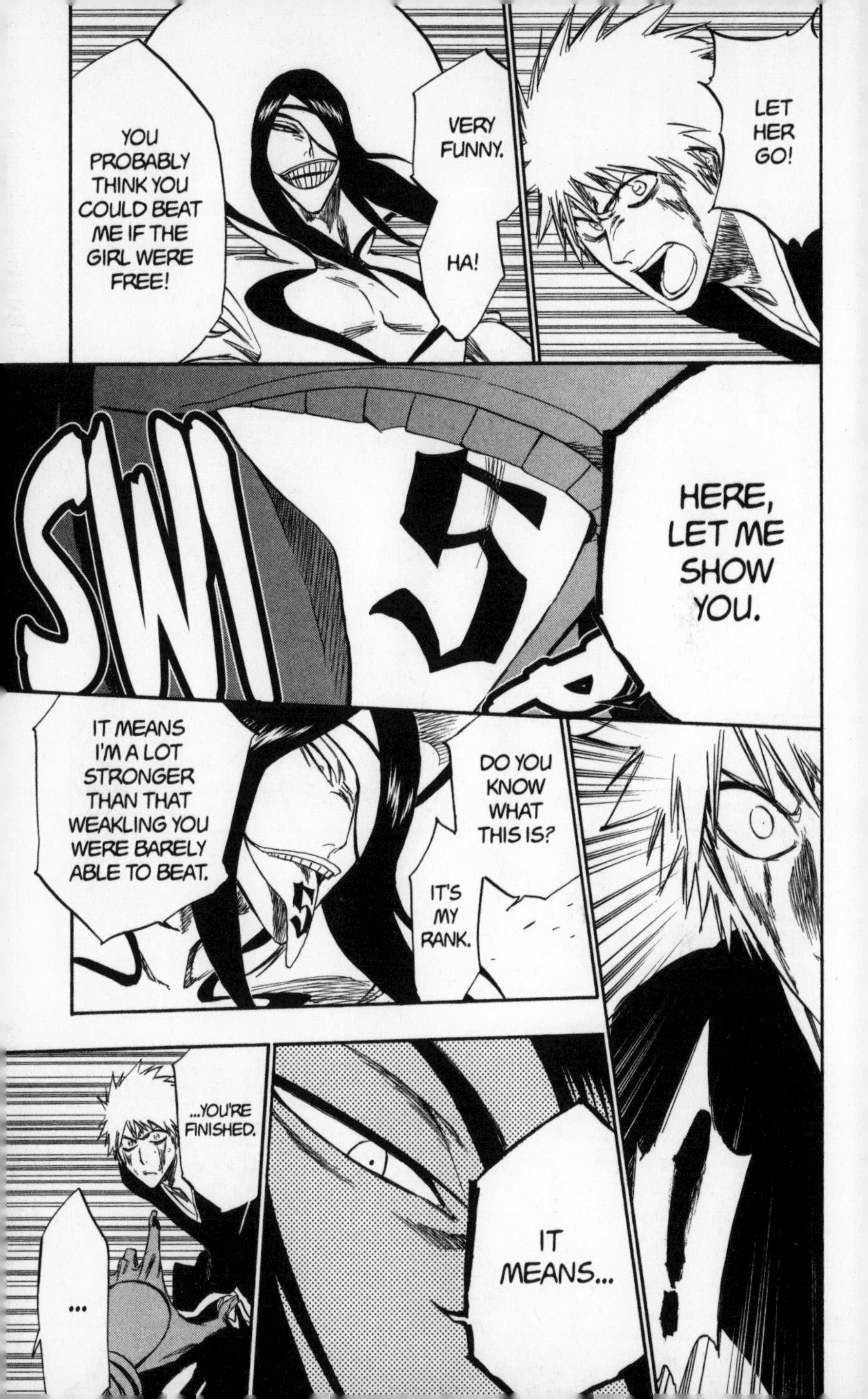
LET HER GO!
VERY FUNNY.
HA!
YOU PROBABLY THINK YOU COULD BEAT ME IF THE GIRL WERE FREE!
HERE, LET ME SHOW YOU.
DO YOU KNOW WHAT THIS IS?
IT'S MY RANK.
IT MEANS I'M A LOT STRONGER THAN THAT WEAKLING YOU WERE BARELY ABLE TO BEAT.
IT MEANS...
...YOU'RE FINISHED.
...

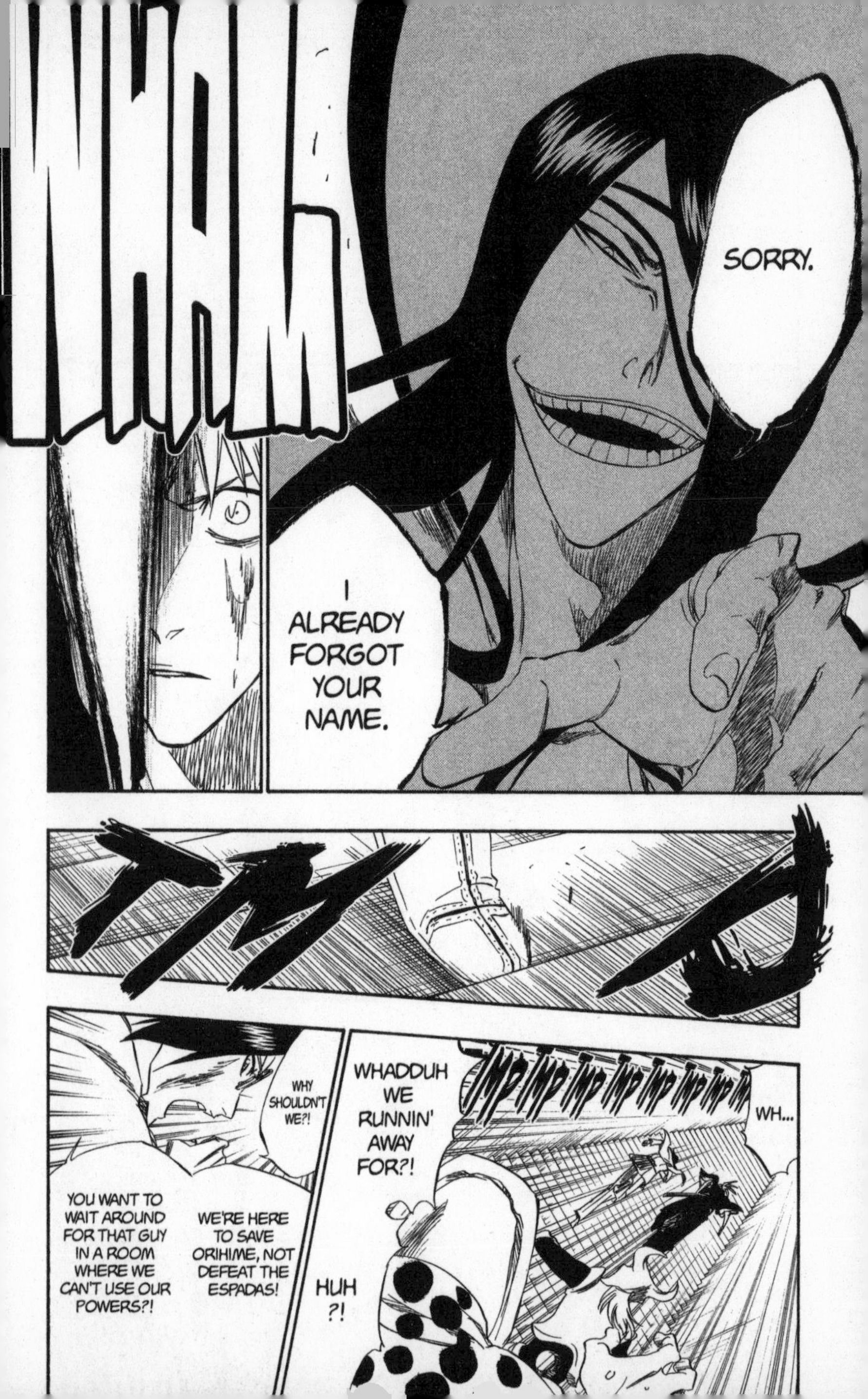
WHAM
SORRY.
I ALREADY FORGOT YOUR NAME.
TMP
WH...
WHADDUH WE RUNNIN' AWAY FOR?!
HUH ?!
WHY SHOULDN'T WE?!
WE'RE HERE TO SAVE ORIHIME, NOT DEFEAT THE ESPADAS!
YOU WANT TO WAIT AROUND FOR THAT GUY IN A ROOM WHERE WE CAN'T USE OUR POWERS?!

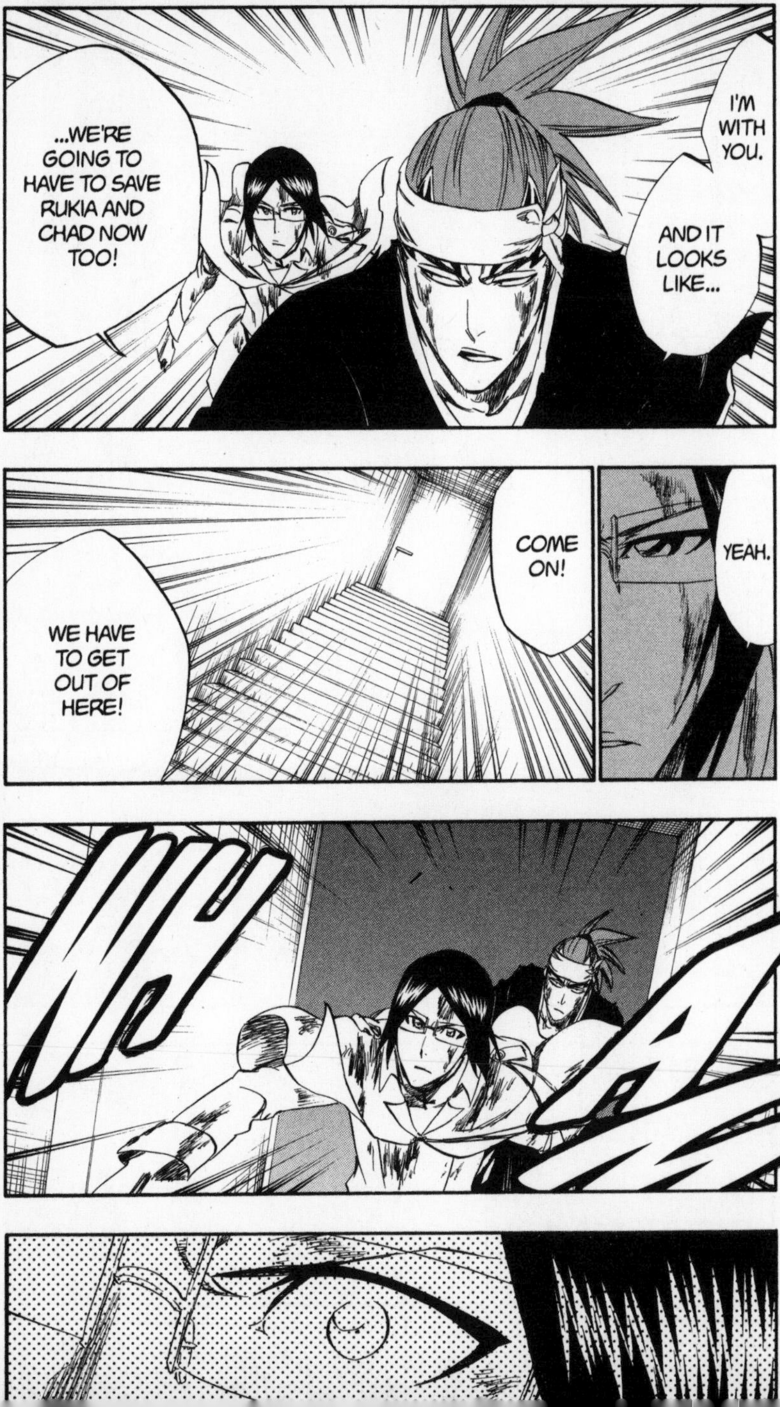
I'M WITH YOU.
AND IT LOOKS LIKE...
...WE'RE GOING TO HAVE TO SAVE RUKIA AND CHAD NOW TOO!
YEAH.
COME ON!
WE HAVE TO GET OUT OF HERE!

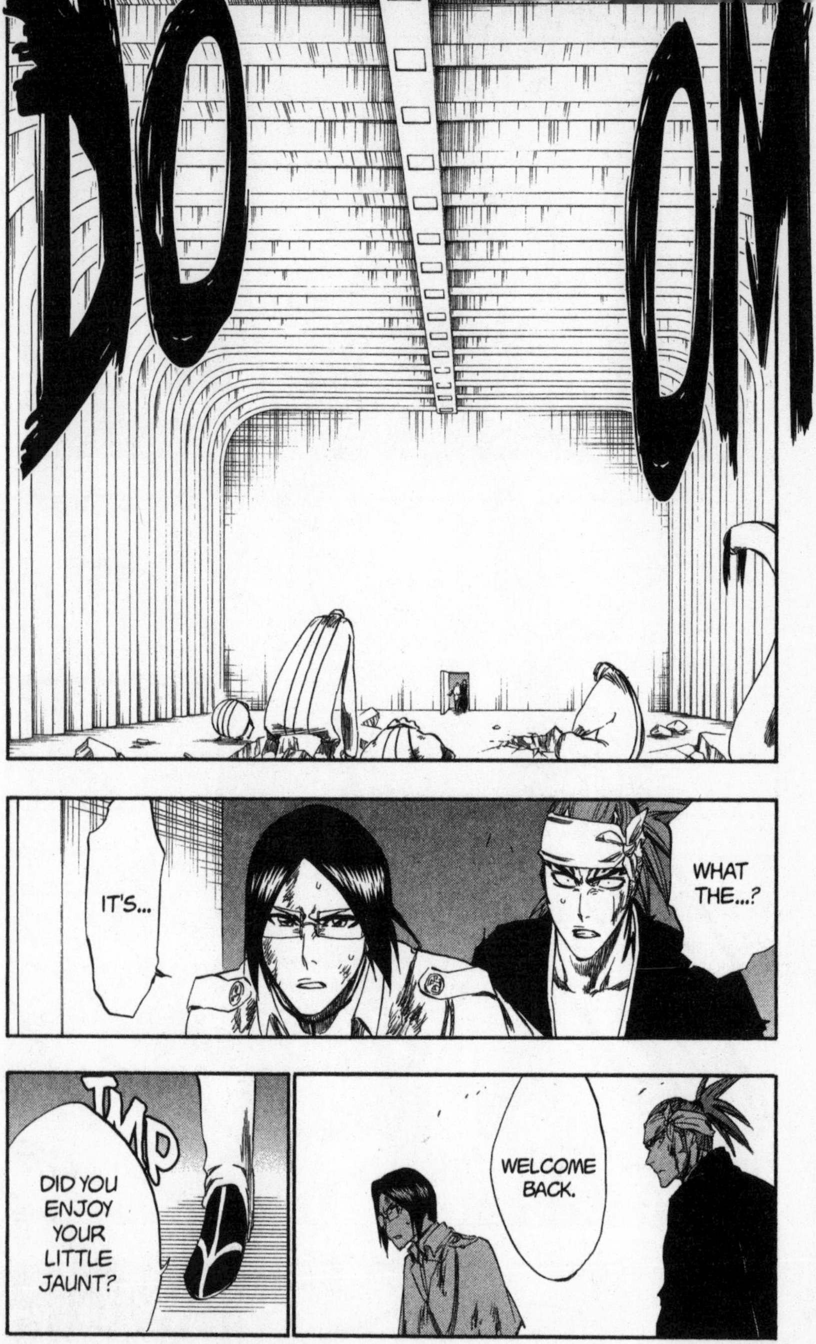
DO OM
WHAT THE...?
IT'S...
WELCOME BACK.
TMP
DID YOU ENJOY YOUR LITTLE JAUNT?

NOW THEN...

SHALL WE BEGIN THE SECOND ACT?

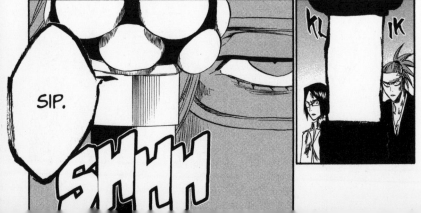

SIP.

SHHH

KL IK

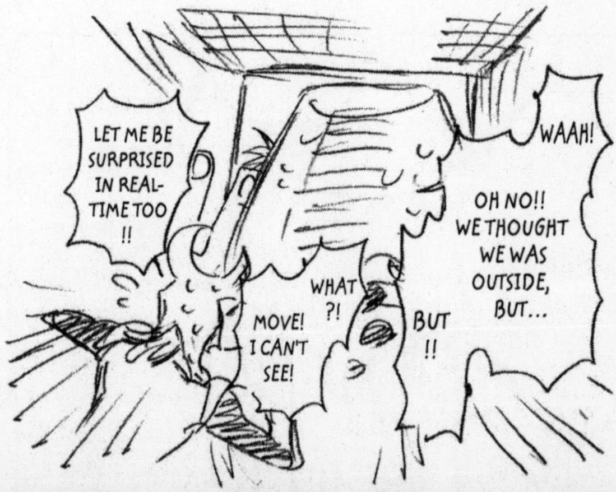
WAAH!
OH NO!! WE THOUGHT WE WAS OUTSIDE, BUT...
BUT !!
LET ME BE SURPRISED IN REAL-TIME TOO !!
WHAT ?!
MOVE! I CAN'T SEE!

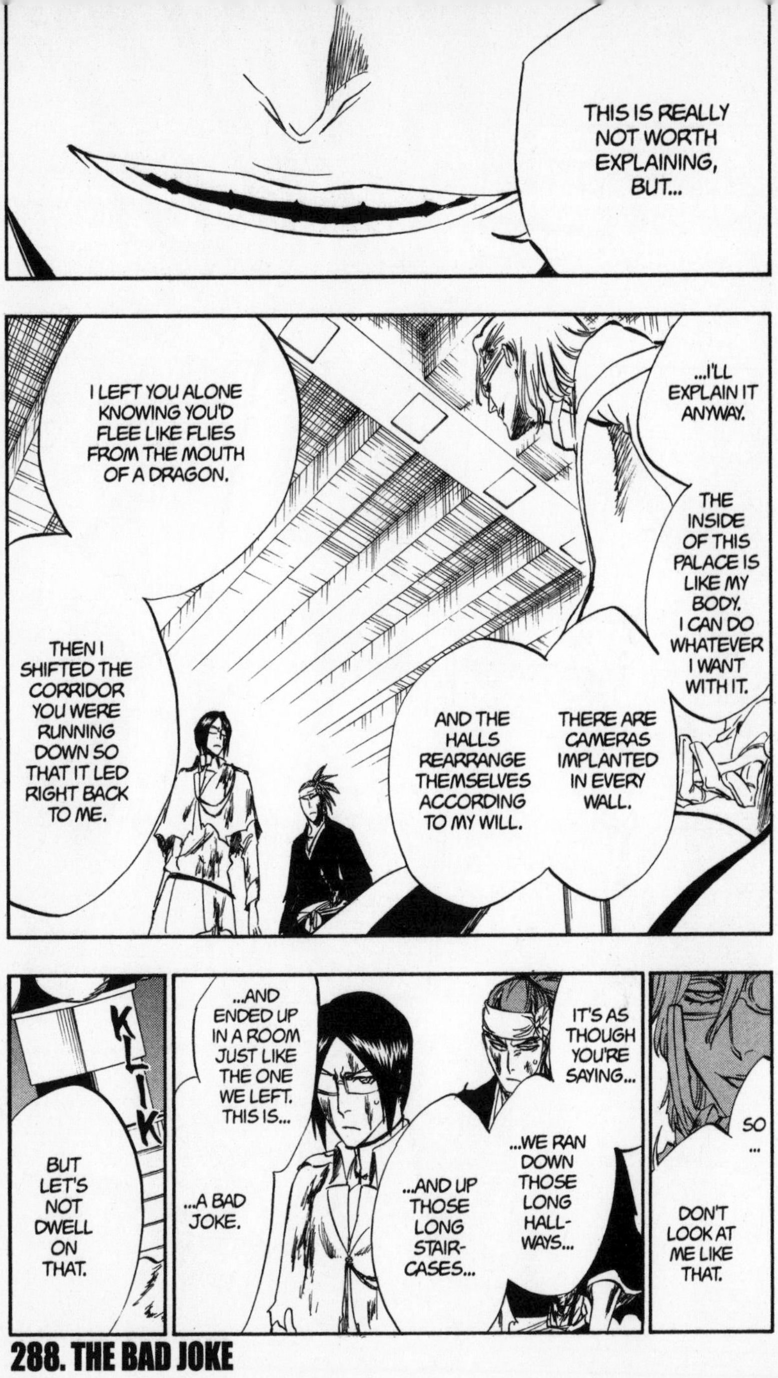
THIS IS REALLY NOT WORTH EXPLAINING, BUT...
...I'LL EXPLAIN IT ANYWAY.
THE INSIDE OF THIS PALACE IS LIKE MY BODY. I CAN DO WHATEVER I WANT WITH IT.
THERE ARE CAMERAS IMPLANTED IN EVERY WALL.
AND THE HALLS REARRANGE THEMSELVES ACCORDING TO MY WILL.
I LEFT YOU ALONE KNOWING YOU'D FLEE LIKE FLIES FROM THE MOUTH OF A DRAGON.
THEN I SHIFTED THE CORRIDOR YOU WERE RUNNING DOWN SO THAT IT LED RIGHT BACK TO ME.
SO ...
DON'T LOOK AT ME LIKE THAT.
IT'S AS THOUGH YOU'RE SAYING...
...WE RAN DOWN THOSE LONG HALL-WAYS...
...AND UP THOSE LONG STAIR-CASES...
...AND ENDED UP IN A ROOM JUST LIKE THE ONE WE LEFT. THIS IS...
...A BAD JOKE.
KLIK
BUT LET'S NOT DWELL ON THAT.

288. THE BAD JOKE

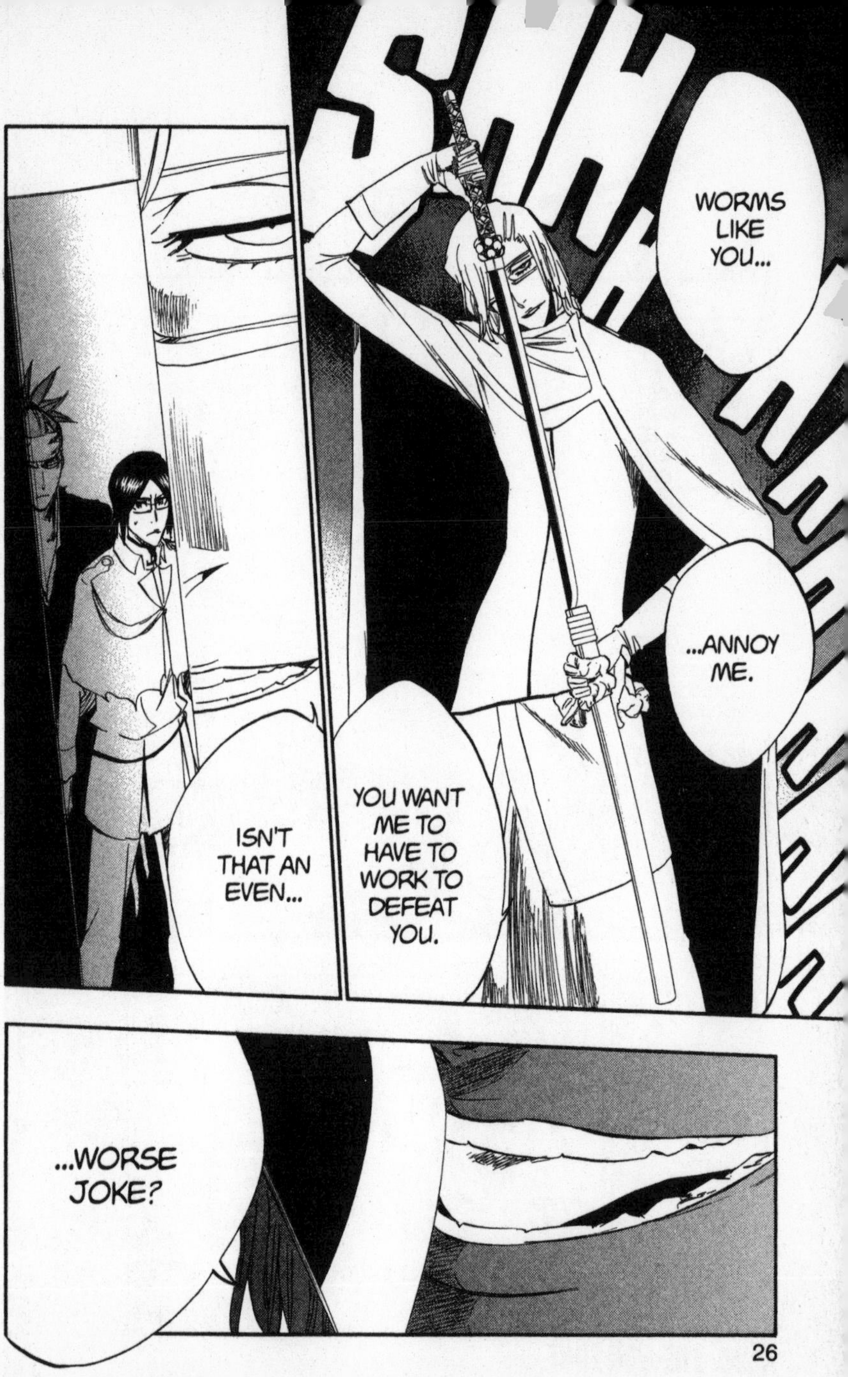
SHH
WORMS LIKE YOU...
...ANNOY ME.
YOU WANT ME TO HAVE TO WORK TO DEFEAT YOU.
ISN'T THAT AN EVEN...
...WORSE JOKE?

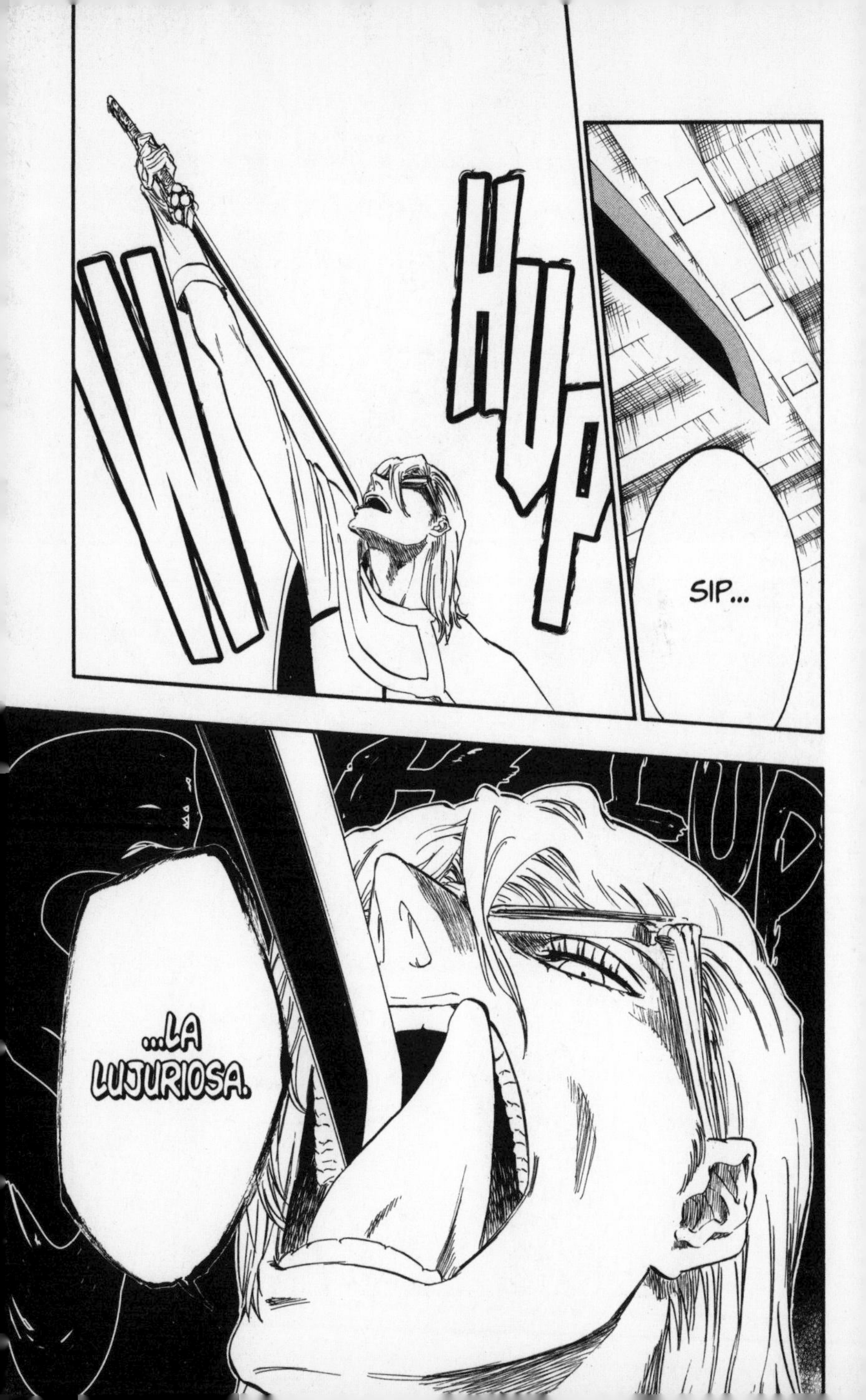
SIP...
WHUP
...LA LUJURIOSA.

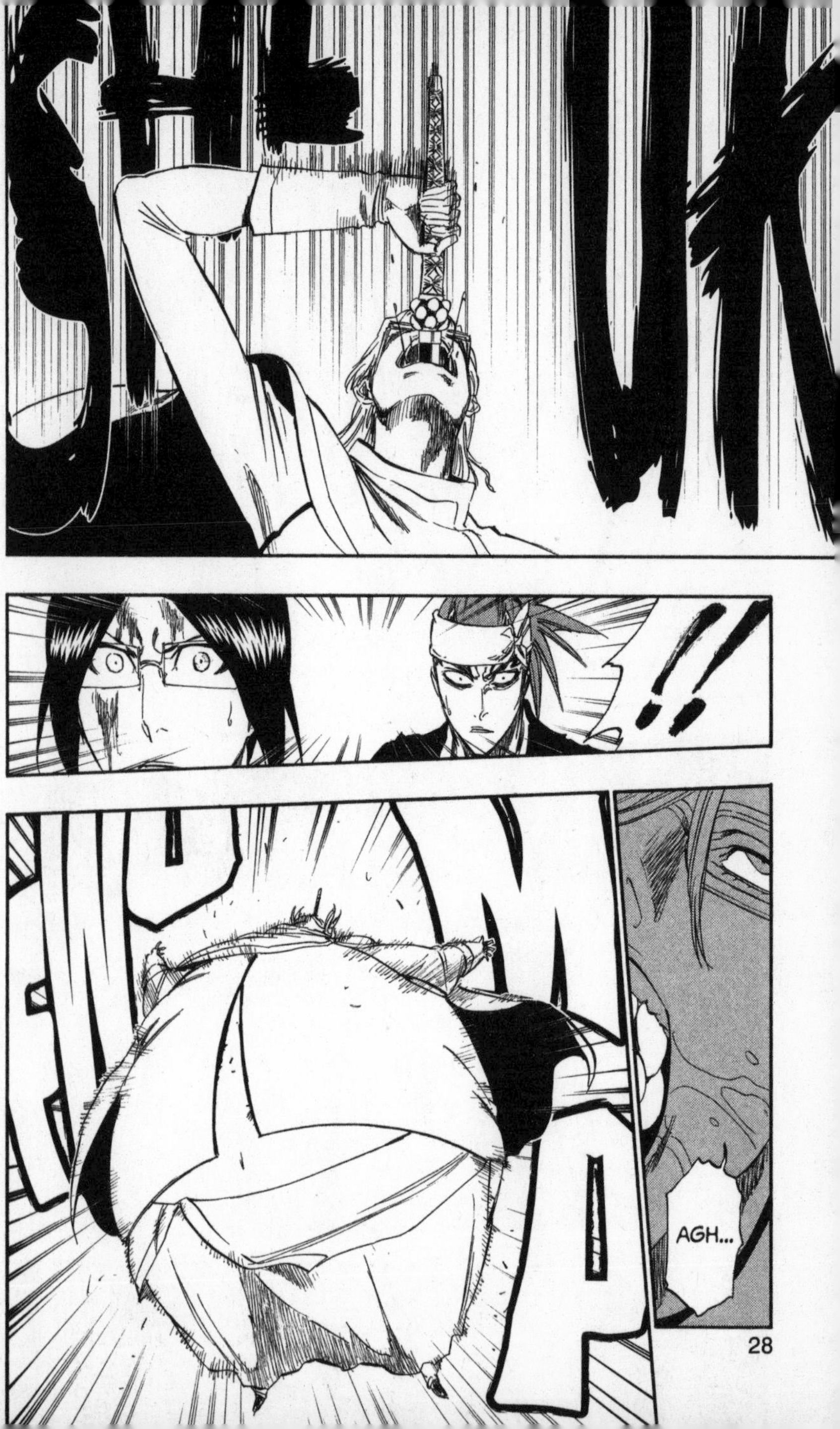
!!
AGH...

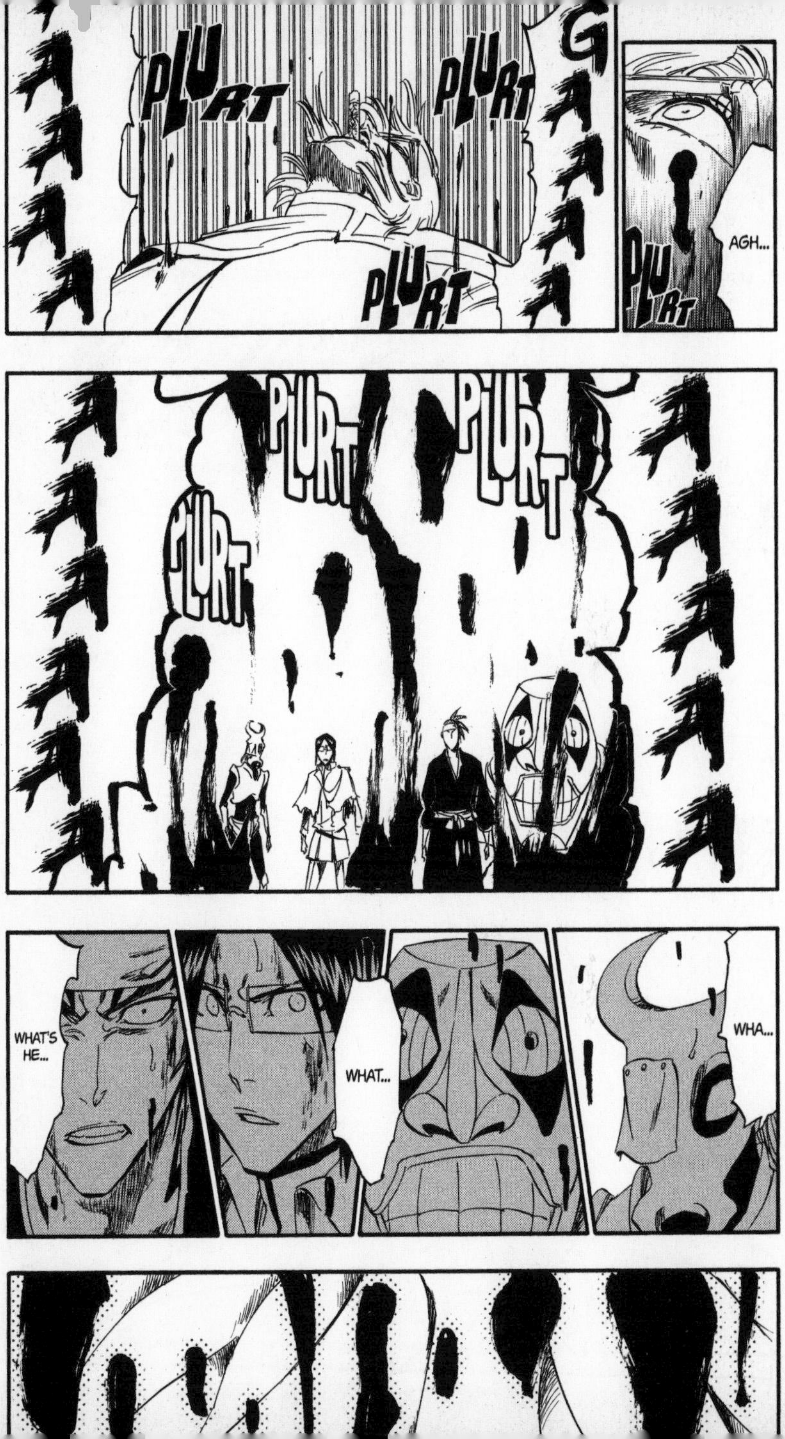

PLURT
AGH...
GAAAA
PLURT
PLURT
PLURT
AAAAA
AAAAAA
PLURT
PLURT
PLURT
AAAAAA
WHA...
WHAT...
WHAT'S HE...

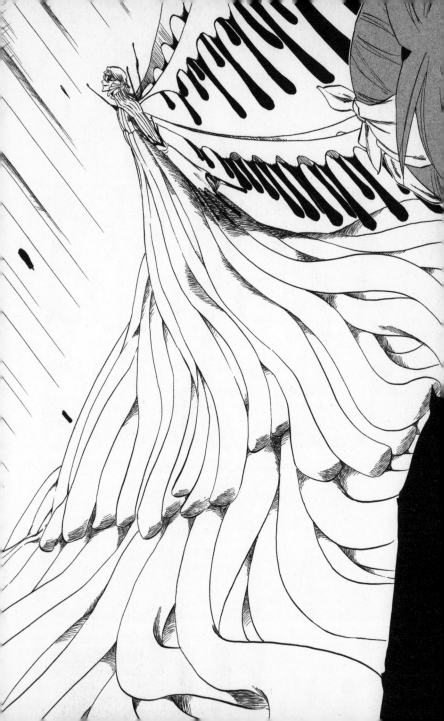

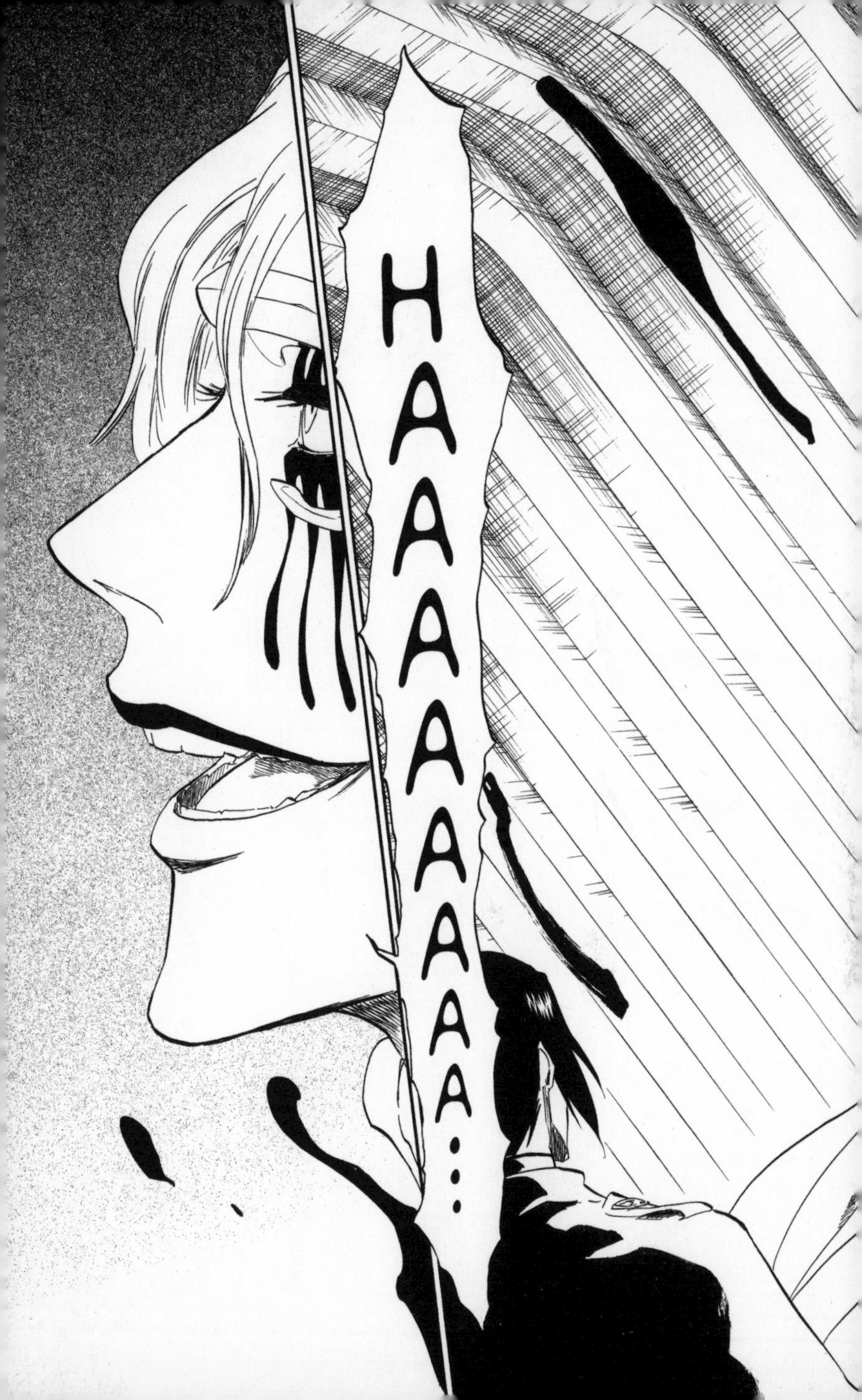
HAAAAAAAA...

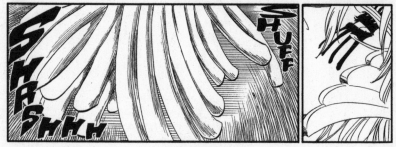

SHRA Shhh

SHUFF

SORRY TO KEEP YOU WAITING.

TMP

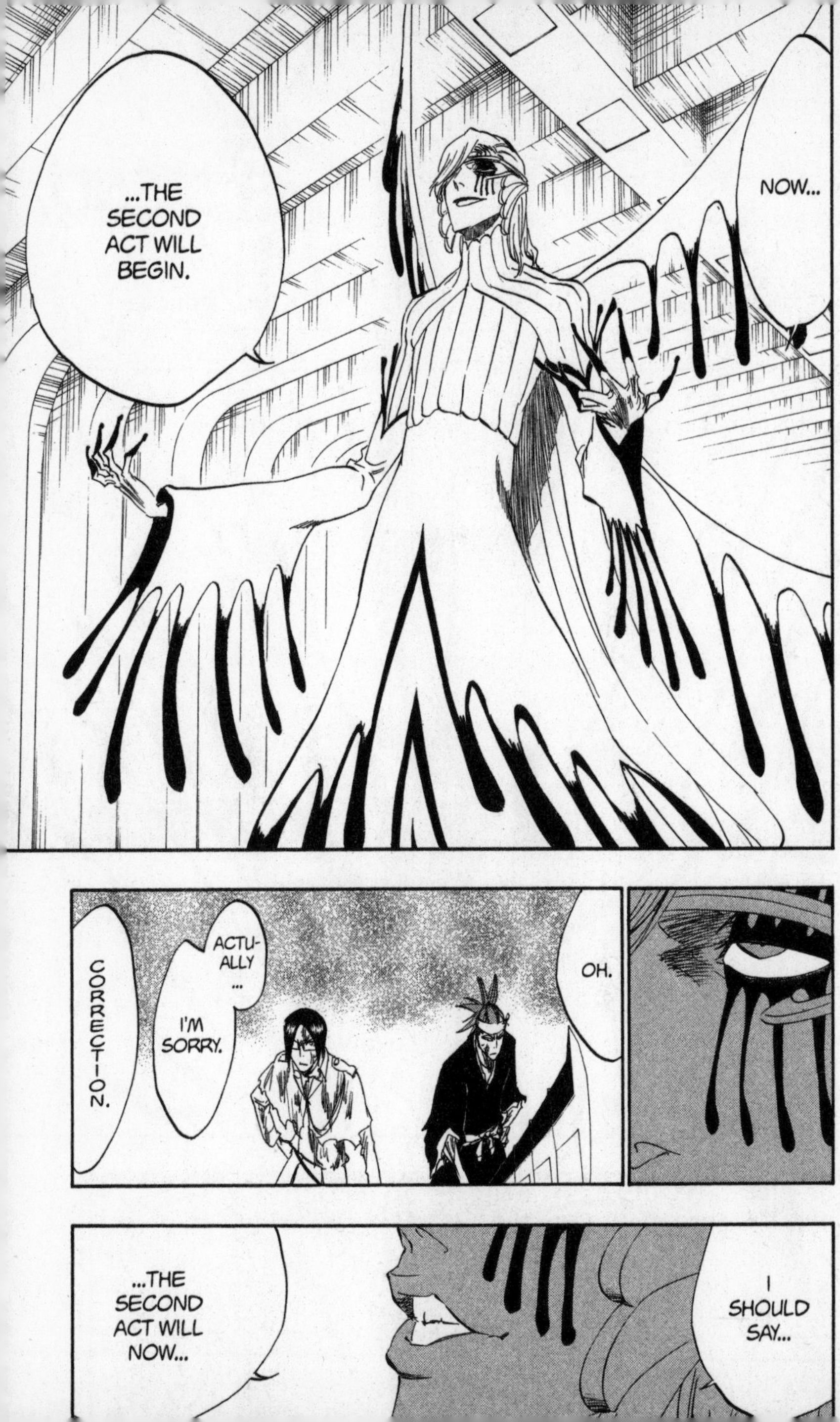
NOW...
...THE SECOND ACT WILL BEGIN.
OH.
ACTU-ALLY... I'M SORRY.
CORRECTION.
I SHOULD SAY...
...THE SECOND ACT WILL NOW...

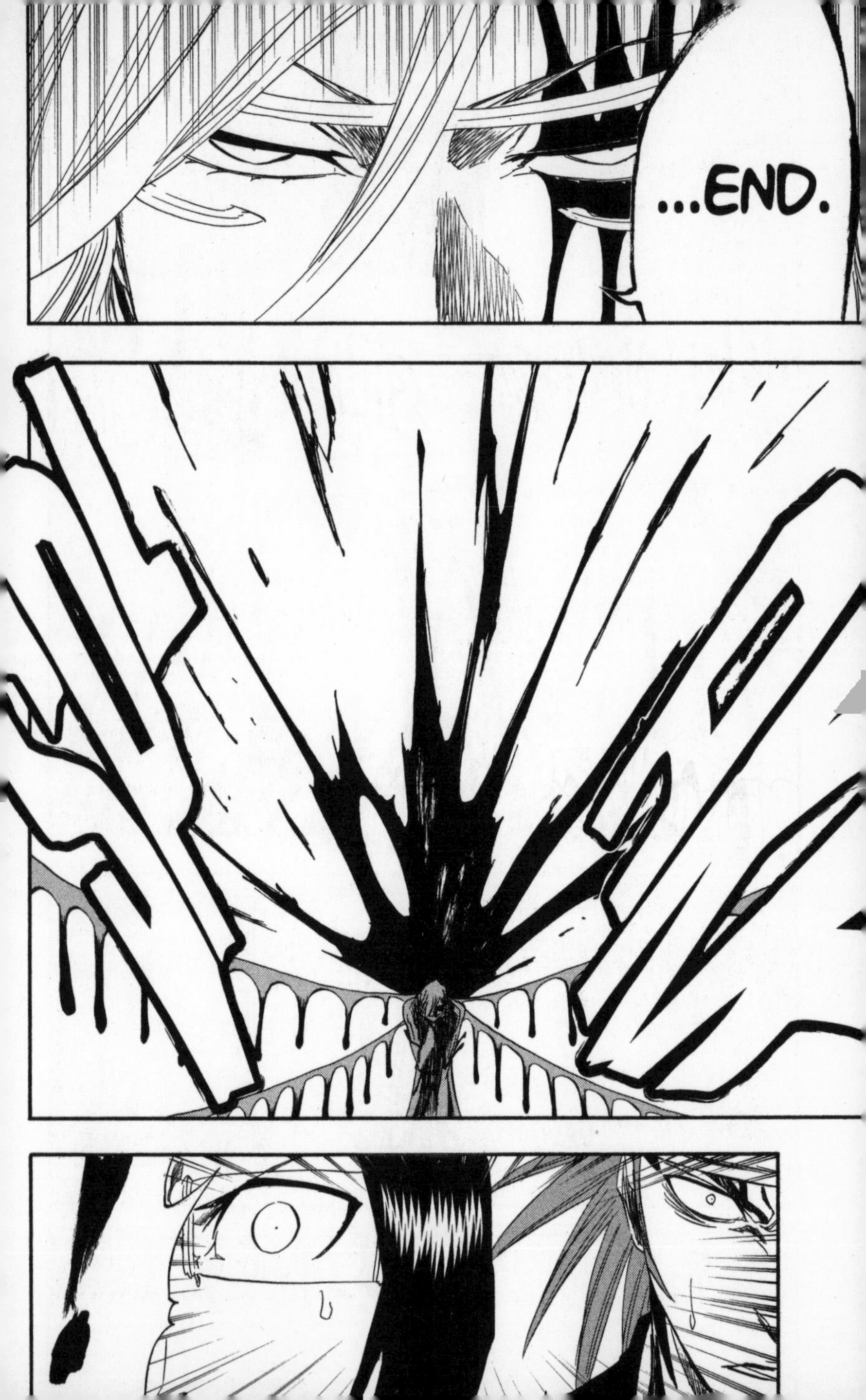
...END.

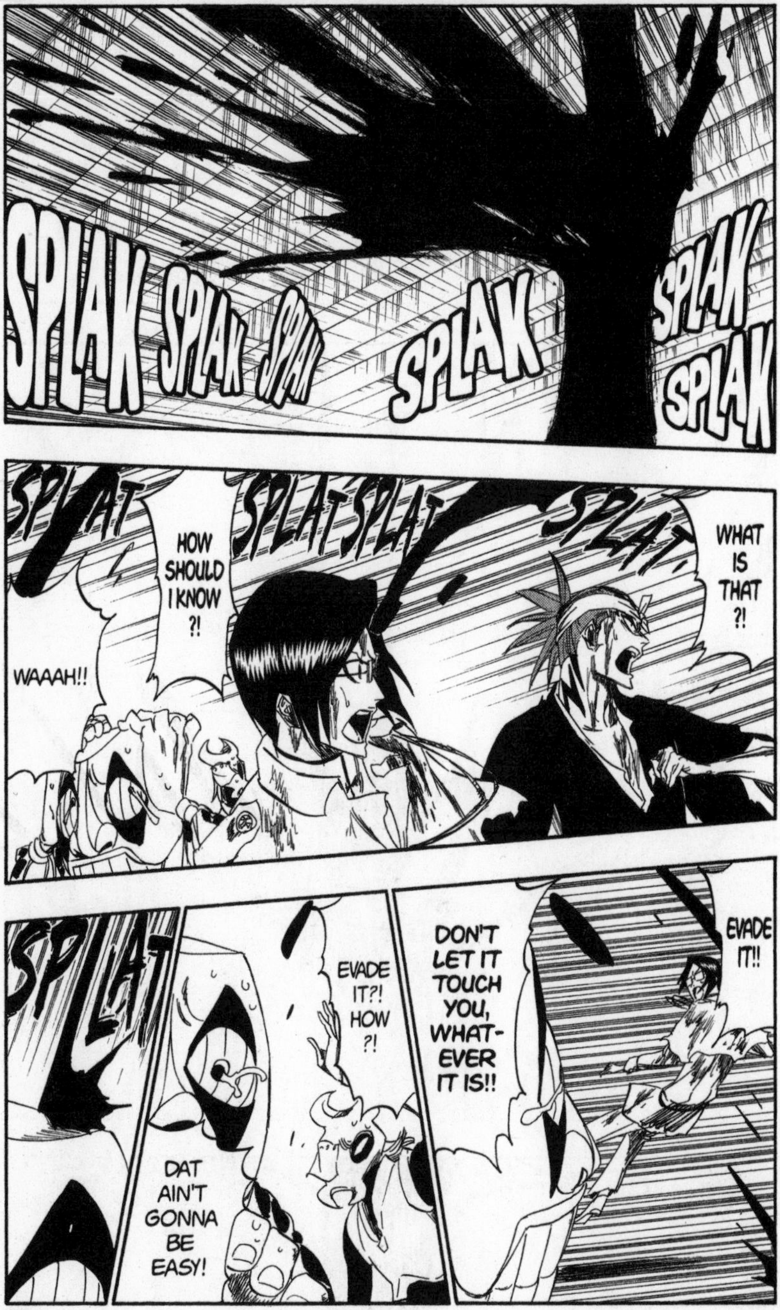
SPLAK
SPLAK
SPLAK
SPLAK
SPLAK
SPLAK
WHAT IS THAT ?!
SPLAT
SPLAT SPLAT
HOW SHOULD I KNOW ?!
SPLAT
WAAAH!!
EVADE IT!!
DON'T LET IT TOUCH YOU, WHATEVER IT IS!!
EVADE IT?! HOW ?!
DAT AIN'T GONNA BE EASY!
SPLAT

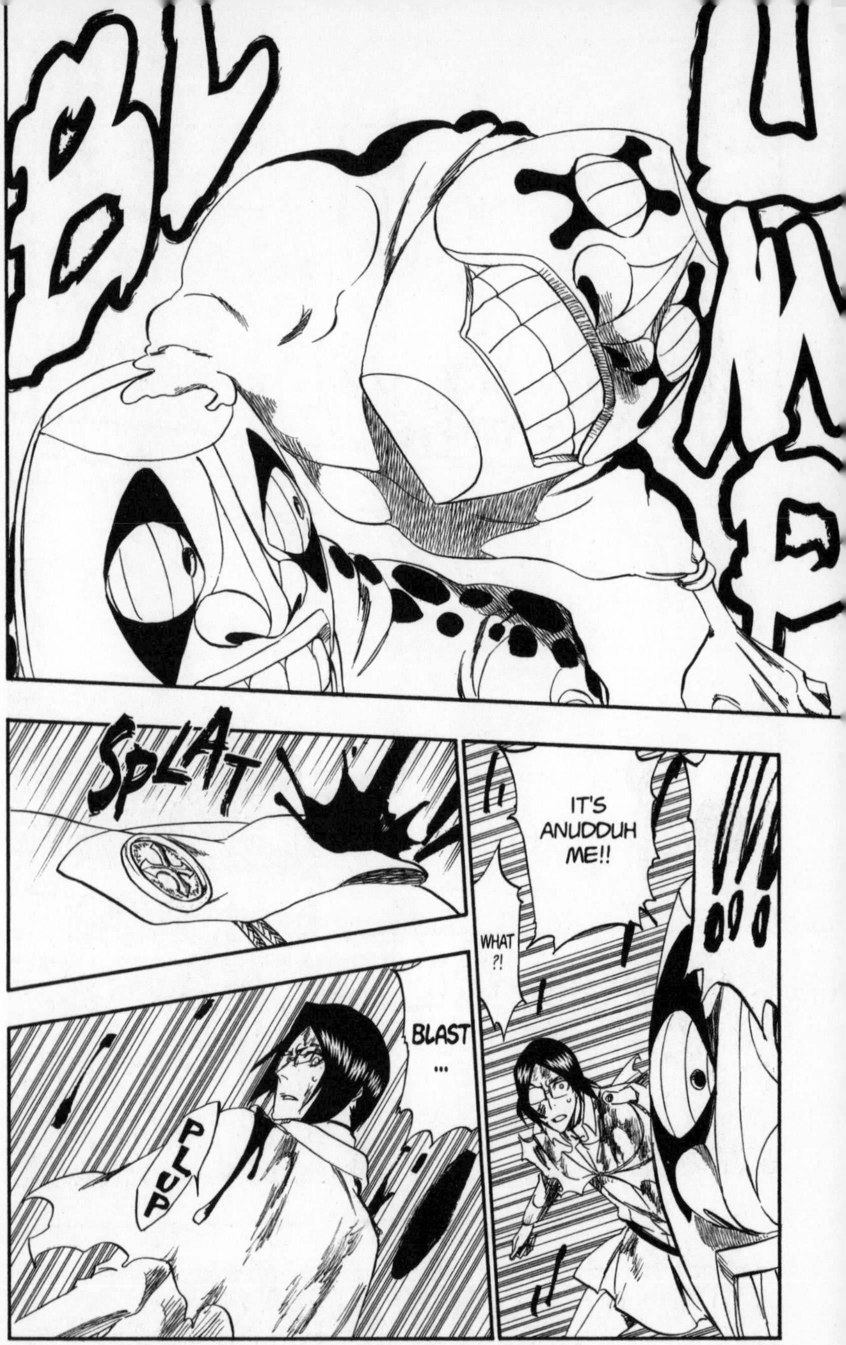
IT'S ANUDDUH ME!!
WHAT ?!
SPLAT
BLAST ...
PLUP

READ THIS WAY

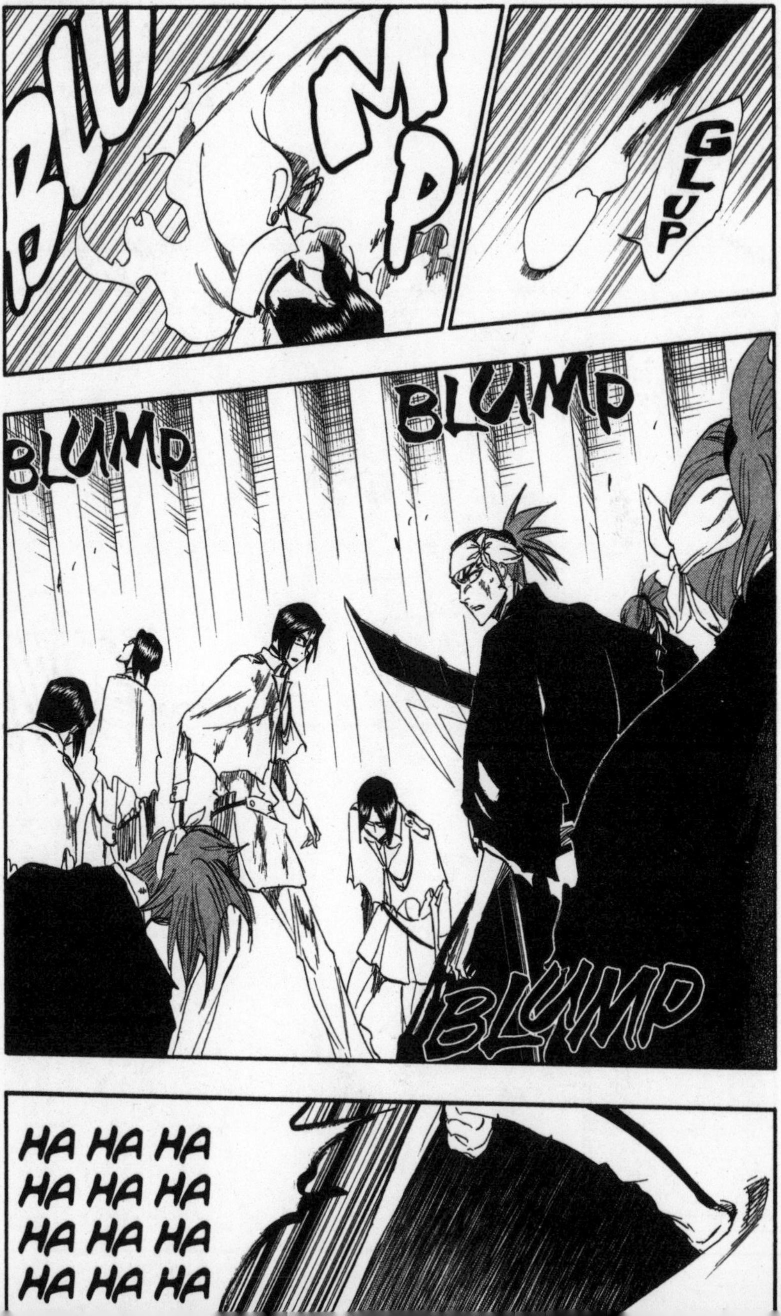
GLUP
BLUMP
BLUMP
BLUMP
BLUMP
HA HA HA
HA HA HA
HA HA HA
HA HA HA

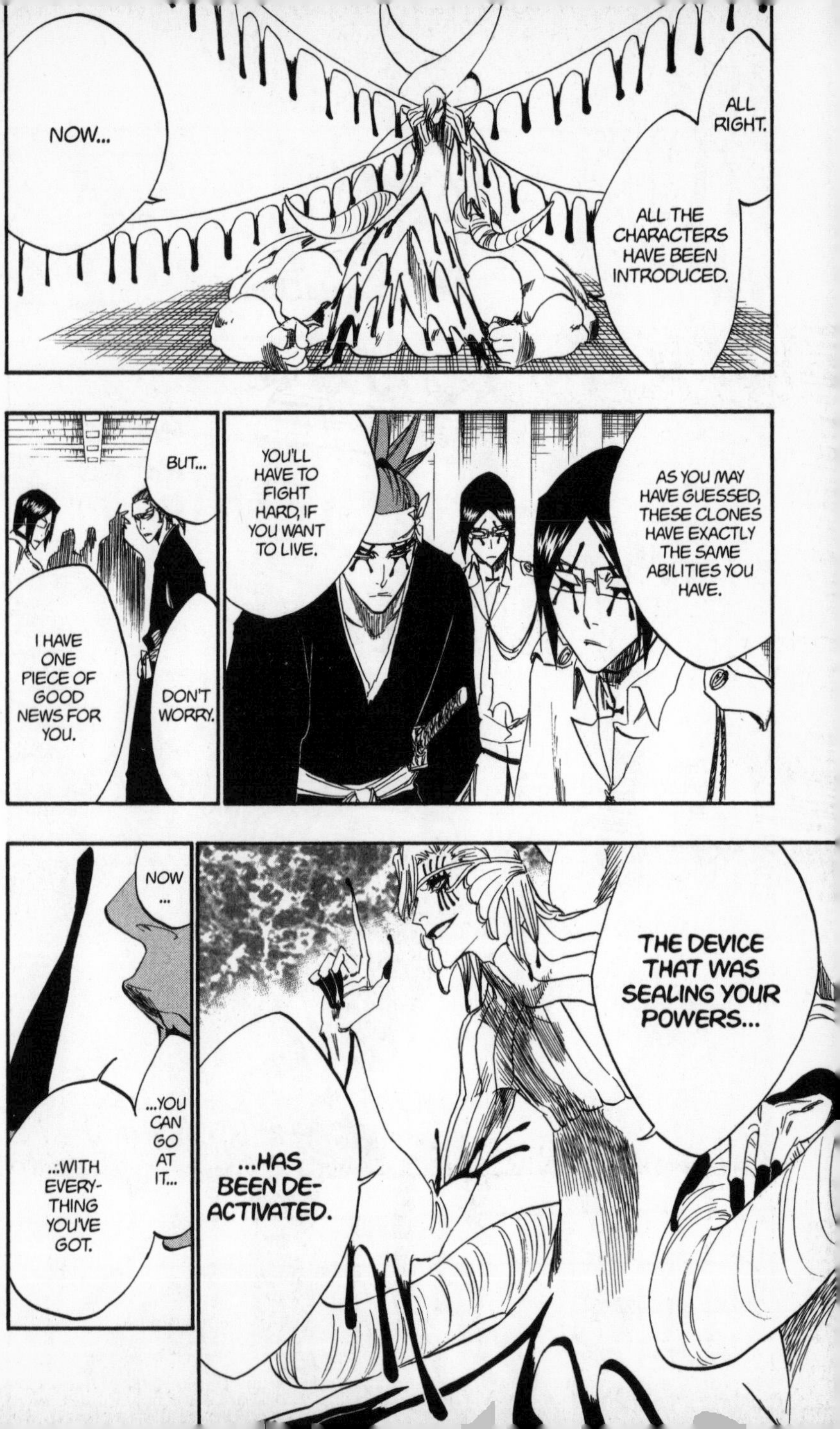
ALL RIGHT.
ALL THE CHARACTERS HAVE BEEN INTRODUCED.
NOW...
AS YOU MAY HAVE GUESSED, THESE CLONES HAVE EXACTLY THE SAME ABILITIES YOU HAVE.
YOU'LL HAVE TO FIGHT HARD, IF YOU WANT TO LIVE.
BUT...
DON'T WORRY.
I HAVE ONE PIECE OF GOOD NEWS FOR YOU.
THE DEVICE THAT WAS SEALING YOUR POWERS...
...HAS BEEN DE-ACTIVATED.
NOW...
...YOU CAN GO AT IT...
...WITH EVERY-THING YOU'VE GOT.

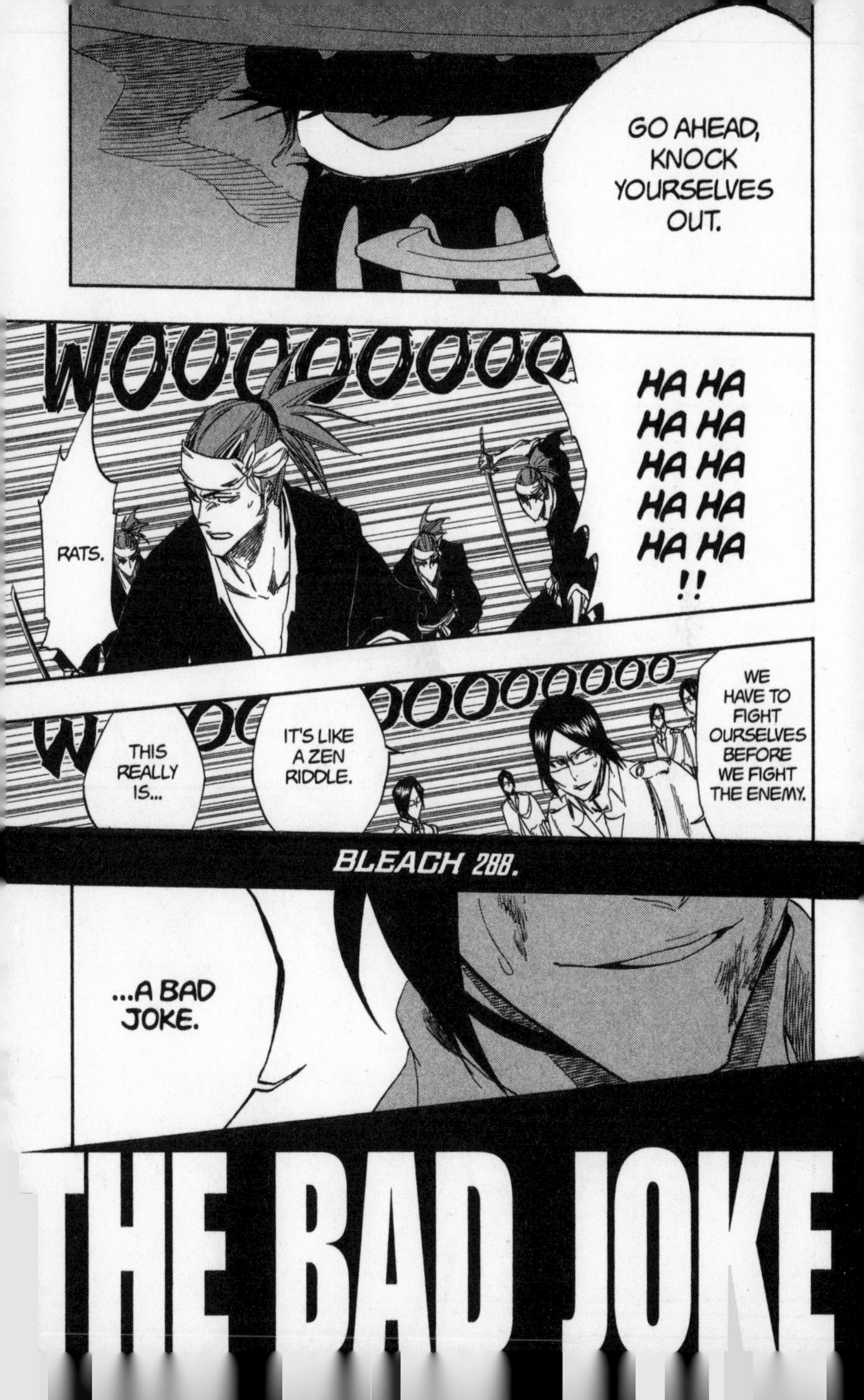
GO AHEAD, KNOCK YOURSELVES OUT.
WOOOOOOOOO
HA HA HA HA HA HA HA HA HA HA !!
RATS.
WOOOOOOOOOOOOO
WE HAVE TO FIGHT OURSELVES BEFORE WE FIGHT THE ENEMY.
IT'S LIKE A ZEN RIDDLE.
THIS REALLY IS...
BLEACH 288.
...A BAD JOKE.
THE BAD JOKE

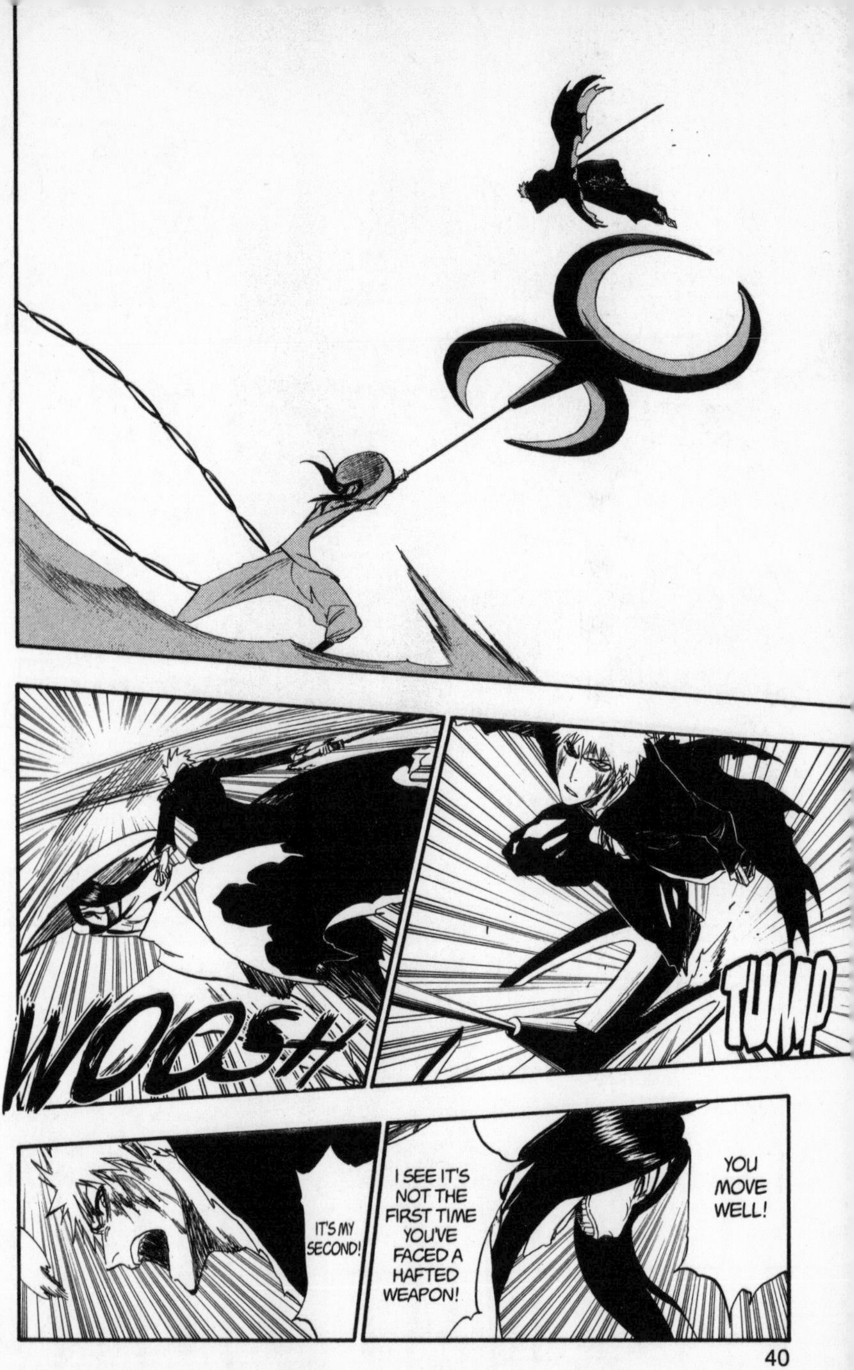
TUMP
WOOSH
YOU MOVE WELL!
I SEE IT'S NOT THE FIRST TIME YOU'VE FACED A HAFTED WEAPON!
IT'S MY SECOND!

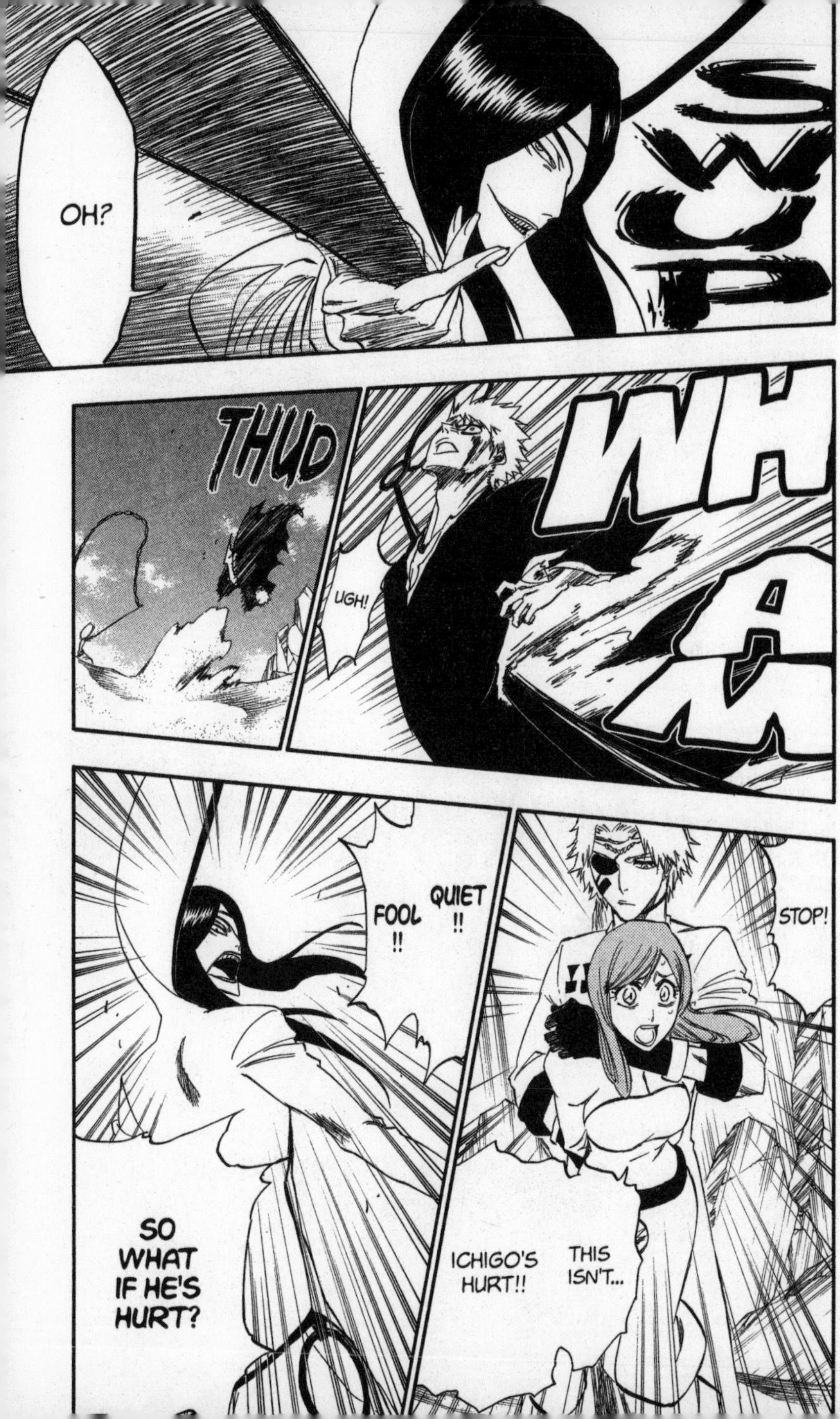
OH?
WHAM
UGH!
THUD
STOP!
THIS ISN'T...
ICHIGO'S HURT!!
QUIET!!
FOOL!!
SO WHAT IF HE'S HURT?

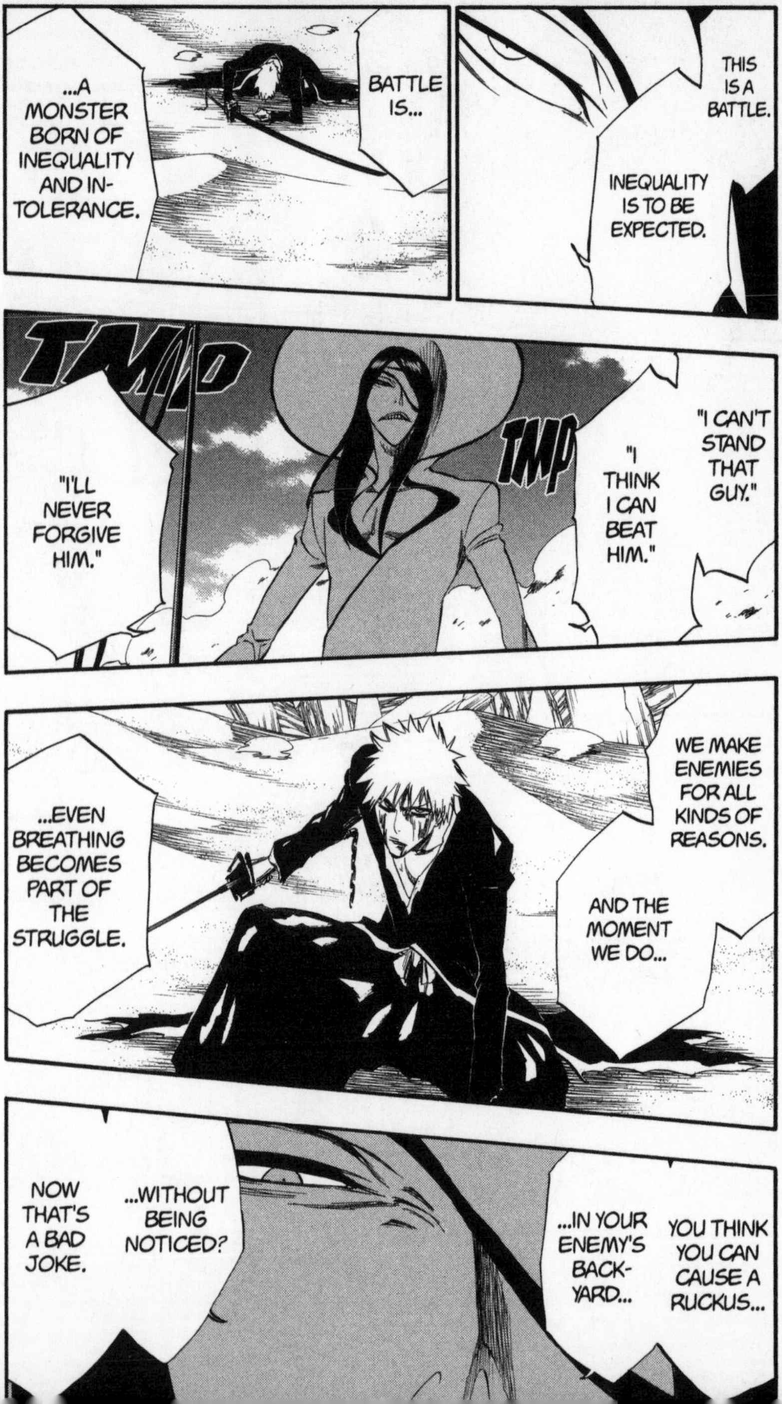
THIS IS A BATTLE.
INEQUALITY IS TO BE EXPECTED.
BATTLE IS...
...A MONSTER BORN OF INEQUALITY AND IN-TOLERANCE.
"I CAN'T STAND THAT GUY."
"I THINK I CAN BEAT HIM."
TMP
TMD
"I'LL NEVER FORGIVE HIM."
WE MAKE ENEMIES FOR ALL KINDS OF REASONS.
AND THE MOMENT WE DO...
...EVEN BREATHING BECOMES PART OF THE STRUGGLE.
YOU THINK YOU CAN CAUSE A RUCKUS...
...IN YOUR ENEMY'S BACK-YARD...
...WITHOUT BEING NOTICED?
NOW THAT'S A BAD JOKE.

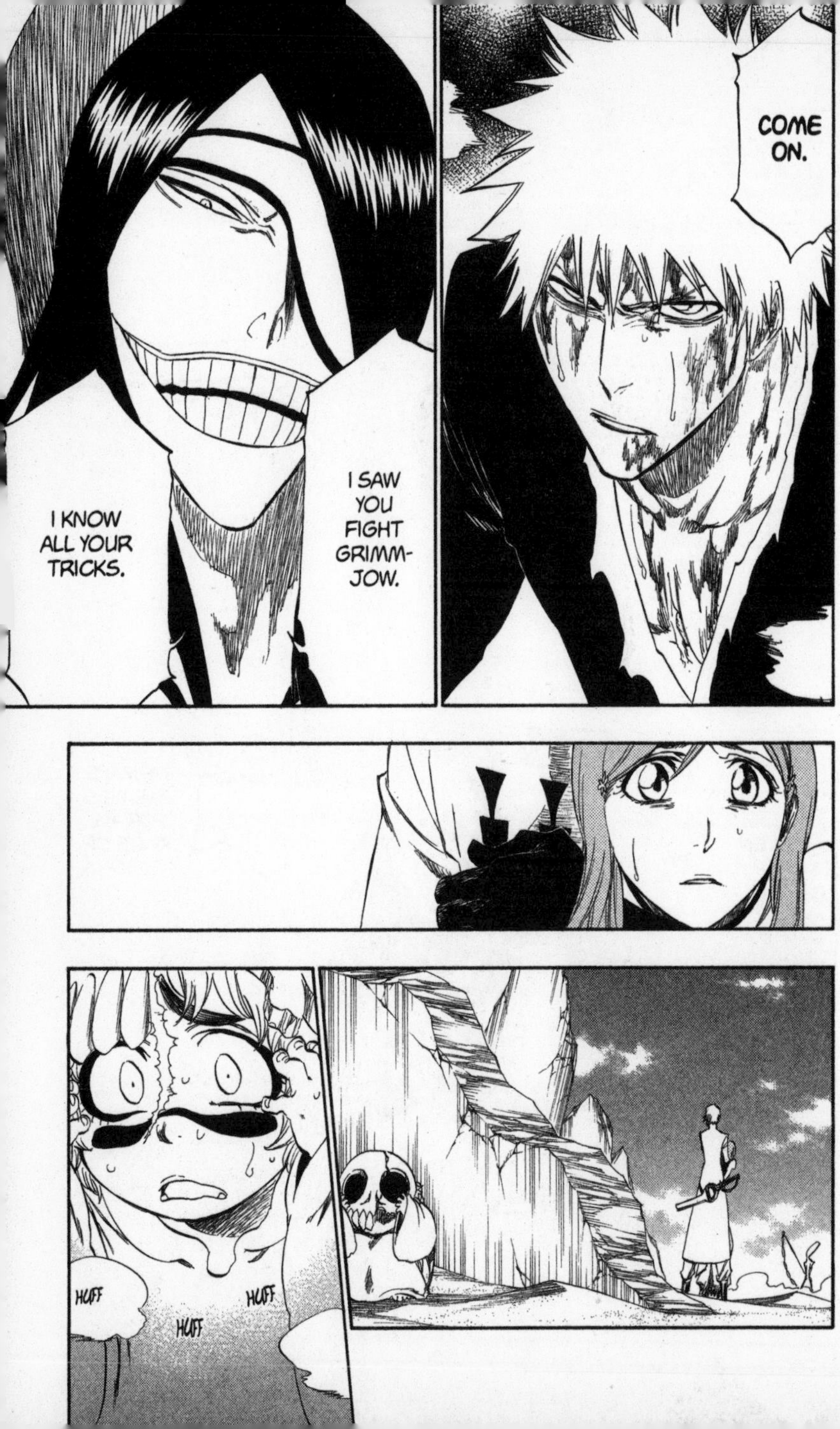
COME ON.
I SAW YOU FIGHT GRIMM-JOW.
I KNOW ALL YOUR TRICKS.
HUFF
HUFF
HUFF

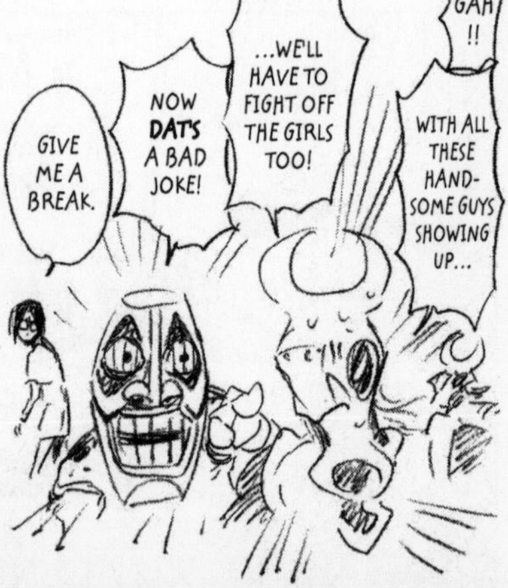
GAH!!
WITH ALL THESE HAND-SOME GUYS SHOWING UP...
...WE'LL HAVE TO FIGHT OFF THE GIRLS TOO!
NOW **DAT'S** A BAD JOKE!
GIVE ME A BREAK.

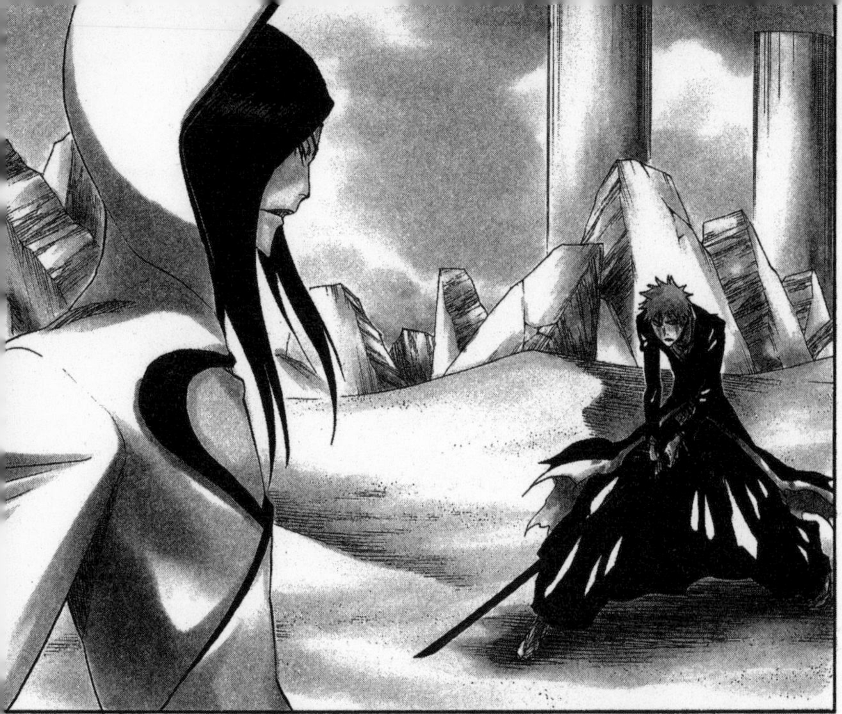

289. The Scarmask

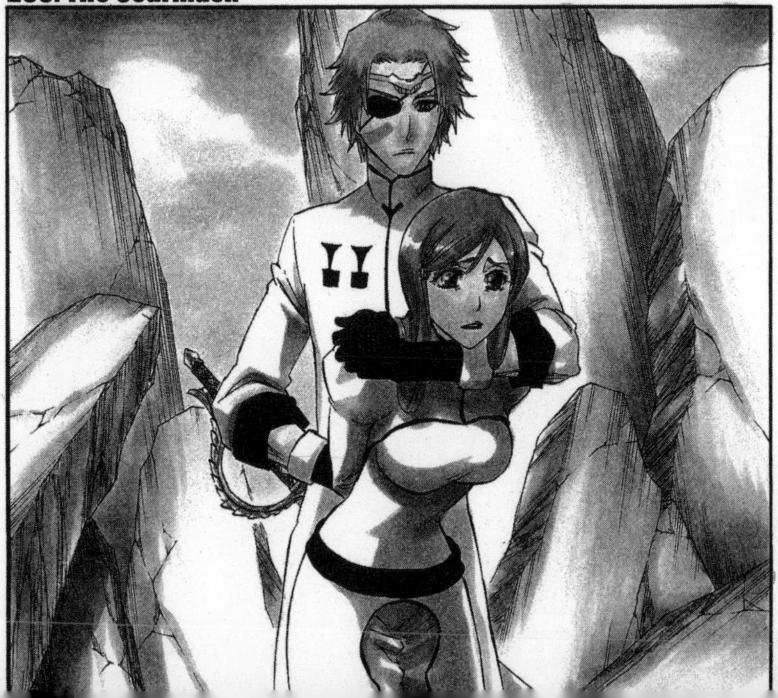

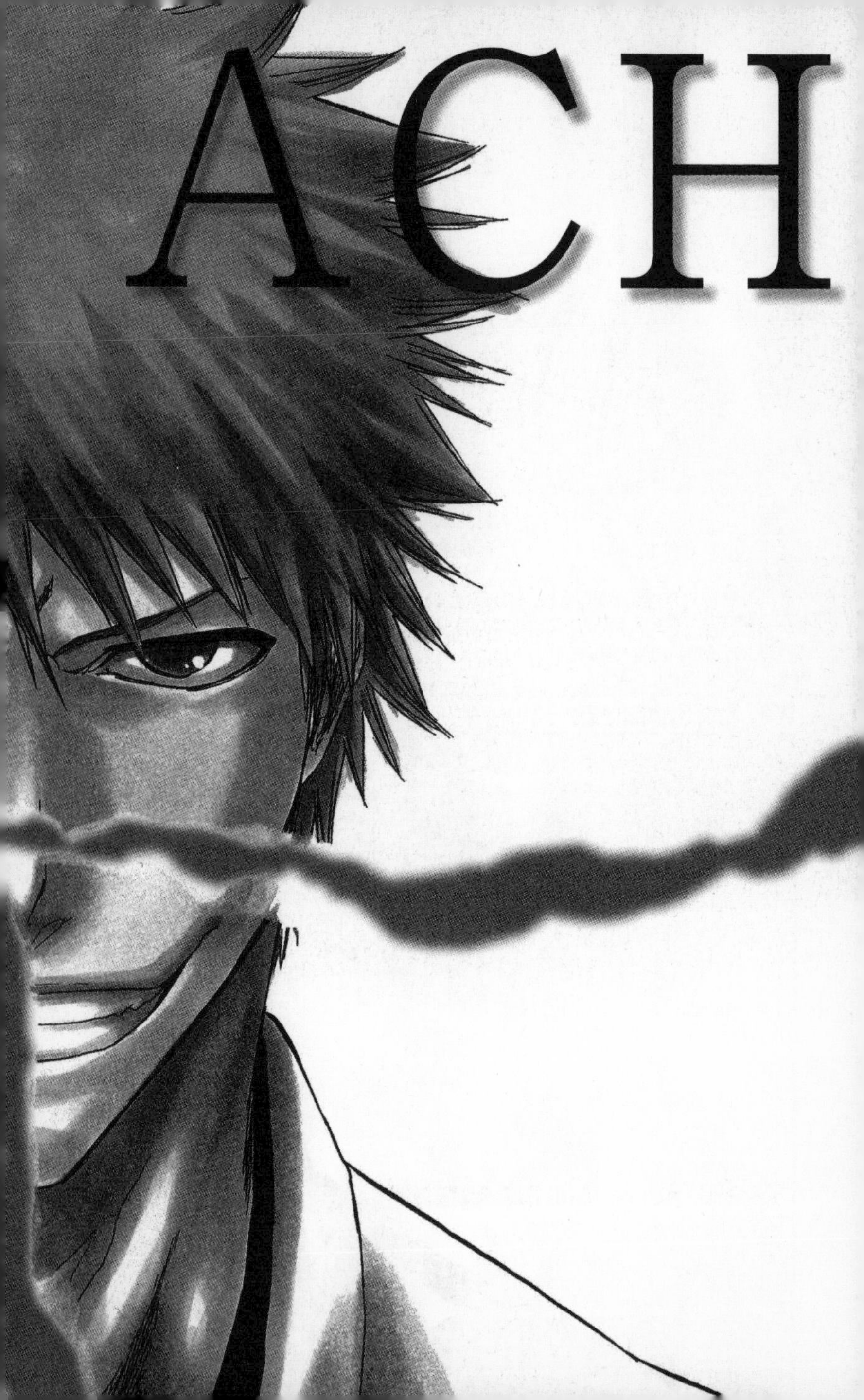
ACH

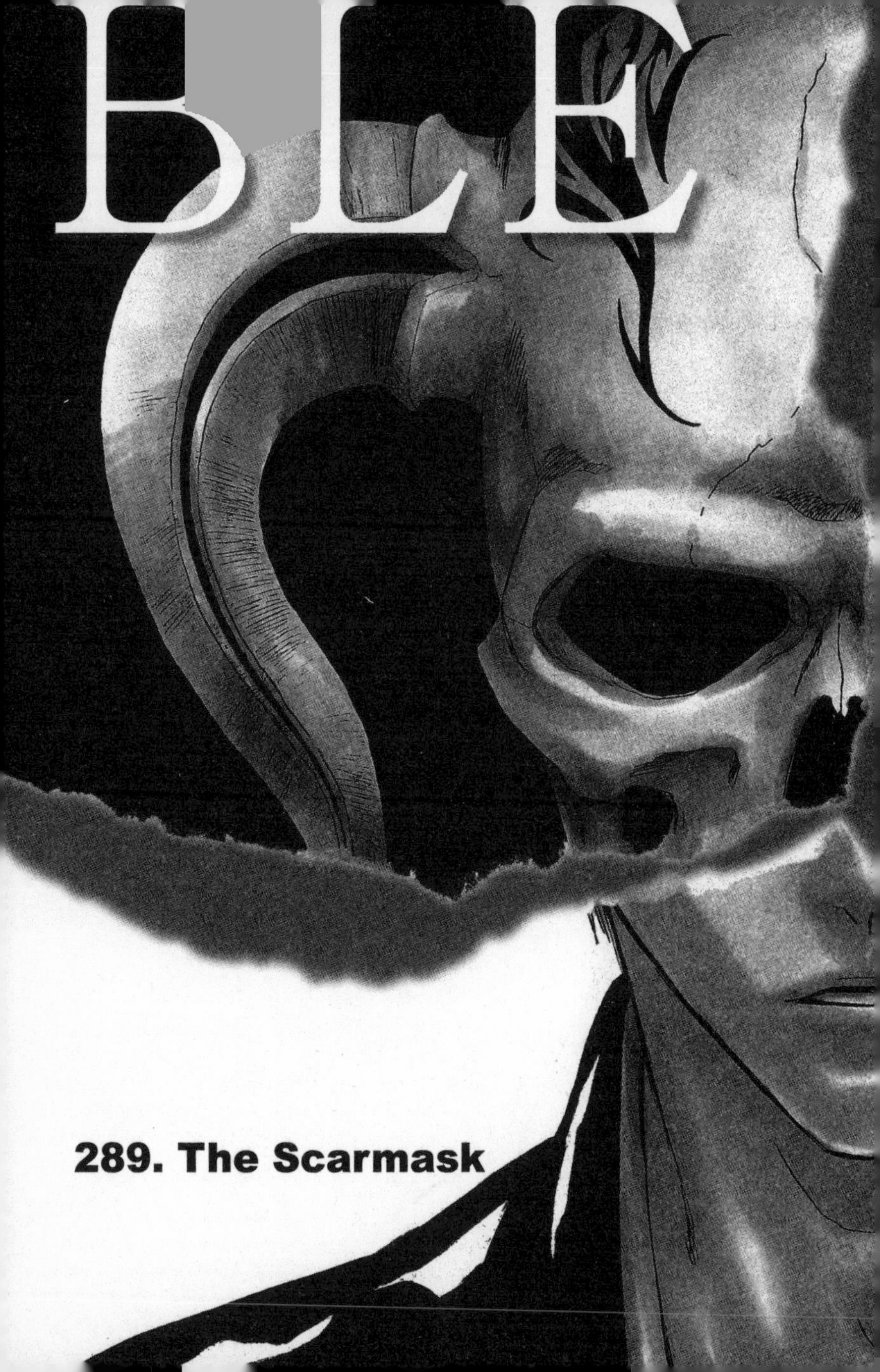
BLE
289. The Scarmask

BLEACH
ブリーチ

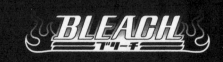

HUFF

HUFF

HUFF

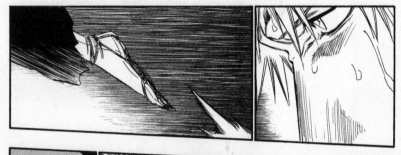

SLOW.

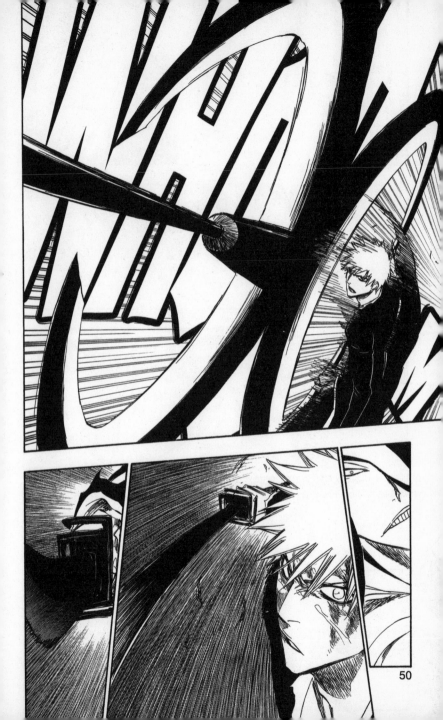

50

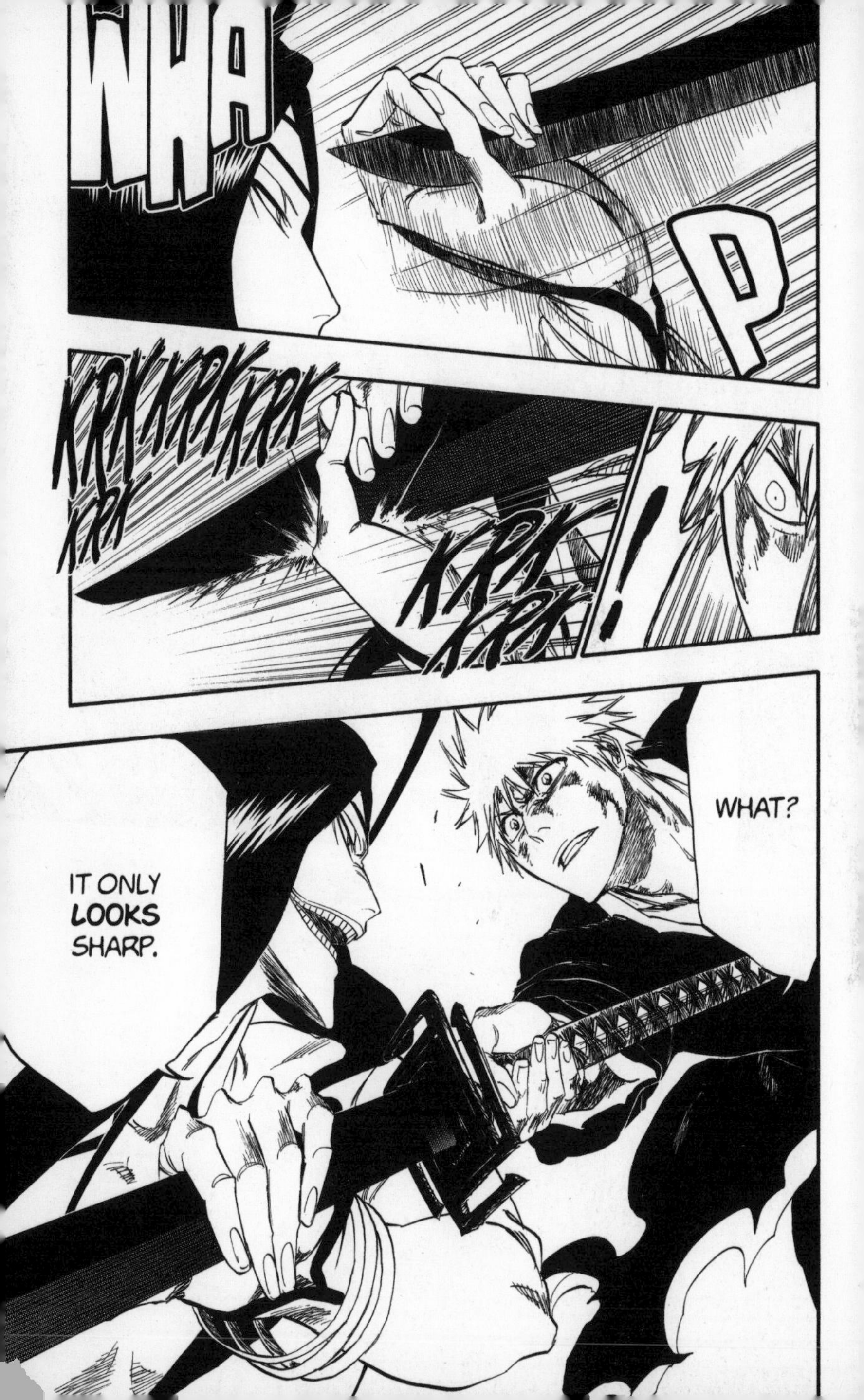

WHAP
!
KRK KRK KRK KRK
KRK KRK
WHAT?
IT ONLY **LOOKS** SHARP.

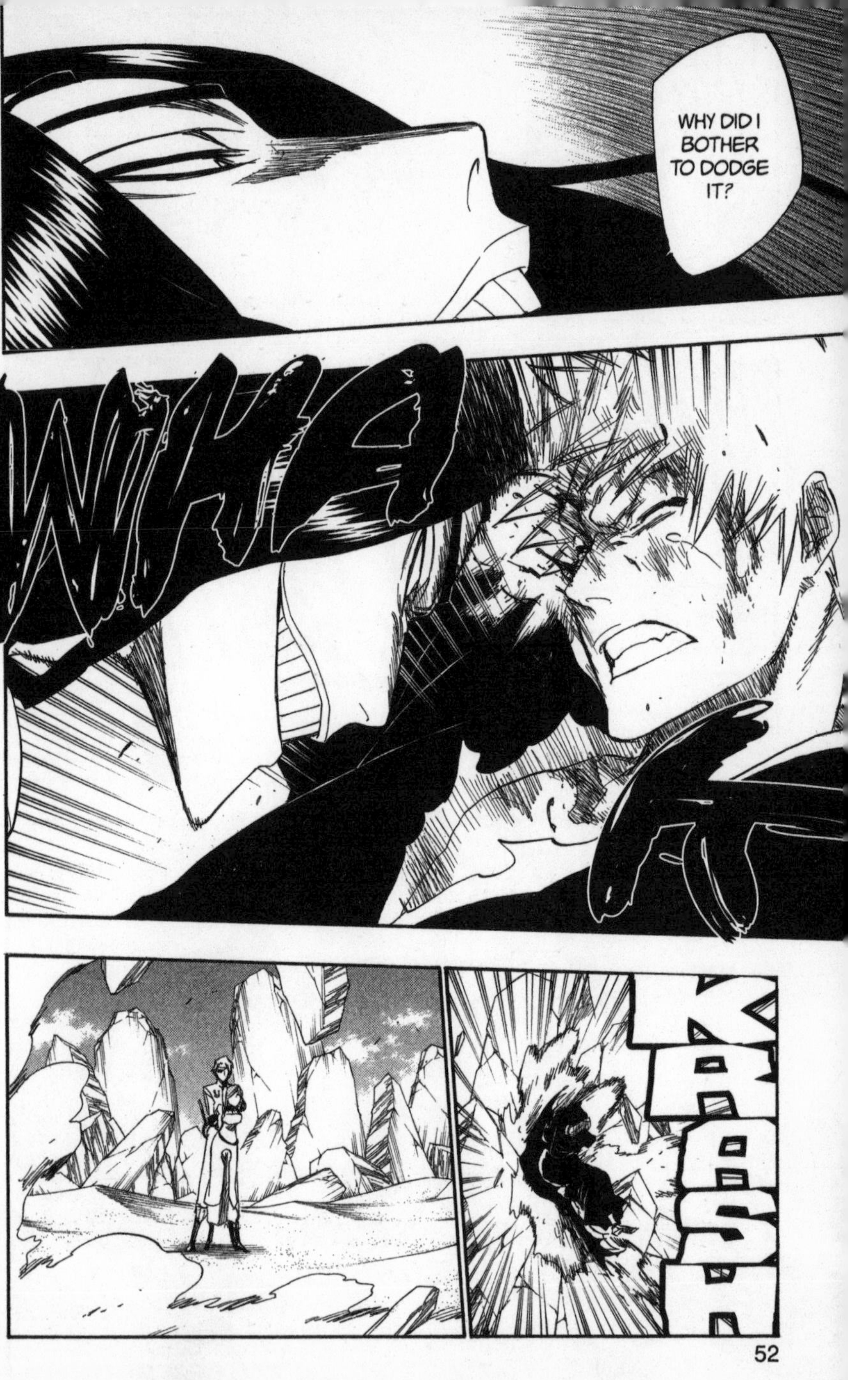
WHY DID I BOTHER TO DODGE IT?
WHAM
KRASH

READ THIS WAY

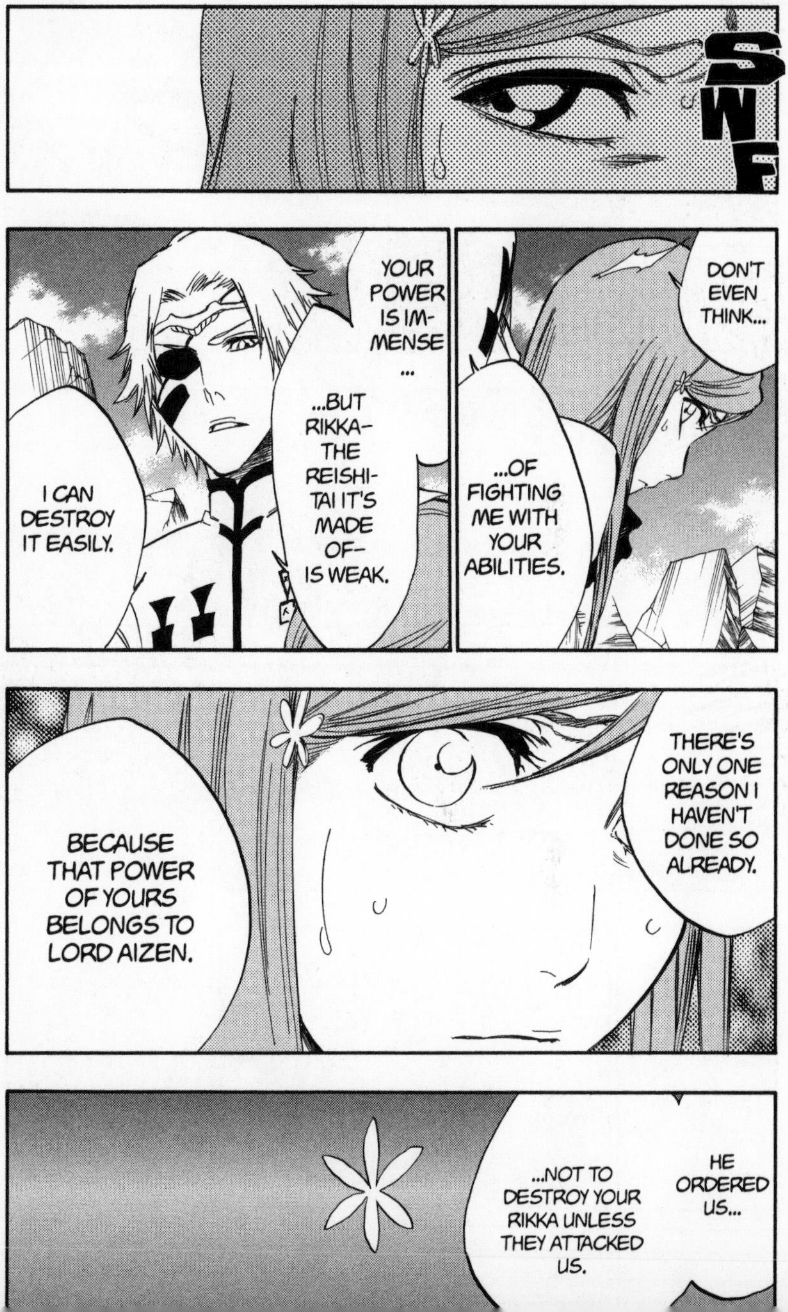
SWF
DON'T EVEN THINK...
...OF FIGHTING ME WITH YOUR ABILITIES.
YOUR POWER IS IMMENSE...
...BUT RIKKA-THE REISHITAI IT'S MADE OF-IS WEAK.
I CAN DESTROY IT EASILY.
THERE'S ONLY ONE REASON I HAVEN'T DONE SO ALREADY.
BECAUSE THAT POWER OF YOURS BELONGS TO LORD AIZEN.
HE ORDERED US...
...NOT TO DESTROY YOUR RIKKA UNLESS THEY ATTACKED US.

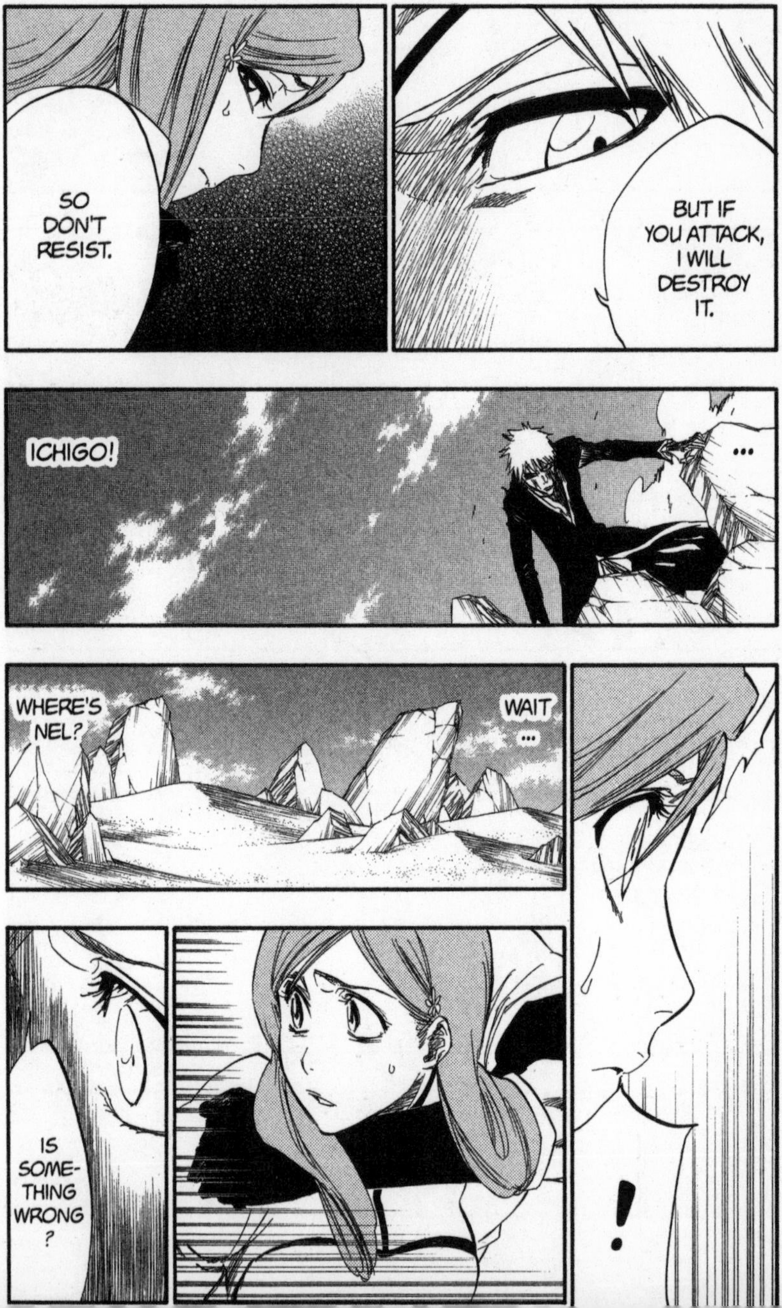
BUT IF YOU ATTACK, I WILL DESTROY IT.
SO DON'T RESIST.
...
ICHIGO!
!
WAIT ...
WHERE'S NEL?
IS SOME-THING WRONG?

READ THIS WAY

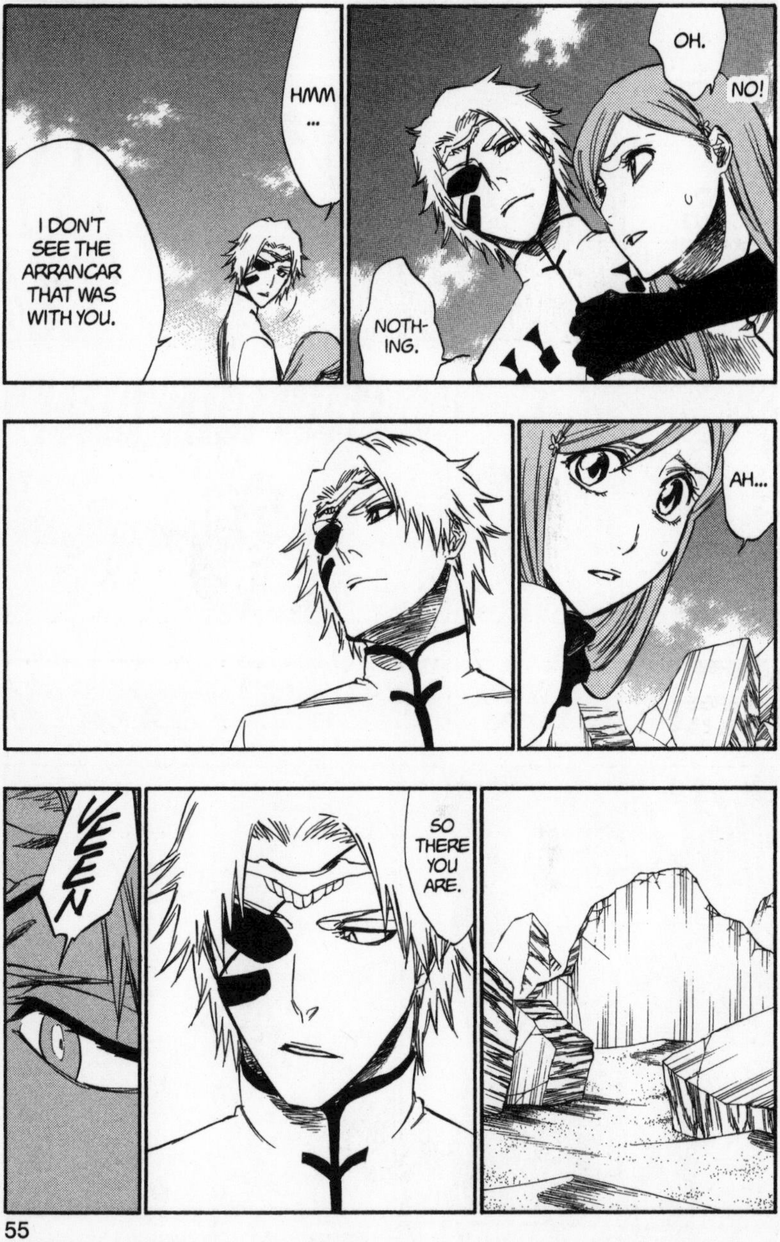

OH.
NO!
NOTH-ING.
HMM ...
I DON'T SEE THE ARRANCAR THAT WAS WITH YOU.
AH...
SO THERE YOU ARE.
VEEEN

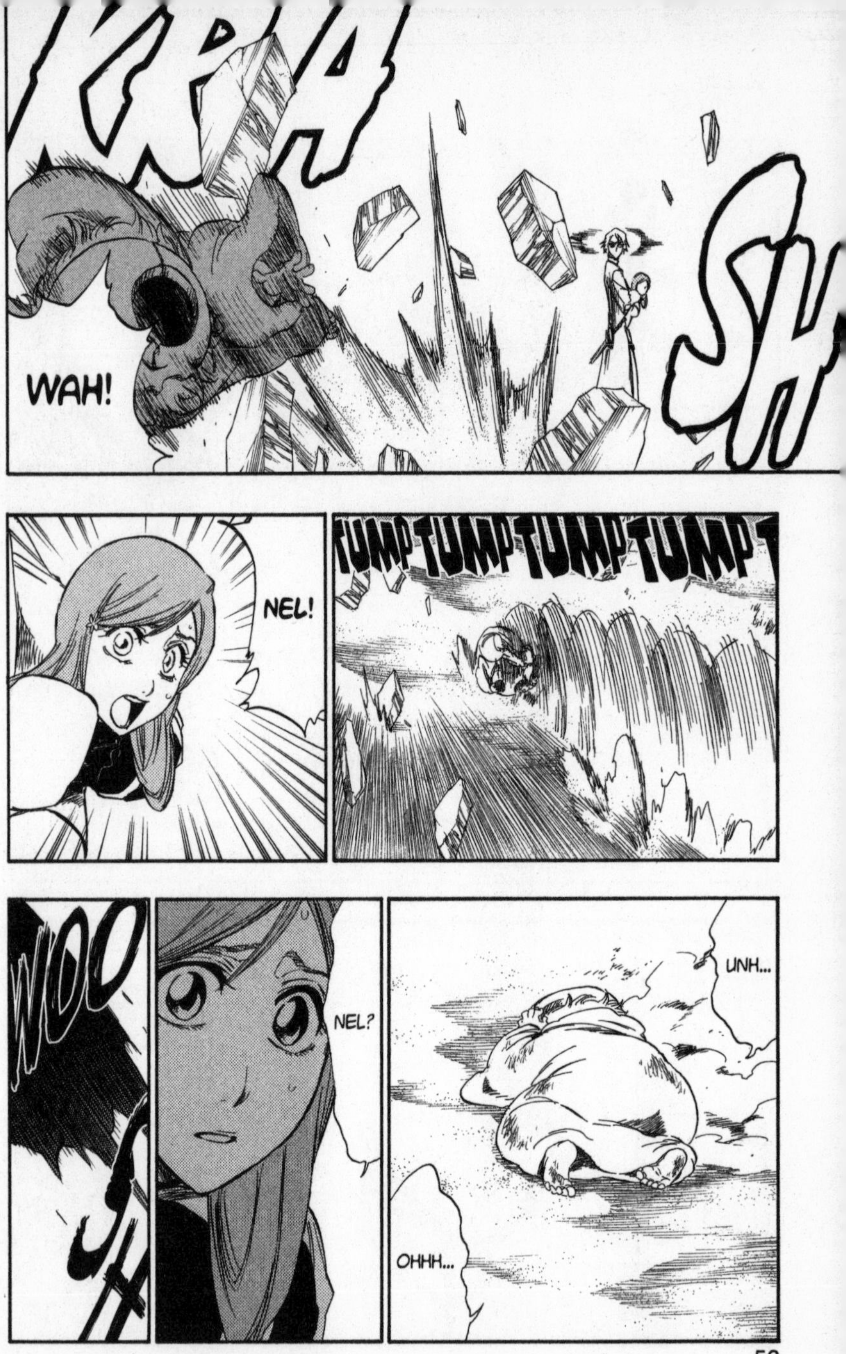
SH
WAH!
TUMP TUMP TUMP TUMP
NEL!
UNH...
OHHH...
NEL?
WOO

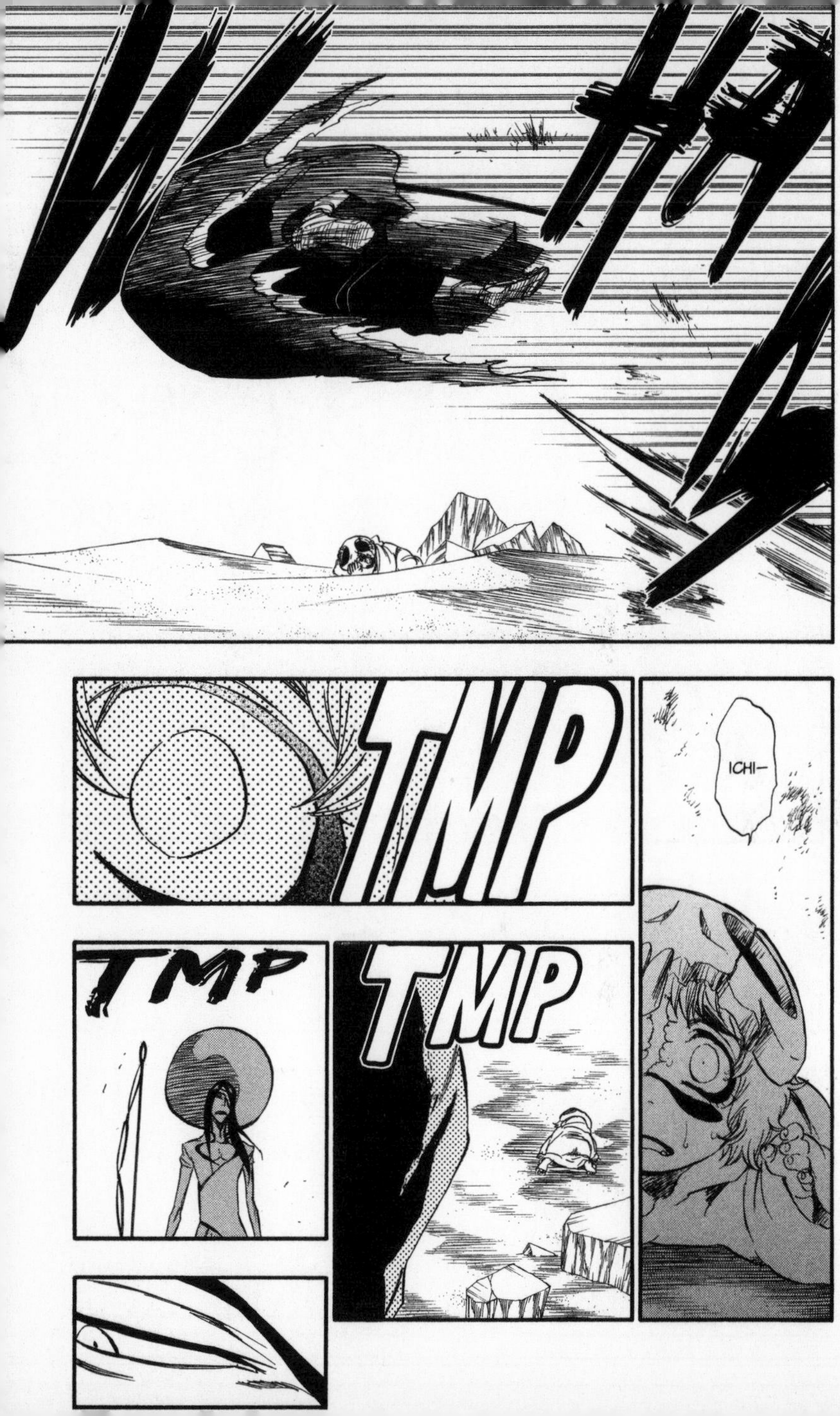
WHAM
ICHI—
TMP
TMP
TMP

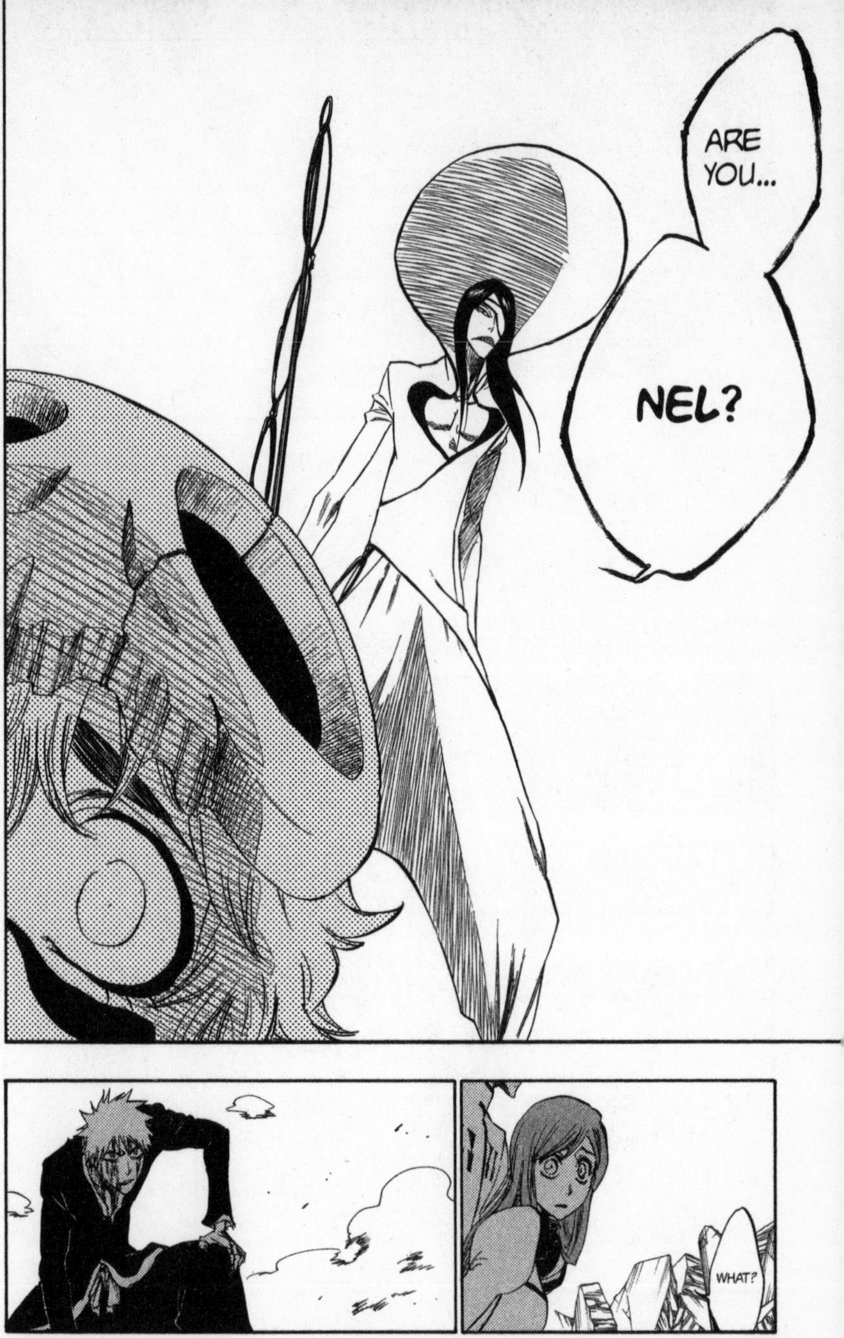
ARE YOU...
NEL?
WHAT?

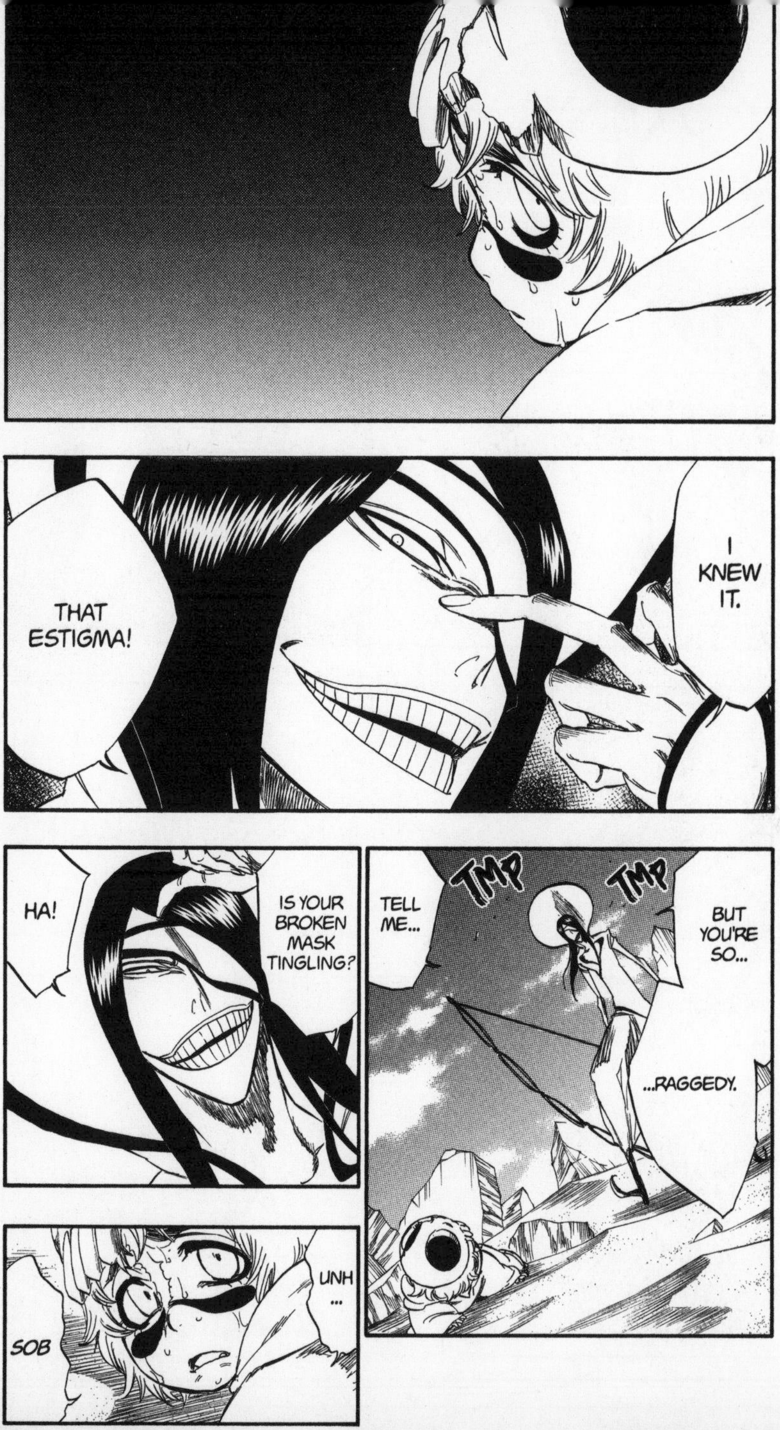
I KNEW IT.
THAT ESTIGMA!
TMP
TMP
BUT YOU'RE SO...
...RAGGEDY.
TELL ME...
IS YOUR BROKEN MASK TINGLING?
HA!
UNH ...
SOB

...KNOW NEL?

YOU...

WHAT'S GOING ON?

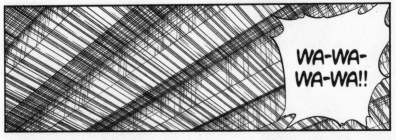

WA-WA-WA-WA!!

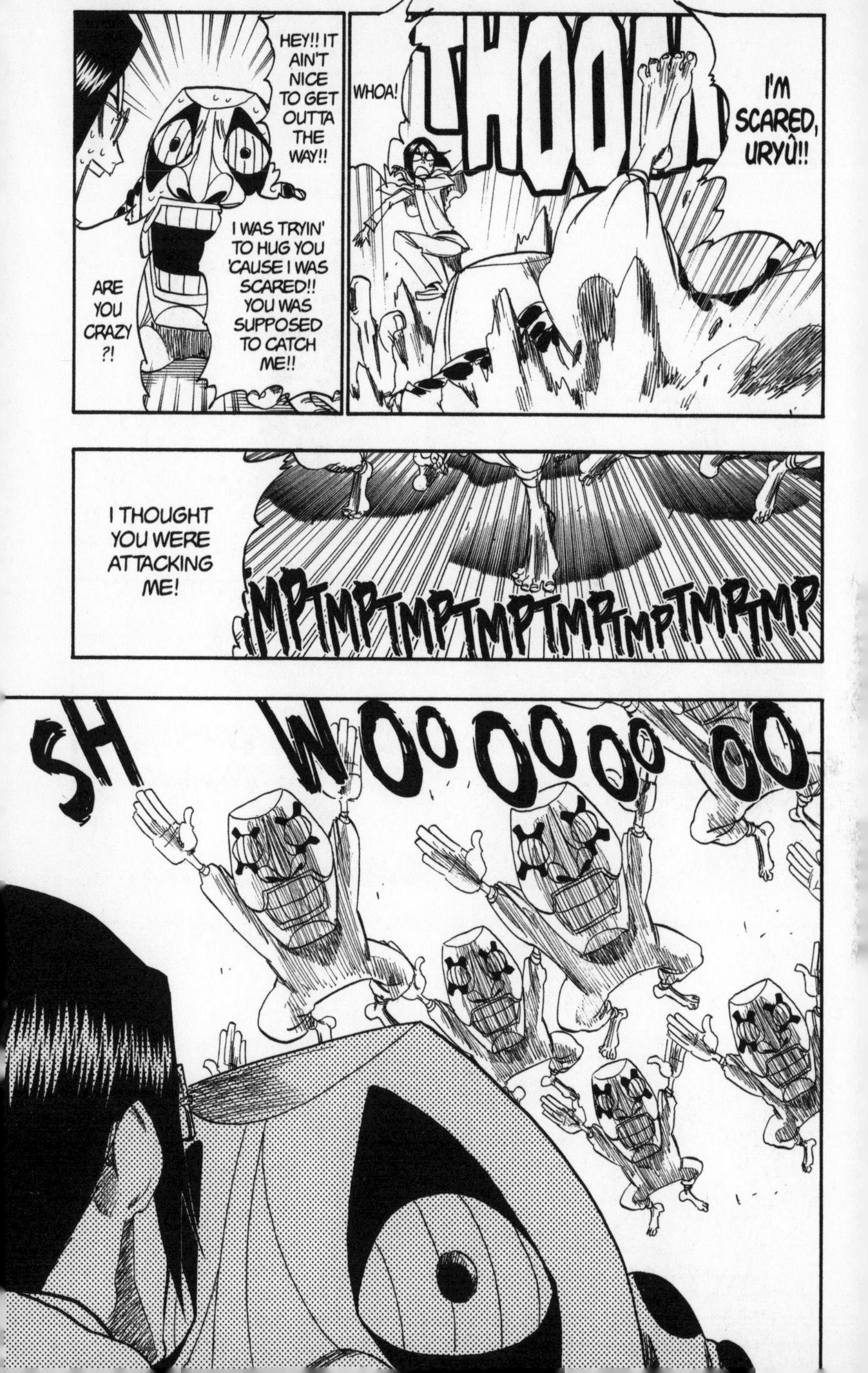
I'M SCARED, URYÛ!!
THOOM
WHOA!
HEY!! IT AIN'T NICE TO GET OUTTA THE WAY!!
I WAS TRYIN' TO HUG YOU 'CAUSE I WAS SCARED!! YOU WAS SUPPOSED TO CATCH ME!!
ARE YOU CRAZY ?!
TMPTMPTMPTMPTMPTMPTMPTMPTMP
I THOUGHT YOU WERE ATTACKING ME!
SHWOOOOOOOO

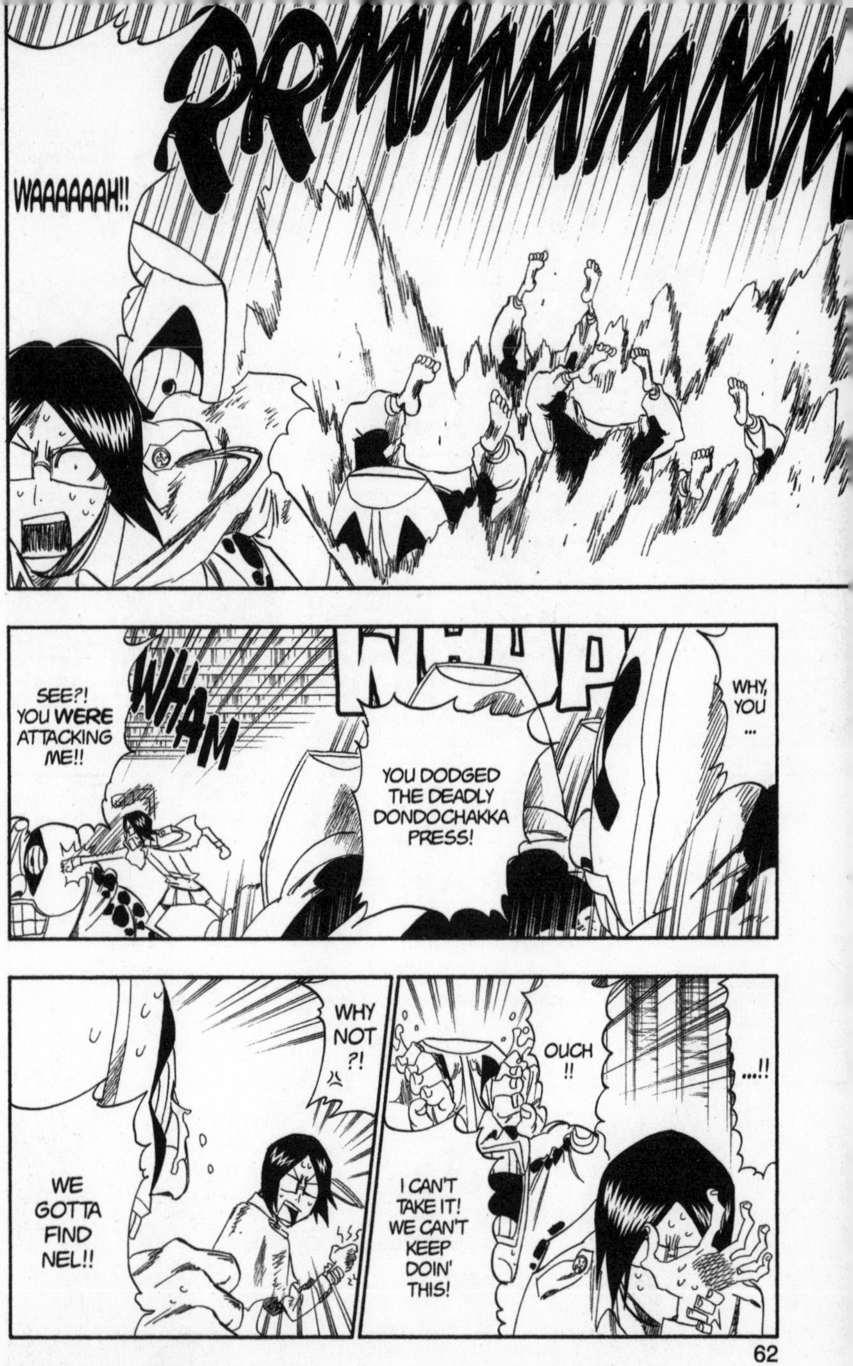
PRMMMMMM
WAAAAAAH!!
WHY, YOU ...
YOU DODGED THE DEADLY DONDOCHAKKA PRESS!
WHAM
SEE?! YOU **WERE** ATTACKING ME!!
...!!
OUCH !!
I CAN'T TAKE IT! WE CAN'T KEEP DOIN' THIS!
WHY NOT ?!
WE GOTTA FIND NEL!!

READ THIS WAY

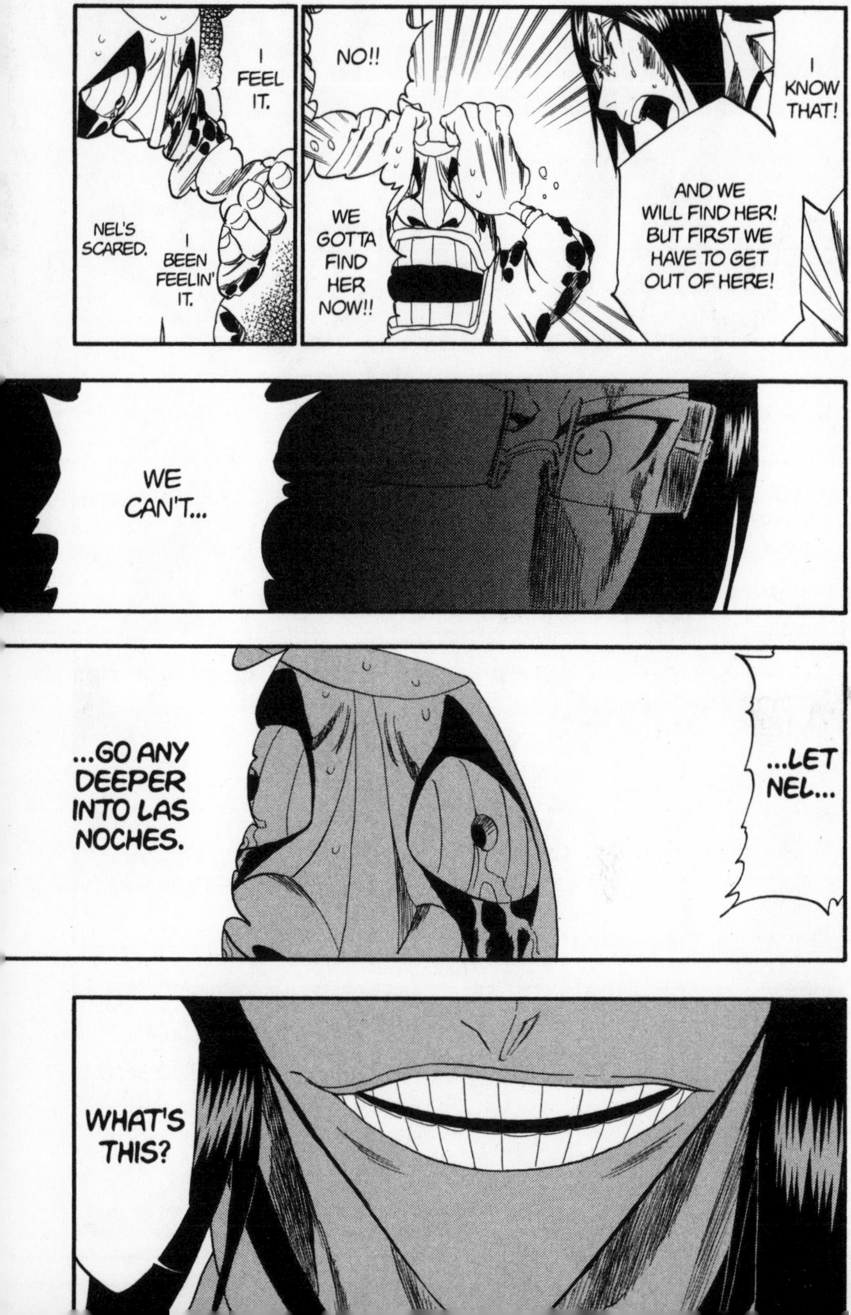
I KNOW THAT!
AND WE WILL FIND HER! BUT FIRST WE HAVE TO GET OUT OF HERE!
NO!!
WE GOTTA FIND HER NOW!!
I FEEL IT.
I BEEN FEELIN' IT.
NEL'S SCARED.
WE CAN'T...
...LET NEL...
...GO ANY DEEPER INTO LAS NOCHES.
WHAT'S THIS?

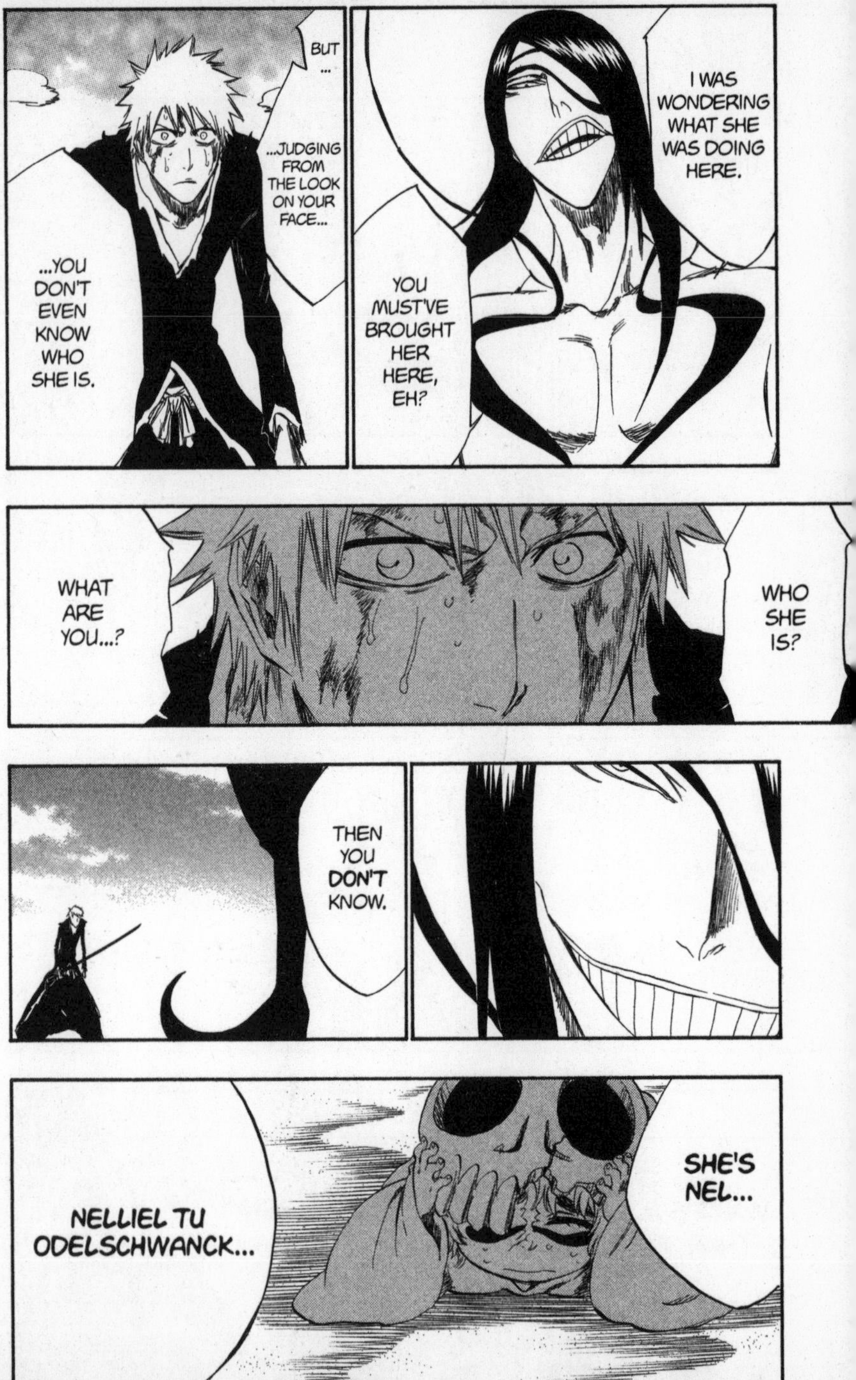
I WAS WONDERING WHAT SHE WAS DOING HERE.
YOU MUST'VE BROUGHT HER HERE, EH?
BUT ...
...JUDGING FROM THE LOOK ON YOUR FACE...
...YOU DON'T EVEN KNOW WHO SHE IS.
WHO SHE IS?
WHAT ARE YOU...?
THEN YOU DON'T KNOW.
SHE'S NEL...
NELLIEL TU ODELSCHWANCK...

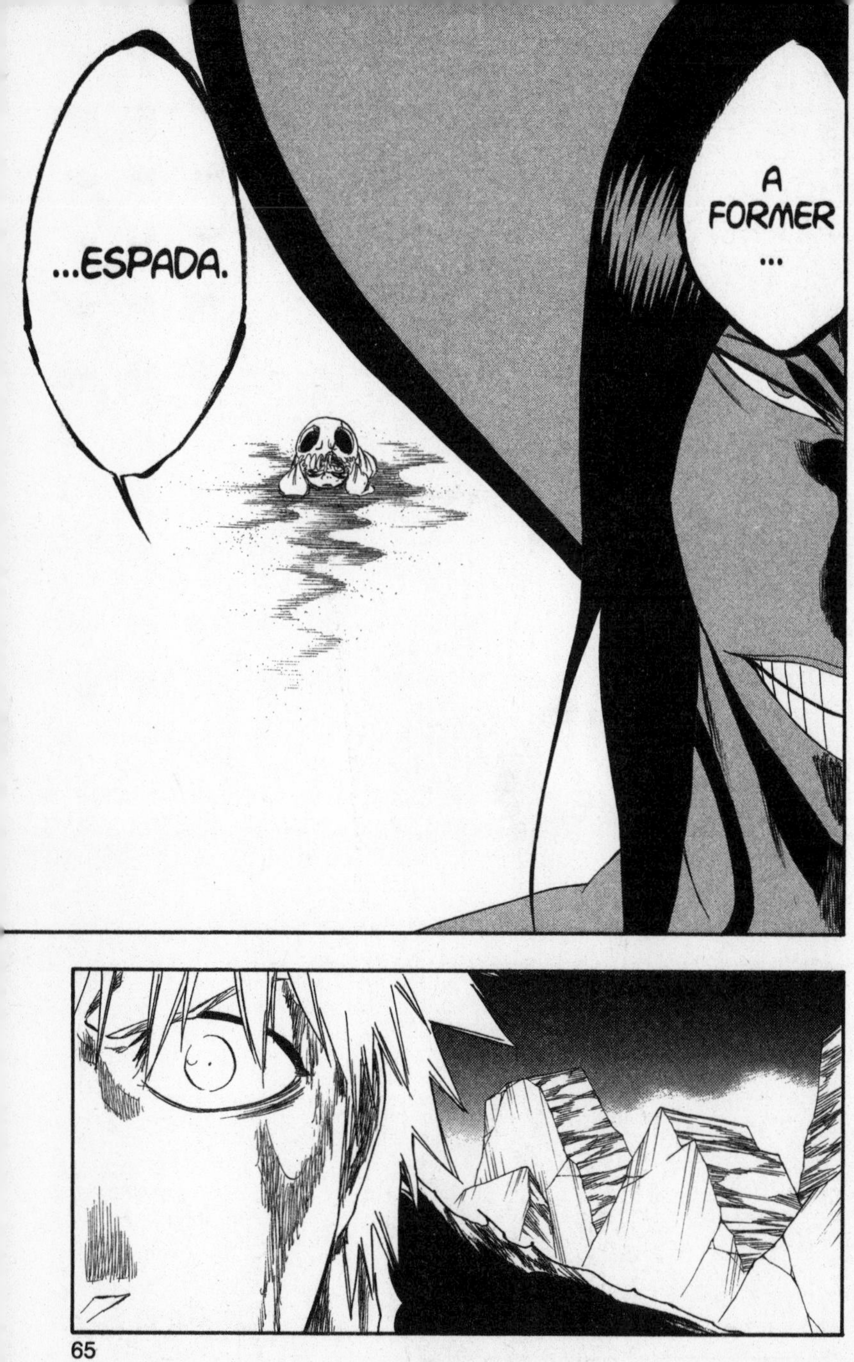
A FORMER ...
...ESPADA.

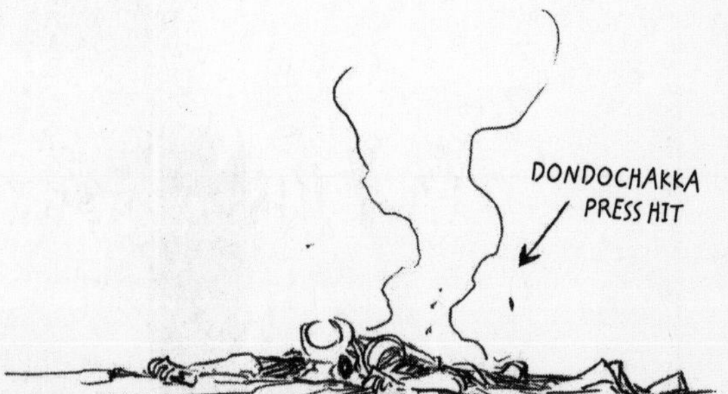
DONDOCHAKKA
PRESS HIT

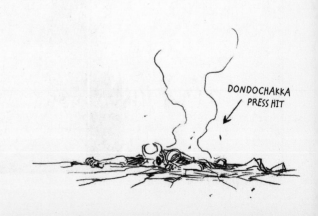

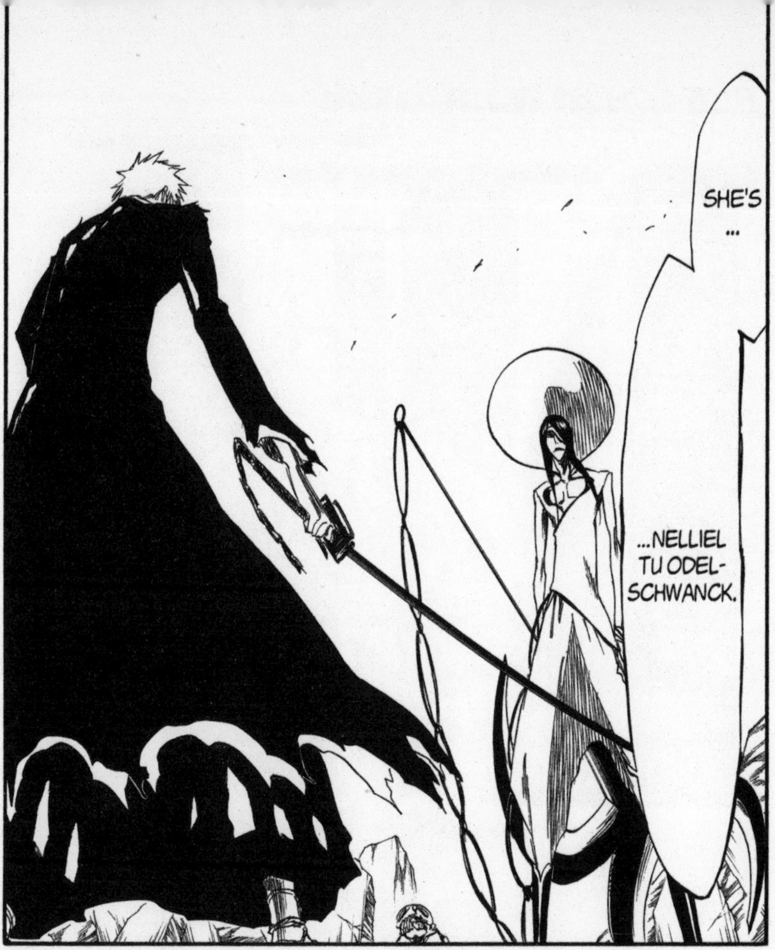
SHE'S ...
...NELLIEL TU ODEL-SCHWANCK.

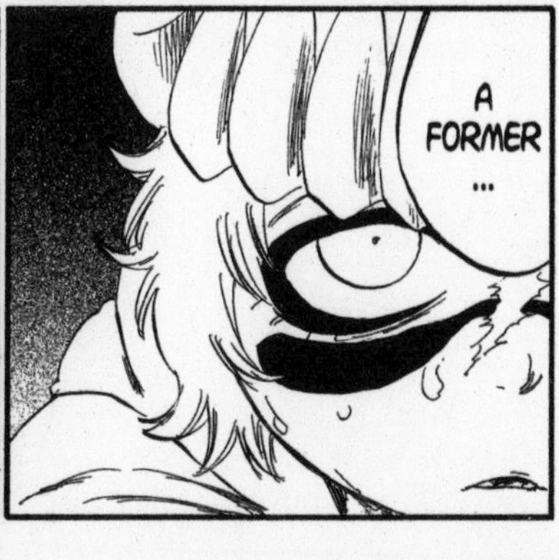
A FORMER ...

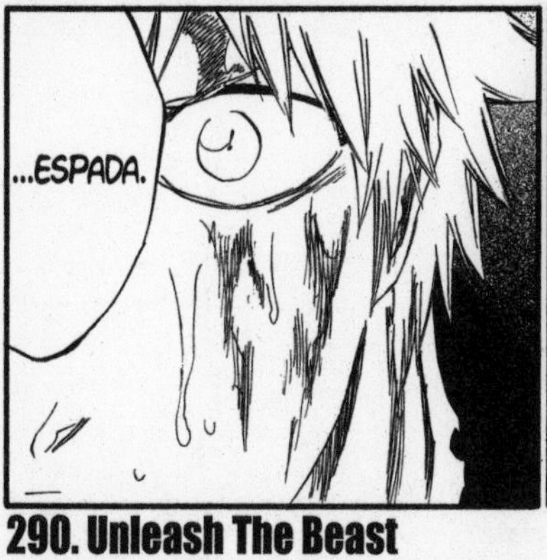
...ESPADA.

290. Unleash The Beast

BLEACH 290. Unleash The Beast

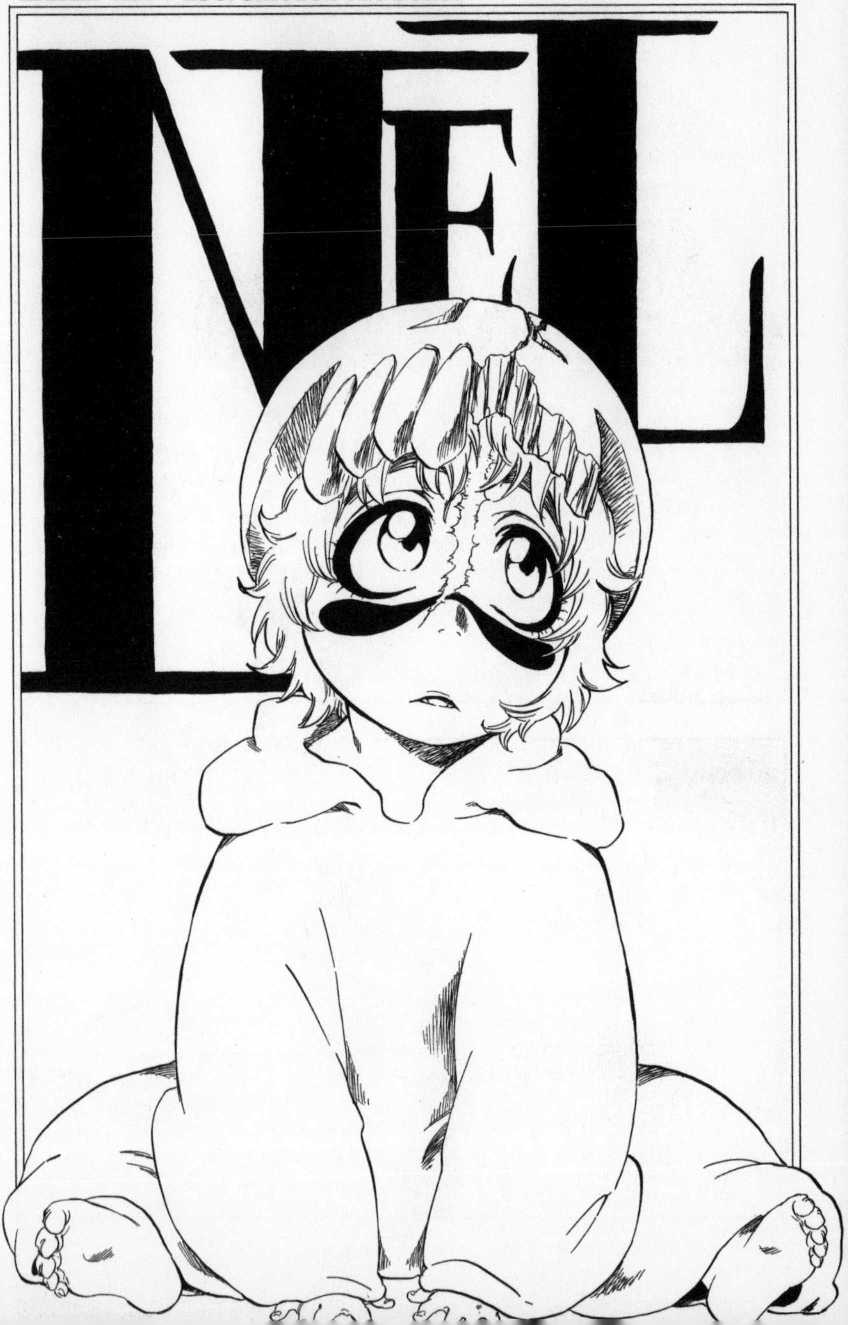
NEL

READ THIS WAY

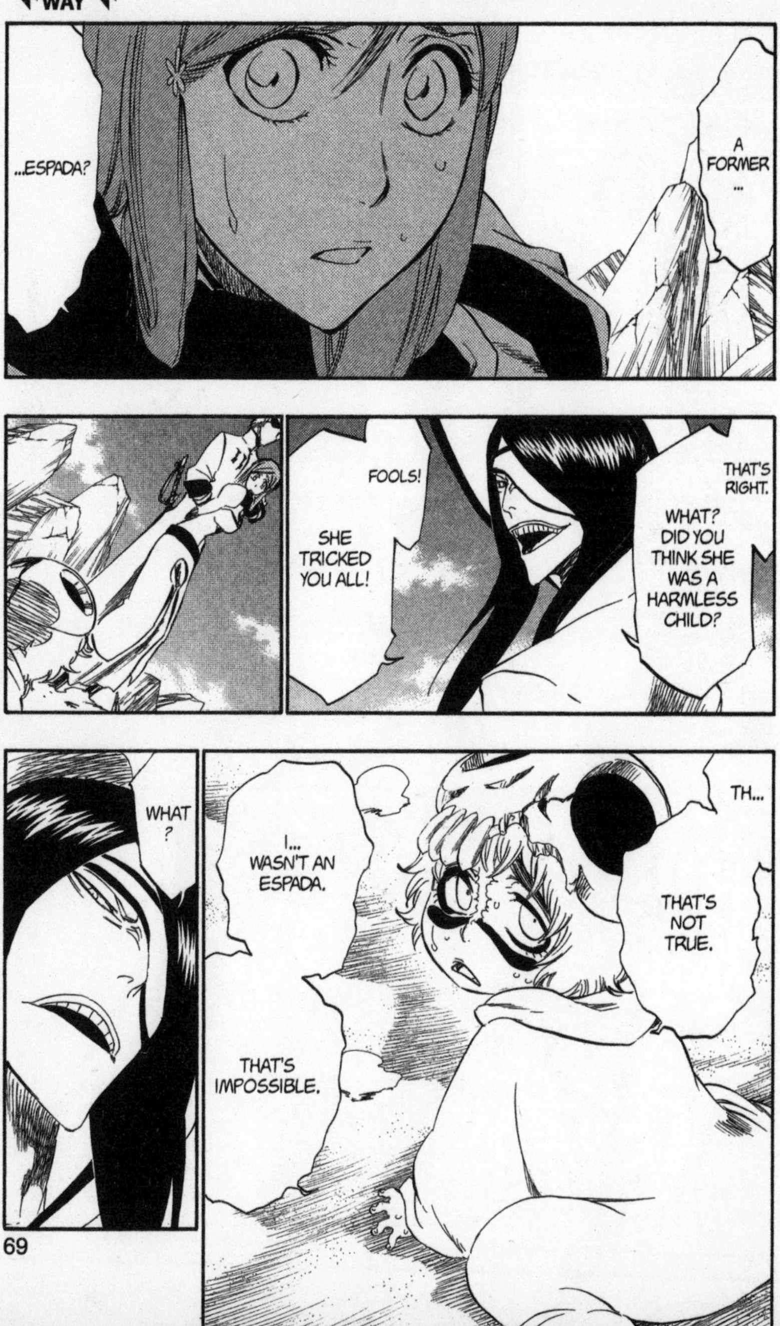
A FORMER ...
...ESPADA?
THAT'S RIGHT.
WHAT? DID YOU THINK SHE WAS A HARMLESS CHILD?
FOOLS!
SHE TRICKED YOU ALL!
TH...
THAT'S NOT TRUE.
I... WASN'T AN ESPADA.
THAT'S IMPOSSIBLE.
WHAT?

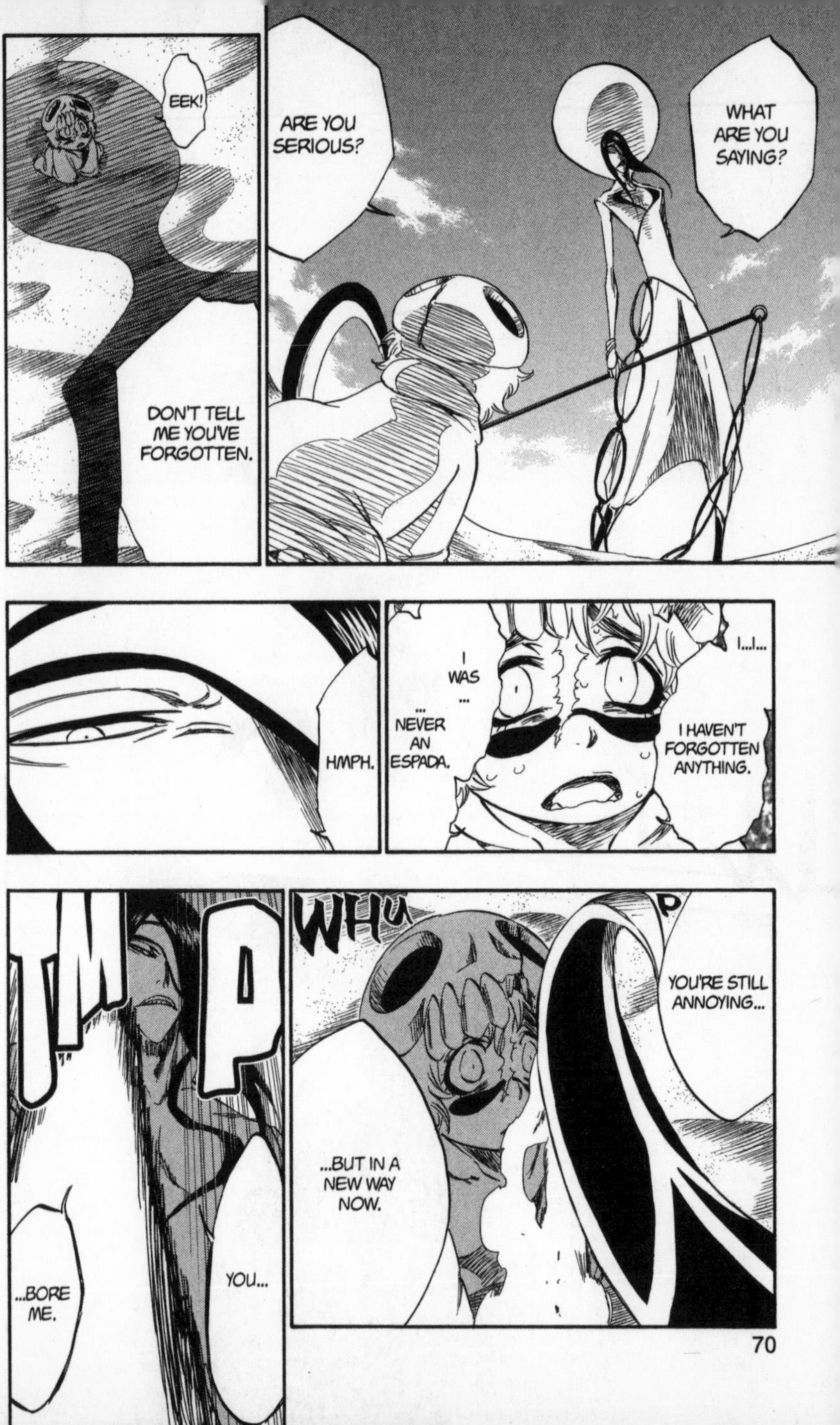
WHAT ARE YOU SAYING?
ARE YOU SERIOUS?
EEK!
DON'T TELL ME YOU'VE FORGOTTEN.
I...I...
I HAVEN'T FORGOTTEN ANYTHING.
I WAS...
...NEVER AN ESPADA.
HMPH.
YOU'RE STILL ANNOYING...
...BUT IN A NEW WAY NOW.
YOU...
...BORE ME.

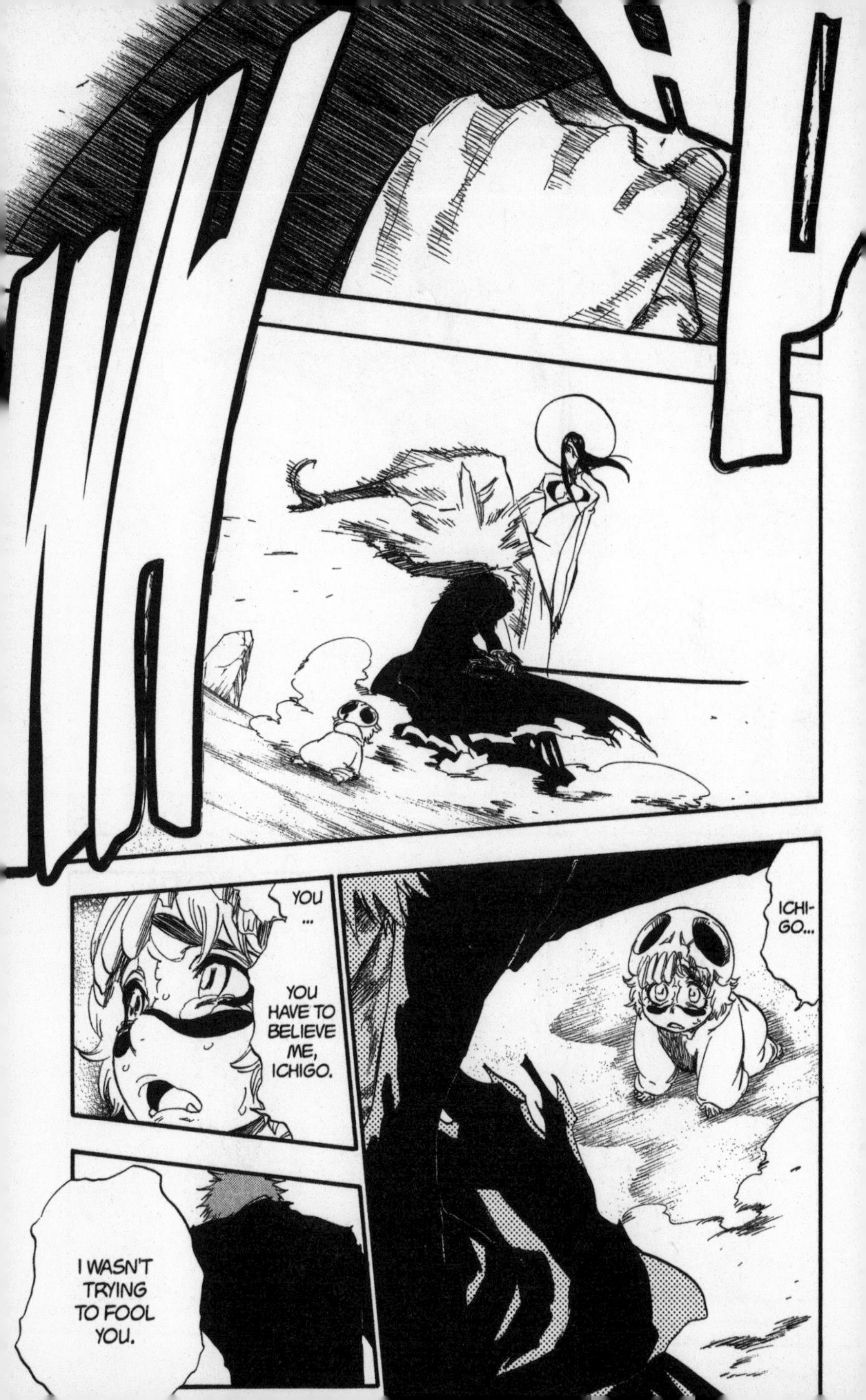
ICHI-GO...
YOU ...
YOU HAVE TO BELIEVE ME, ICHIGO.
I WASN'T TRYING TO FOOL YOU.

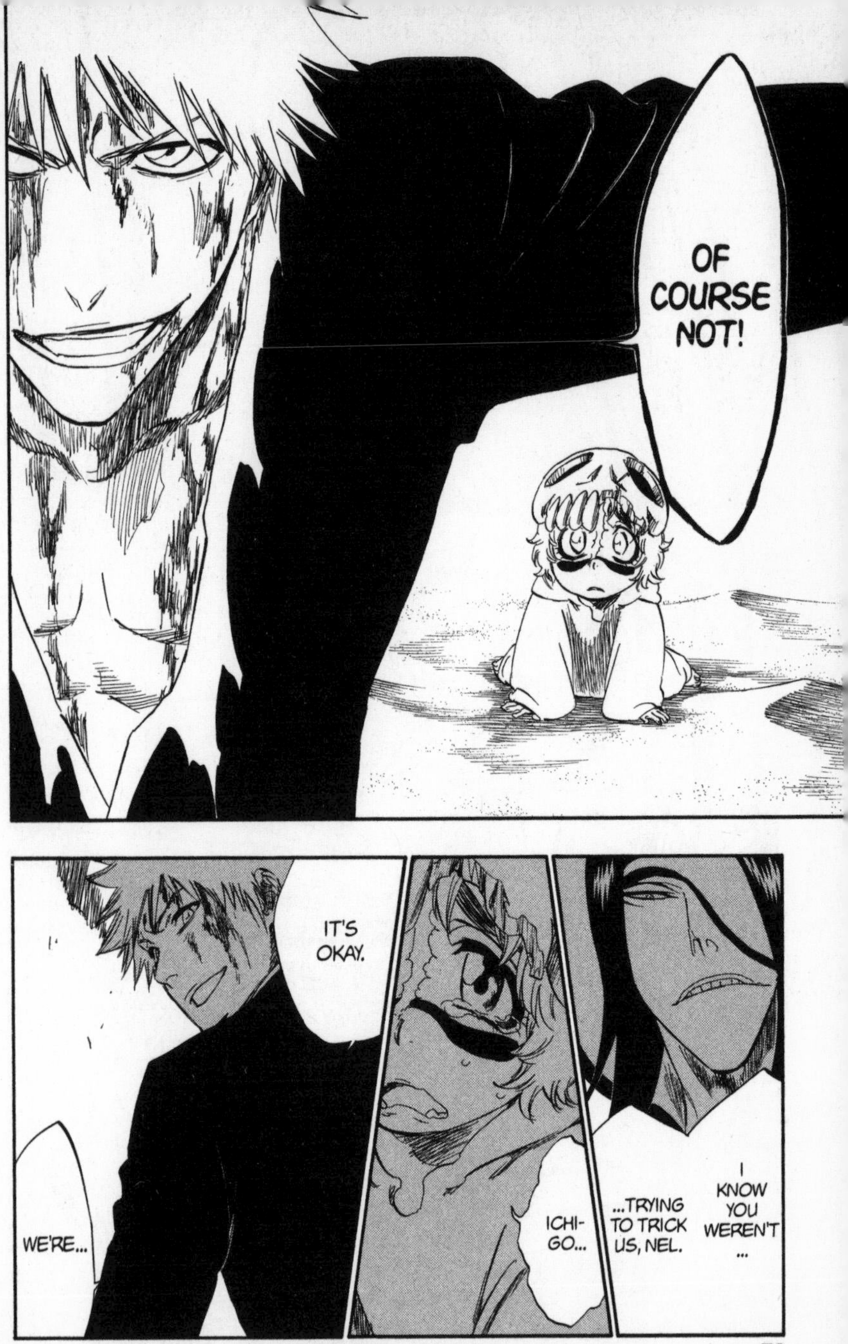
OF COURSE NOT!
I KNOW YOU WEREN'T ...
...TRYING TO TRICK US, NEL.
ICHI-GO...
IT'S OKAY.
WE'RE...

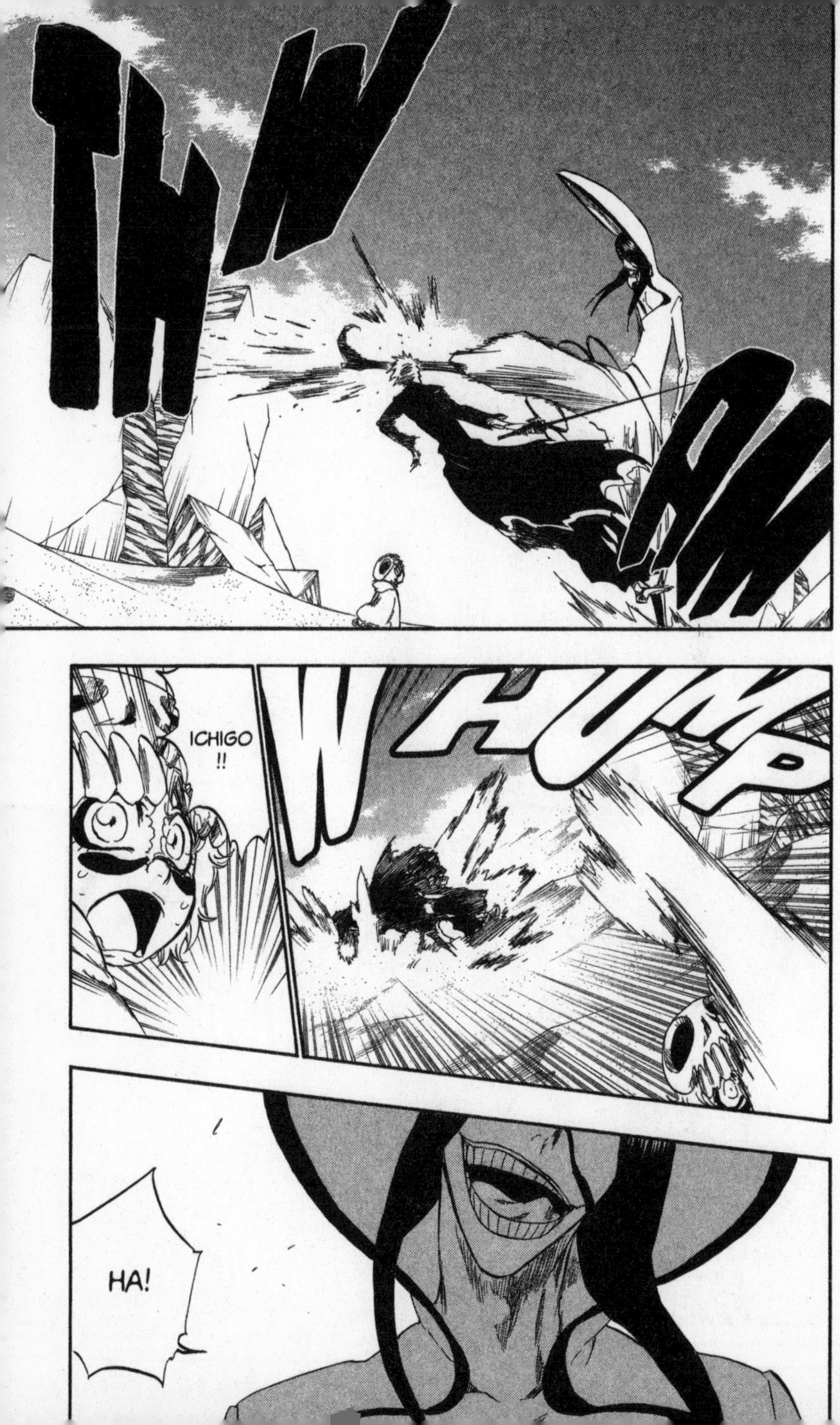
THWAM
WHUMP
ICHIGO !!
HA!

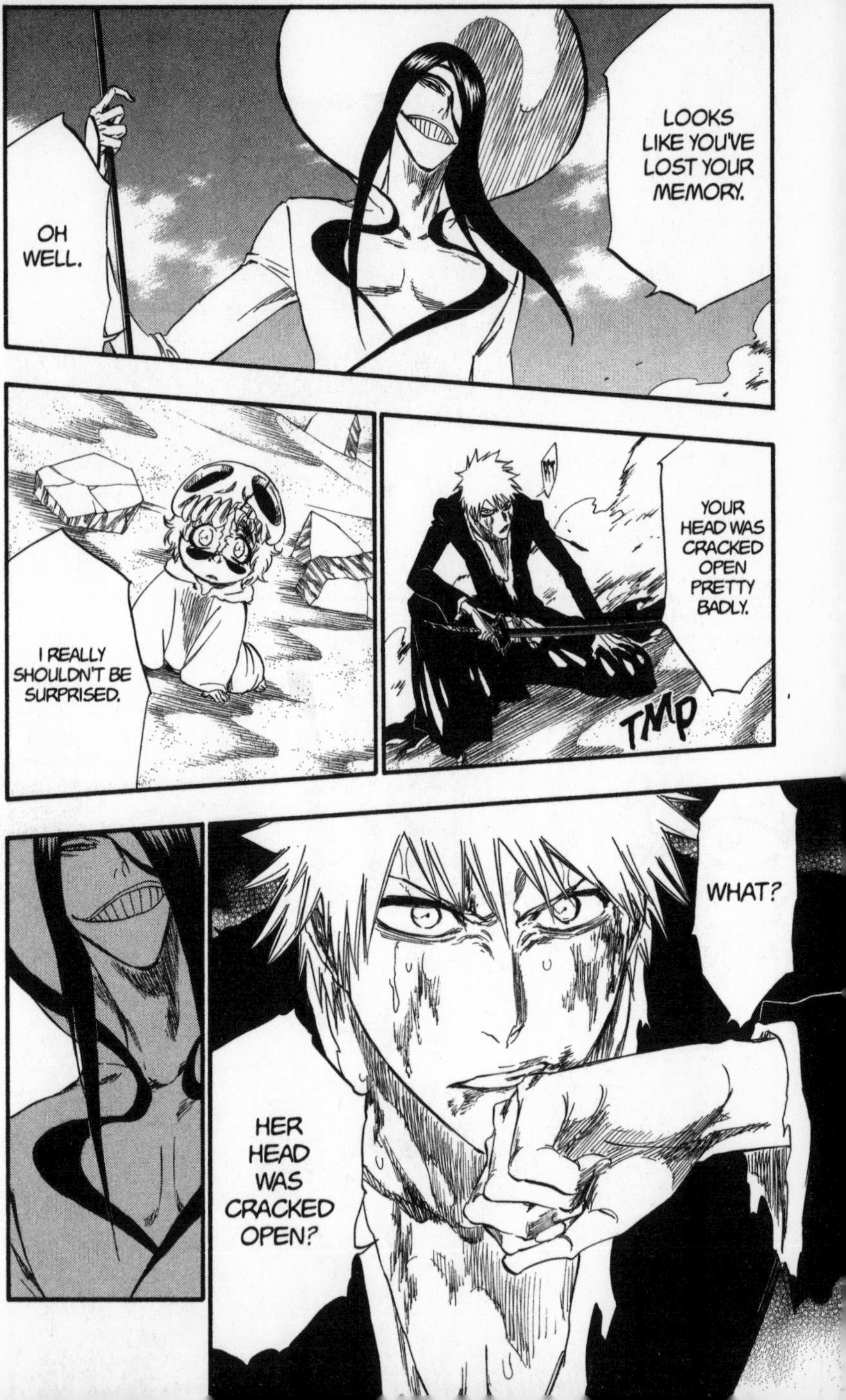
LOOKS LIKE YOU'VE LOST YOUR MEMORY.
OH WELL.
YOUR HEAD WAS CRACKED OPEN PRETTY BADLY.
TMP
I REALLY SHOULDN'T BE SURPRISED.
WHAT?
HER HEAD WAS CRACKED OPEN?

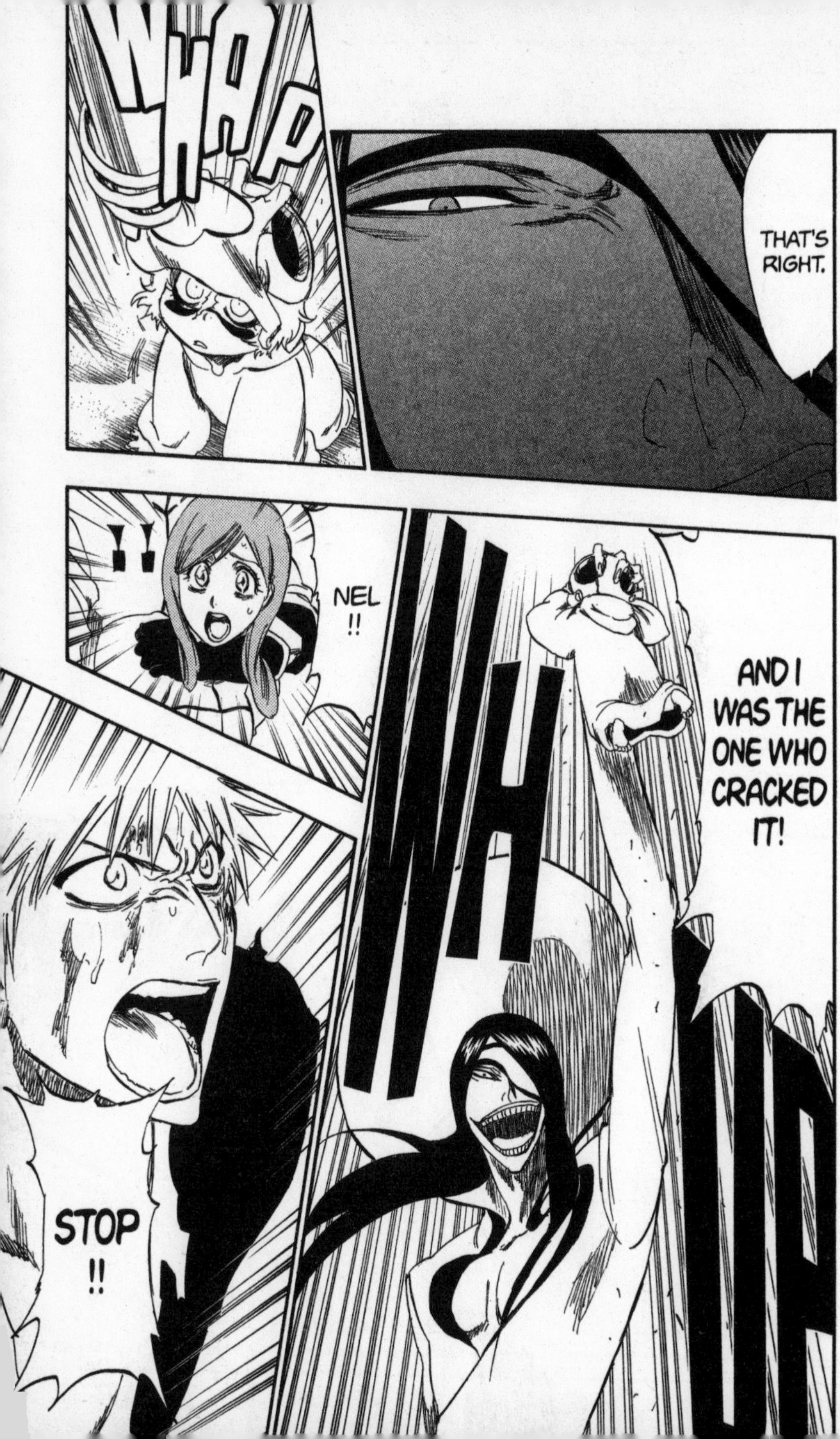
THAT'S RIGHT.
WHAP
AND I WAS THE ONE WHO CRACKED IT!
WHAP
NEL!!
STOP!!

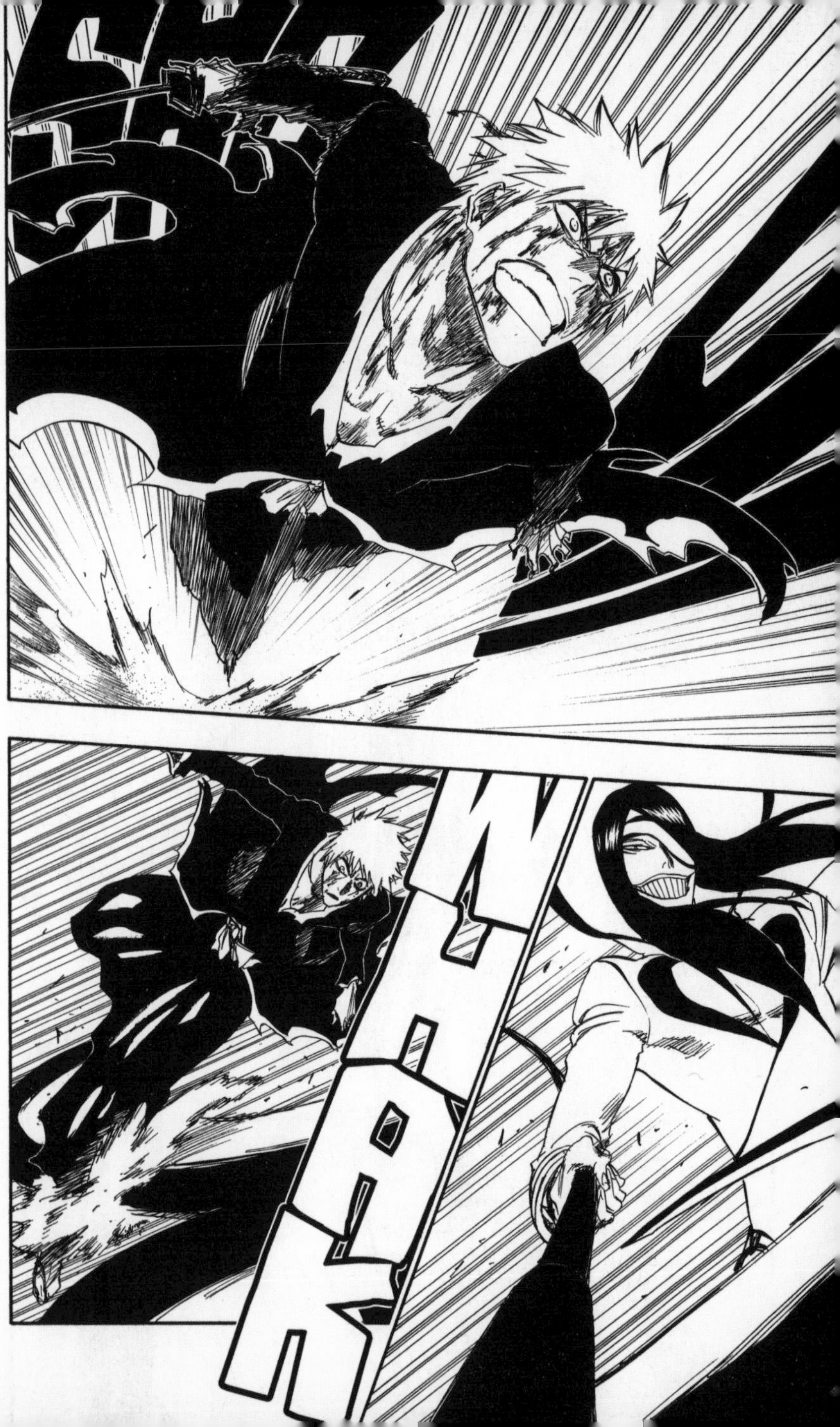
WHACK

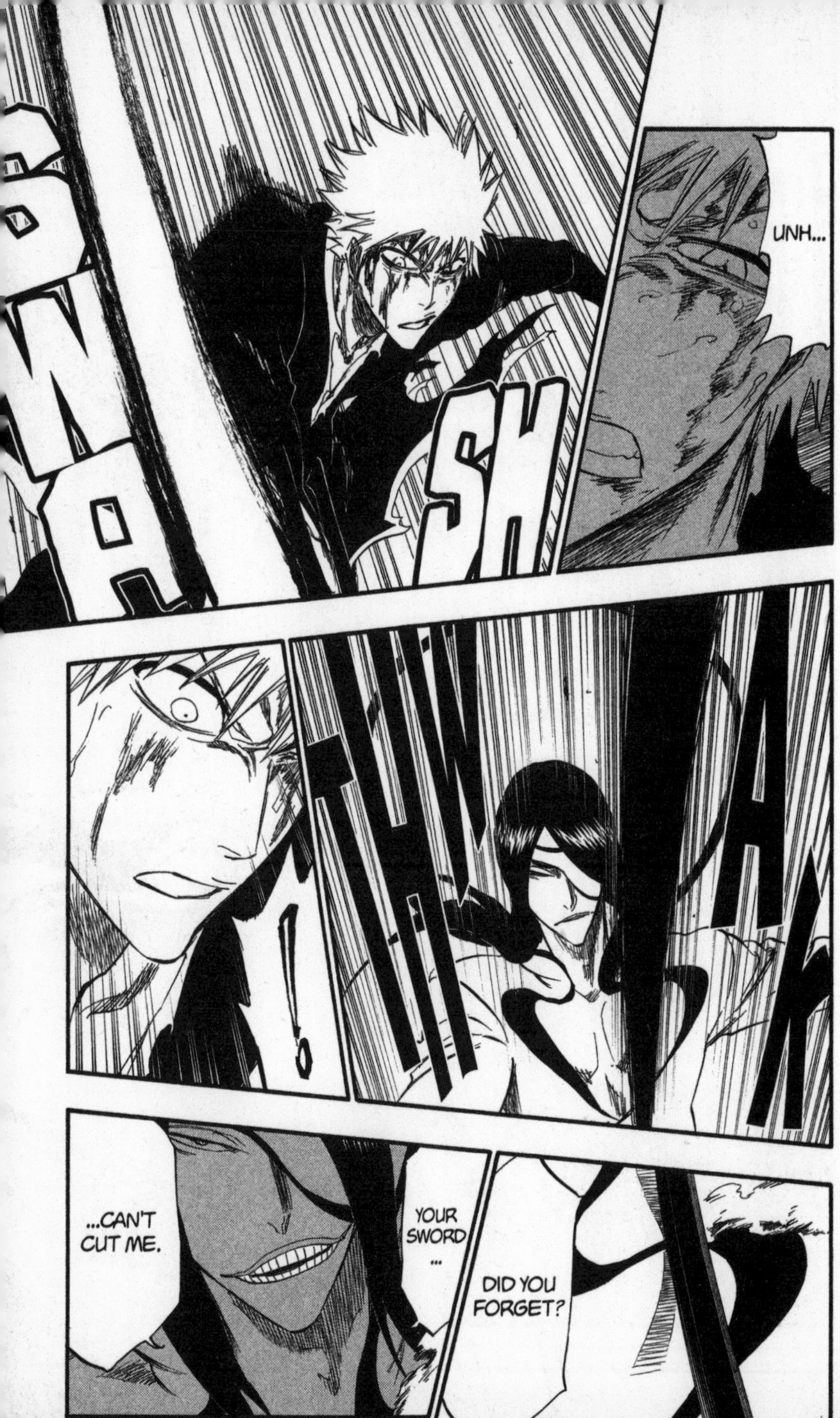
UNH...
SH
THWAK
!
DID YOU FORGET?
YOUR SWORD ...
...CAN'T CUT ME.

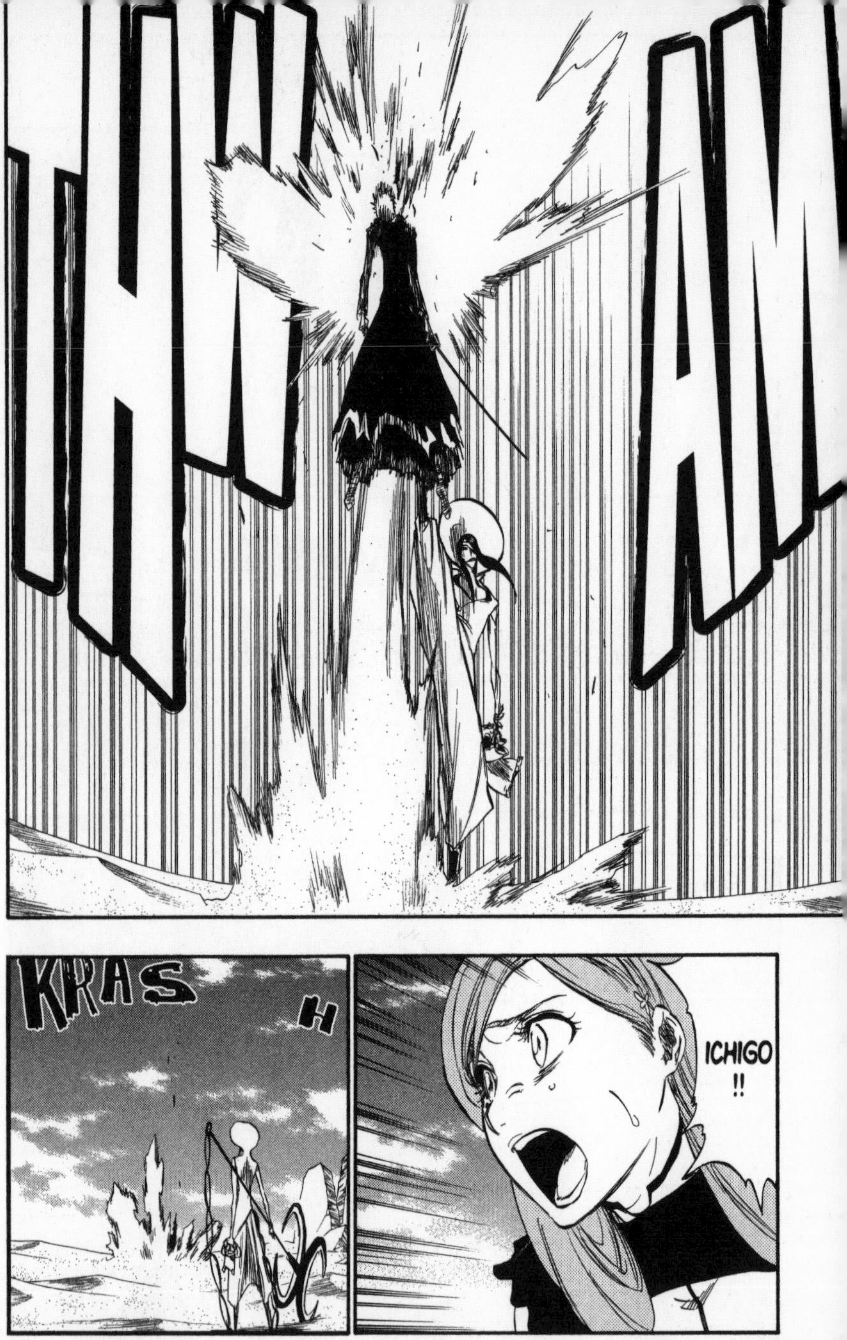
ICHIGO !!
KRASH

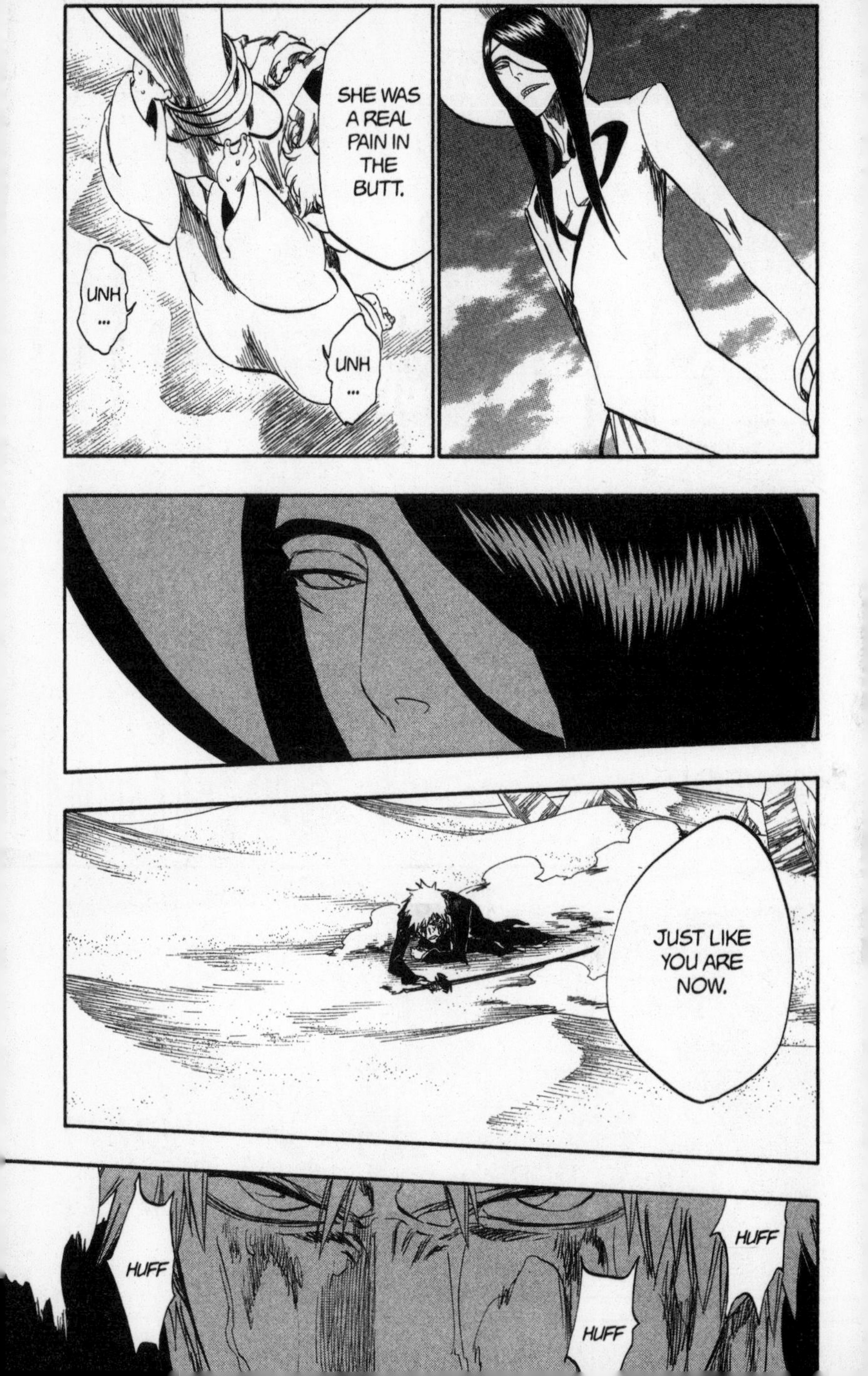
SHE WAS A REAL PAIN IN THE BUTT.
UNH ...
UNH ...
JUST LIKE YOU ARE NOW.
HUFF
HUFF
HUFF

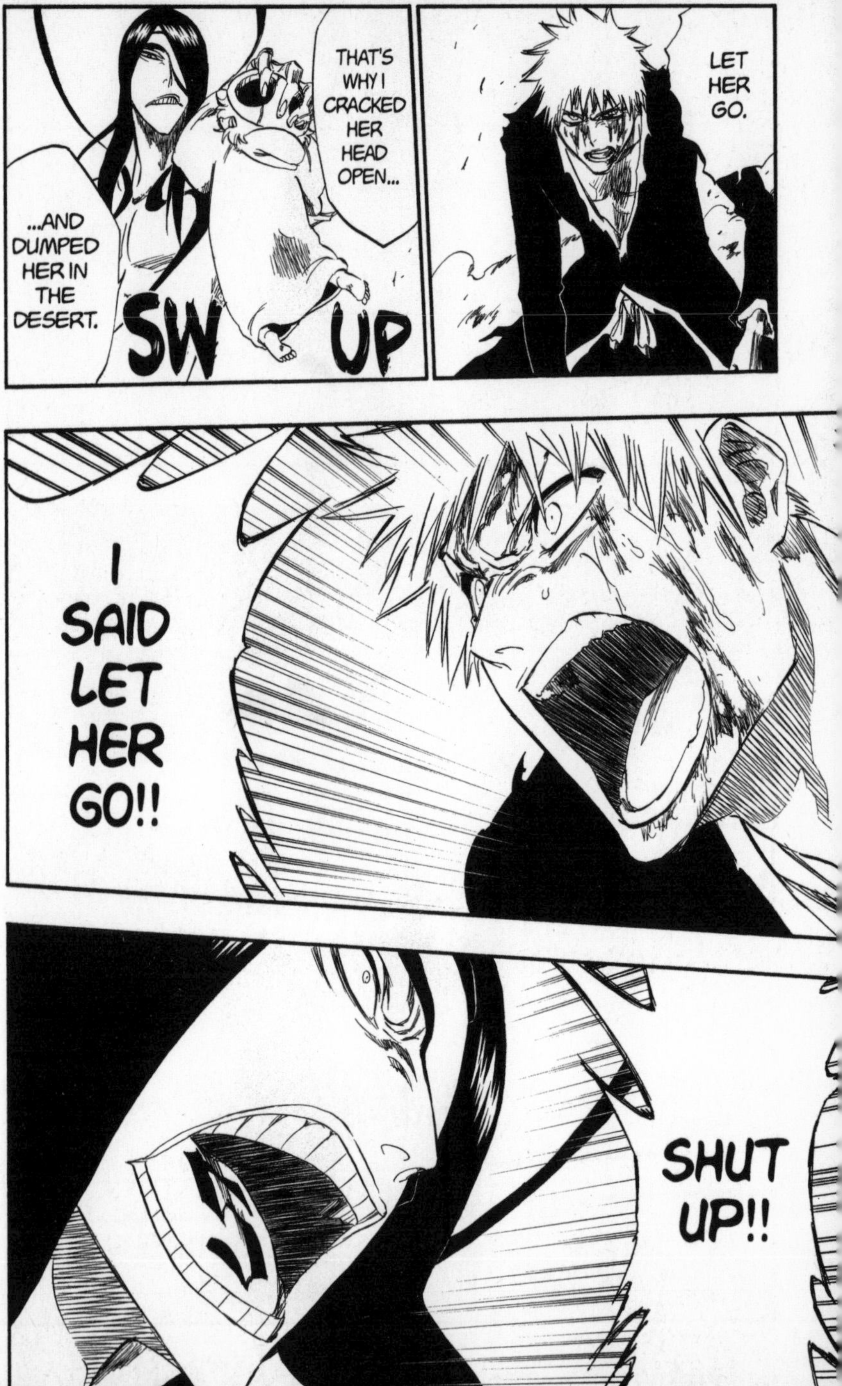
LET HER GO.
THAT'S WHY I CRACKED HER HEAD OPEN...
...AND DUMPED HER IN THE DESERT.
SW UP
I SAID LET HER GO!!
SHUT UP!!

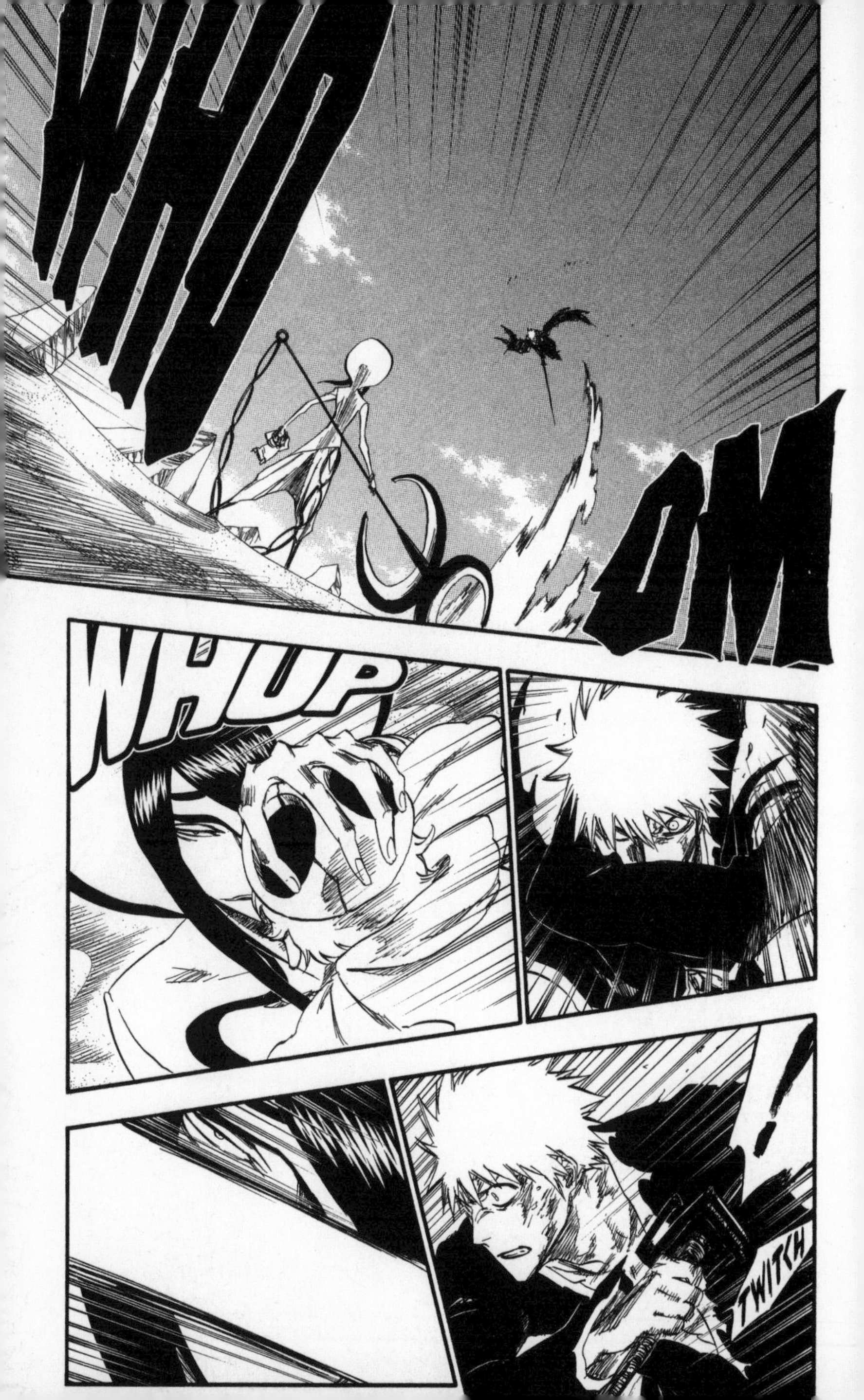
WHOOM
WHUP
!
TWITCH

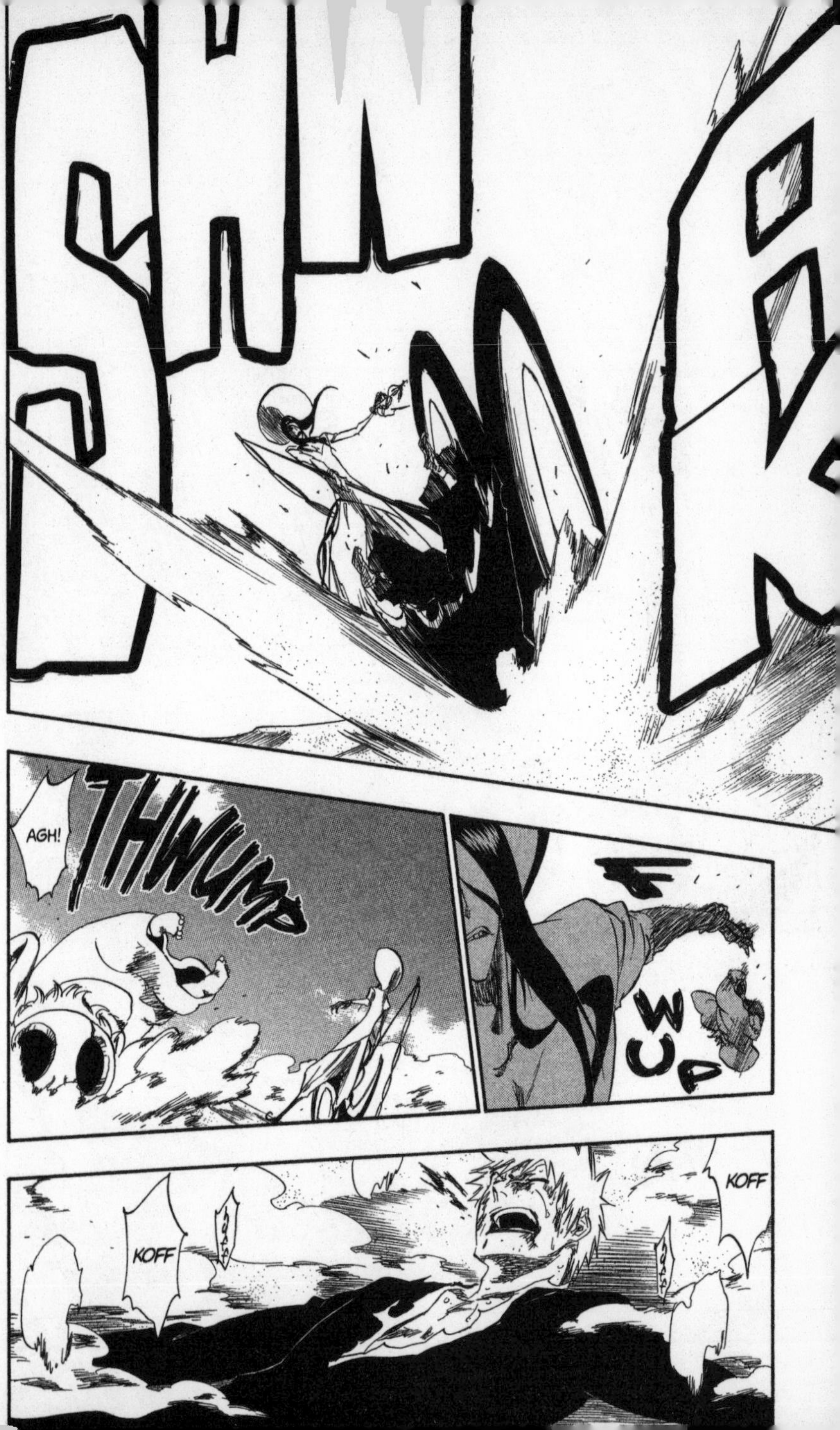
WUP
AGH!
THWUMP
KOFF
KOFF

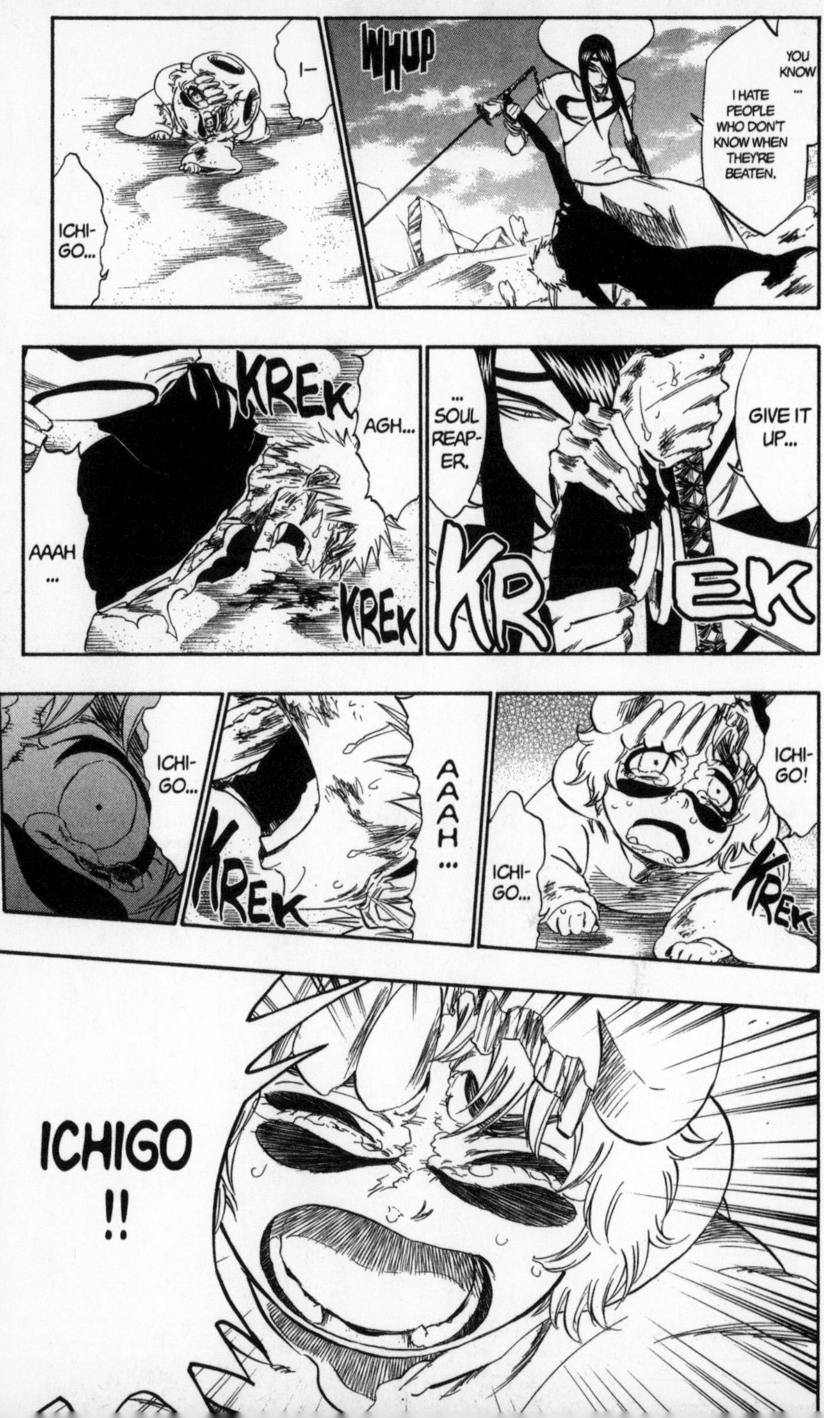
YOU KNOW...
I HATE PEOPLE WHO DON'T KNOW WHEN THEY'RE BEATEN.
WHUP
I—
ICHI-GO...
GIVE IT UP...
...SOUL REAPER.
KREK
KREK
AGH...
AAAH...
KREK
ICHI-GO!
ICHI-GO...
KREK
AAAH...
KREK
ICHI-GO...
ICHIGO!!

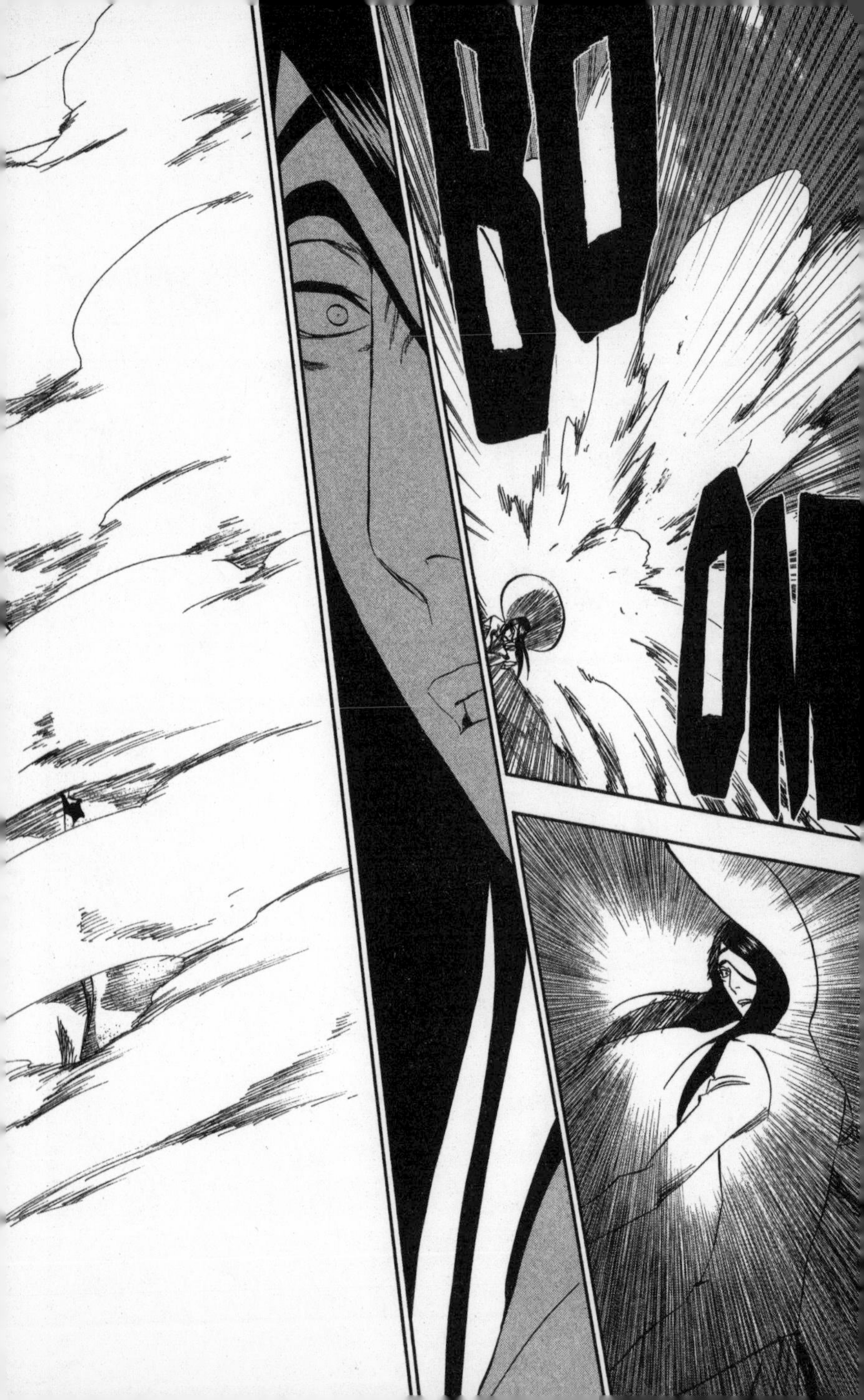
BOOM

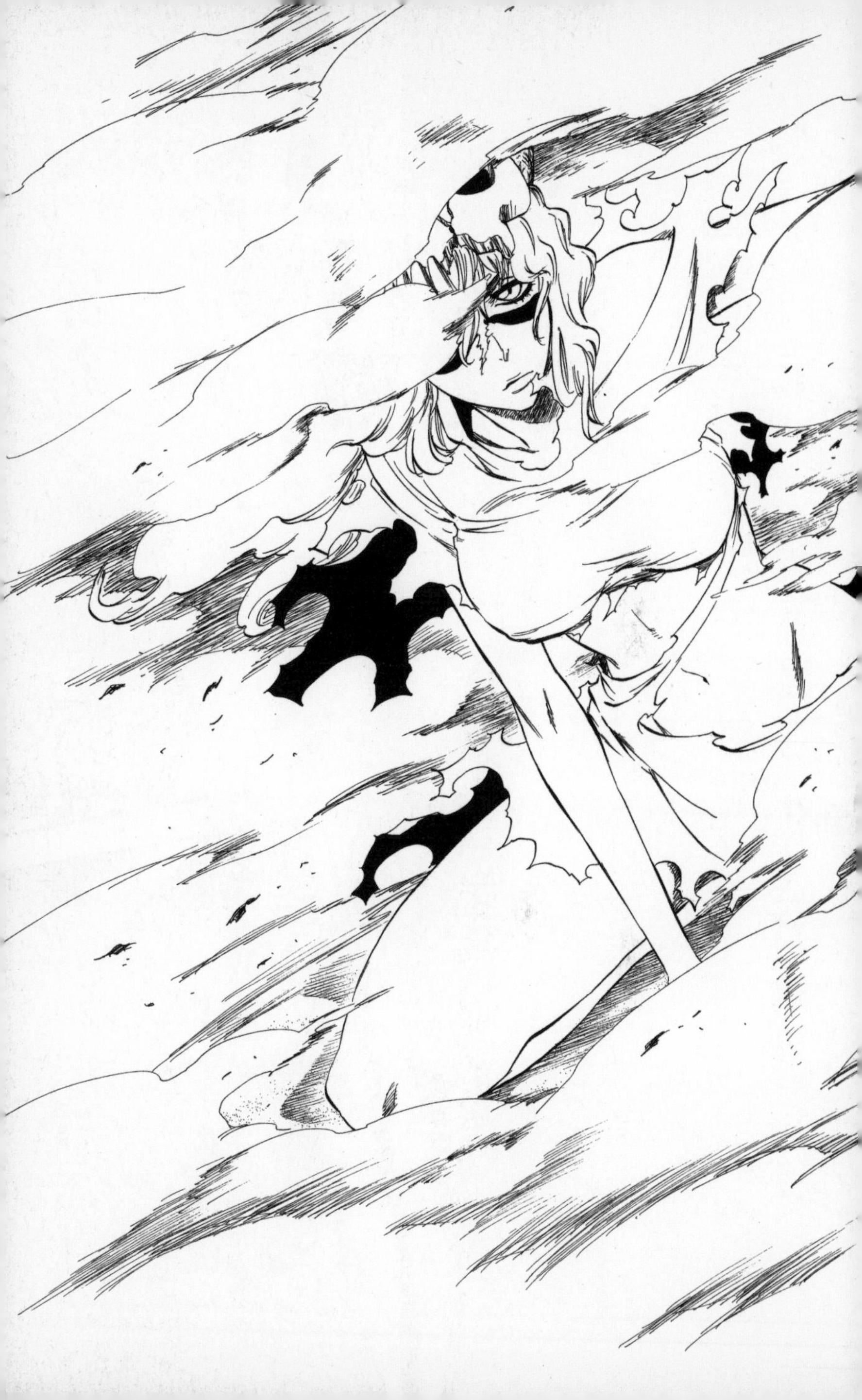

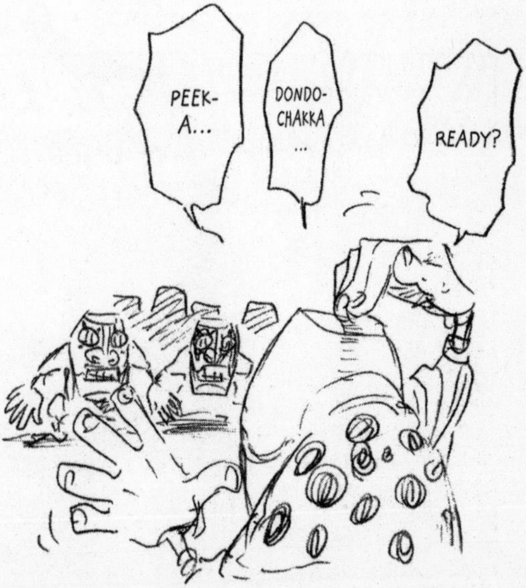
READY?
DONDO-CHAKKA ...
PEEK-A...

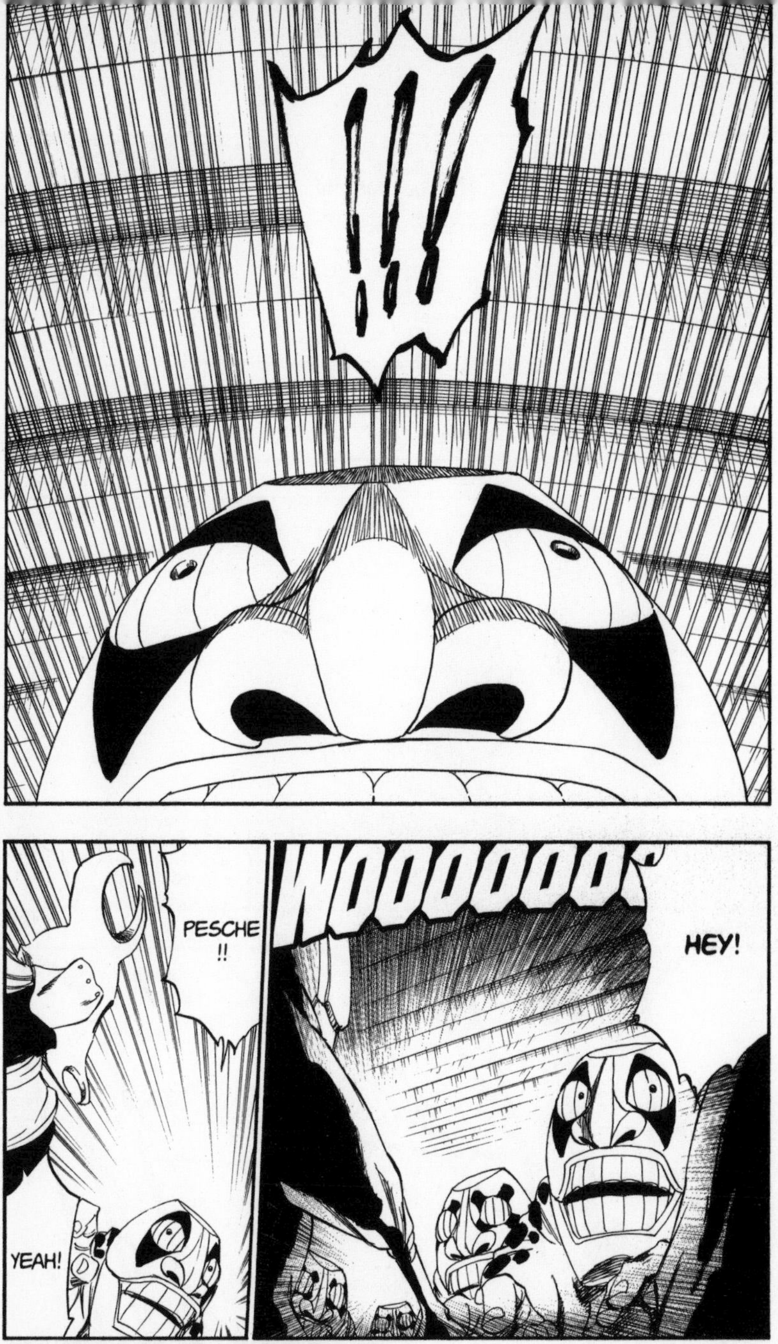
!!?
WOOOOOO
HEY!
PESCHE !!
YEAH!

291. Thank You For Defending Me

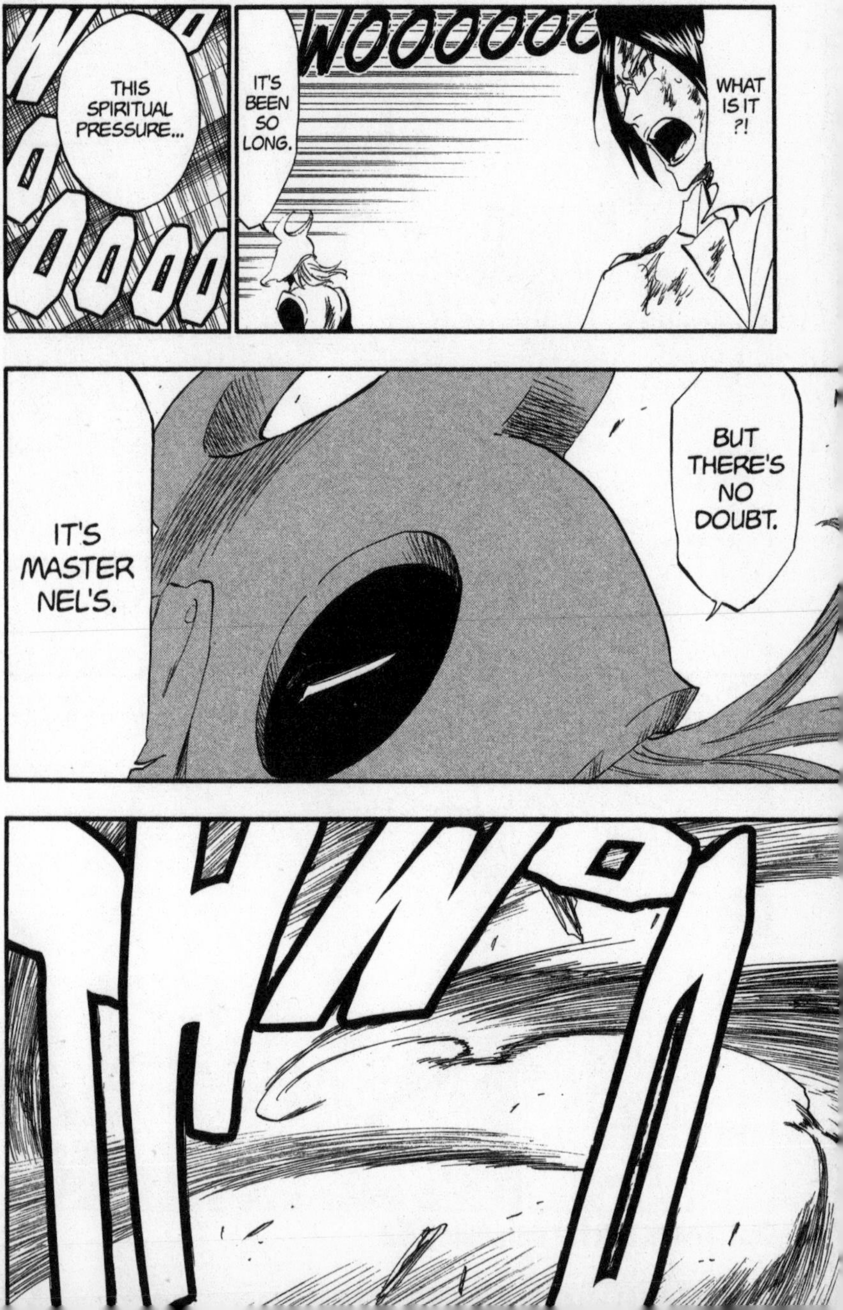
WHAT IS IT ?!
IT'S BEEN SO LONG.
THIS SPIRITUAL PRESSURE...
BUT THERE'S NO DOUBT.
IT'S MASTER NEL'S.

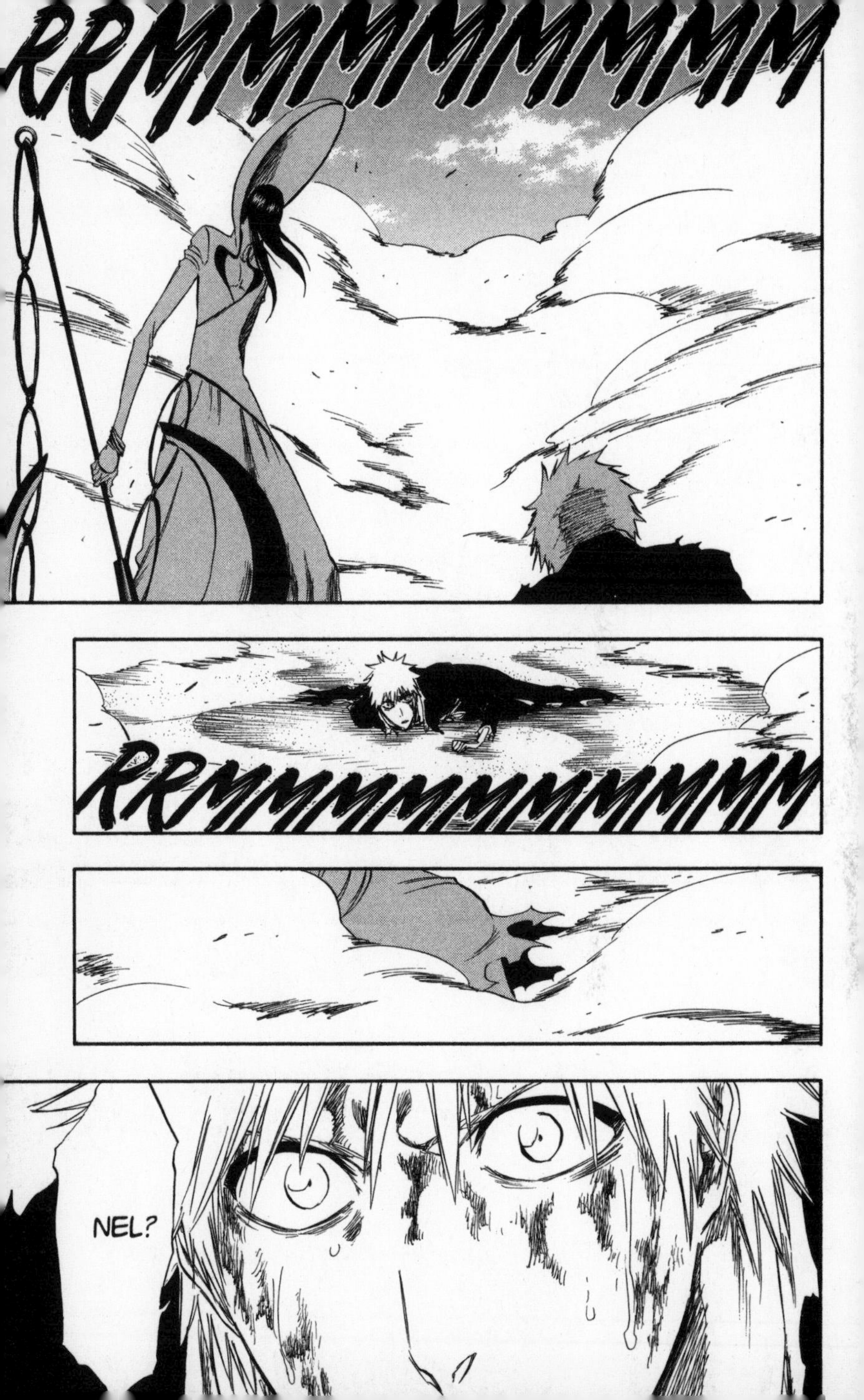
RRMMMMMMMMMMM
RRMMMMMMMMMMMM
NEL?

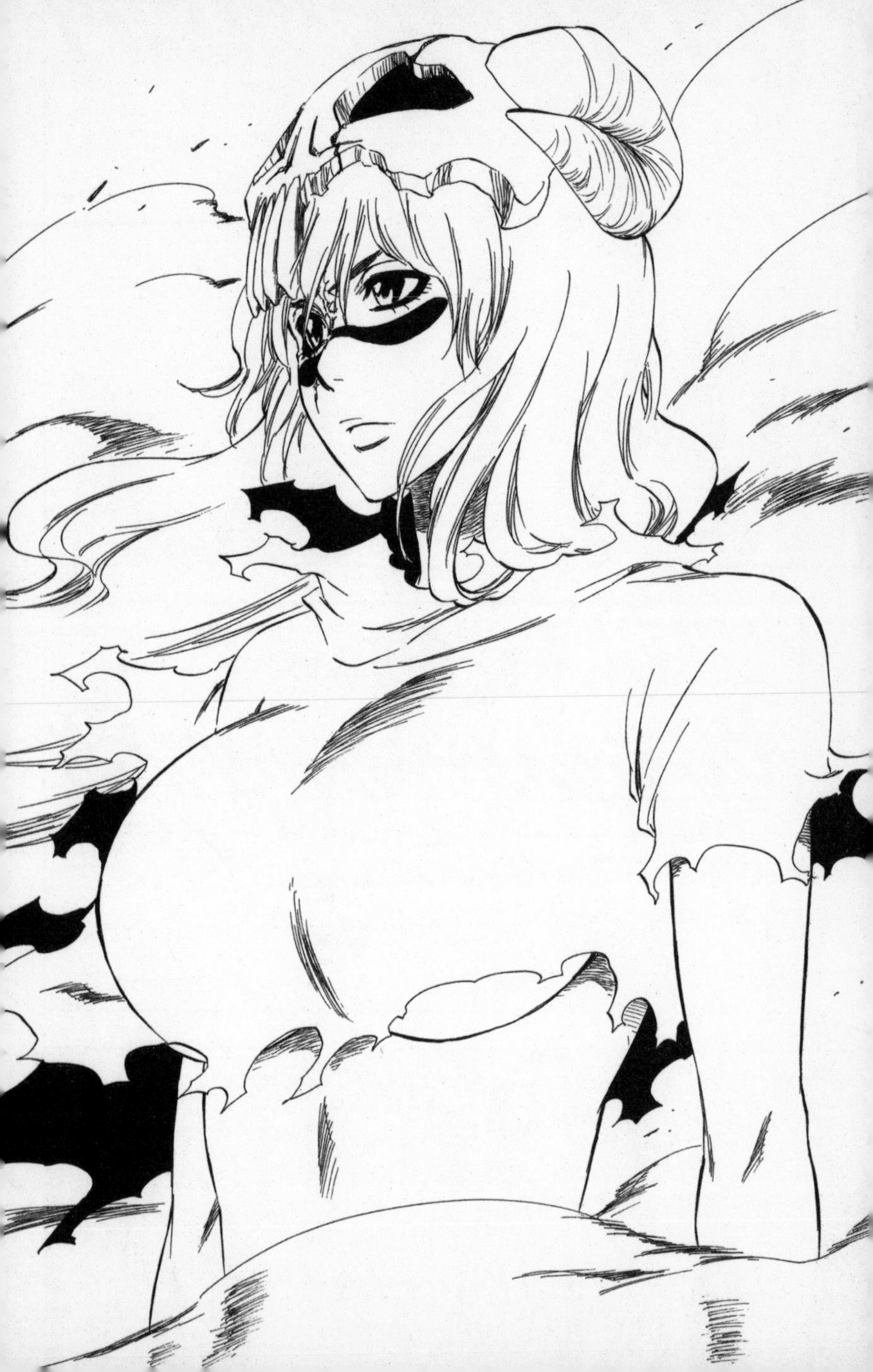

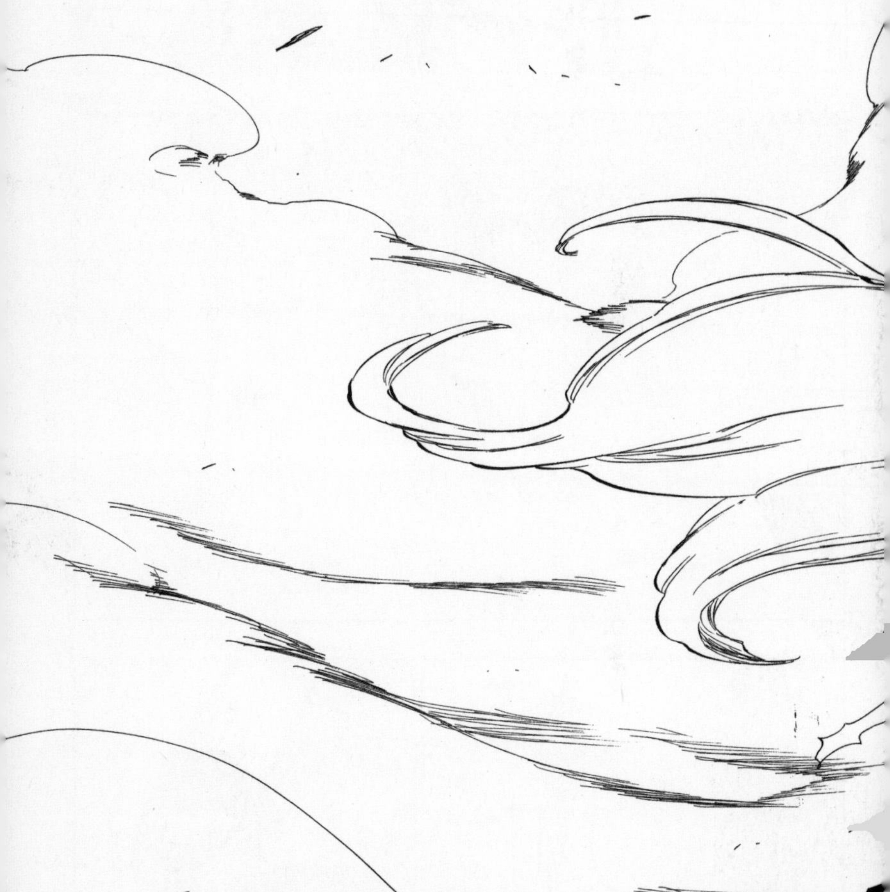

BLEACH 291. Thank You For Defending Me

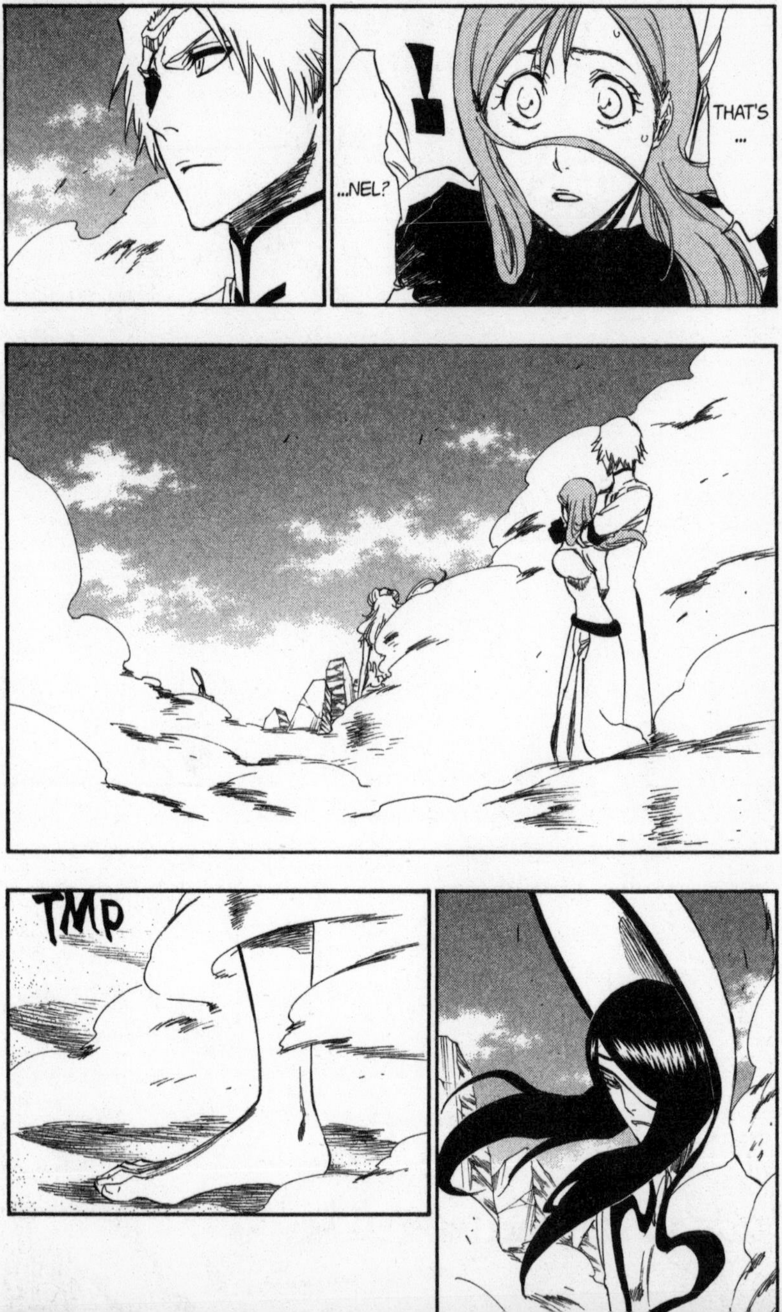

THAT'S ...
!
...NEL?
TMP

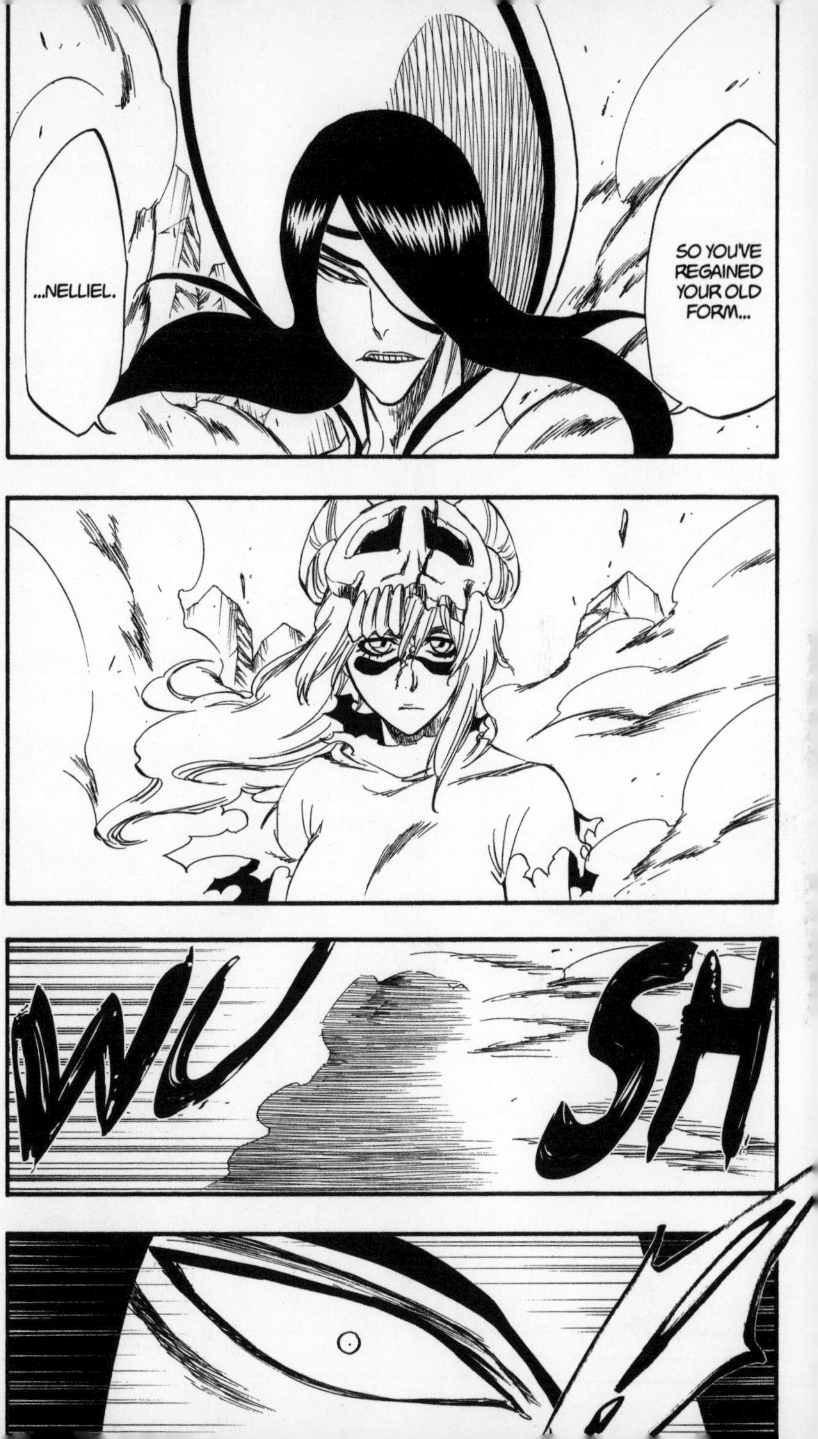
SO YOU'VE REGAINED YOUR OLD FORM...
...NELLIEL.
WU SH

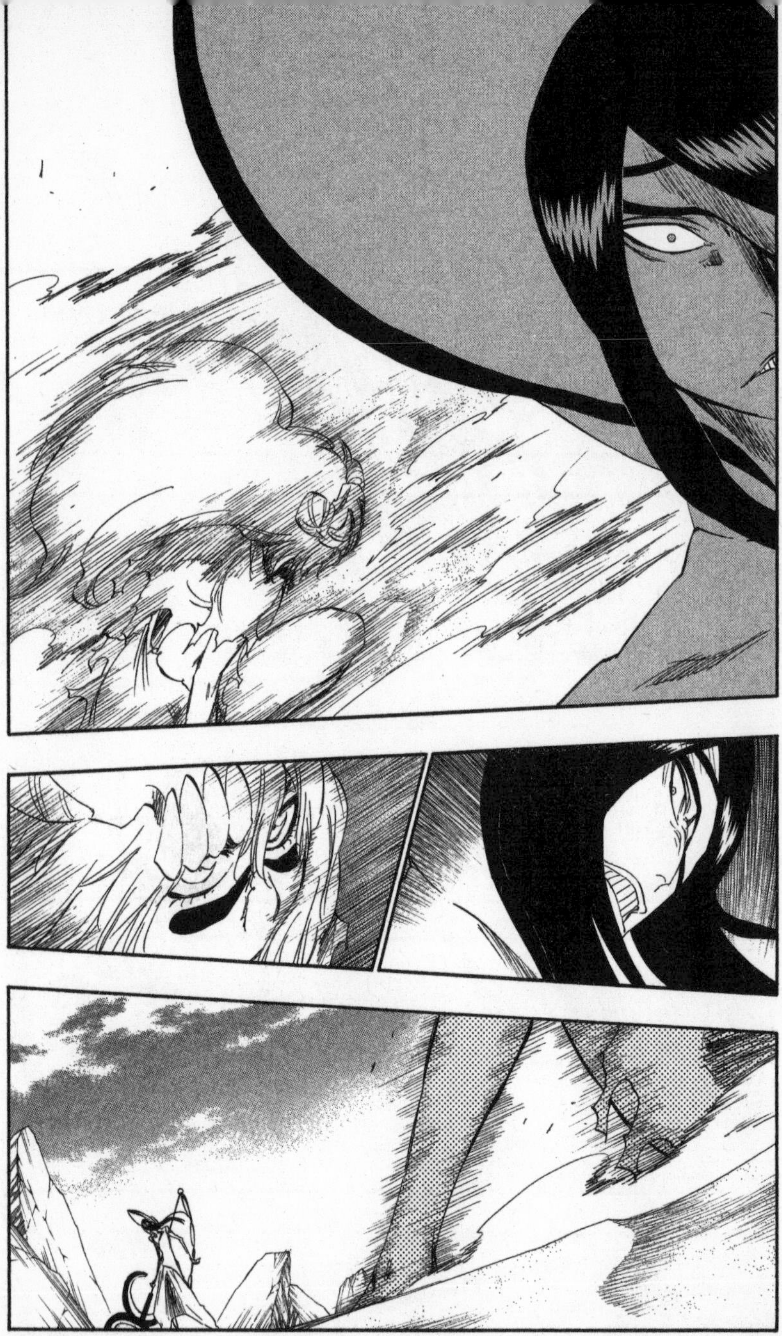

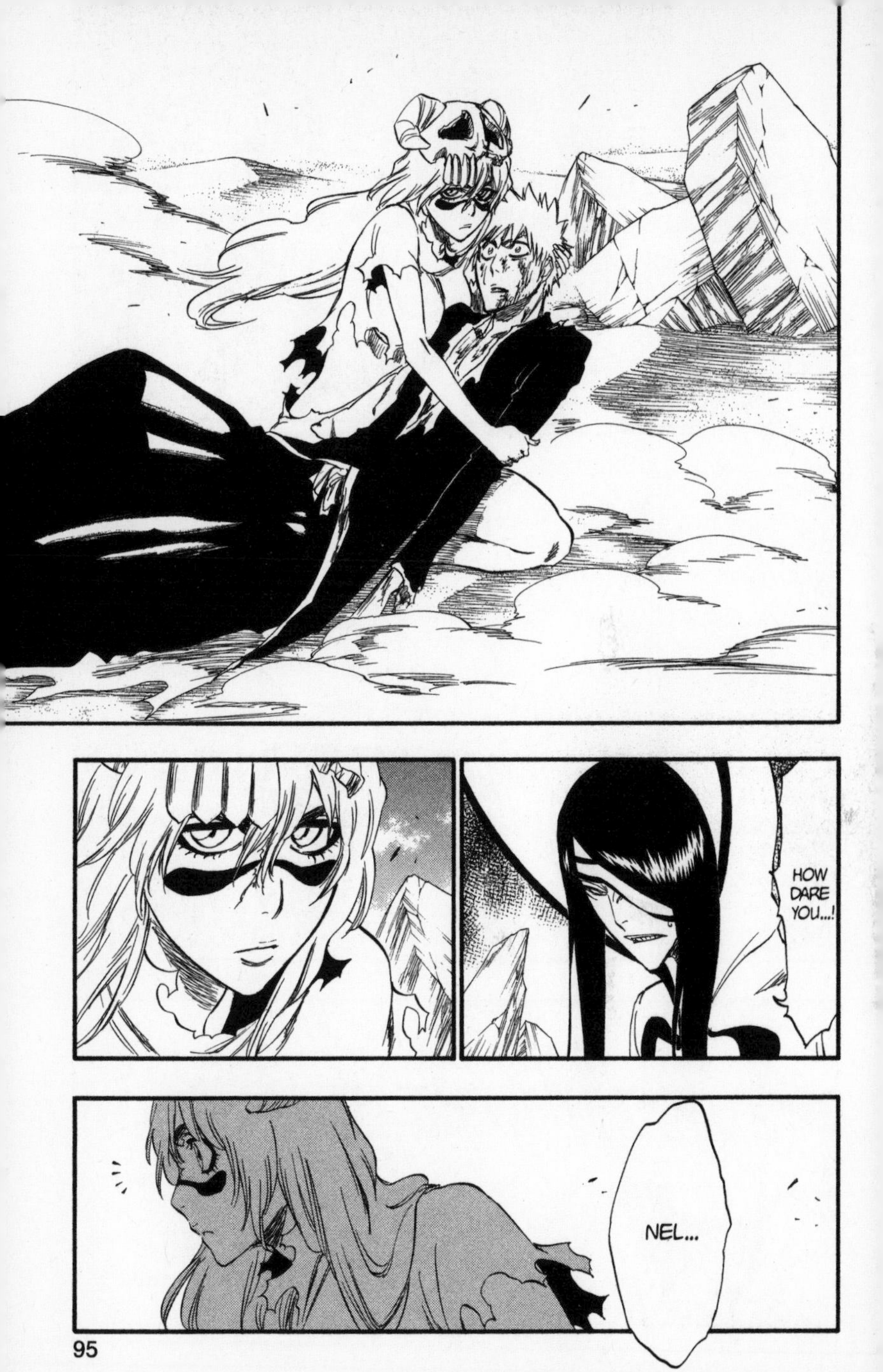
HOW DARE YOU...!
NEL...

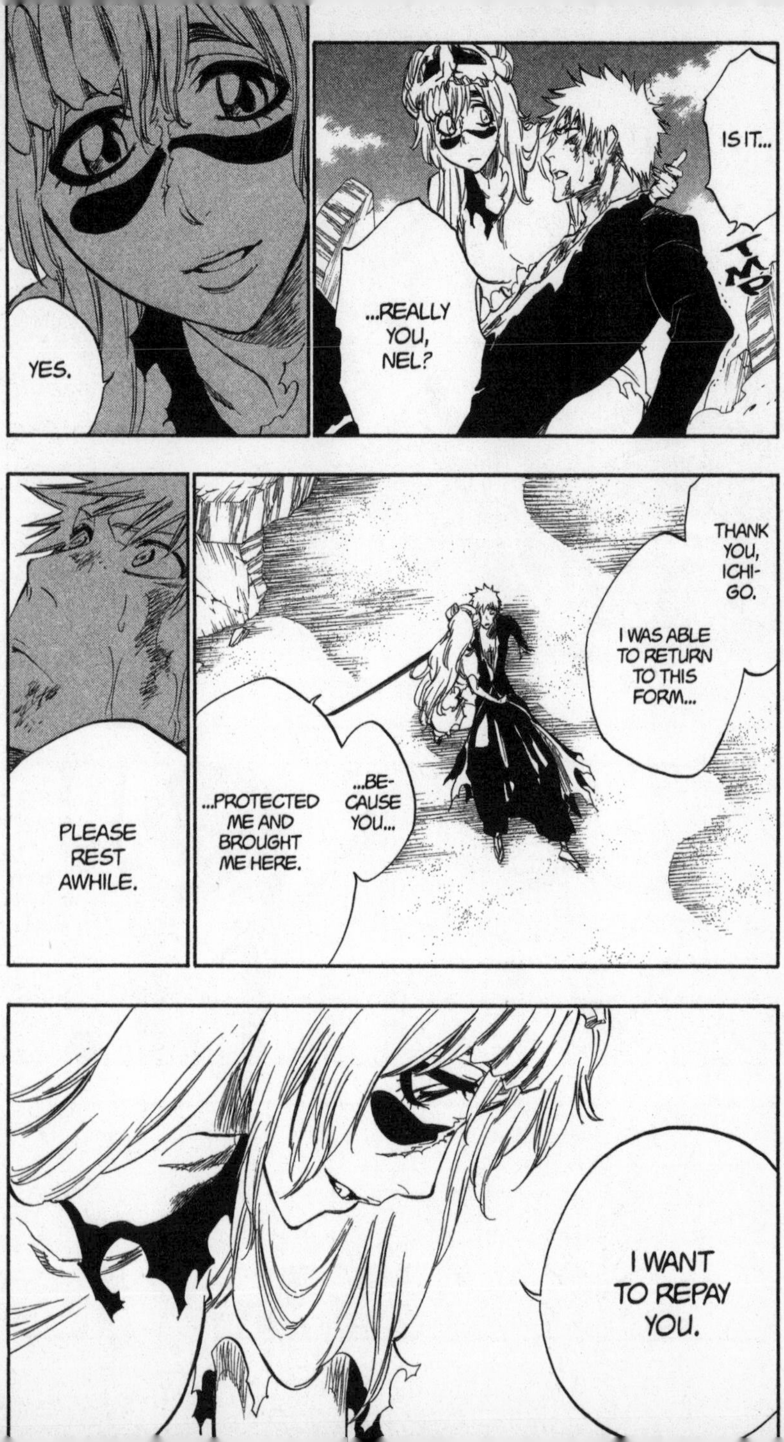
IS IT...
TMP
...REALLY YOU, NEL?
YES.
THANK YOU, ICHI-GO.
I WAS ABLE TO RETURN TO THIS FORM...
...BE-CAUSE YOU...
...PROTECTED ME AND BROUGHT ME HERE.
PLEASE REST AWHILE.
I WANT TO REPAY YOU.

READ THIS WAY

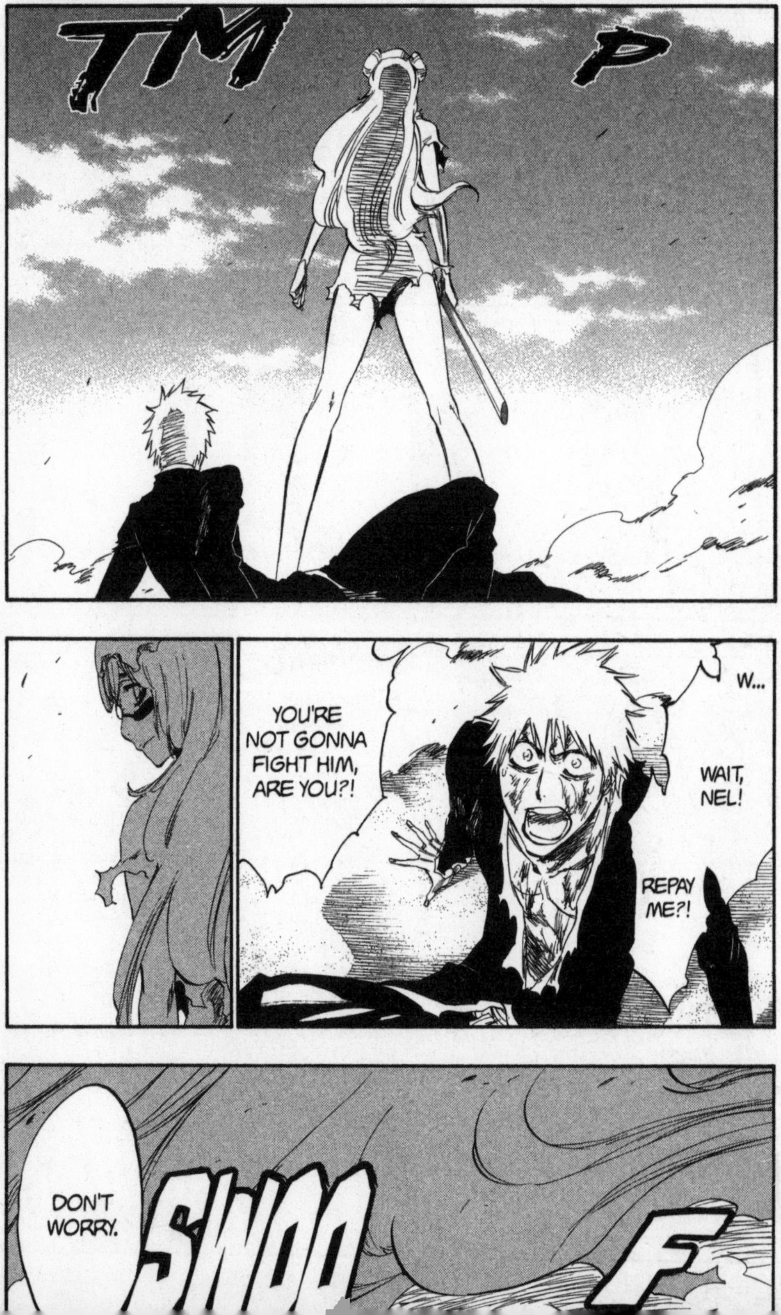
TMP
W...
WAIT, NEL!
REPAY ME?!
YOU'RE NOT GONNA FIGHT HIM, ARE YOU?!
SWOOF
DON'T WORRY.

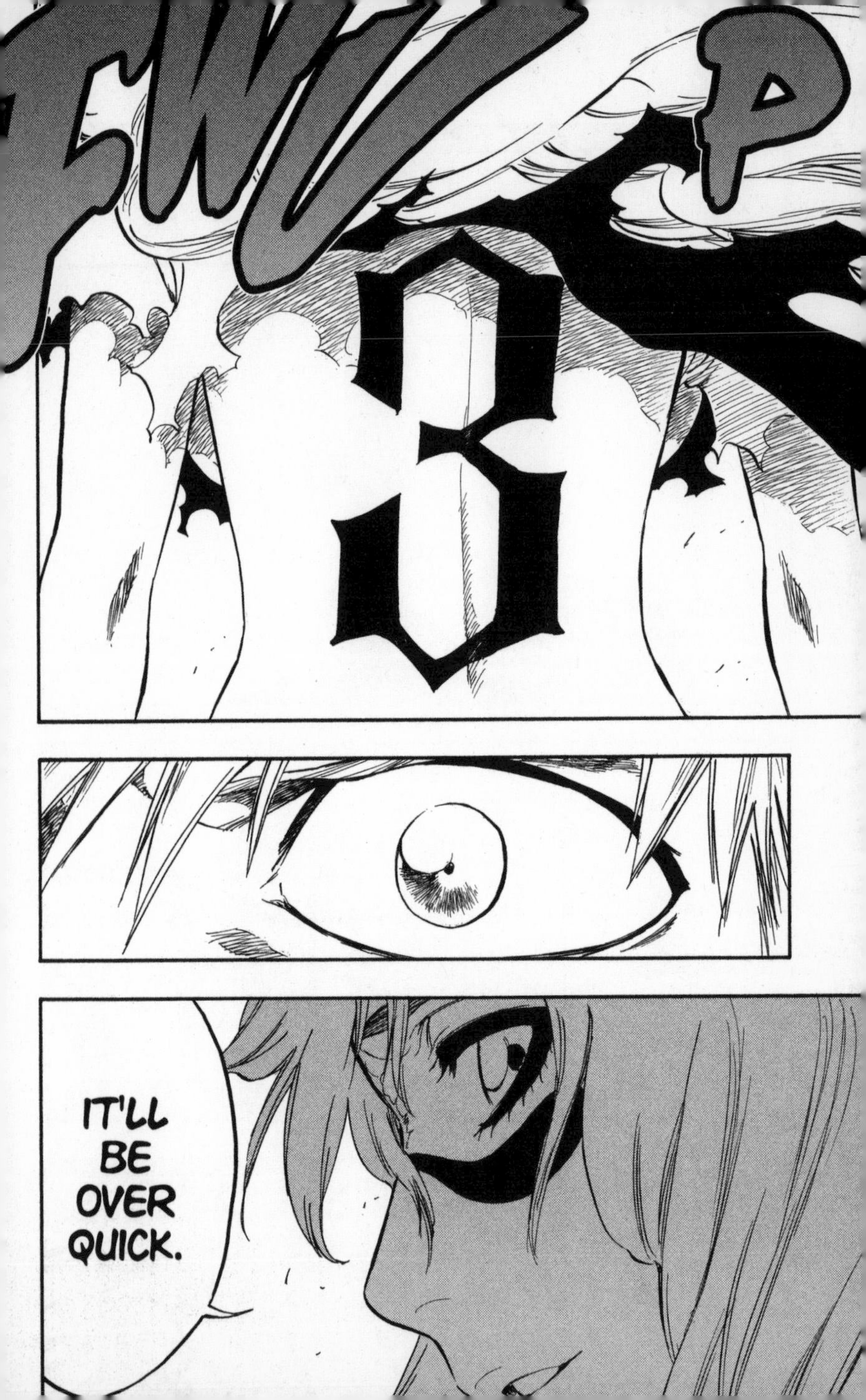
FWUP
3
IT'LL BE OVER QUICK.

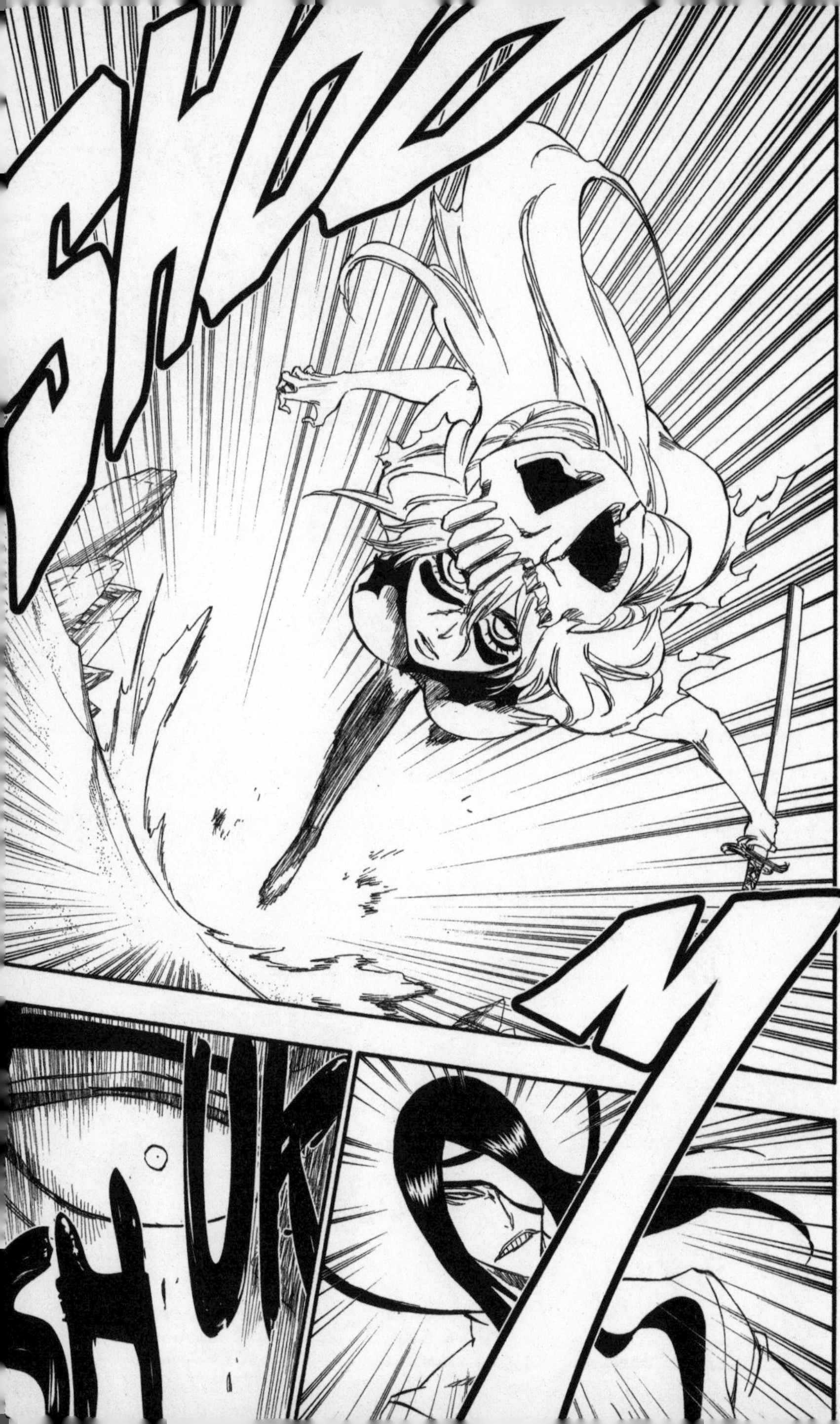
SHUK

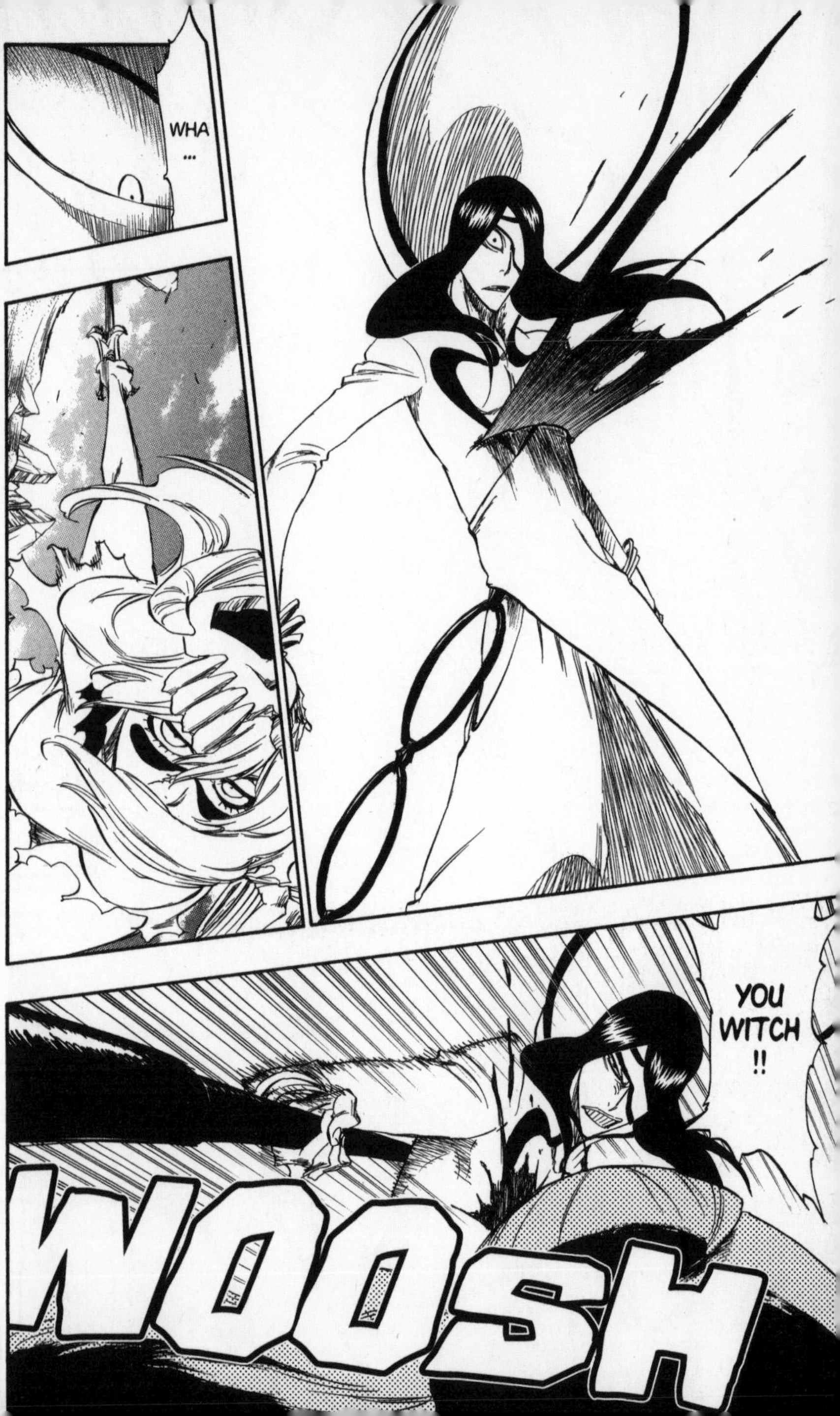
WHA
...
YOU WITCH
!!
WOOSH

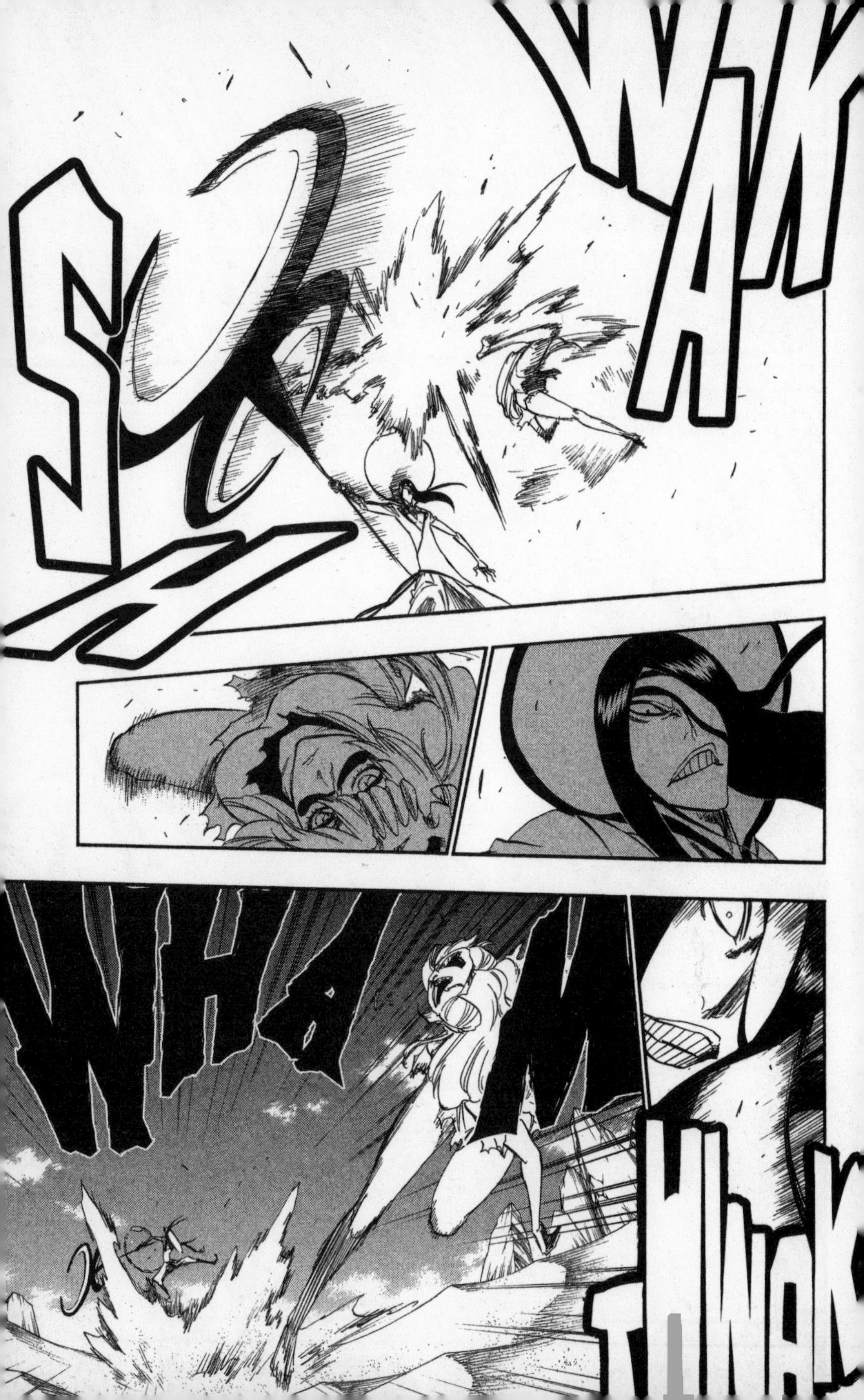
WHAK
SH
THWAK
WHAM

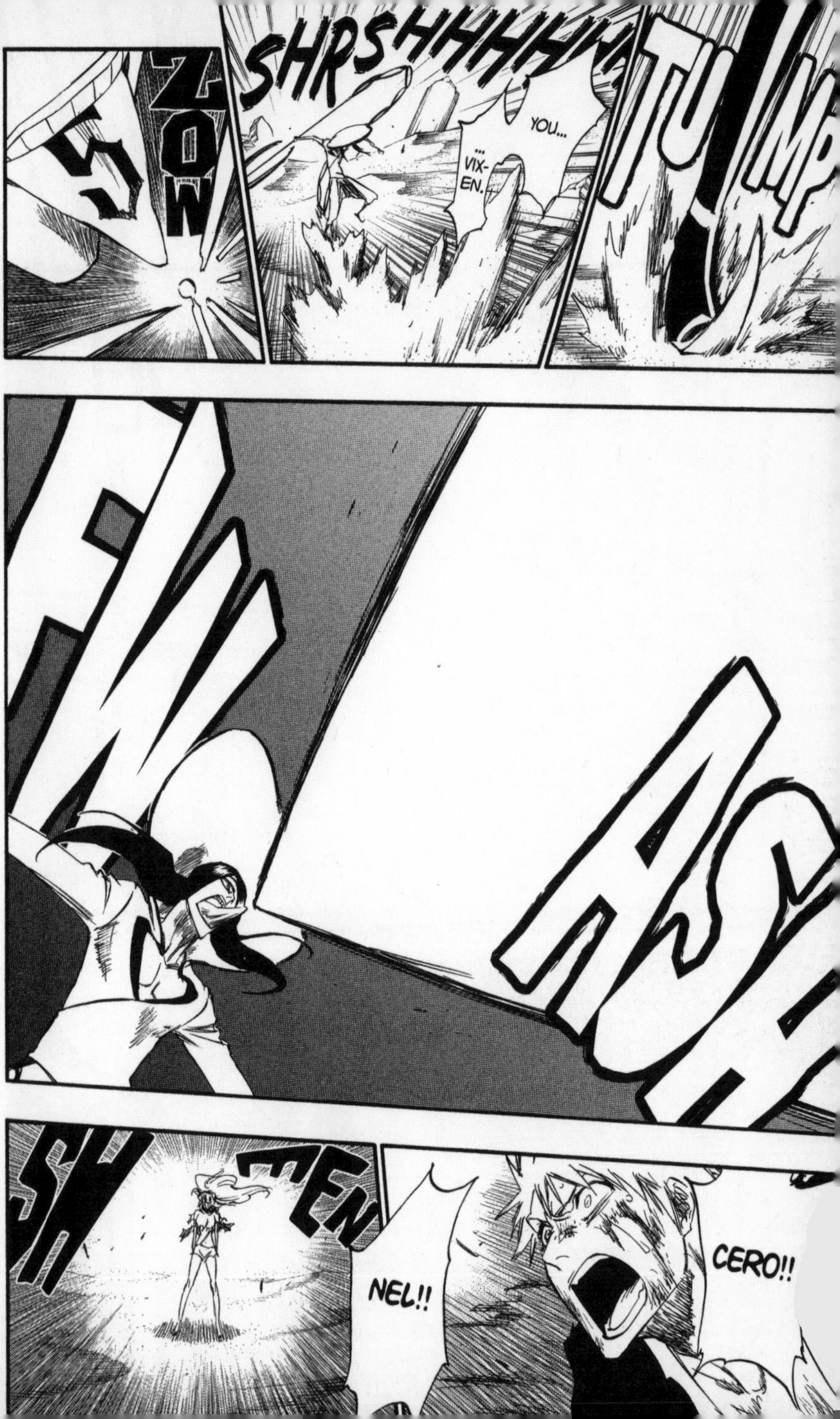
YOU...
...VIX-EN.
ZOW
CERO!!
NEL!!

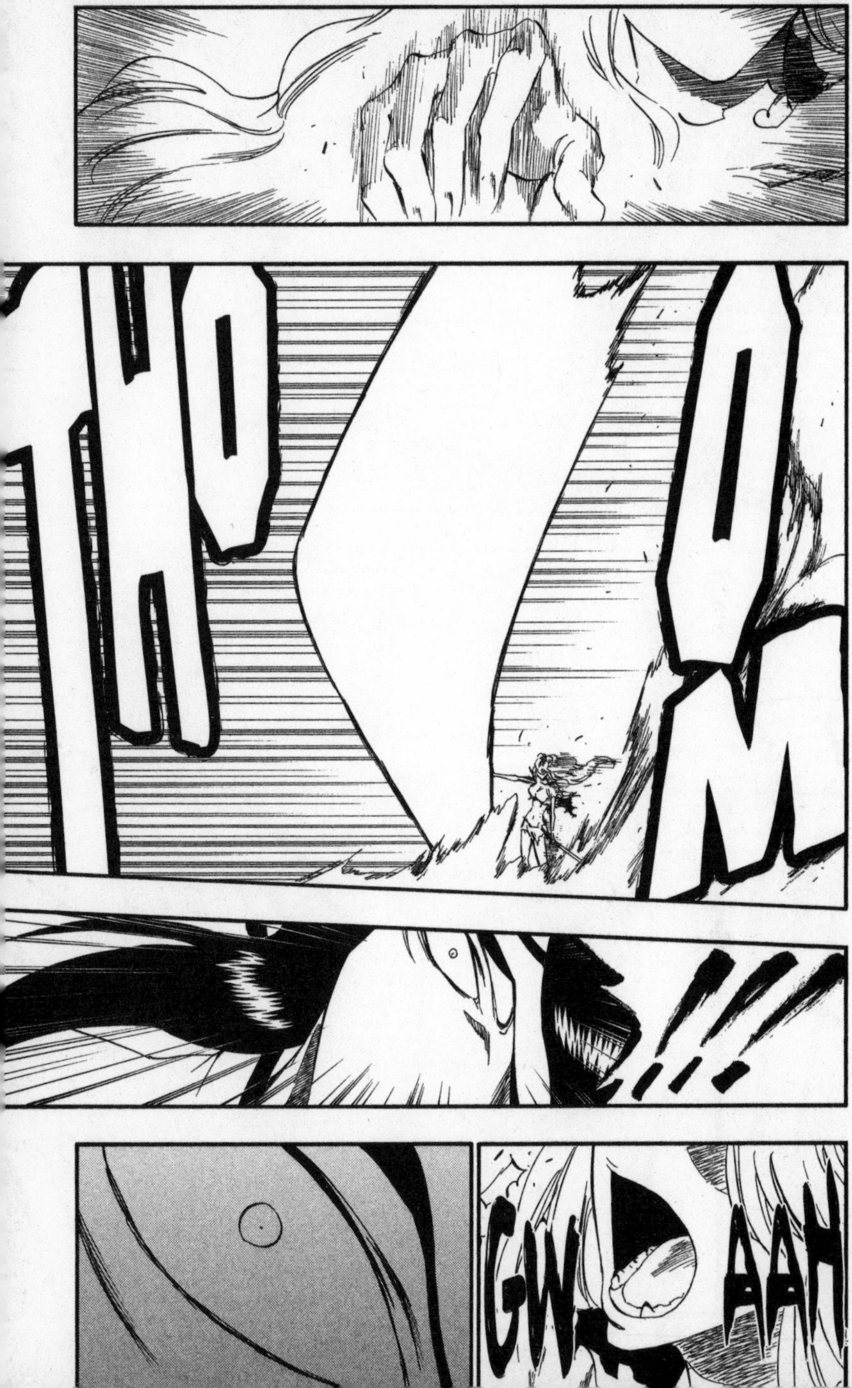
THOOM
!!
GWAAH

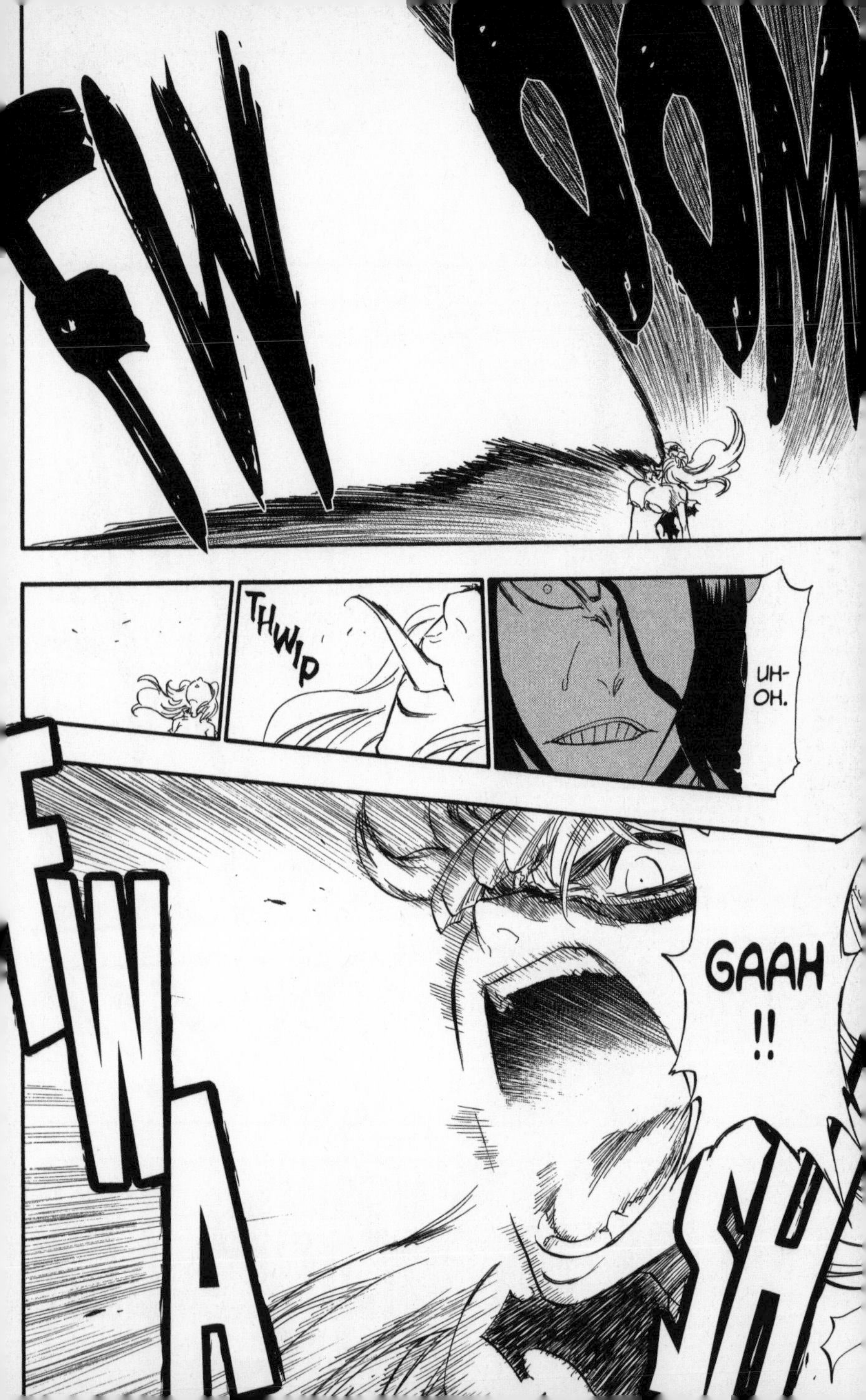
FWOOM
UH-OH.
THWIP
GAAH!!
FWASH

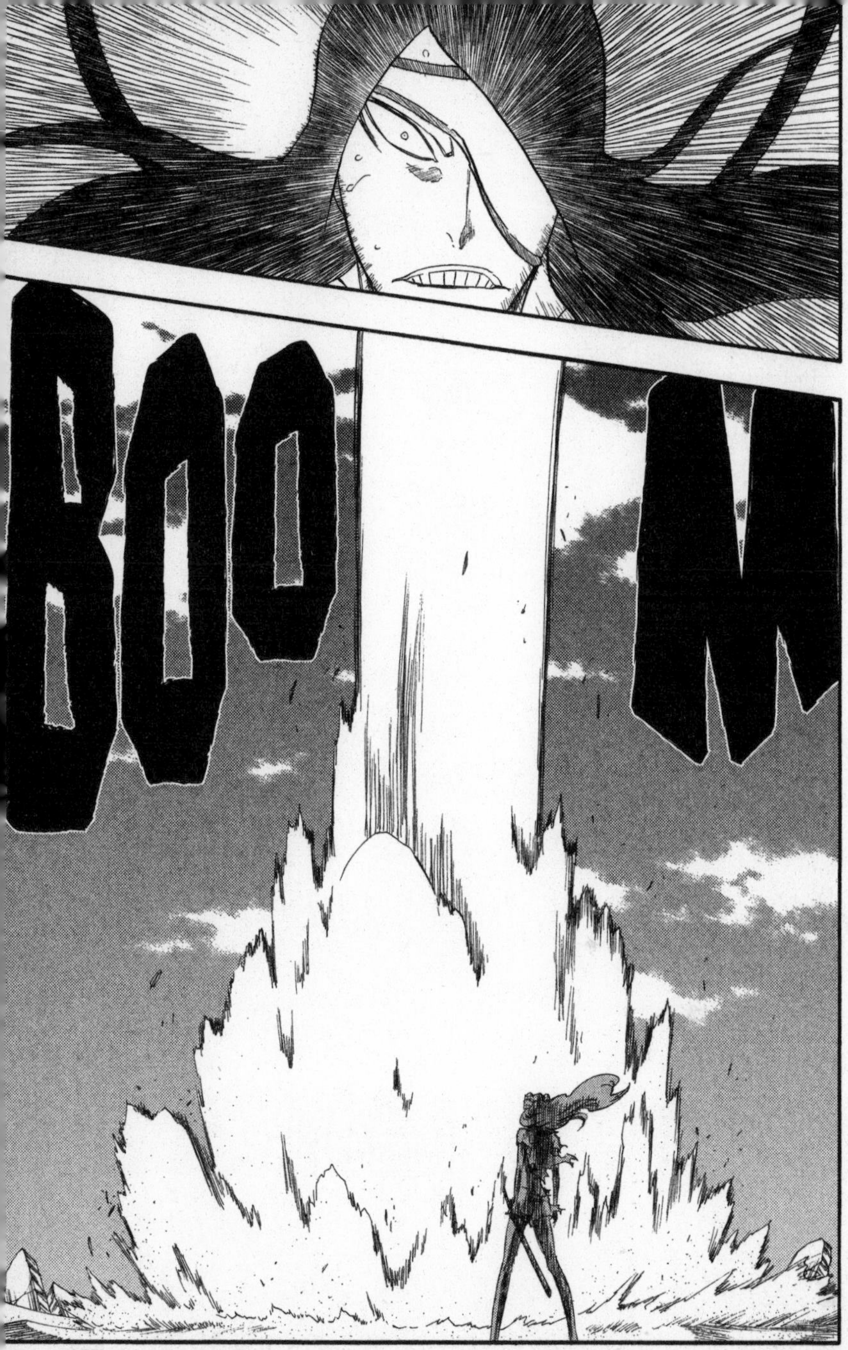
BOOM

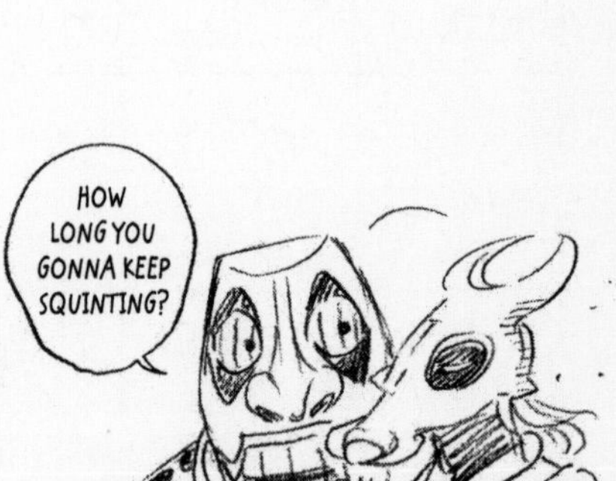
HOW LONG YOU GONNA KEEP SQUINTING?

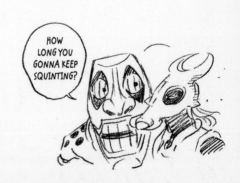

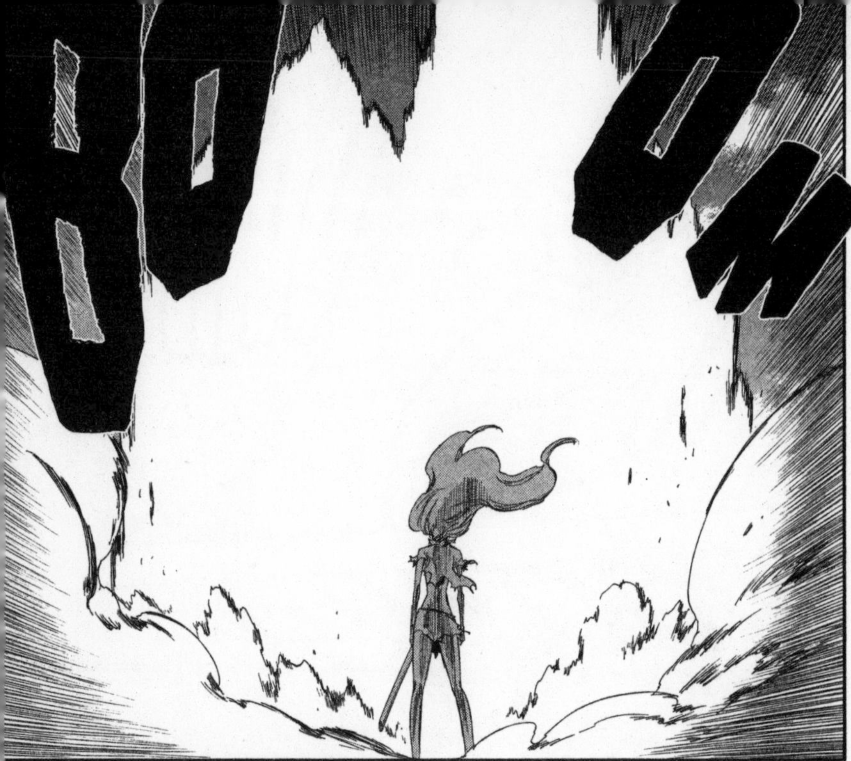
BOOM

292. Rupture My Replica

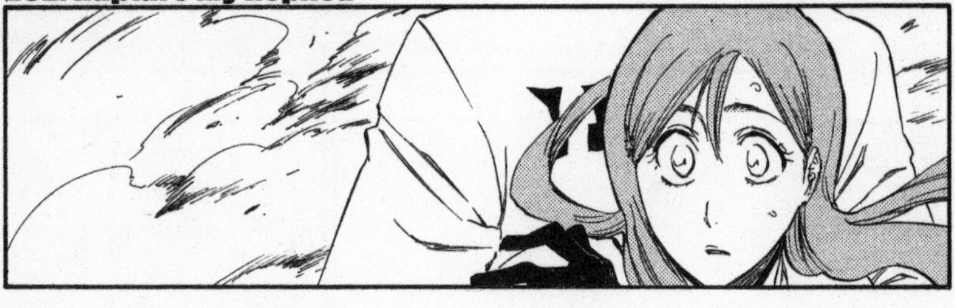

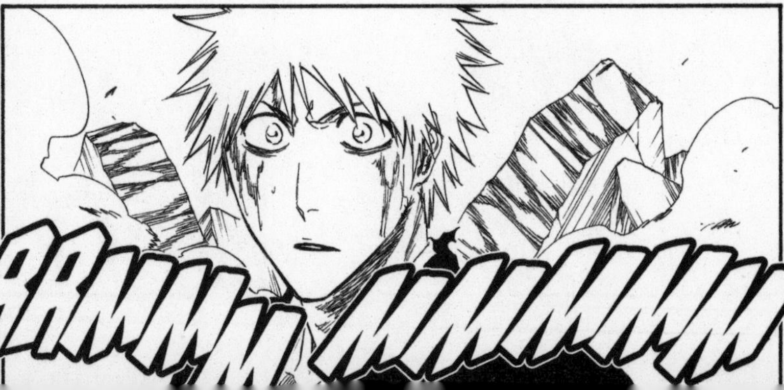
RRMMMM MMMMMMM

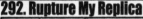

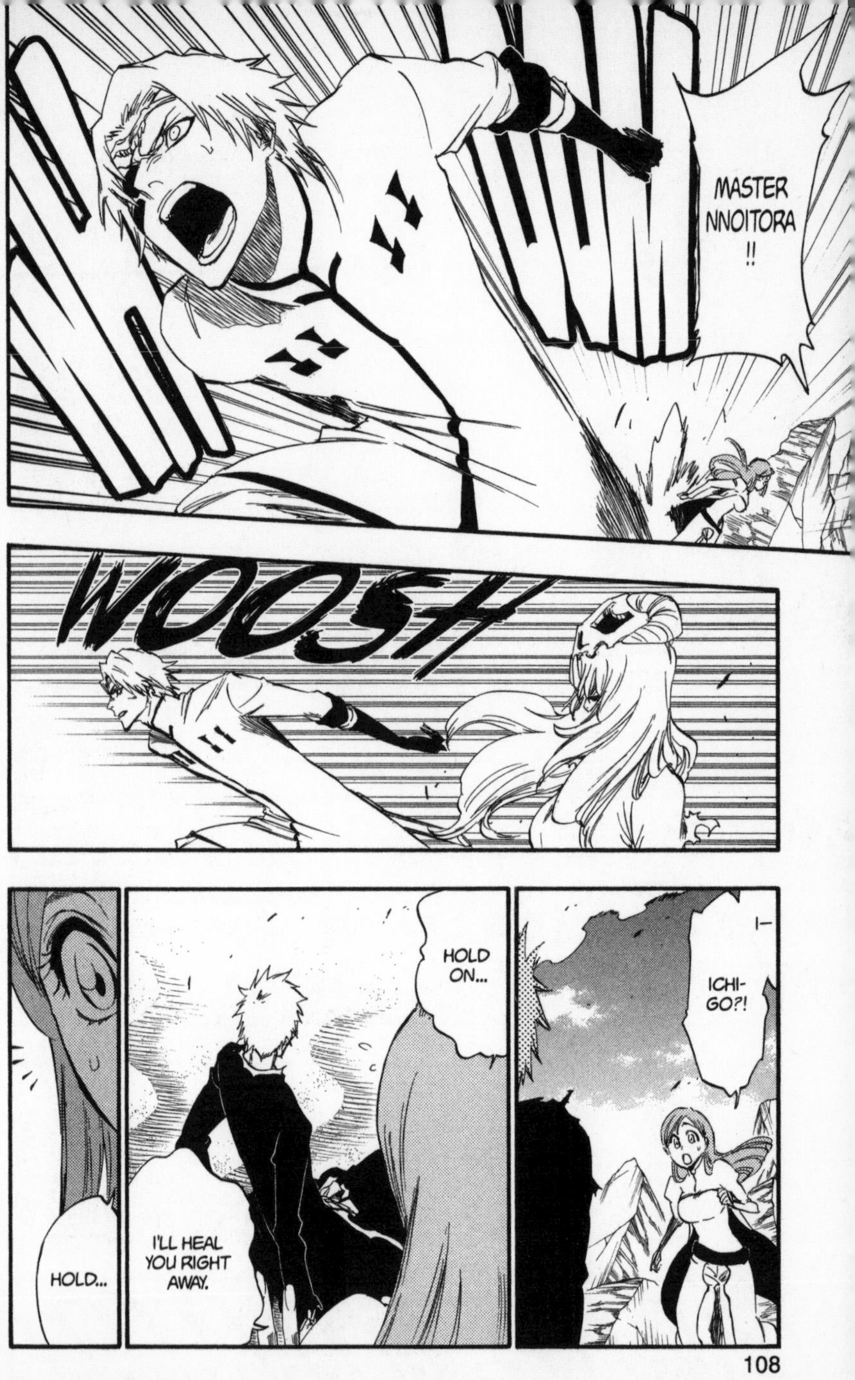
MASTER NNOITORA !!
WOOSH
I—
ICHI-GO?!
HOLD ON...
I'LL HEAL YOU RIGHT AWAY.
HOLD...

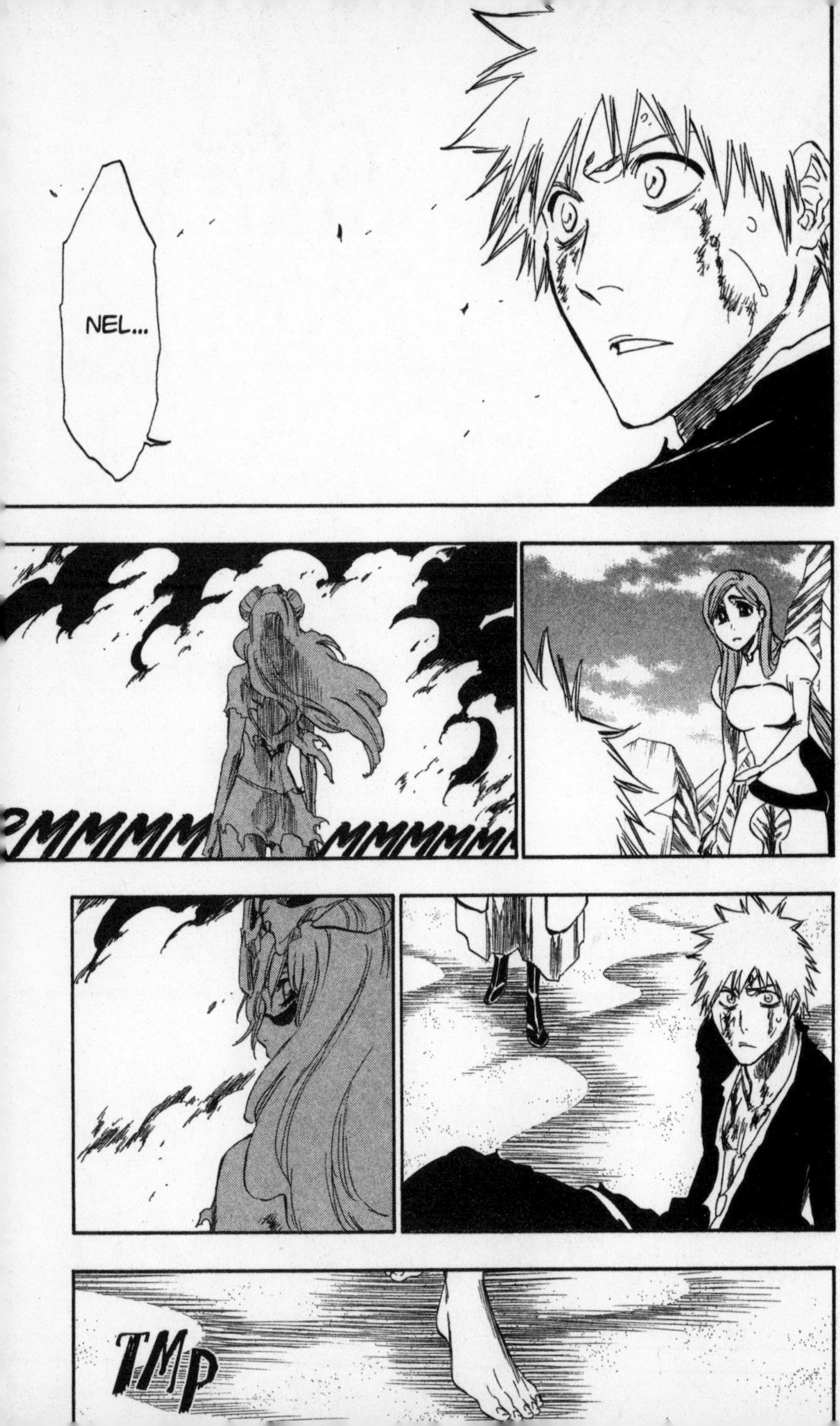
NEL...
MMMMM MMMMMM
TMP

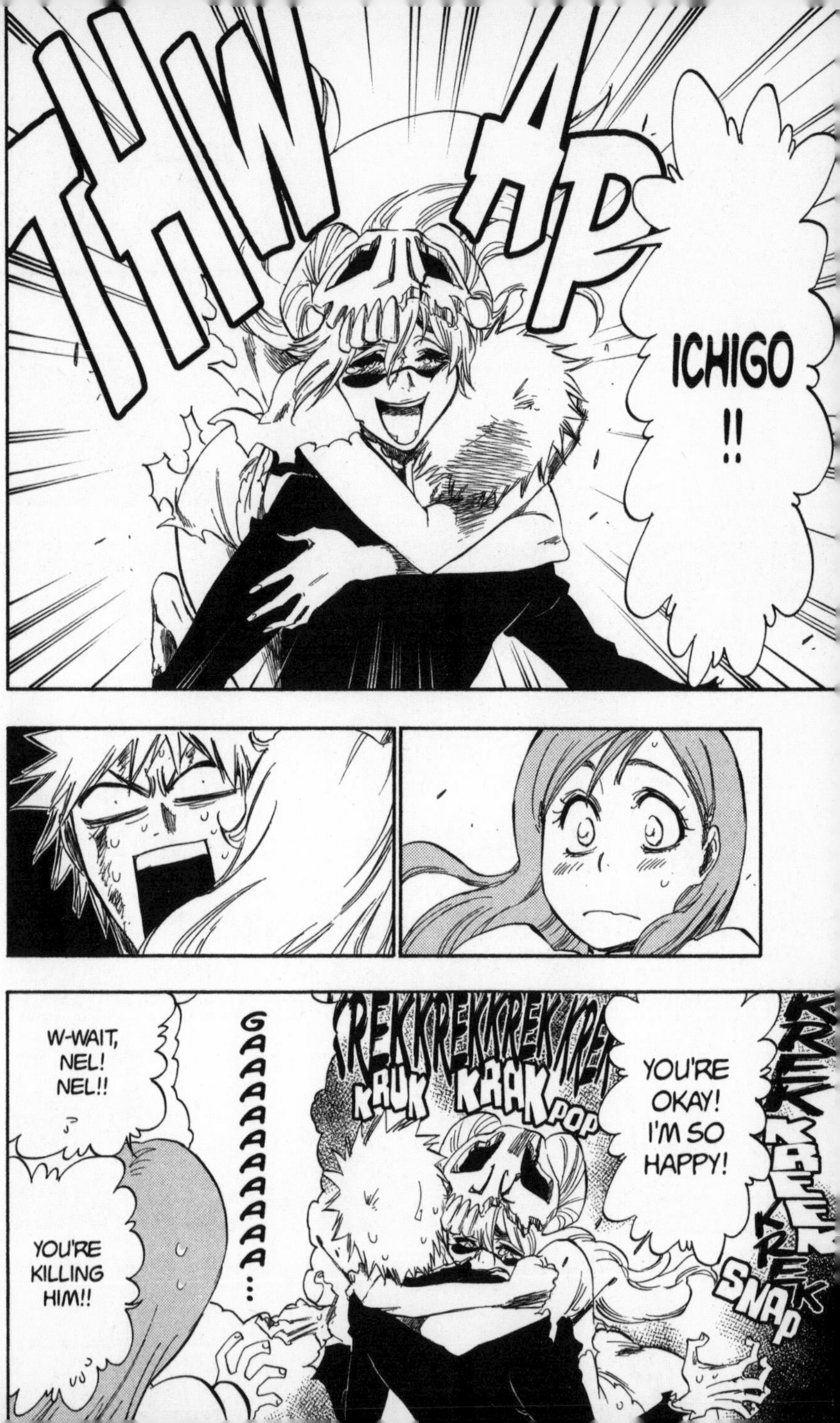
THWAP
ICHIGO !!
YOU'RE OKAY! I'M SO HAPPY!
KRUK KRAK POP
GAAAAAAAAAAAA...
W-WAIT, NEL! NEL!!
YOU'RE KILLING HIM!!
SNAP

READ THIS WAY

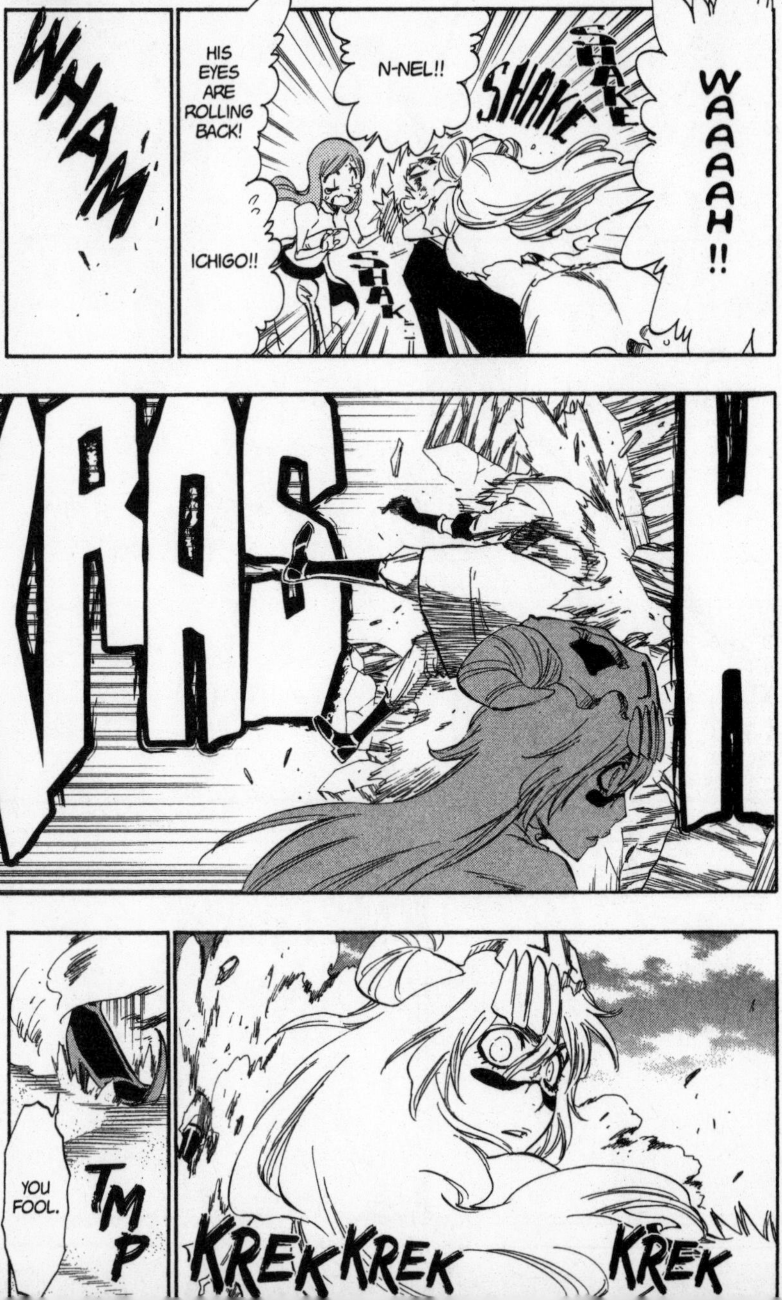

WAAAAH!!
SHAKE
SHAKE
N-NEL!!
HIS EYES ARE ROLLING BACK!
ICHIGO!!
SHAK
WHAM
KRASH
KREK
KREKKREK
YOU FOOL.
TMP

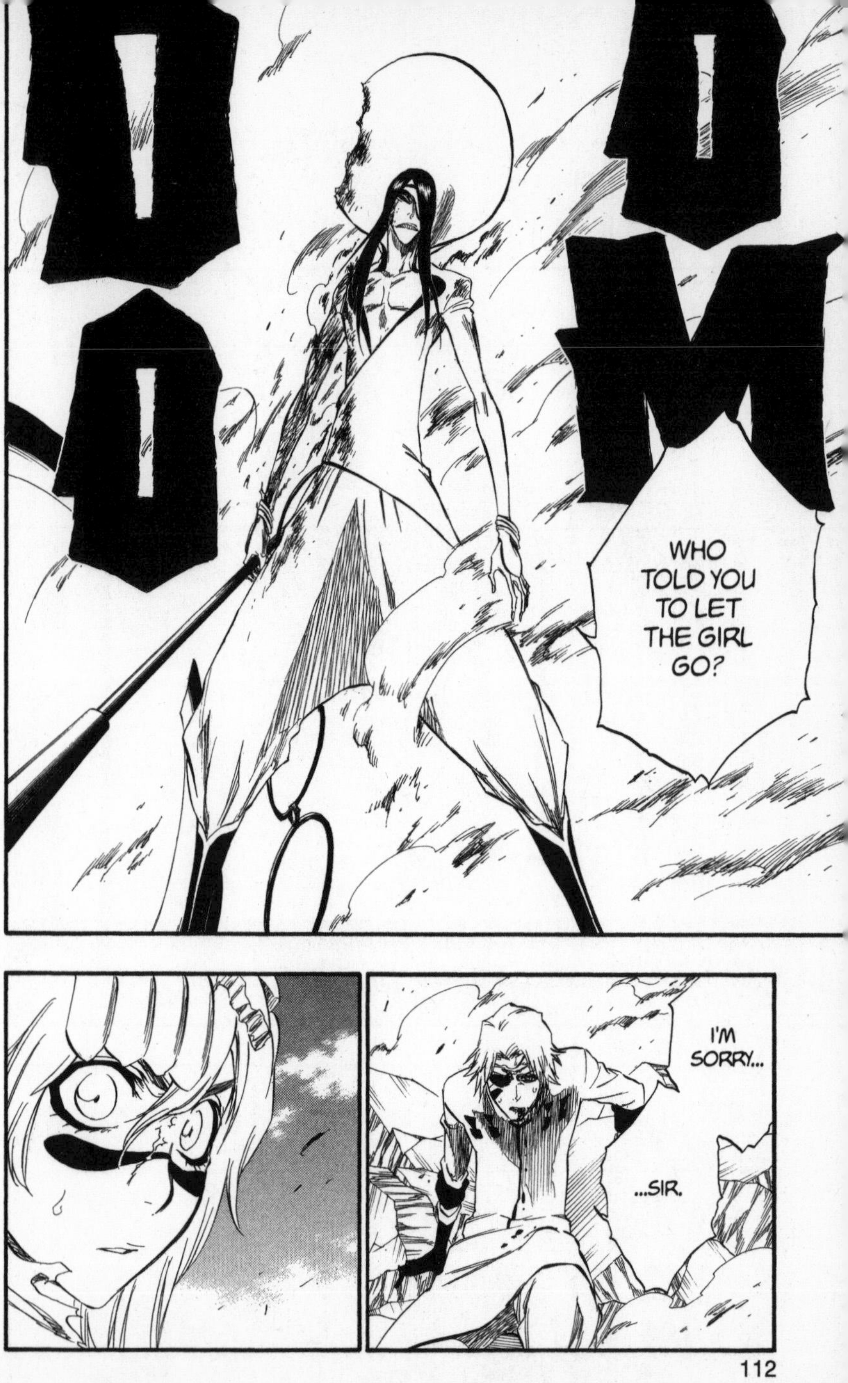
DOOM
WHO TOLD YOU TO LET THE GIRL GO?
I'M SORRY...
...SIR.

READ THIS WAY

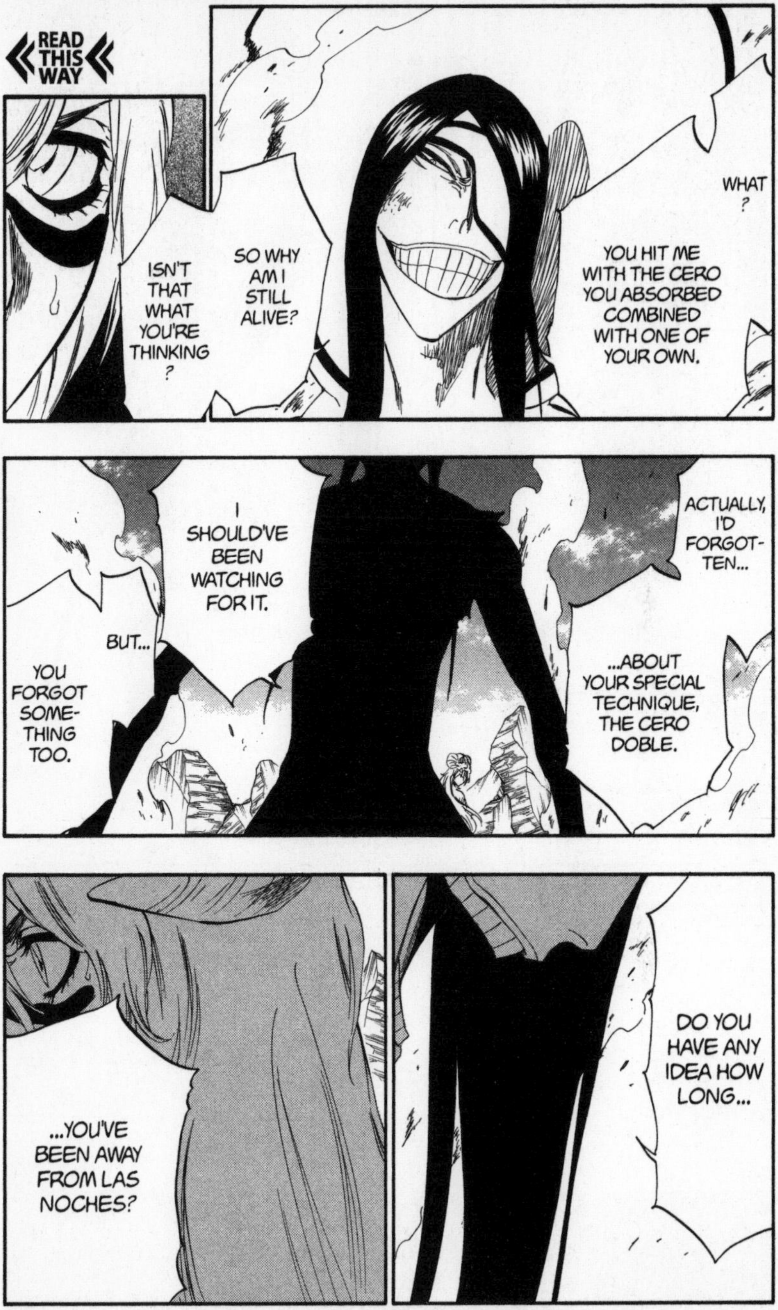
WHAT?
YOU HIT ME WITH THE CERO YOU ABSORBED COMBINED WITH ONE OF YOUR OWN.
SO WHY AM I STILL ALIVE?
ISN'T THAT WHAT YOU'RE THINKING?
ACTUALLY, I'D FORGOT-TEN...
...ABOUT YOUR SPECIAL TECHNIQUE, THE CERO DOBLE.
I SHOULD'VE BEEN WATCHING FOR IT.
BUT...
YOU FORGOT SOME-THING TOO.
DO YOU HAVE ANY IDEA HOW LONG...
...YOU'VE BEEN AWAY FROM LAS NOCHES?

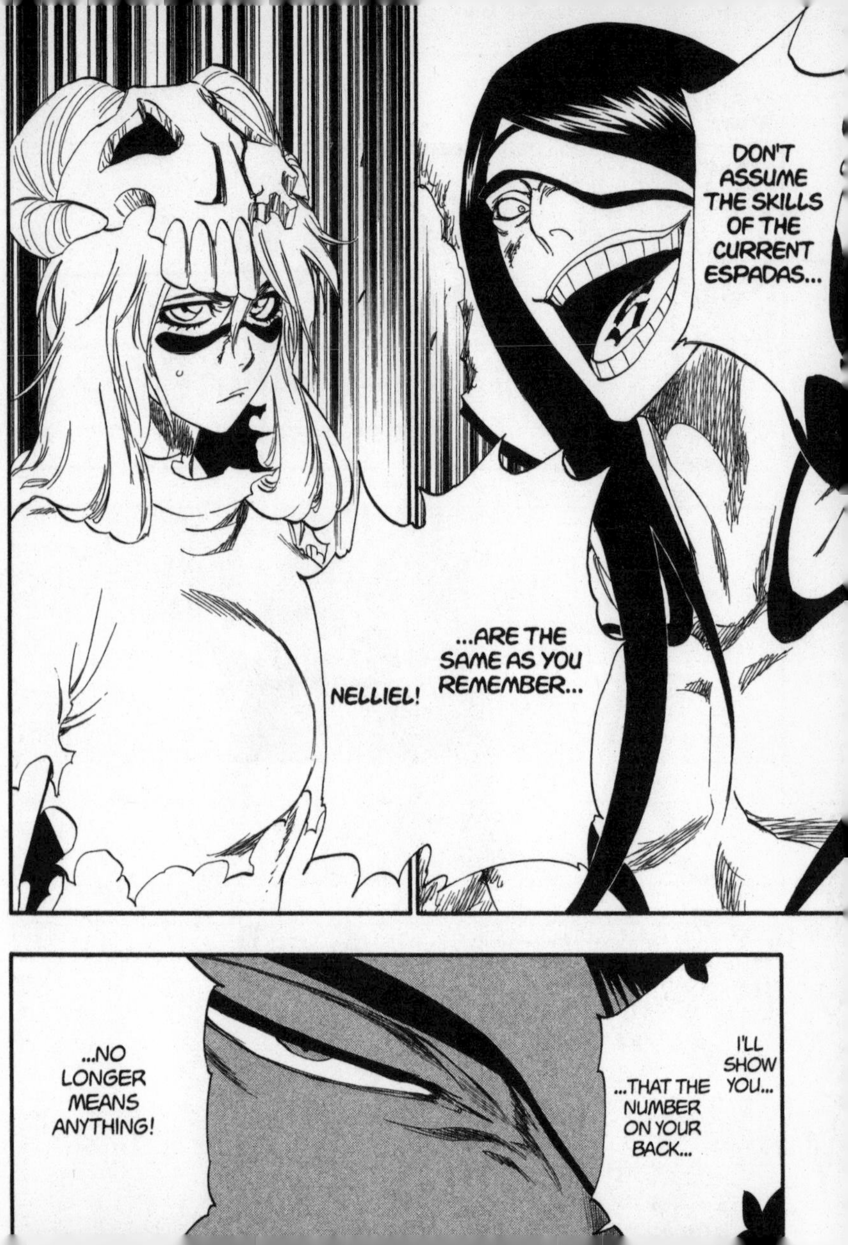
DON'T ASSUME THE SKILLS OF THE CURRENT ESPADAS...
...ARE THE SAME AS YOU REMEMBER...
NELLIEL!
I'LL SHOW YOU...
...THAT THE NUMBER ON YOUR BACK...
...NO LONGER MEANS ANYTHING!

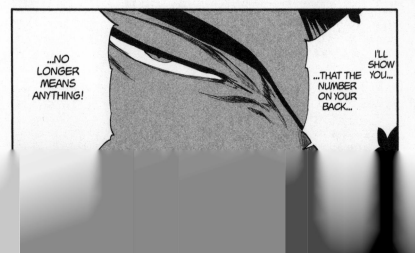

READ THIS WAY

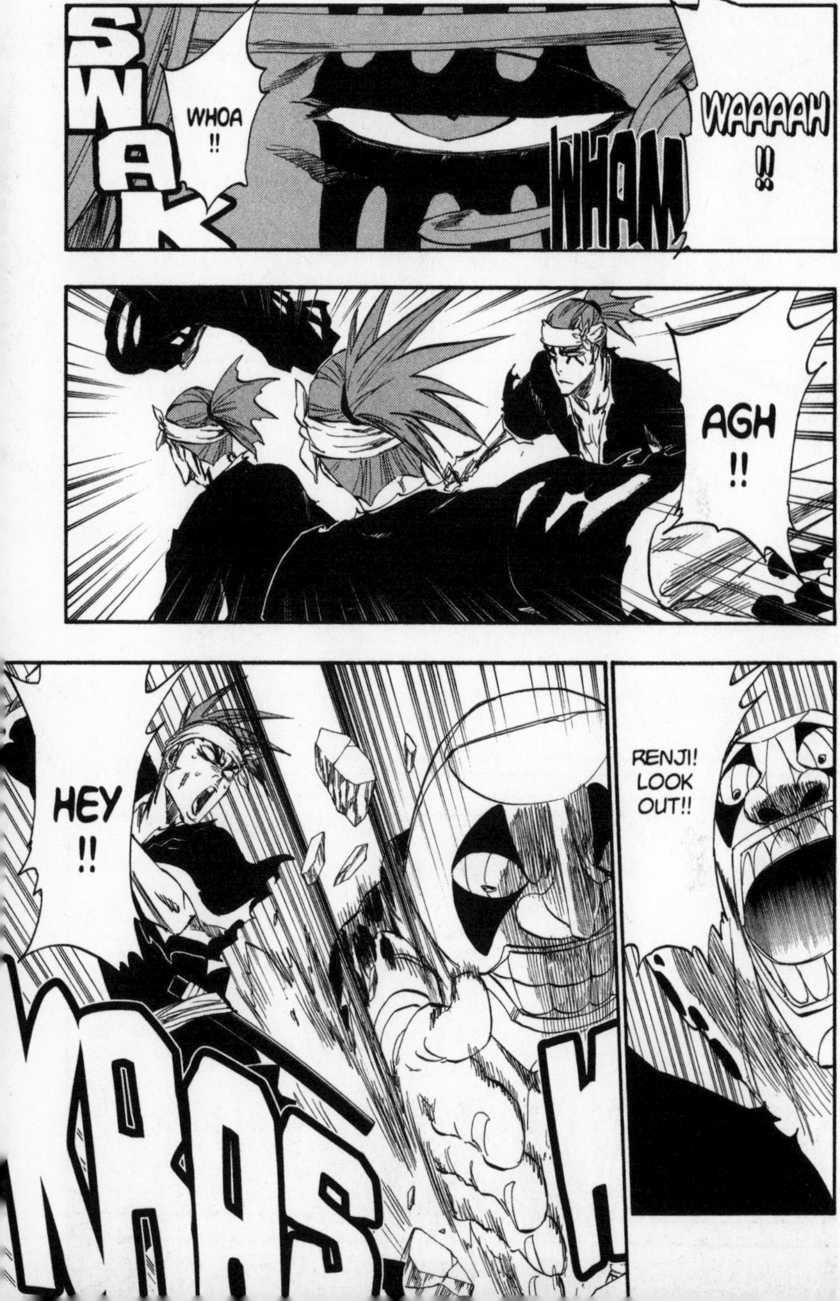
WAAAAH!!
WHAM
WHOA!!
SWAK
AGH!!
RENJI! LOOK OUT!!
HEY!!
KRASH

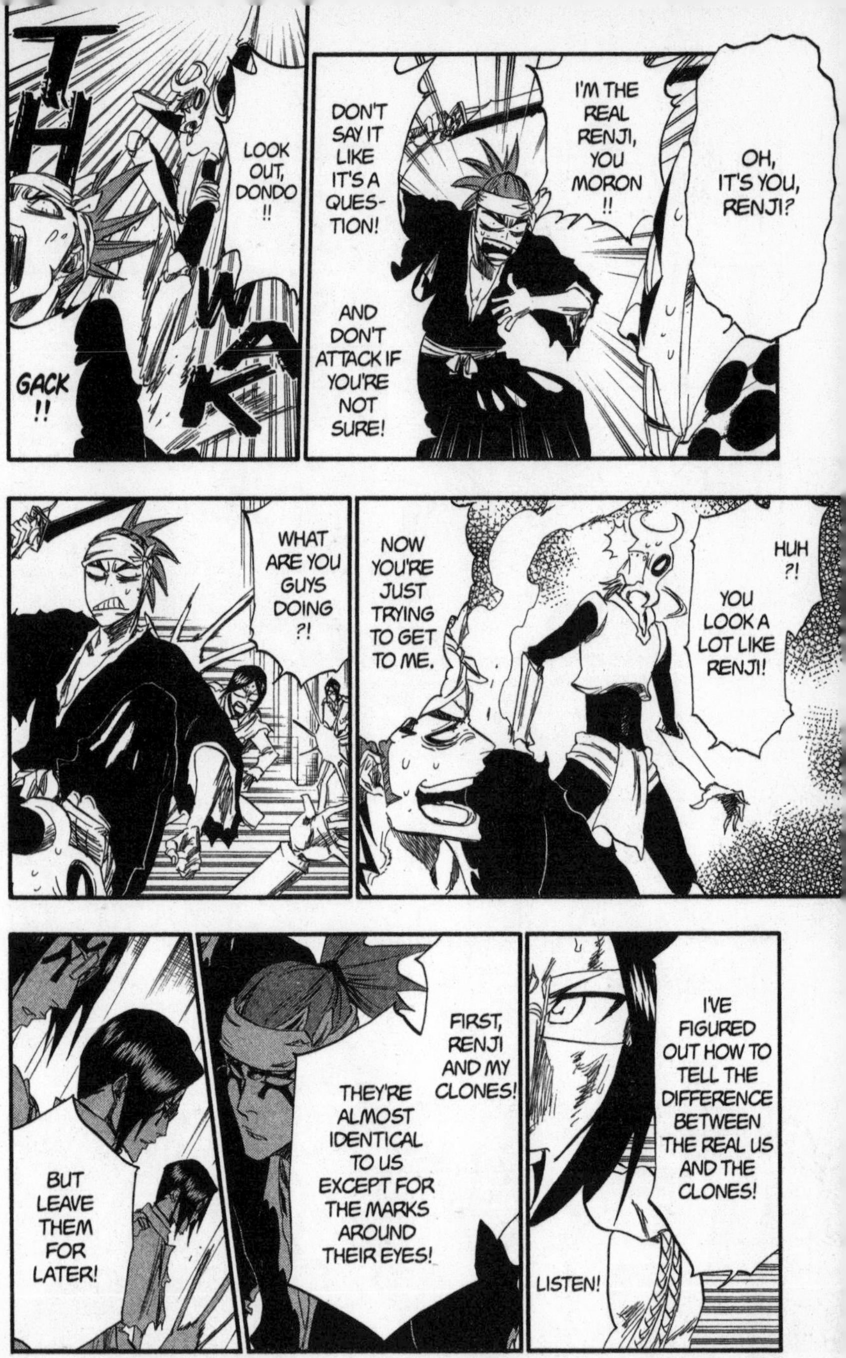
OH, IT'S YOU, RENJI?
I'M THE REAL RENJI, YOU MORON !!
DON'T SAY IT LIKE IT'S A QUES-TION!
AND DON'T ATTACK IF YOU'RE NOT SURE!
LOOK OUT, DONDO !!
THWAK
GACK !!
HUH ?!
YOU LOOK A LOT LIKE RENJI!
NOW YOU'RE JUST TRYING TO GET TO ME.
WHAT ARE YOU GUYS DOING ?!
I'VE FIGURED OUT HOW TO TELL THE DIFFERENCE BETWEEN THE REAL US AND THE CLONES!
LISTEN!
FIRST, RENJI AND MY CLONES!
THEY'RE ALMOST IDENTICAL TO US EXCEPT FOR THE MARKS AROUND THEIR EYES!
BUT LEAVE THEM FOR LATER!

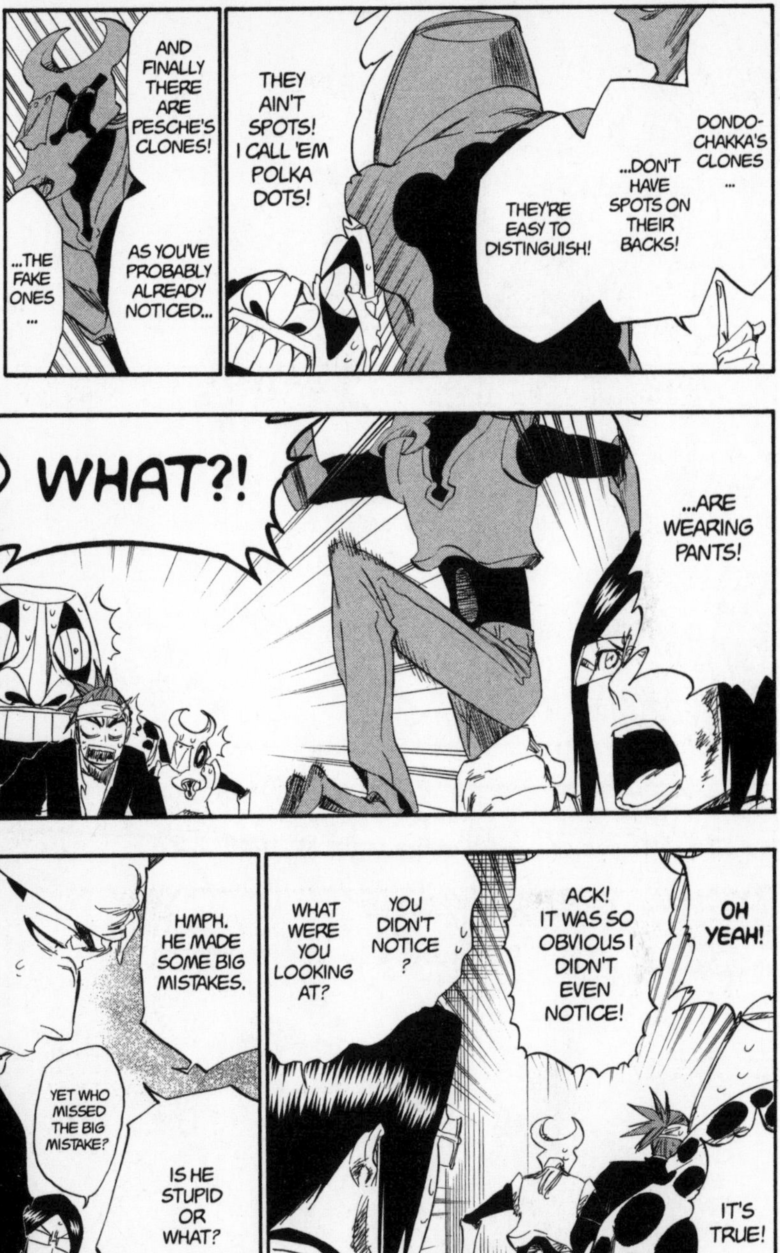
DONDO-CHAKKA'S CLONES ...
...DON'T HAVE SPOTS ON THEIR BACKS!
THEY'RE EASY TO DISTINGUISH!
THEY AIN'T SPOTS! I CALL 'EM POLKA DOTS!
AND FINALLY THERE ARE PESCHE'S CLONES!
AS YOU'VE PROBABLY ALREADY NOTICED...
...THE FAKE ONES ...
...ARE WEARING PANTS!
WHAT?!
OH YEAH!
ACK! IT WAS SO OBVIOUS I DIDN'T EVEN NOTICE!
YOU DIDN'T NOTICE ?
WHAT WERE YOU LOOKING AT?
IT'S TRUE!
HMPH. HE MADE SOME BIG MISTAKES.
YET WHO MISSED THE BIG MISTAKE?
IS HE STUPID OR WHAT?

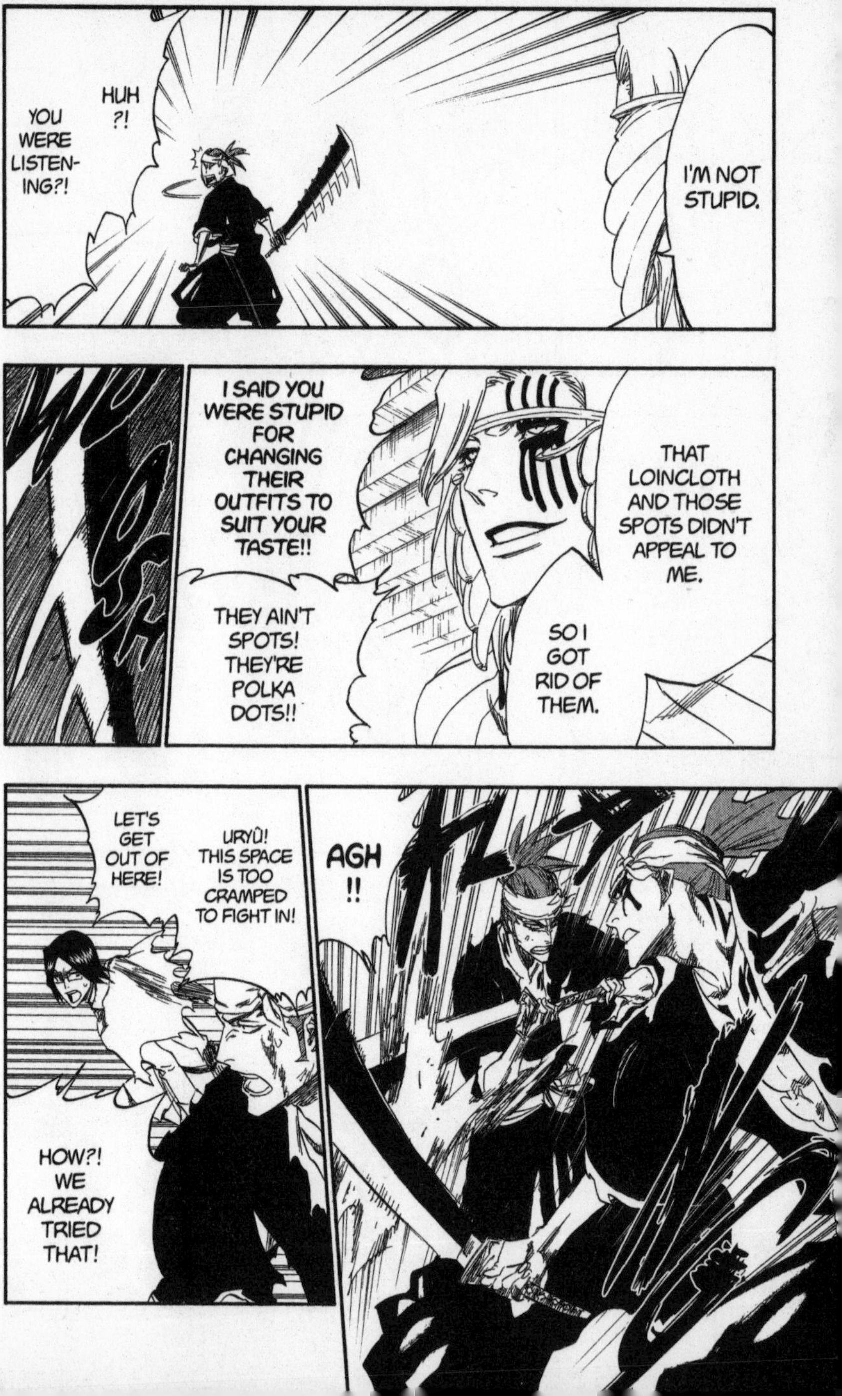
I'M NOT STUPID.
HUH ?!
YOU WERE LISTENING?!
THAT LOINCLOTH AND THOSE SPOTS DIDN'T APPEAL TO ME.
SO I GOT RID OF THEM.
I SAID YOU WERE STUPID FOR CHANGING THEIR OUTFITS TO SUIT YOUR TASTE!!
THEY AIN'T SPOTS! THEY'RE POLKA DOTS!!
AGH !!
URYÛ! THIS SPACE IS TOO CRAMPED TO FIGHT IN!
LET'S GET OUT OF HERE!
HOW?! WE ALREADY TRIED THAT!

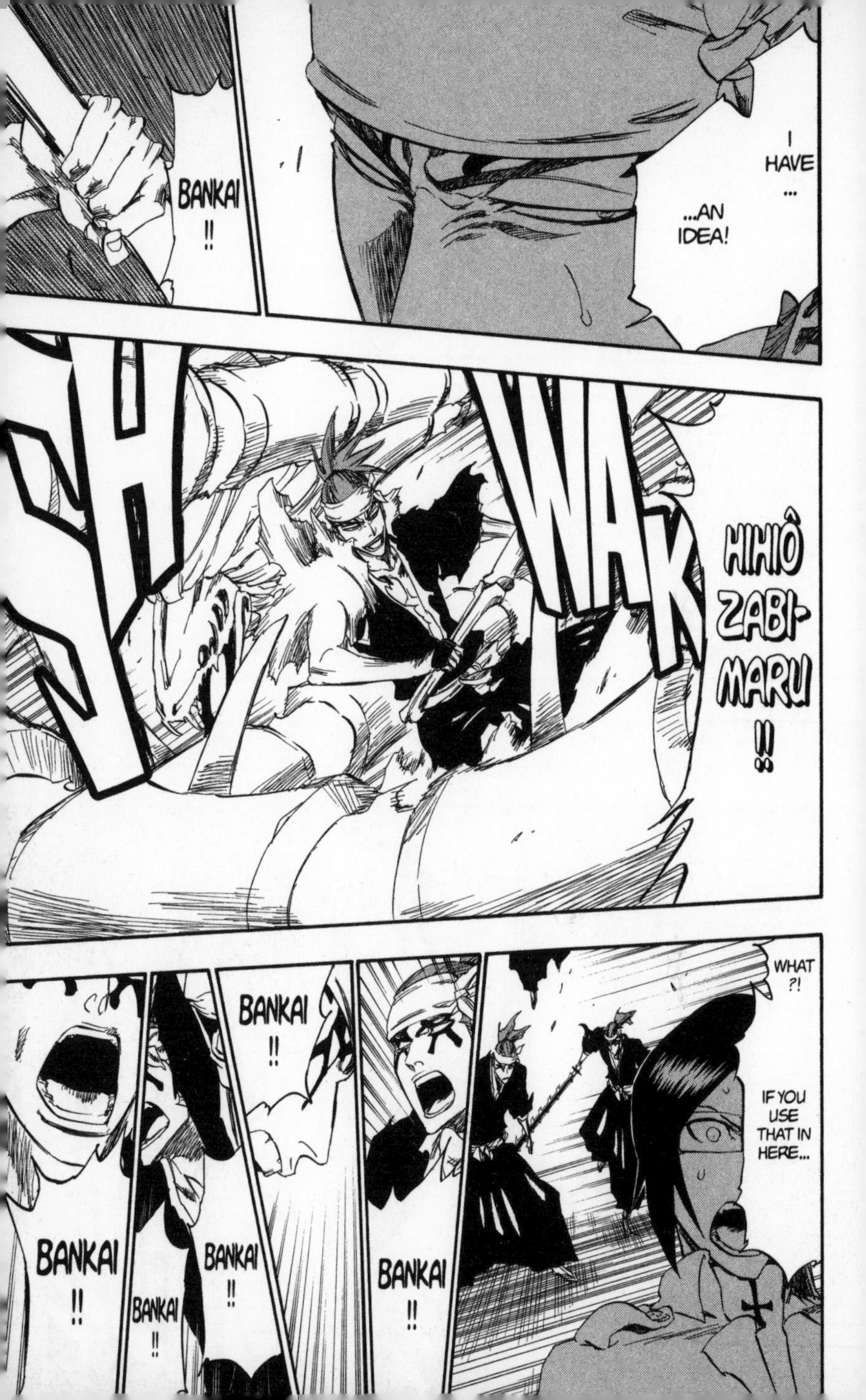
I HAVE...
...AN IDEA!
BANKAI!!
HIHIÔ ZABIMARU!!
SHWAK
WHAT?!
IF YOU USE THAT IN HERE...
BANKAI!!
BANKAI!!
BANKAI!!
BANKAI!!
BANKAI!!

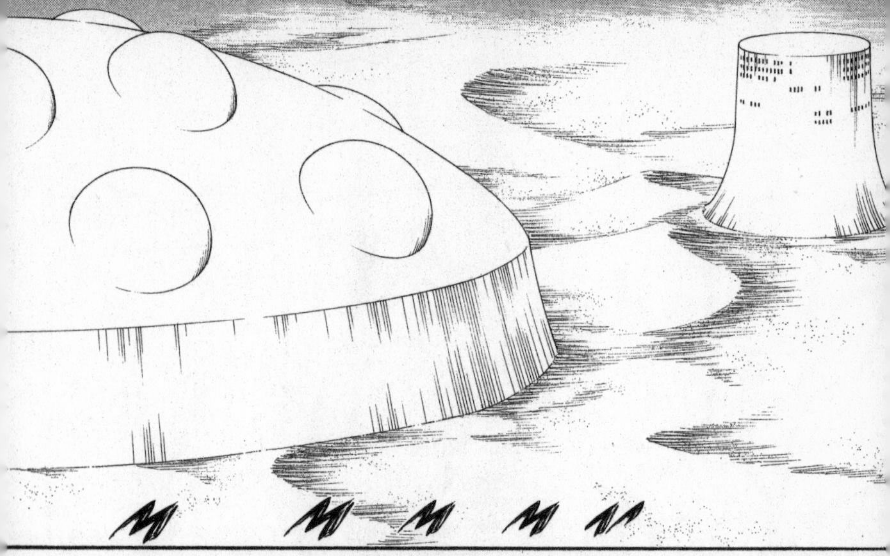

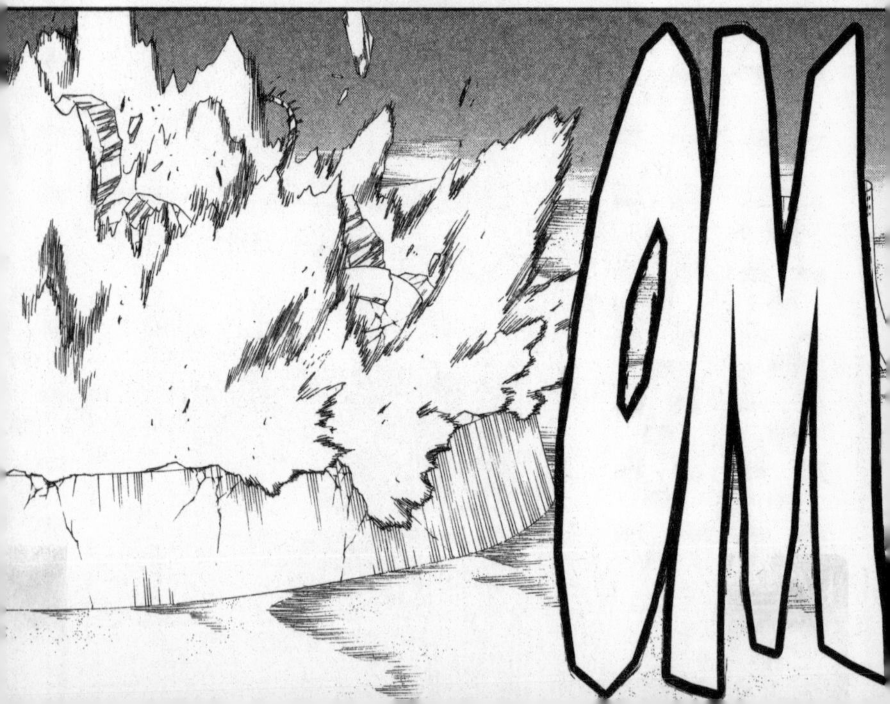
OM

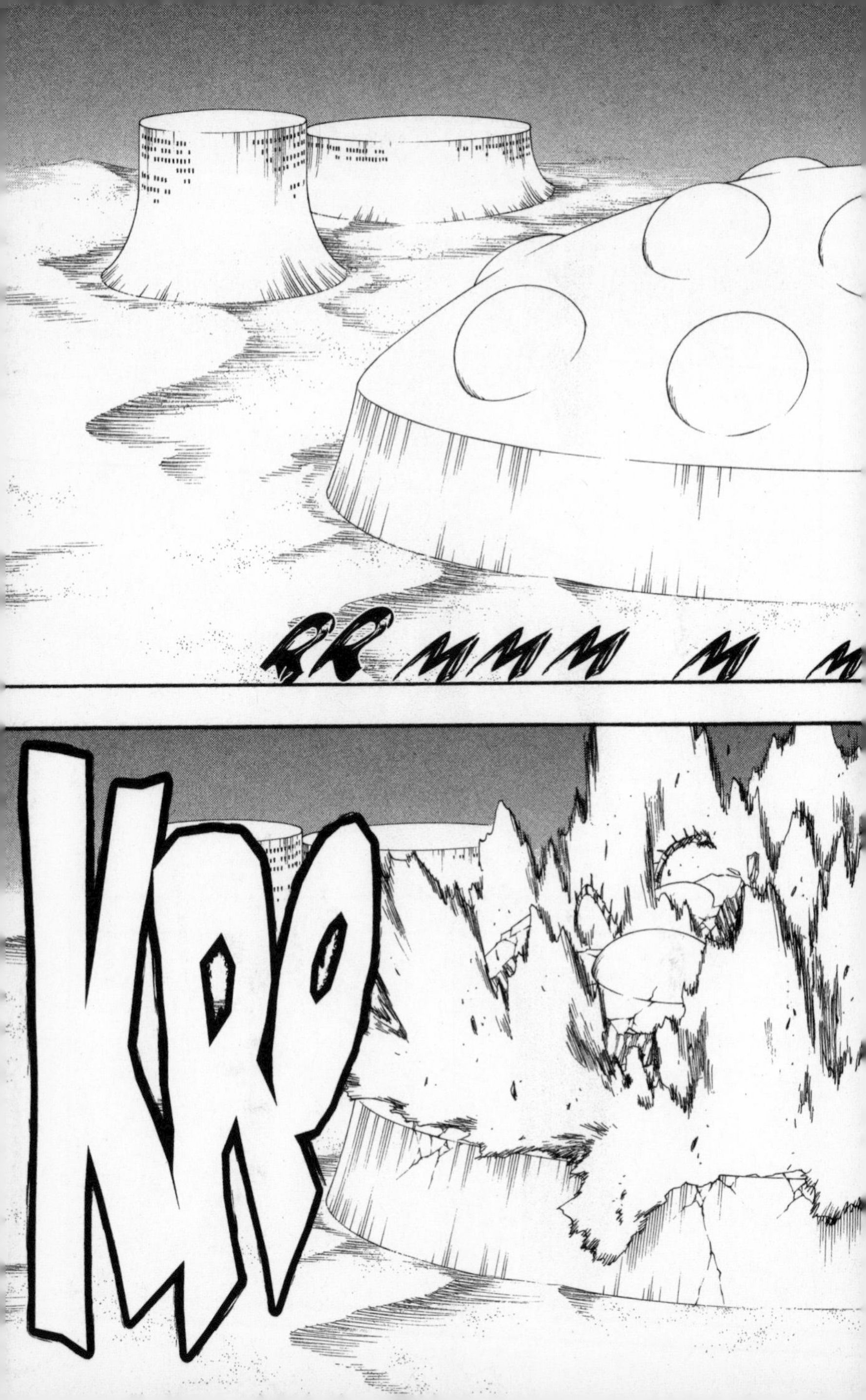
RRMMMM M M
KRO

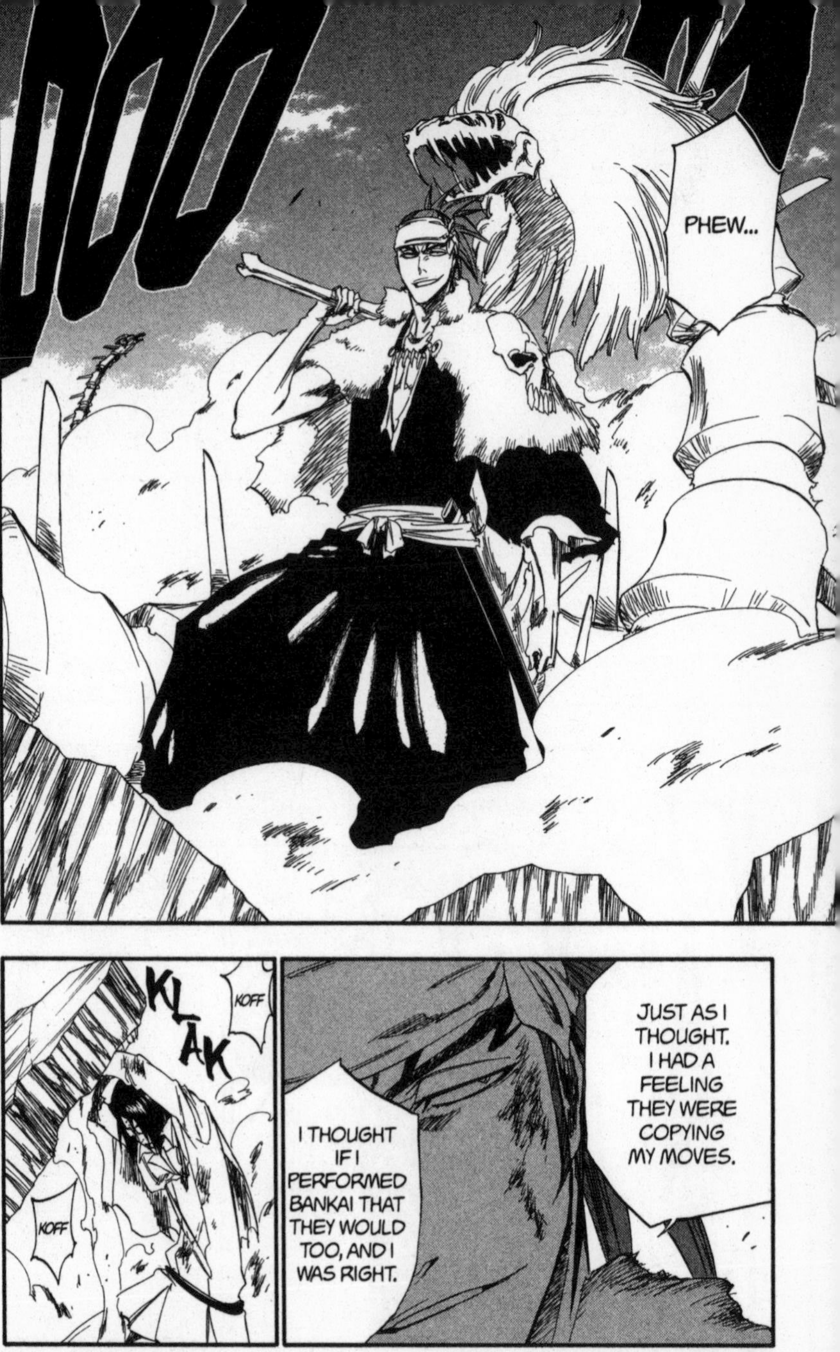
PHEW...
JUST AS I THOUGHT. I HAD A FEELING THEY WERE COPYING MY MOVES.
I THOUGHT IF I PERFORMED BANKAI THAT THEY WOULD TOO, AND I WAS RIGHT.
KLAK
KOFF
KOFF

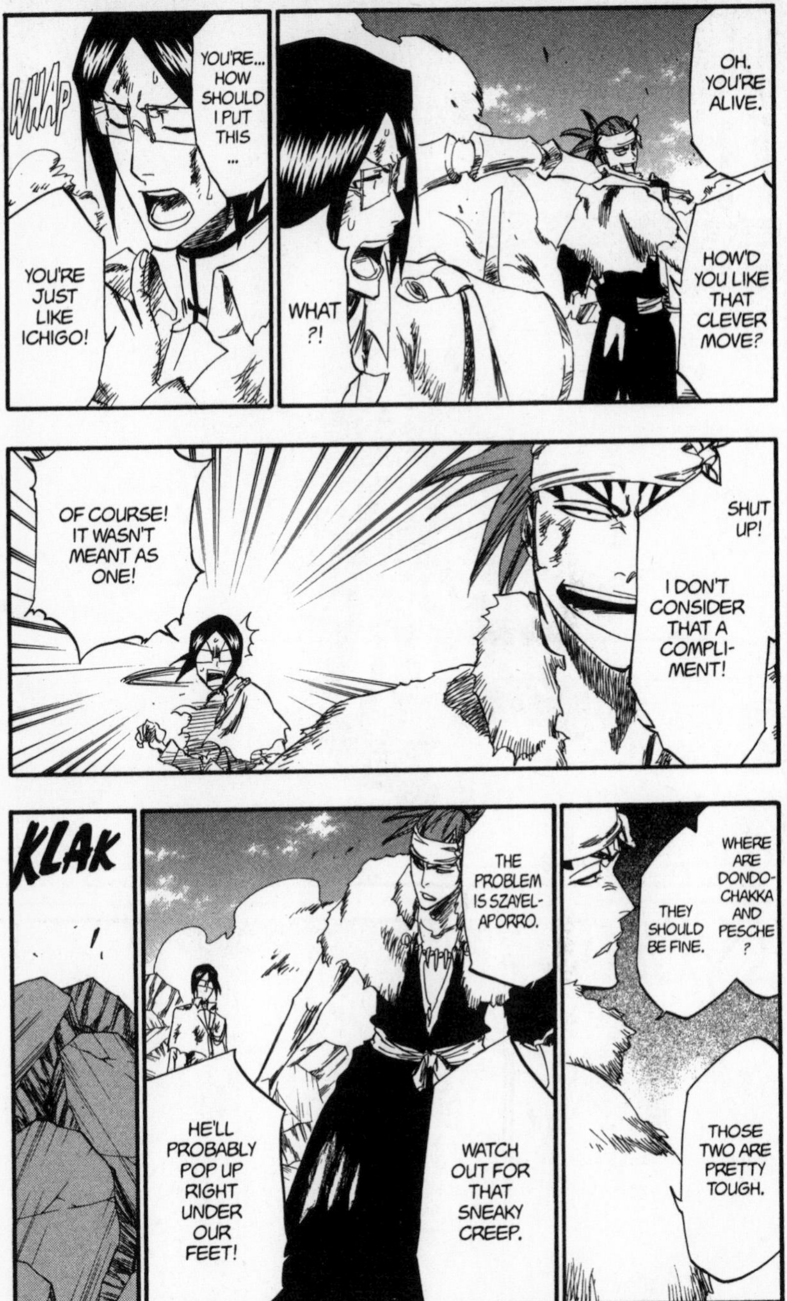
OH. YOU'RE ALIVE.
HOW'D YOU LIKE THAT CLEVER MOVE?
WHAT?!
WHAP
YOU'RE... HOW SHOULD I PUT THIS ...
YOU'RE JUST LIKE ICHIGO!
SHUT UP!
I DON'T CONSIDER THAT A COMPLIMENT!
OF COURSE! IT WASN'T MEANT AS ONE!
WHERE ARE DONDO-CHAKKA AND PESCHE?
THEY SHOULD BE FINE.
THOSE TWO ARE PRETTY TOUGH.
THE PROBLEM IS SZAYEL-APORRO.
WATCH OUT FOR THAT SNEAKY CREEP.
HE'LL PROBABLY POP UP RIGHT UNDER OUR FEET!
KLAK

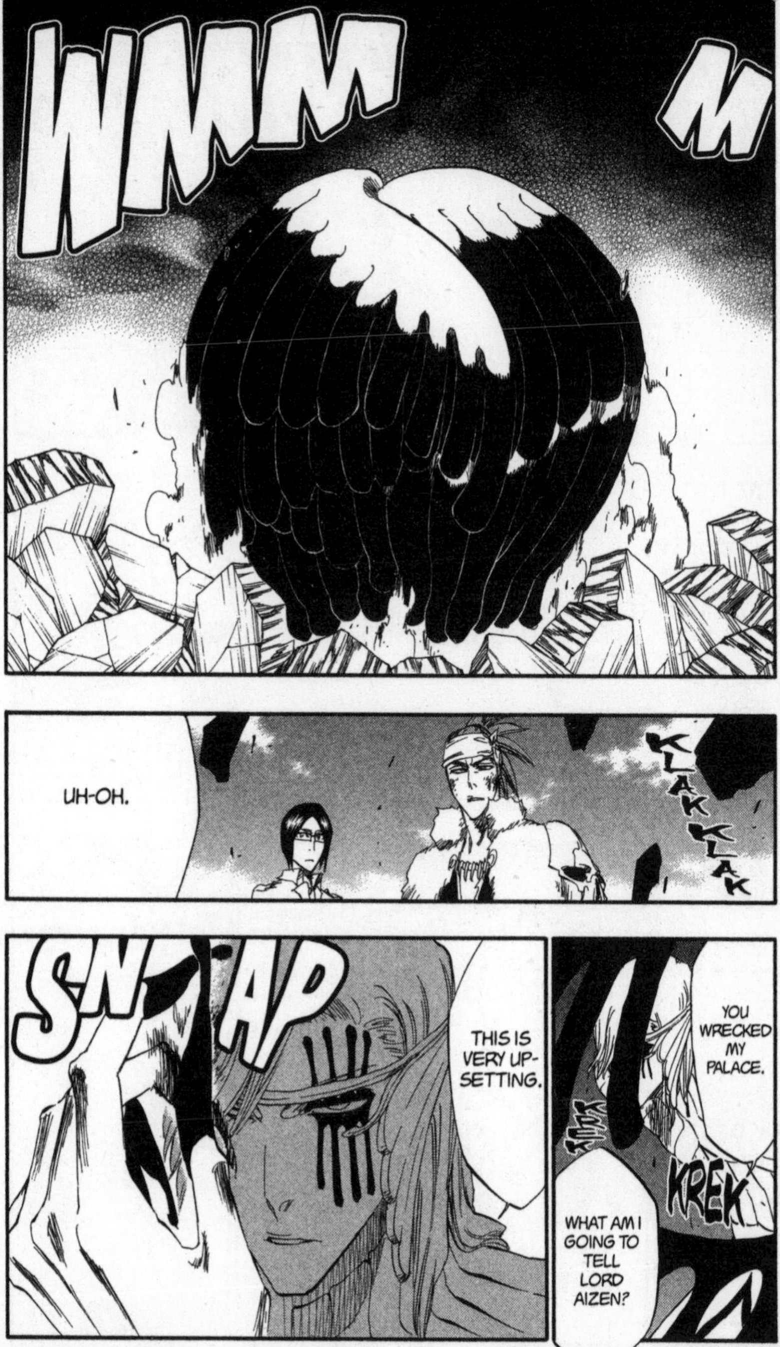
WMMM
M
KLAK KLAK
UH-OH.
YOU WRECKED MY PALACE.
KREK
WHAT AM I GOING TO TELL LORD AIZEN?
SN AP
THIS IS VERY UP-SETTING.

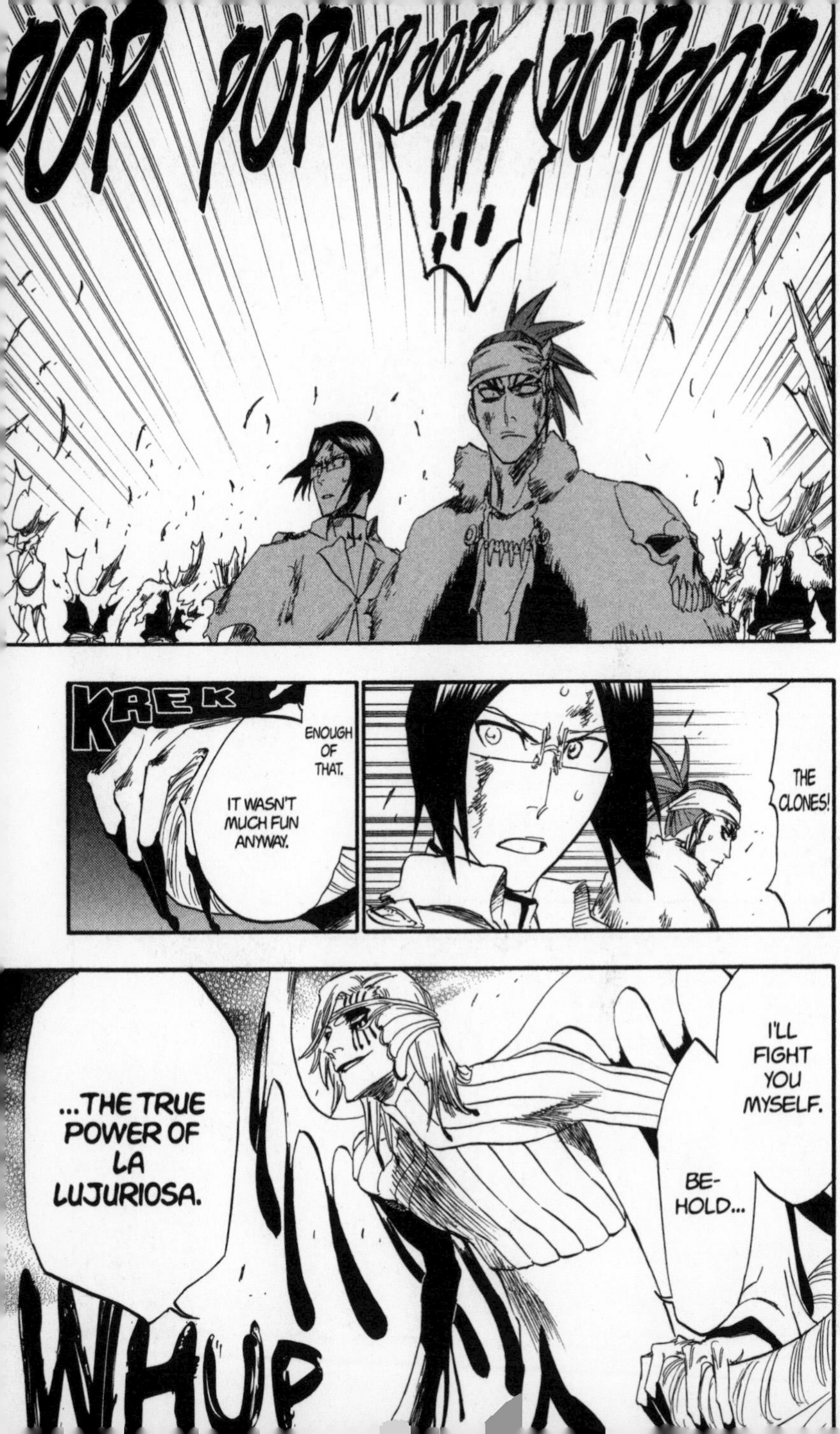

POP POP POP POP!!! POP POP POP
THE CLONES!
KREK
ENOUGH OF THAT.
IT WASN'T MUCH FUN ANYWAY.
I'LL FIGHT YOU MYSELF.
BE-HOLD...
...THE TRUE POWER OF LA LUJURIOSA.
WHUP

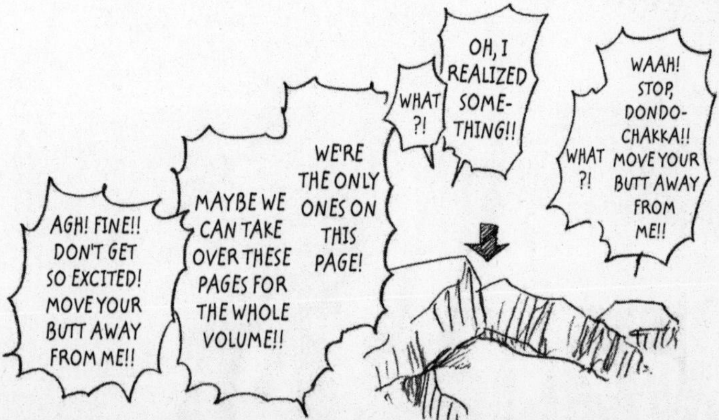
WAAH! STOP, DONDO-CHAKKA!! MOVE YOUR BUTT AWAY FROM ME!!
WHAT ?!
OH, I REALIZED SOME-THING!!
WHAT ?!
WE'RE THE ONLY ONES ON THIS PAGE!
MAYBE WE CAN TAKE OVER THESE PAGES FOR THE WHOLE VOLUME!!
AGH! FINE!! DON'T GET SO EXCITED! MOVE YOUR BUTT AWAY FROM ME!!

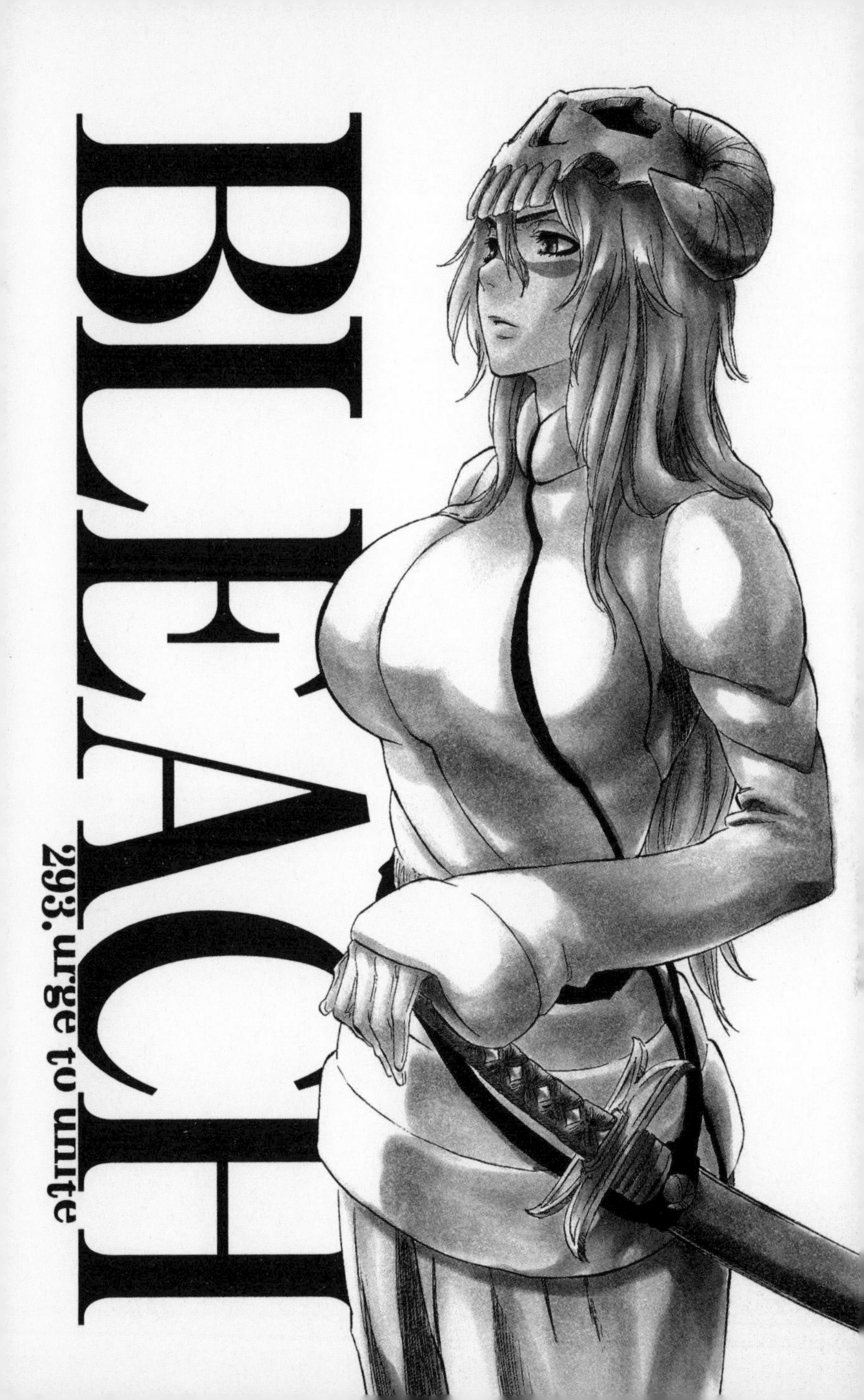
BLEACH
293. urge to unite

BLEACH
ブリーチ

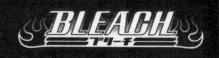

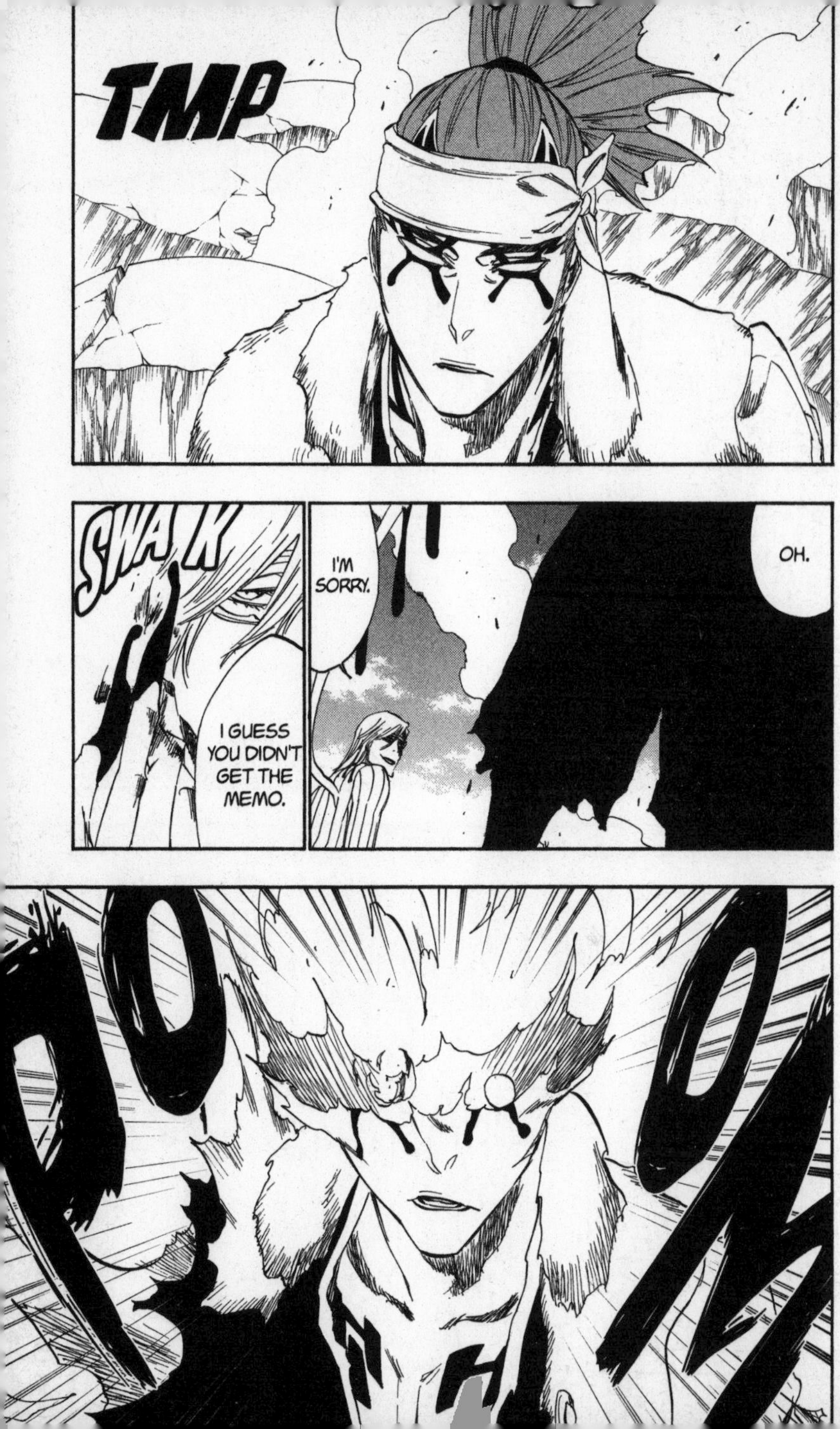
TMP
OH.
I'M SORRY.
SWAK
I GUESS YOU DIDN'T GET THE MEMO.

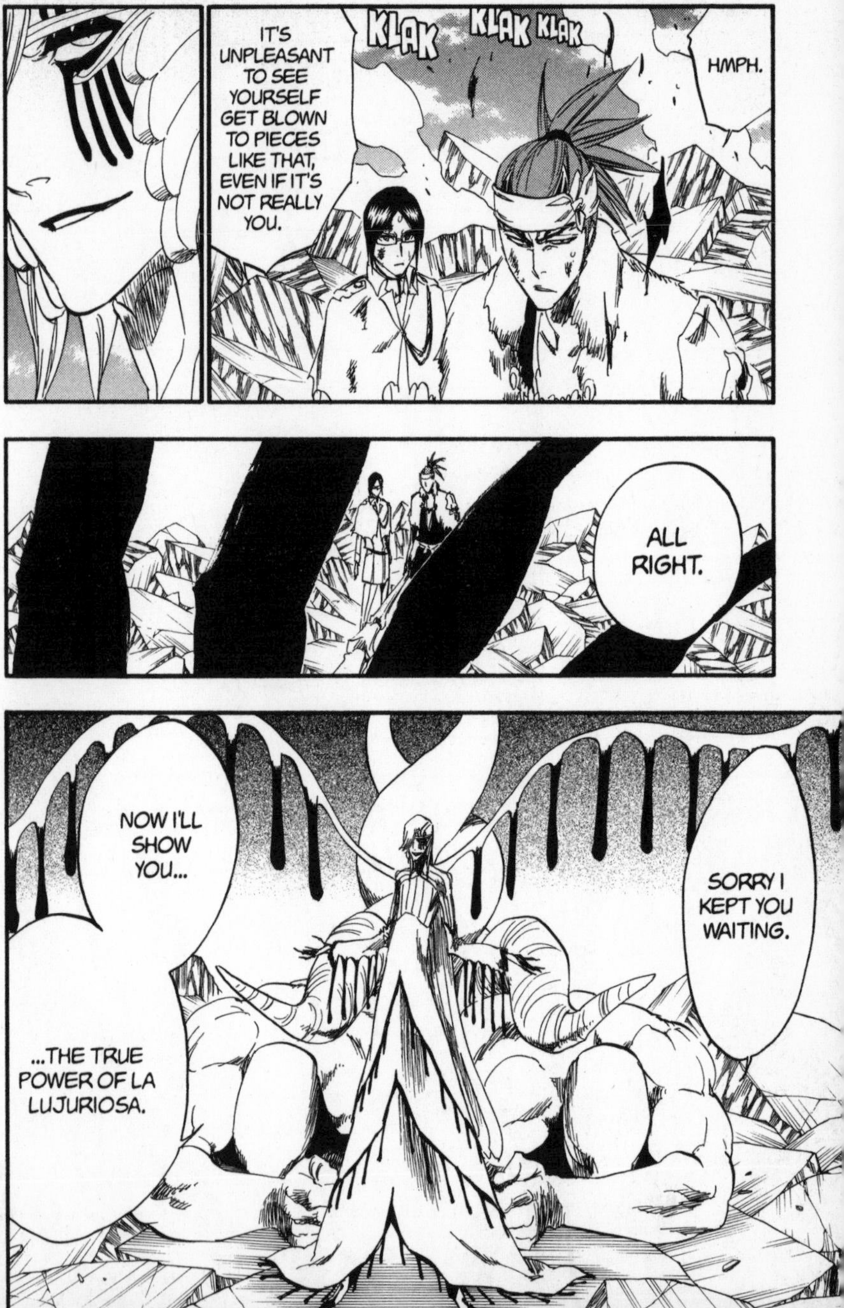
HMPH.
KLAK KLAK
KLAK
IT'S UNPLEASANT TO SEE YOURSELF GET BLOWN TO PIECES LIKE THAT, EVEN IF IT'S NOT REALLY YOU.
ALL RIGHT.
SORRY I KEPT YOU WAITING.
NOW I'LL SHOW YOU...
...THE TRUE POWER OF LA LUJURIOSA.

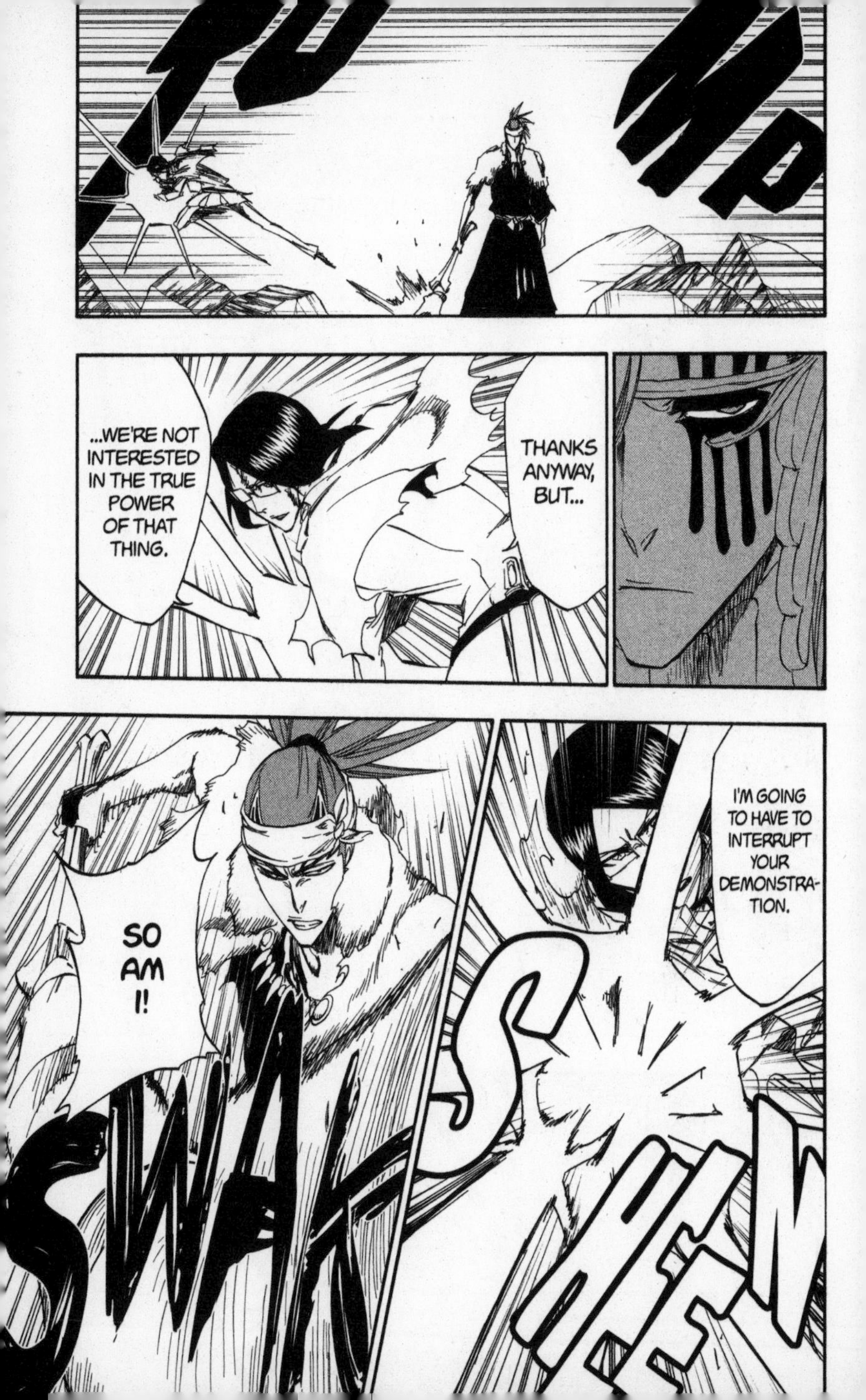
THUMP
THANKS ANYWAY, BUT...
...WE'RE NOT INTERESTED IN THE TRUE POWER OF THAT THING.
I'M GOING TO HAVE TO INTERRUPT YOUR DEMONSTRATION.
SO AM I!

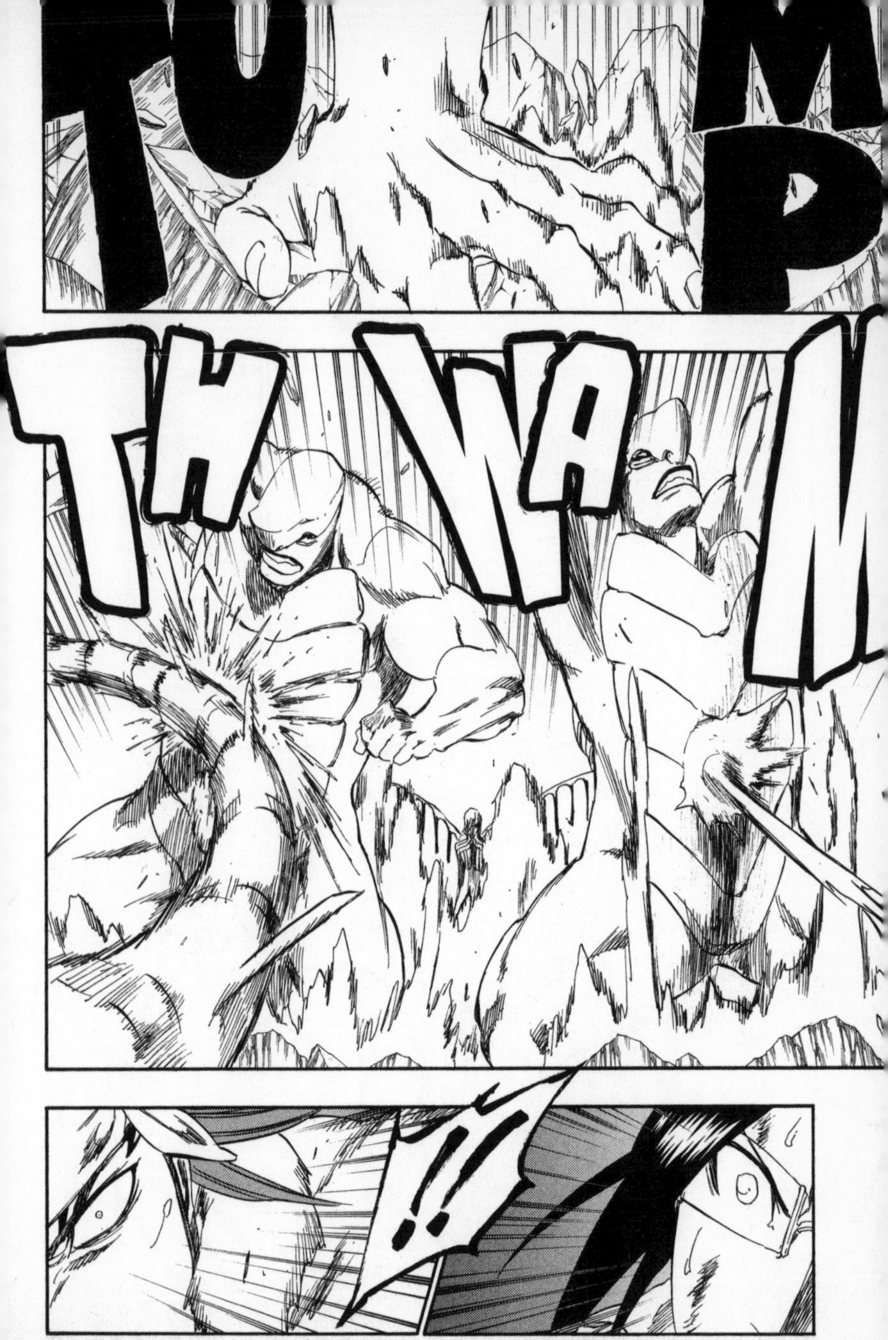
THWAM
!!

READ THIS WAY

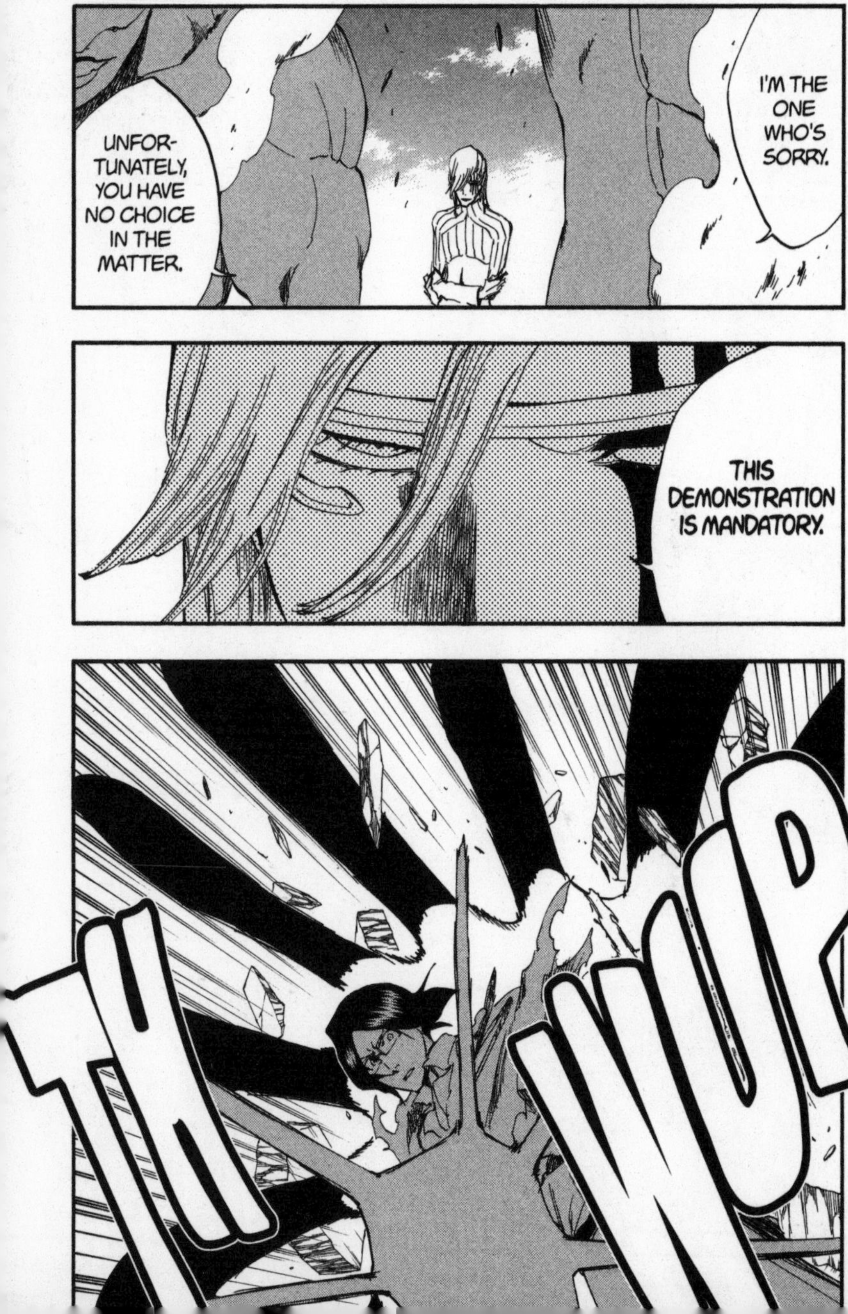
I'M THE ONE WHO'S SORRY.
UNFOR-TUNATELY, YOU HAVE NO CHOICE IN THE MATTER.
THIS DEMONSTRATION IS MANDATORY.
THWUP

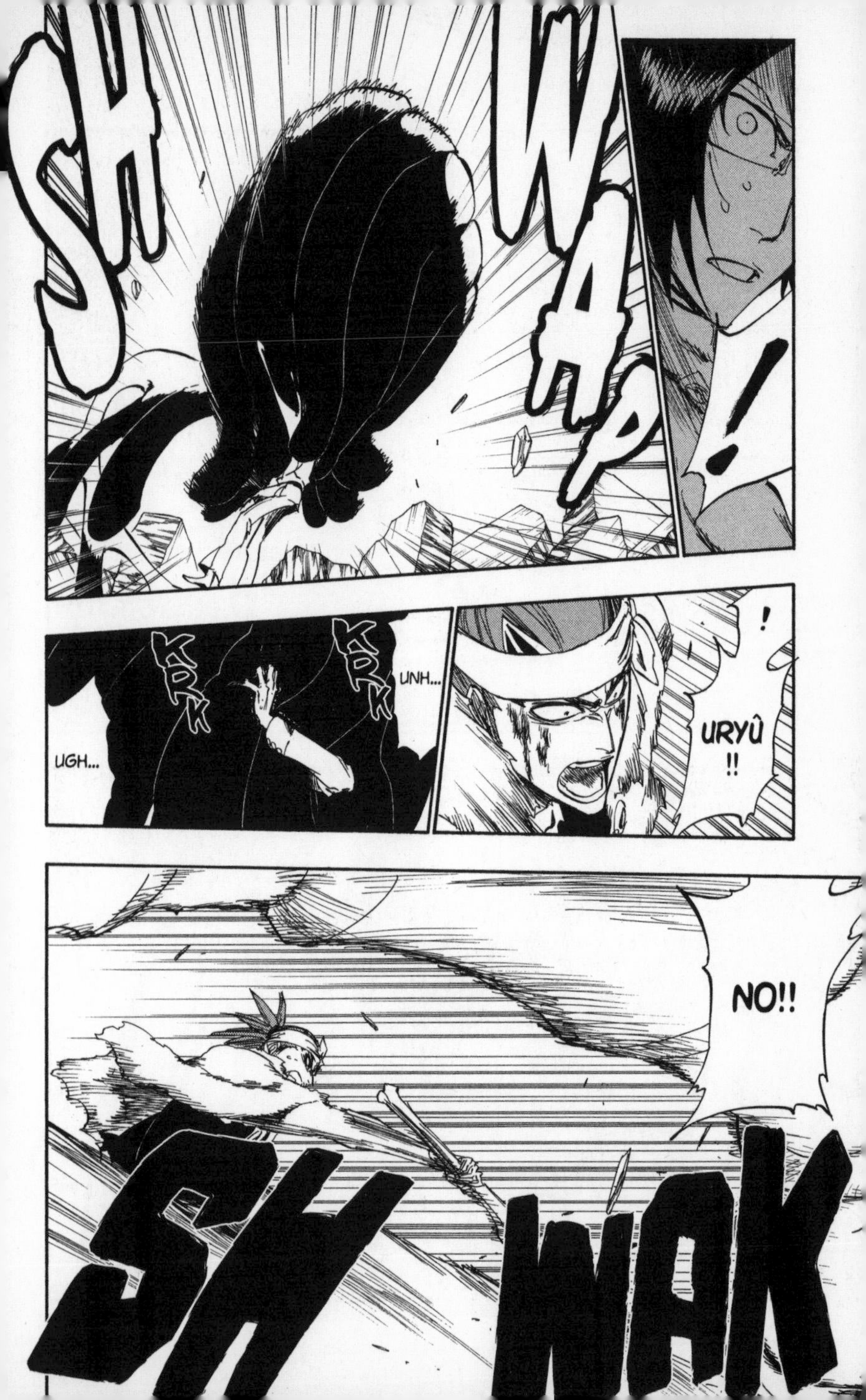
!
SHWAP
!
URYÛ !!
UNH...
KRK
KRK
UGH...
NO!!
SHWAK

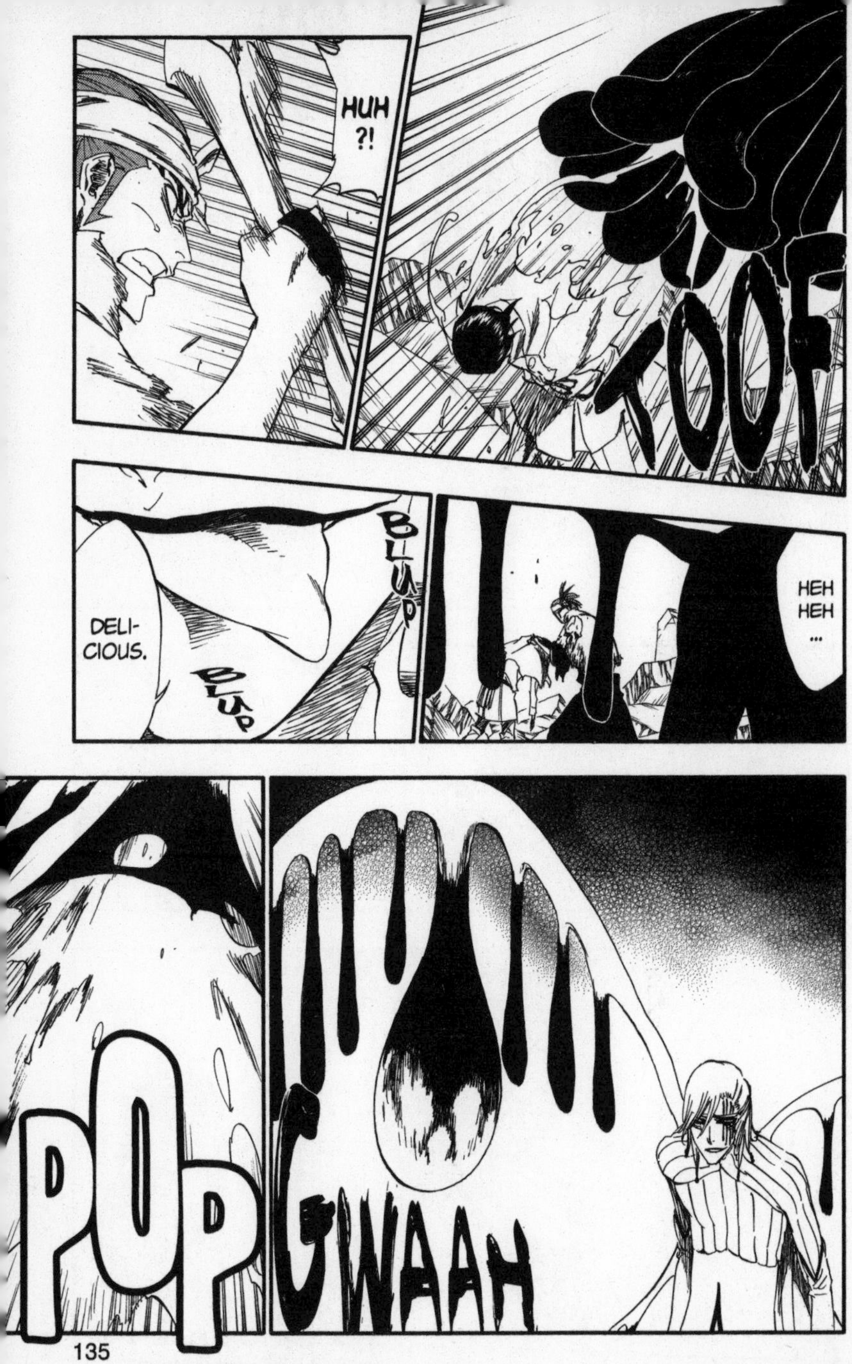
TOOF
HUH ?!
HEH HEH ...
BLUP
BLUP
DELI-CIOUS.
GWAAH
POP

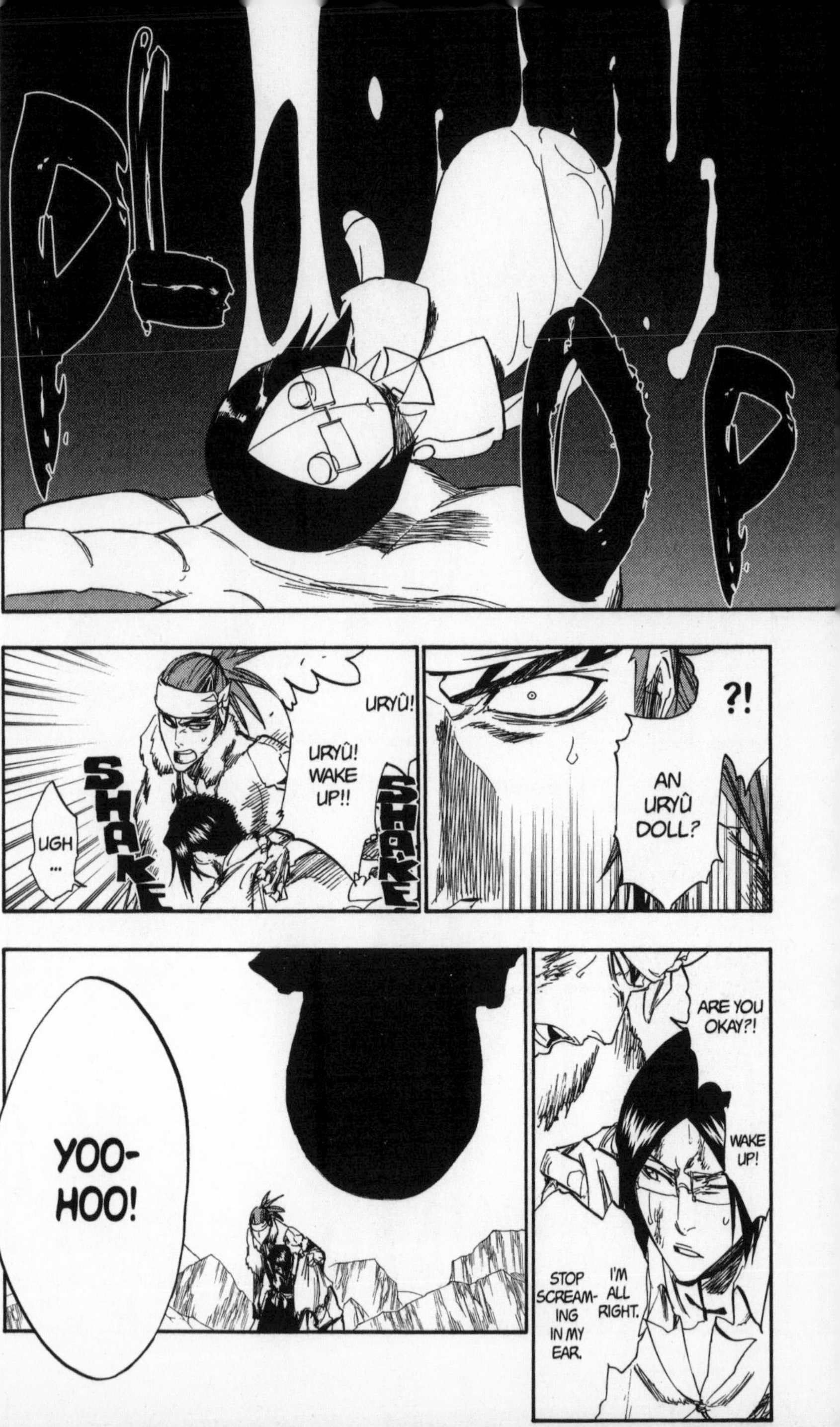
DLOOP
?!
AN URYÛ DOLL?
URYÛ!
URYÛ! WAKE UP!!
SHAKE
SHAKE
UGH ...
ARE YOU OKAY?!
WAKE UP!
I'M ALL RIGHT.
STOP SCREAM-ING IN MY EAR.
YOO-HOO!

READ THIS WAY

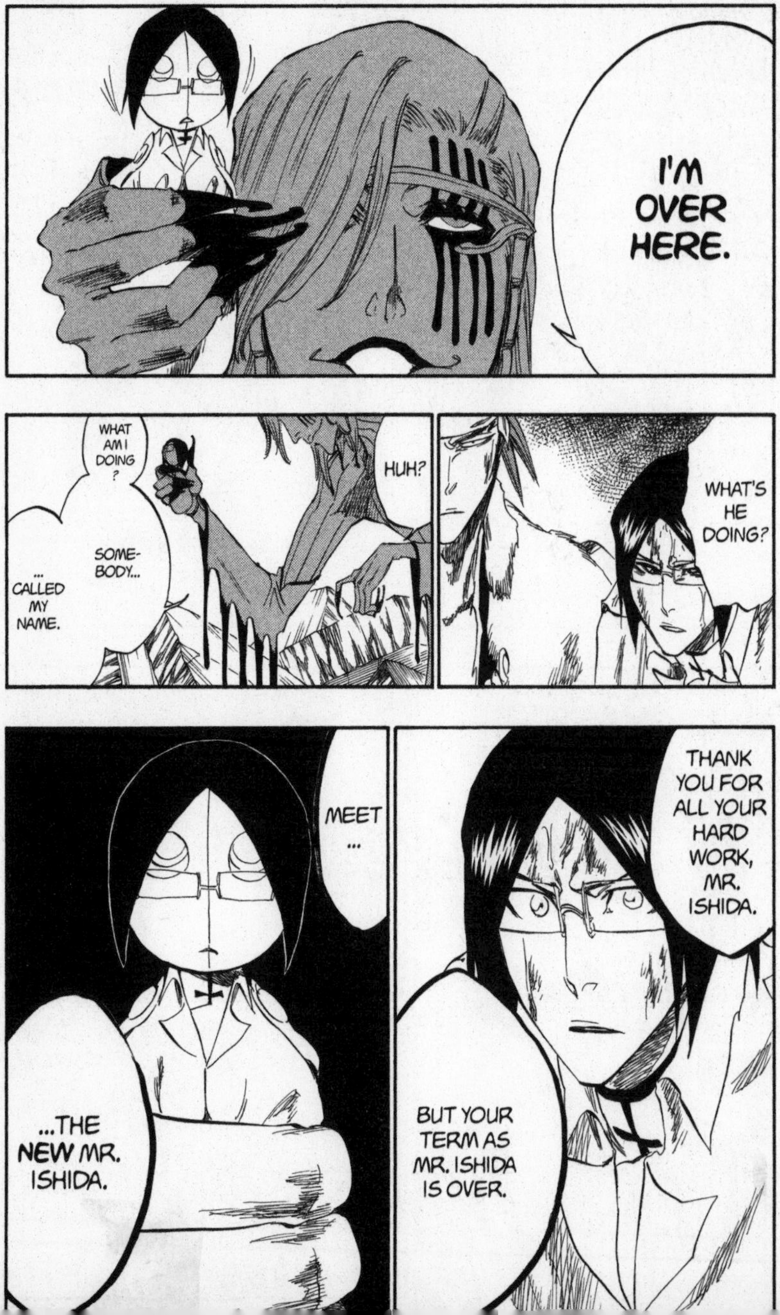
I'M OVER HERE.
WHAT'S HE DOING?
HUH?
WHAT AM I DOING?
SOMEBODY...
...CALLED MY NAME.
THANK YOU FOR ALL YOUR HARD WORK, MR. ISHIDA.
BUT YOUR TERM AS MR. ISHIDA IS OVER.
MEET...
...THE NEW MR. ISHIDA.

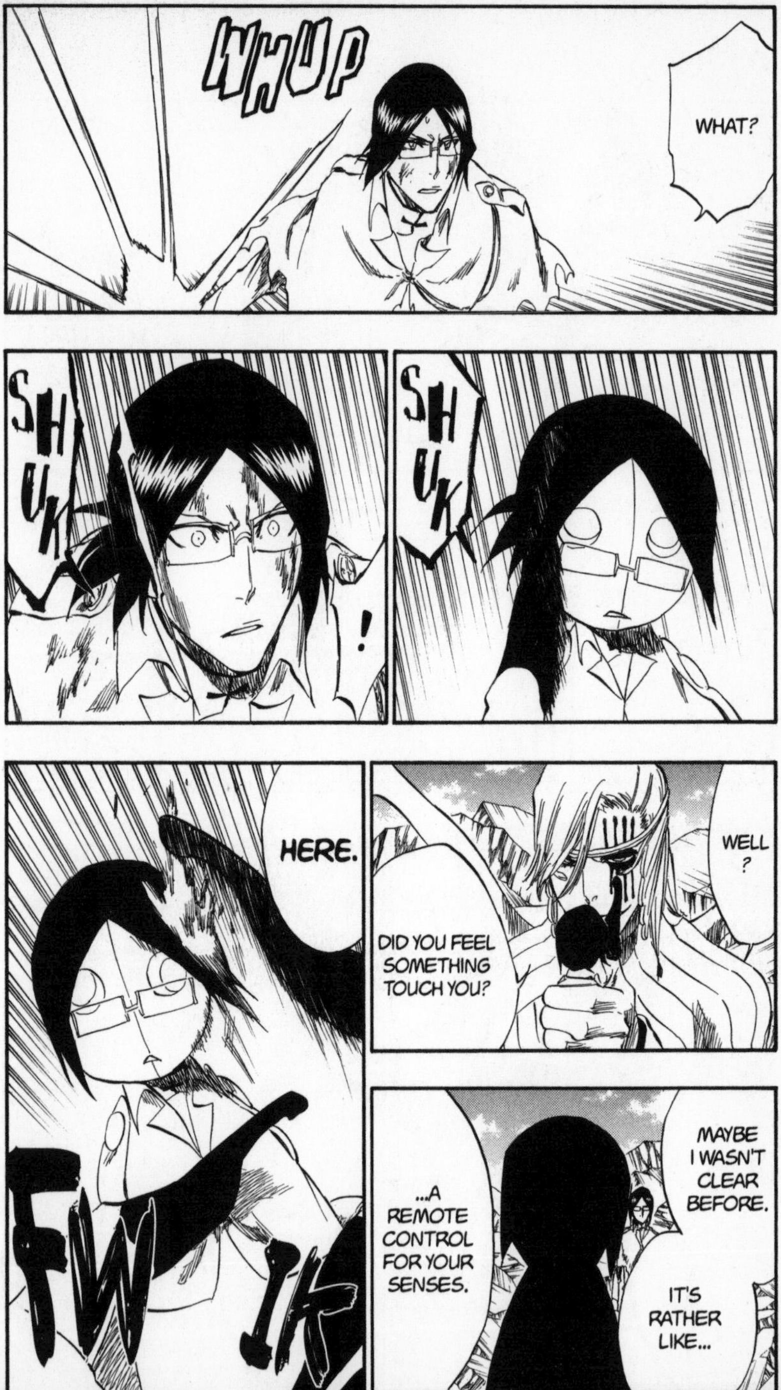

WHUP
WHAT?
SHUK
SHUK
!
WELL?
DID YOU FEEL SOMETHING TOUCH YOU?
MAYBE I WASN'T CLEAR BEFORE.
IT'S RATHER LIKE...
...A REMOTE CONTROL FOR YOUR SENSES.
HERE.
FWIK

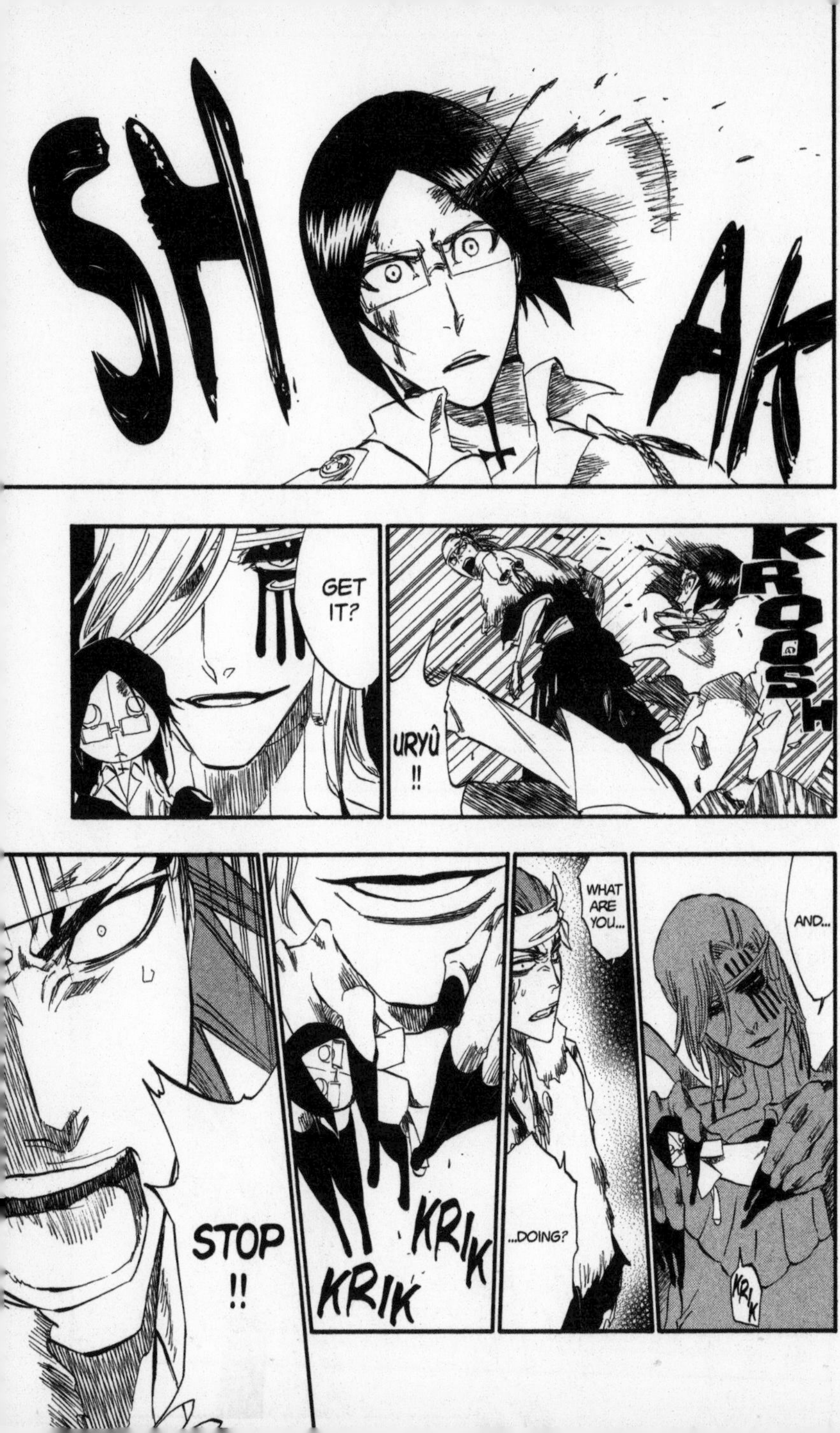
SHAK
KROOSH
URYÛ !!
GET IT?
AND...
KRIK
WHAT ARE YOU...
...DOING?
KRIK
KRIK
STOP !!

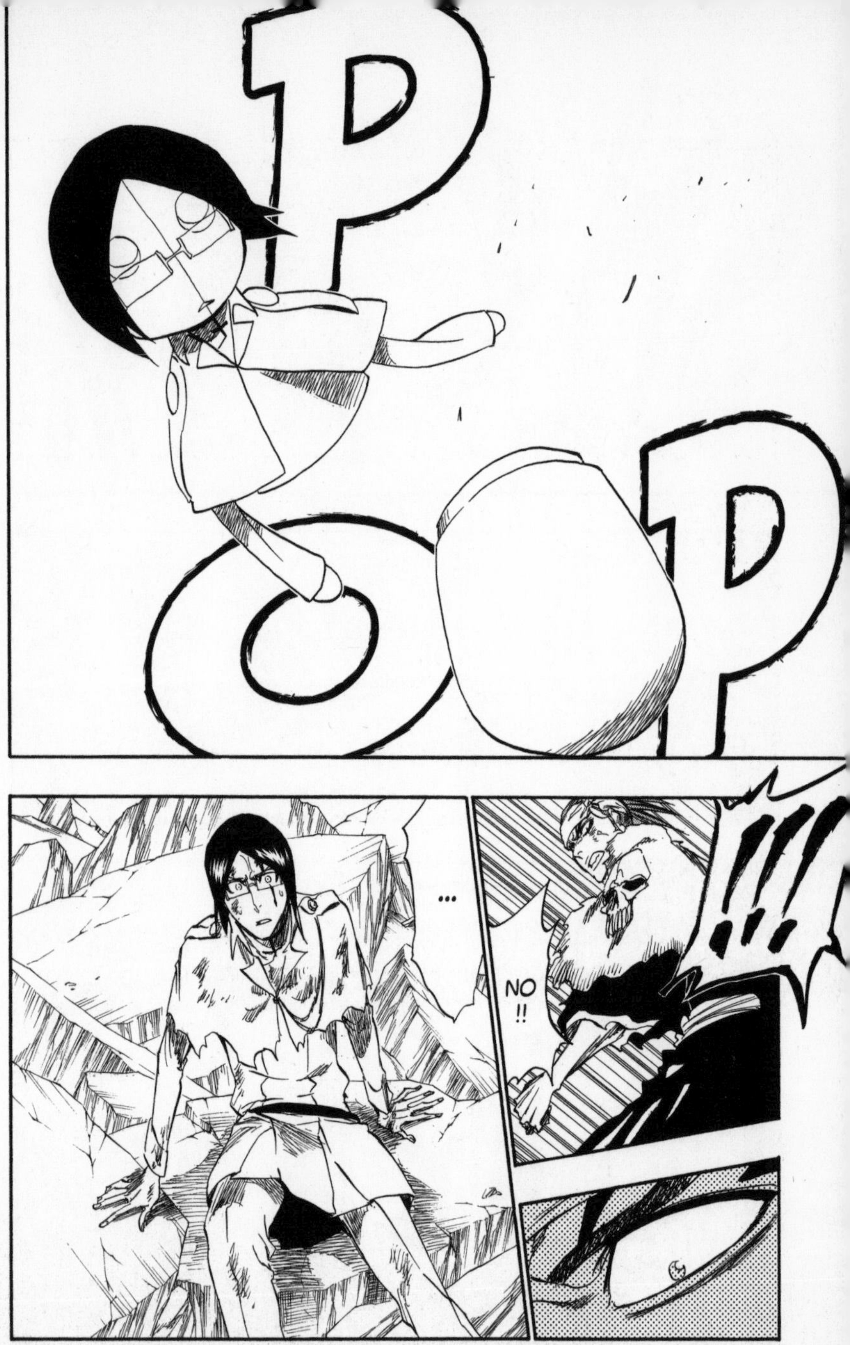
POOP
!!!
NO !!
...

READ THIS WAY

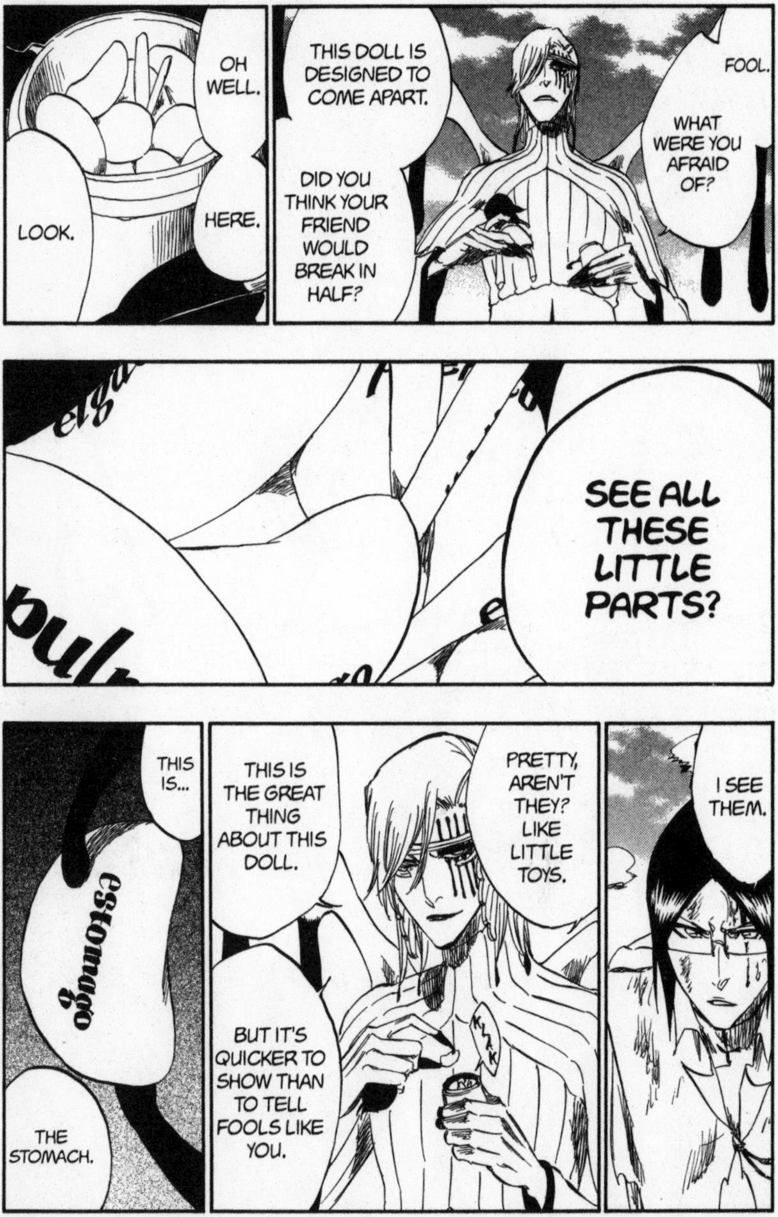
FOOL.
WHAT WERE YOU AFRAID OF?
THIS DOLL IS DESIGNED TO COME APART.
DID YOU THINK YOUR FRIEND WOULD BREAK IN HALF?
OH WELL.
HERE.
LOOK.
SEE ALL THESE LITTLE PARTS?
I SEE THEM.
PRETTY, AREN'T THEY? LIKE LITTLE TOYS.
THIS IS THE GREAT THING ABOUT THIS DOLL.
BUT IT'S QUICKER TO SHOW THAN TO TELL FOOLS LIKE YOU.
KLAK
THIS IS...
estomago
THE STOMACH.

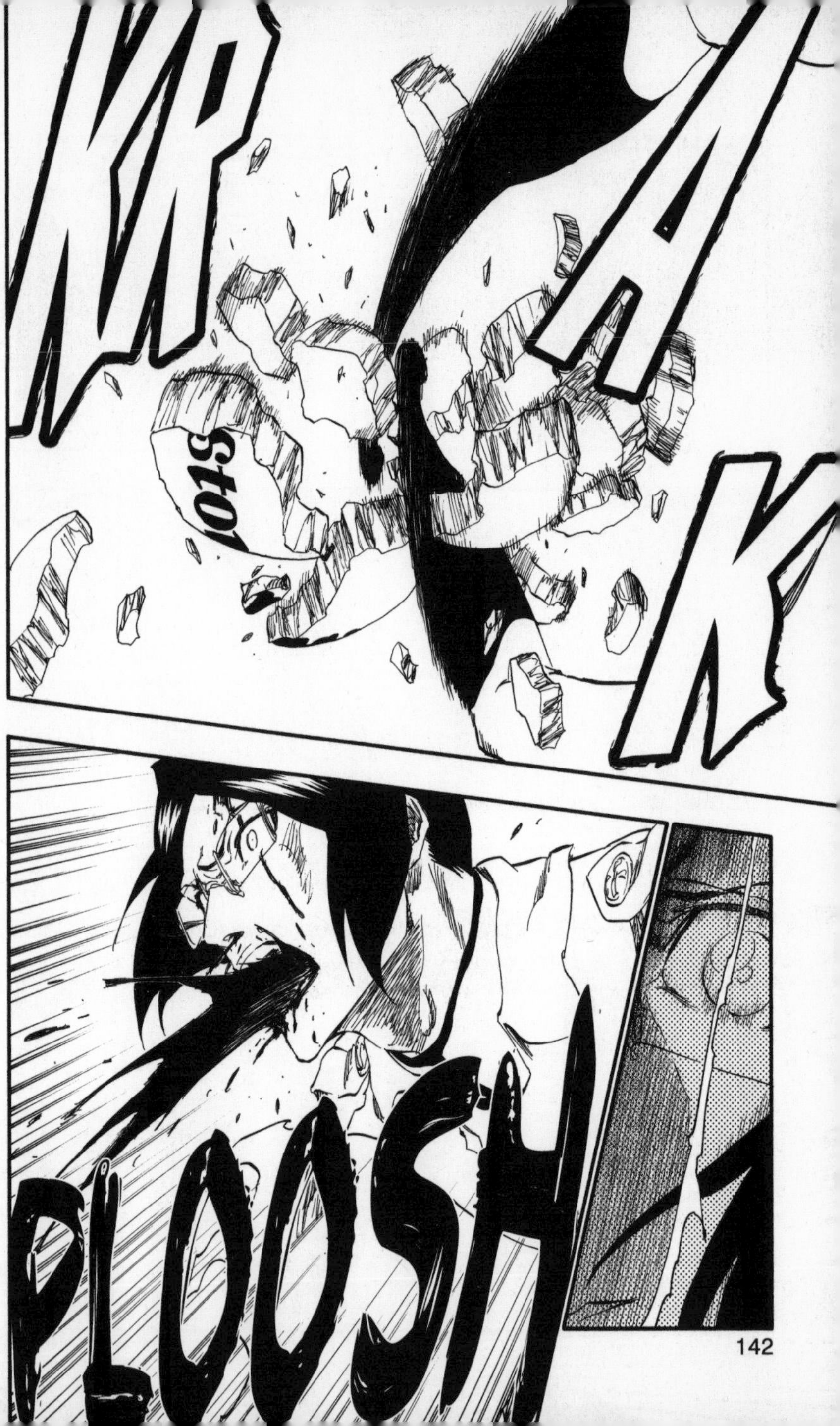
KRAK
PLOOSH

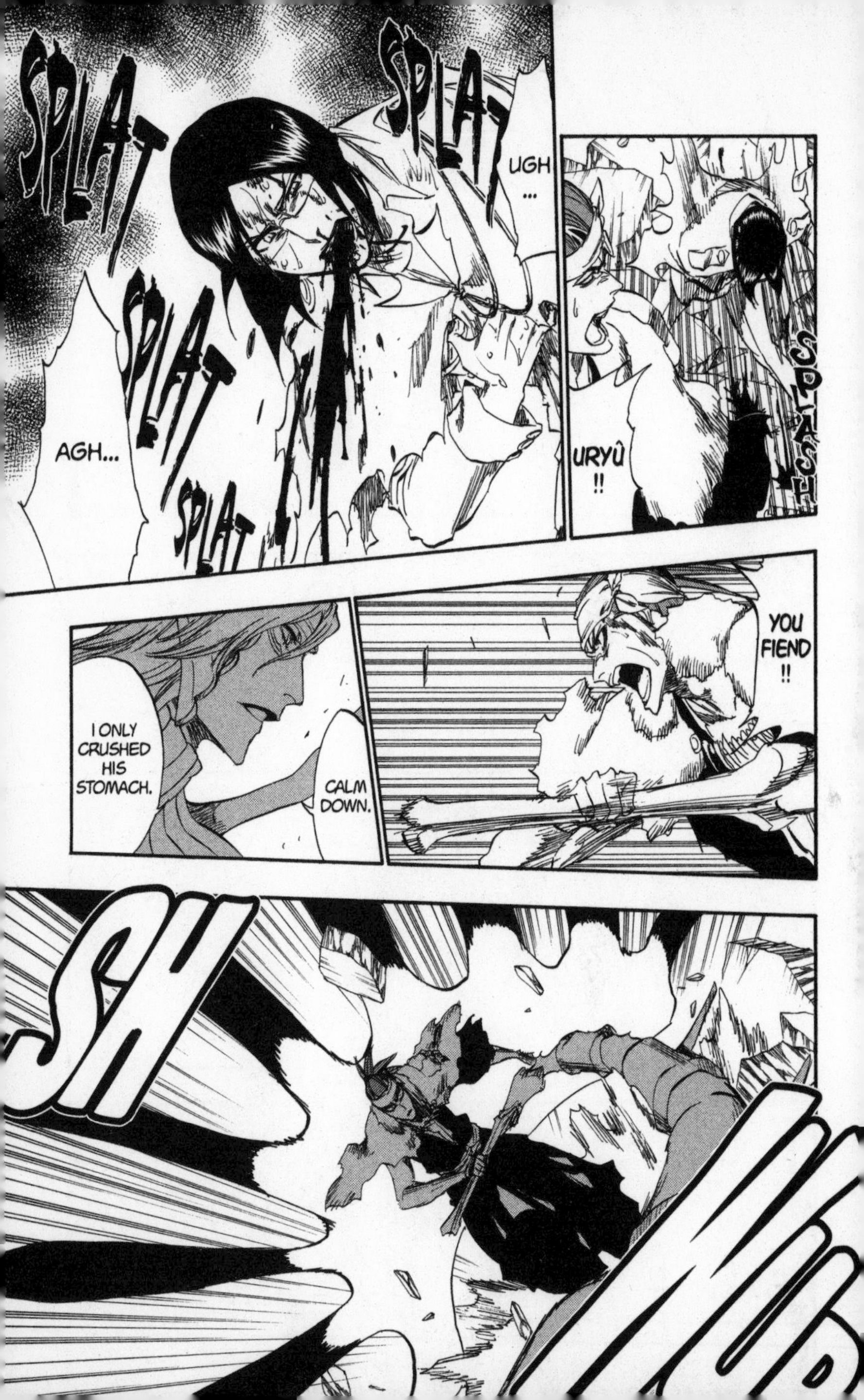
SPLASH
URYÛ!!
SPLAT
UGH...
SPLAT
SPLAT
AGH...
SPLAT
YOU FIEND!!
CALM DOWN.
I ONLY CRUSHED HIS STOMACH.
SH

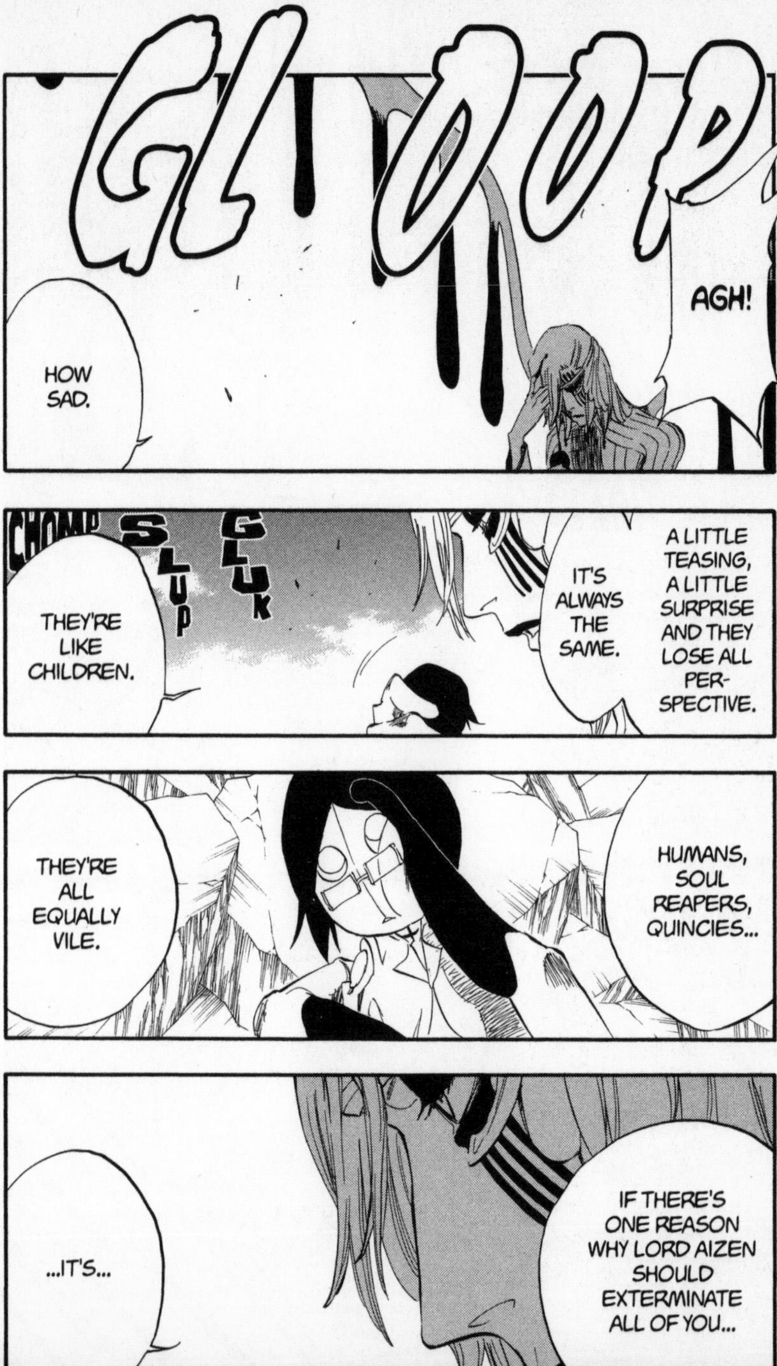
GLOOP
AGH!
HOW SAD.
A LITTLE TEASING, A LITTLE SURPRISE AND THEY LOSE ALL PER-SPECTIVE.
IT'S ALWAYS THE SAME.
GLUK
SLUP
CHOMP
THEY'RE LIKE CHILDREN.
HUMANS, SOUL REAPERS, QUINCIES...
THEY'RE ALL EQUALLY VILE.
IF THERE'S ONE REASON WHY LORD AIZEN SHOULD EXTERMINATE ALL OF YOU...
...IT'S...

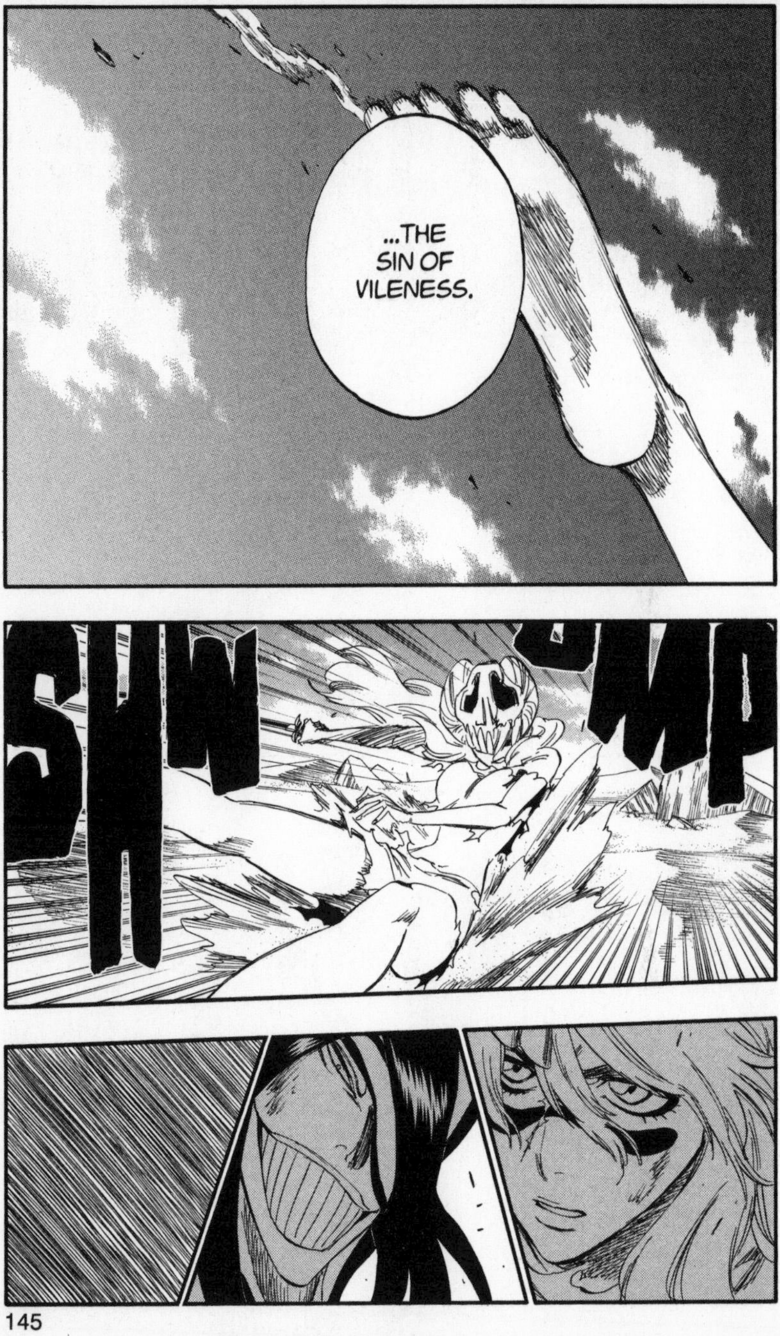
...THE SIN OF VILENESS.
SHWOMP

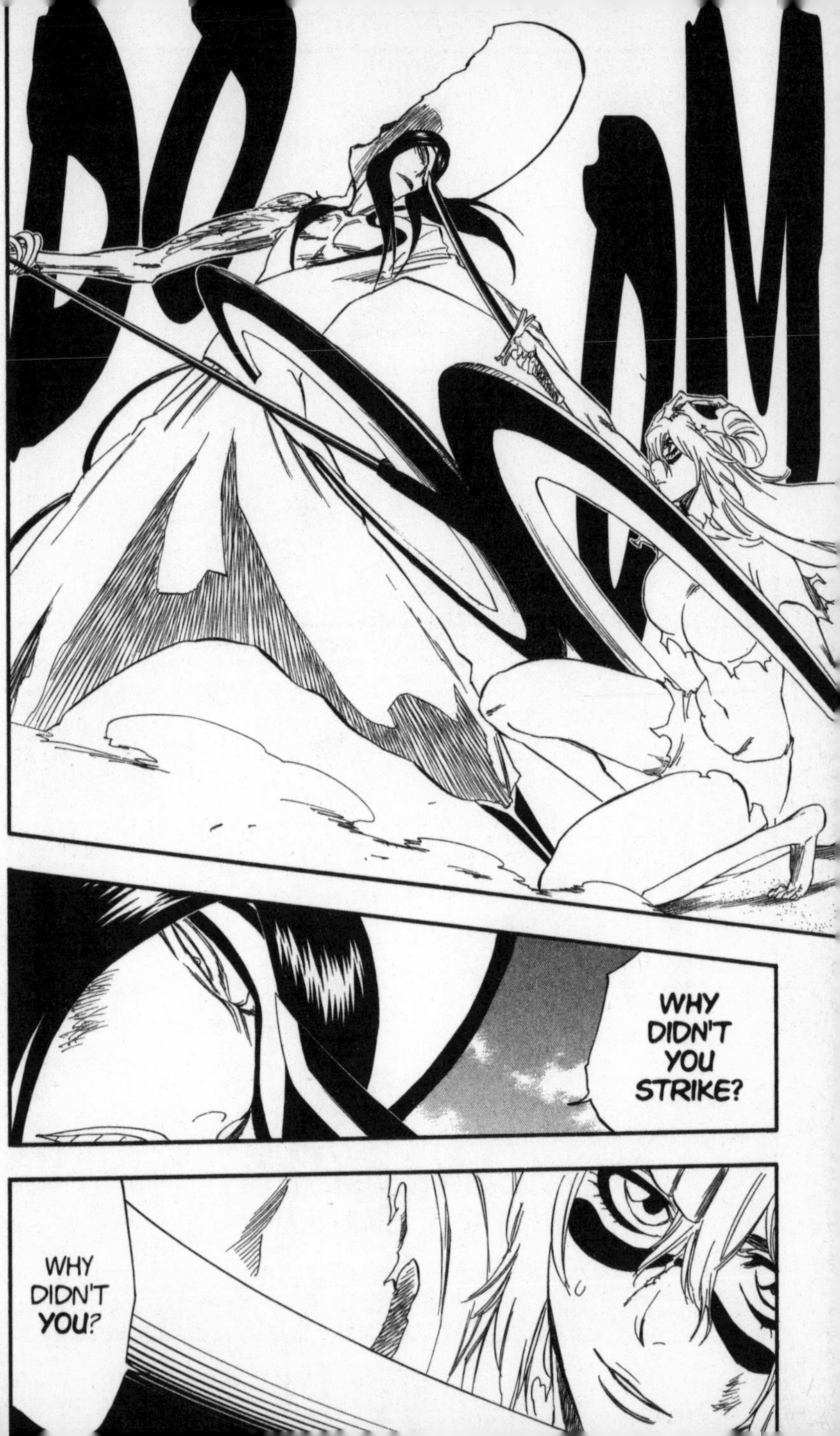
DOOM
WHY DIDN'T YOU STRIKE?
WHY DIDN'T YOU?

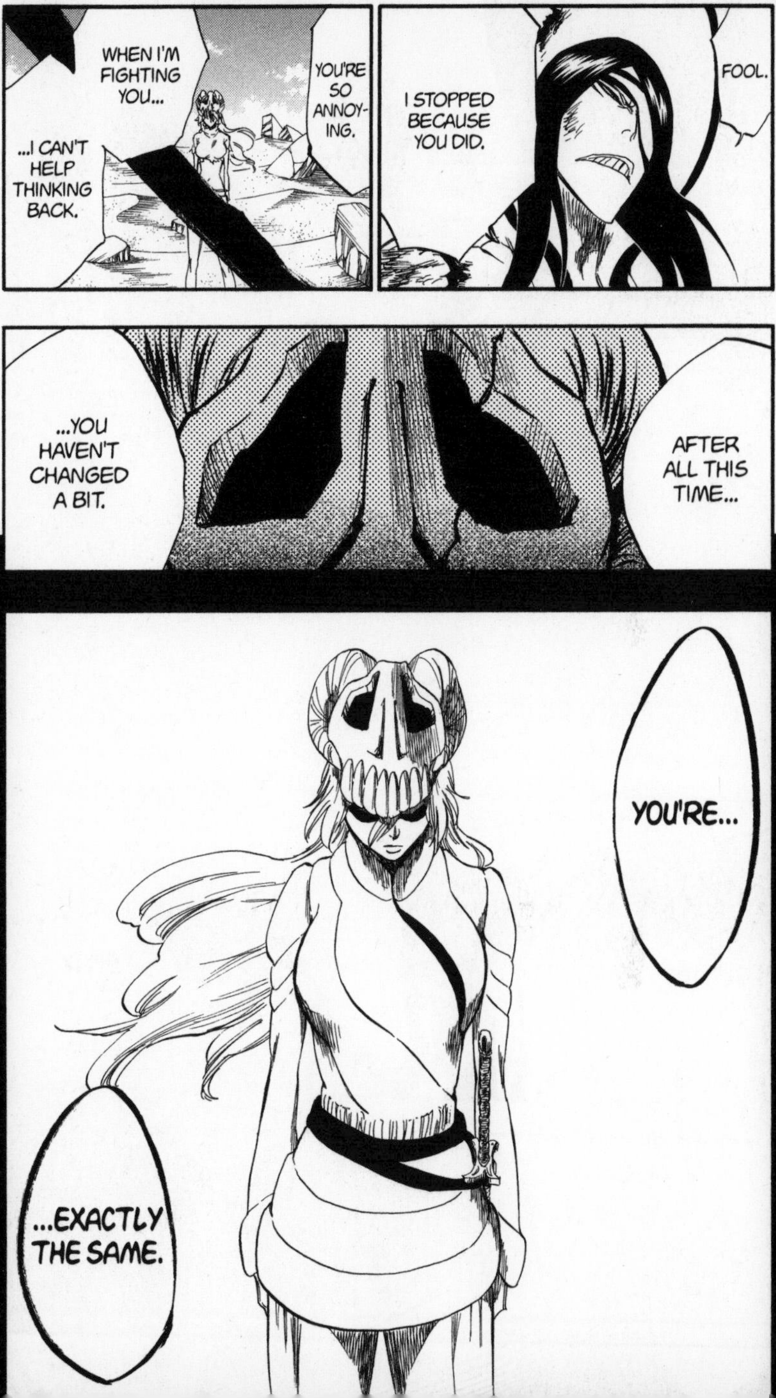
FOOL.
I STOPPED BECAUSE YOU DID.
YOU'RE SO ANNOY-ING.
WHEN I'M FIGHTING YOU...
...I CAN'T HELP THINKING BACK.
AFTER ALL THIS TIME...
...YOU HAVEN'T CHANGED A BIT.
YOU'RE...
...EXACTLY THE SAME.

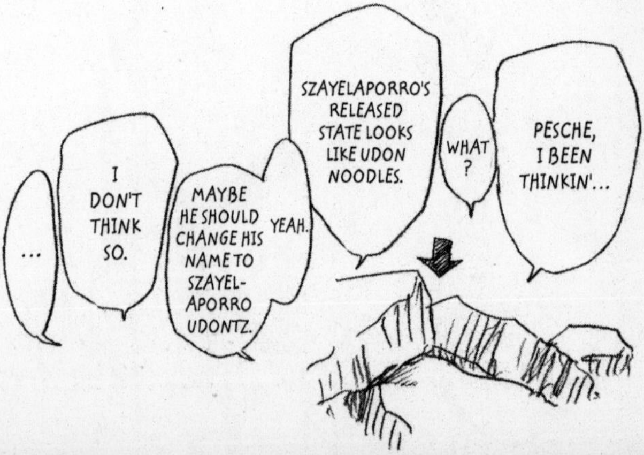
PESCHE, I BEEN THINKIN'...
WHAT?
SZAYELAPORRO'S RELEASED STATE LOOKS LIKE UDON NOODLES.
YEAH.
MAYBE HE SHOULD CHANGE HIS NAME TO SZAYEL-APORRO UDONTZ.
I DON'T THINK SO.
...

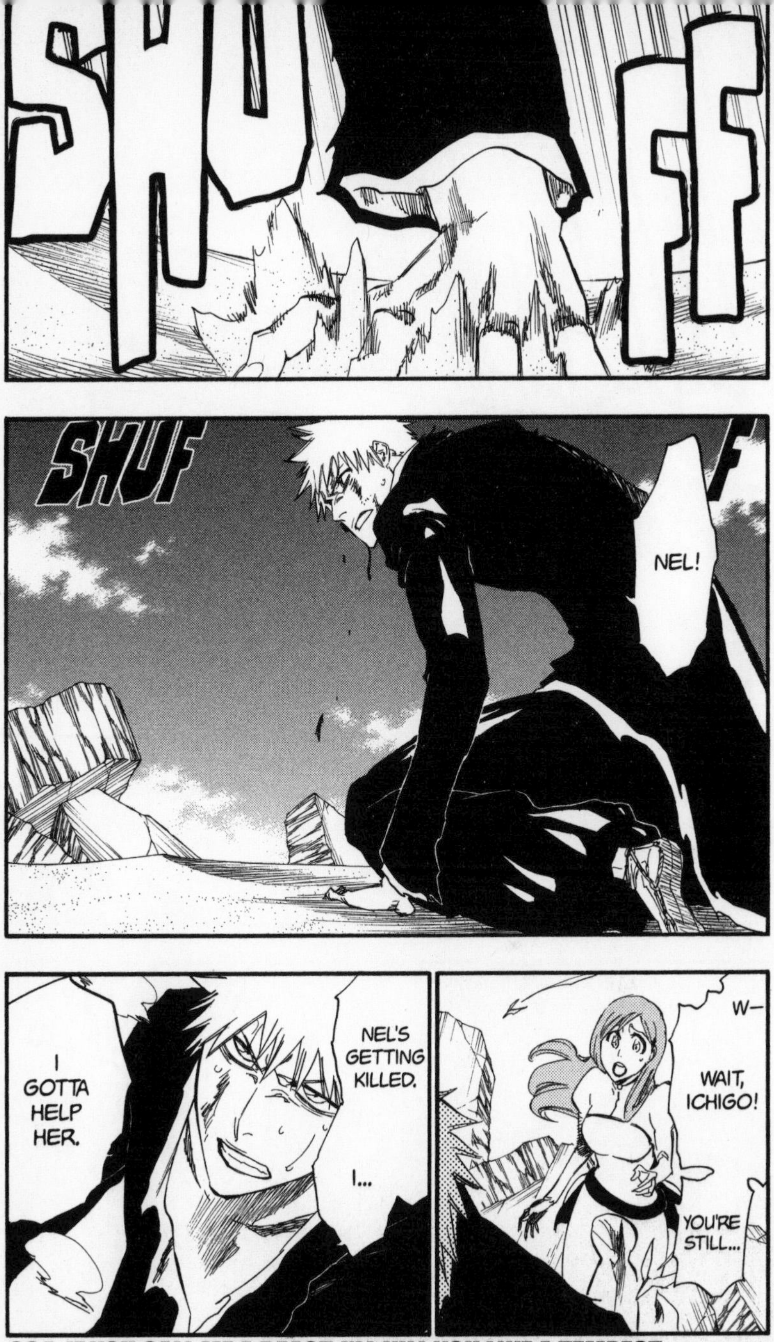
SHUFF
SHUF
NEL!
W—
WAIT, ICHIGO!
YOU'RE STILL...
NEL'S GETTING KILLED.
I...
I GOTTA HELP HER.

294. IF YOU CALL ME A BEAST, I'LL KILL YOU LIKE A TEMPEST

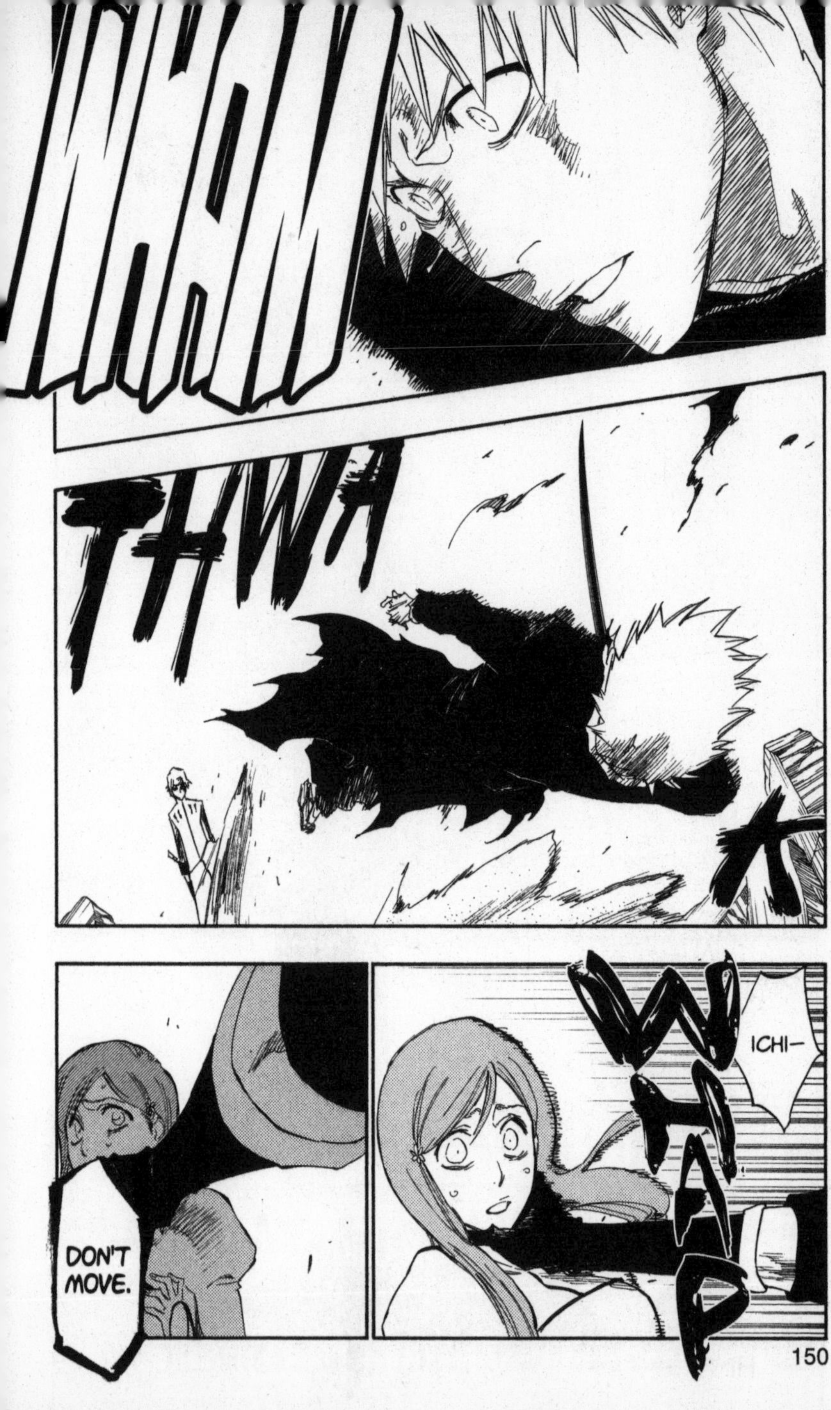
ICHI-
DON'T MOVE.

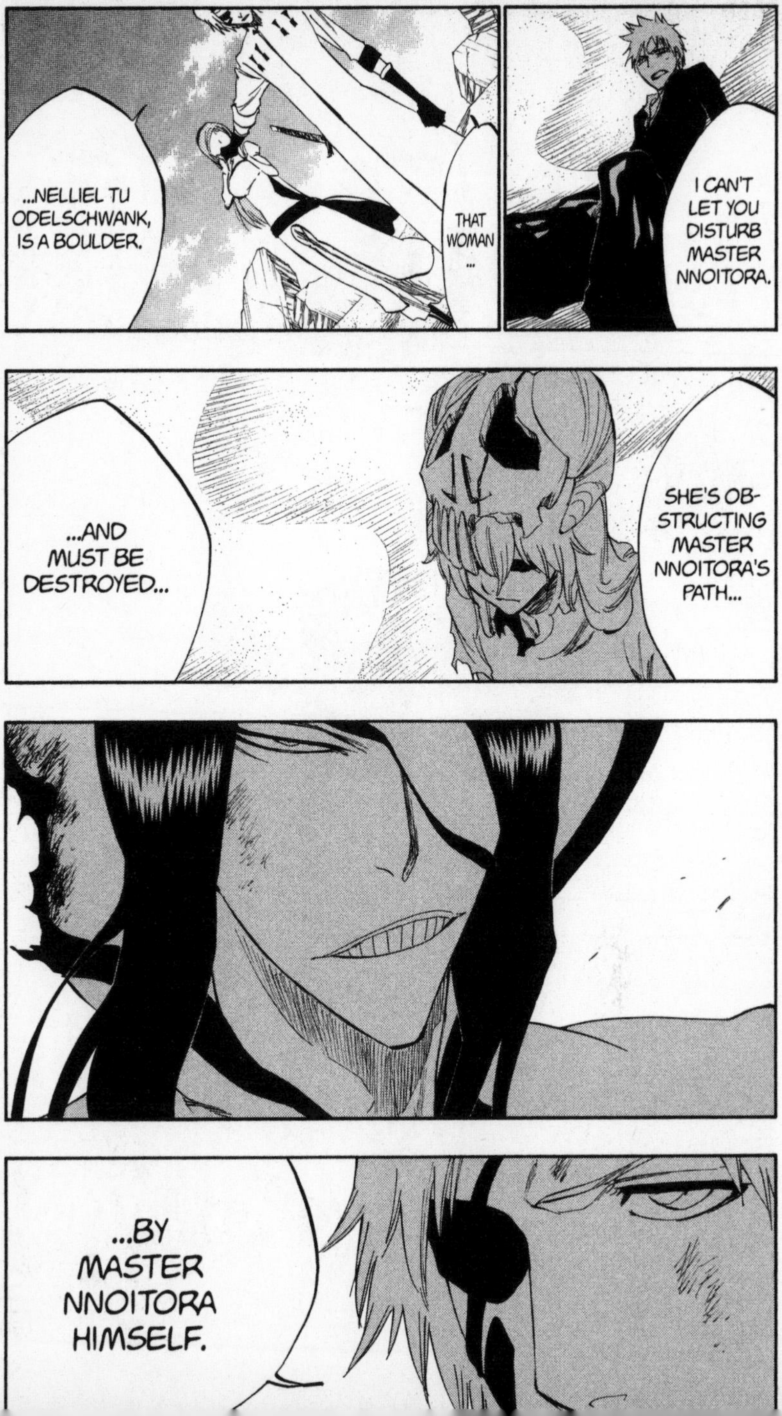
I CAN'T LET YOU DISTURB MASTER NNOITORA.
THAT WOMAN ...
...NELLIEL TU ODELSCHWANK, IS A BOULDER.
SHE'S OB-STRUCTING MASTER NNOITORA'S PATH...
...AND MUST BE DESTROYED...
...BY MASTER NNOITORA HIMSELF.

BLEACH294.

IF YOU CALL ME A BEAST,
I'LL KILL YOU LIKE A TEMPEST

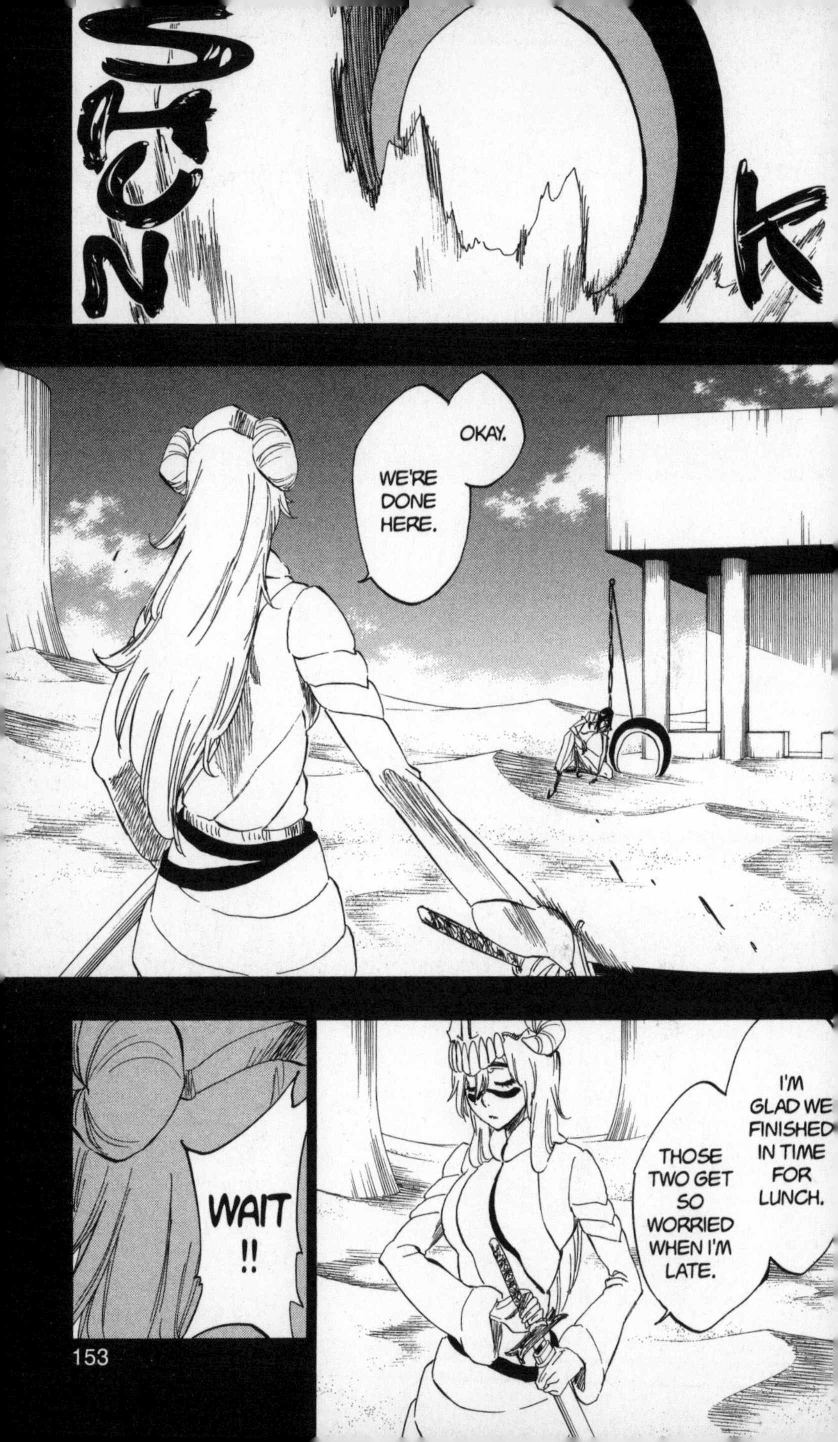
OKAY.
WE'RE DONE HERE.
I'M GLAD WE FINISHED IN TIME FOR LUNCH.
THOSE TWO GET SO WORRIED WHEN I'M LATE.
WAIT!!

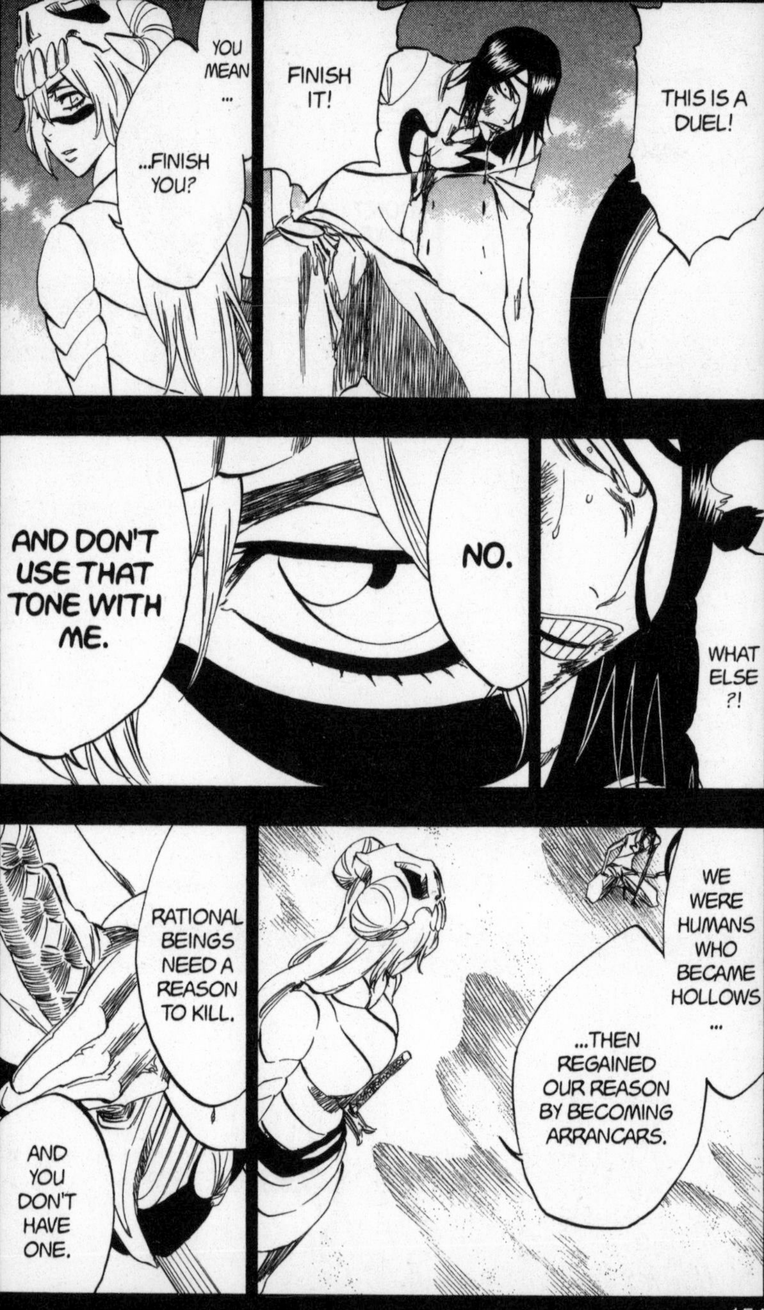
THIS IS A DUEL!
FINISH IT!
YOU MEAN ...
...FINISH YOU?
WHAT ELSE ?!
NO.
AND DON'T USE THAT TONE WITH ME.
WE WERE HUMANS WHO BECAME HOLLOWS ...
...THEN REGAINED OUR REASON BY BECOMING ARRANCARS.
RATIONAL BEINGS NEED A REASON TO KILL.
AND YOU DON'T HAVE ONE.

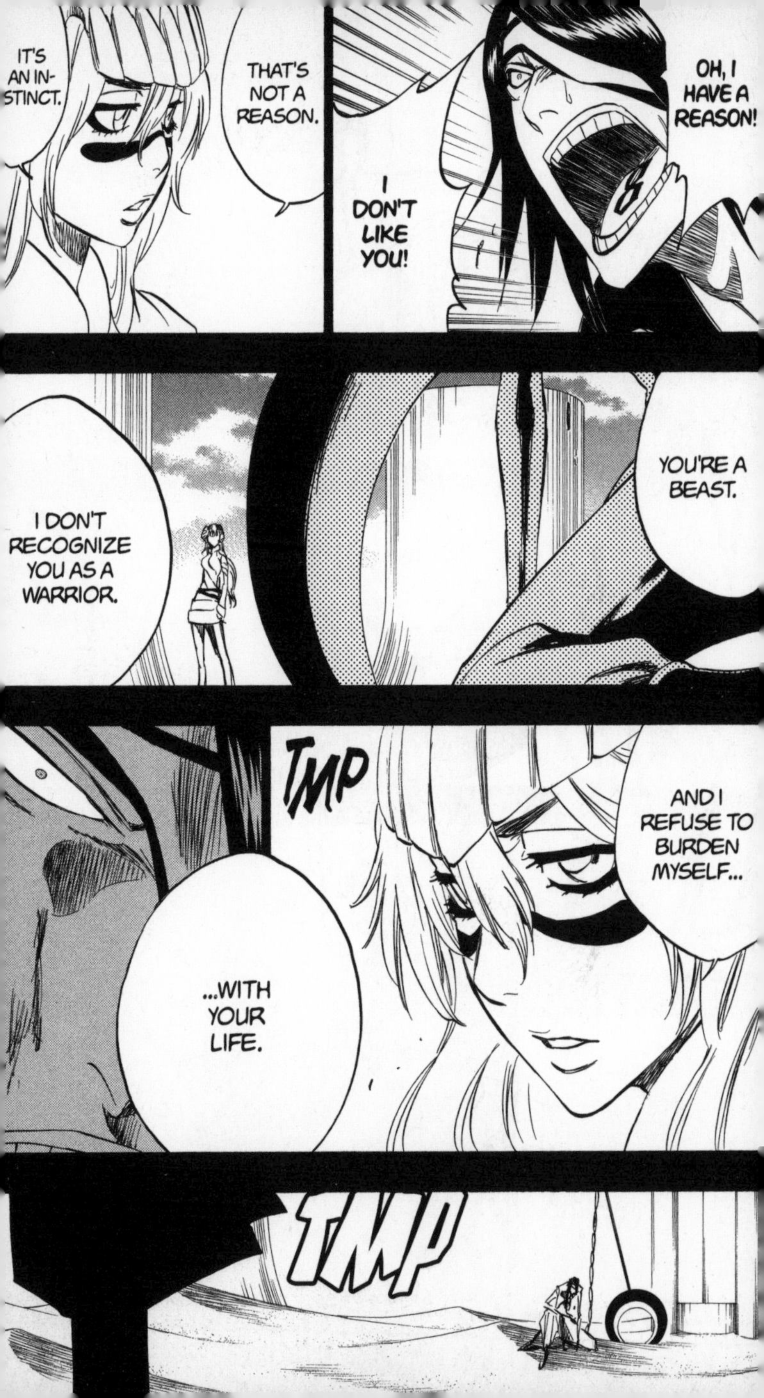
OH, I HAVE A REASON!
I DON'T LIKE YOU!
THAT'S NOT A REASON.
IT'S AN IN-STINCT.
YOU'RE A BEAST.
I DON'T RECOGNIZE YOU AS A WARRIOR.
AND I REFUSE TO BURDEN MYSELF...
TMP
...WITH YOUR LIFE.
TMP

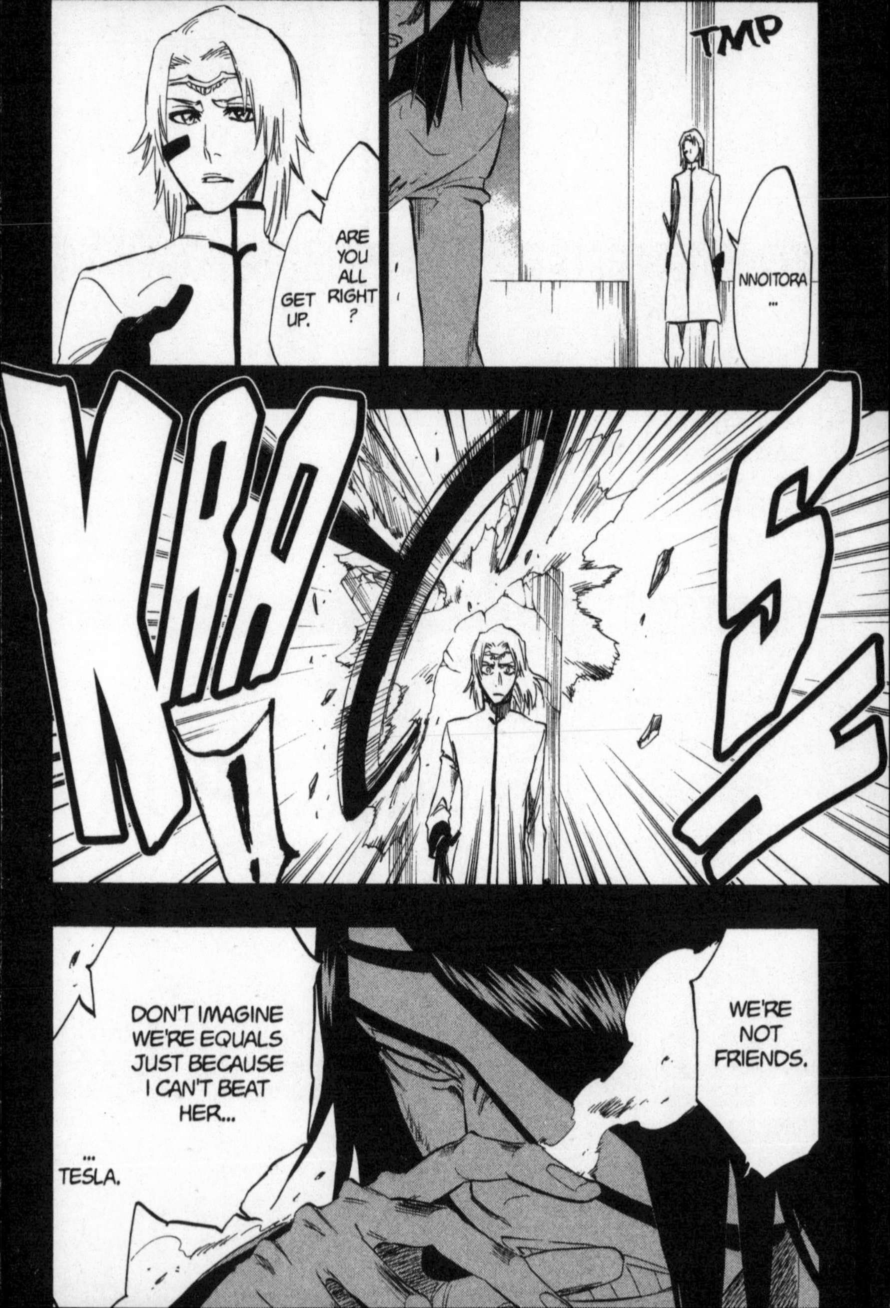
TMP
NNOITORA...
ARE YOU ALL RIGHT?
GET UP.
WE'RE NOT FRIENDS.
DON'T IMAGINE WE'RE EQUALS JUST BECAUSE I CAN'T BEAT HER...
... TESLA.

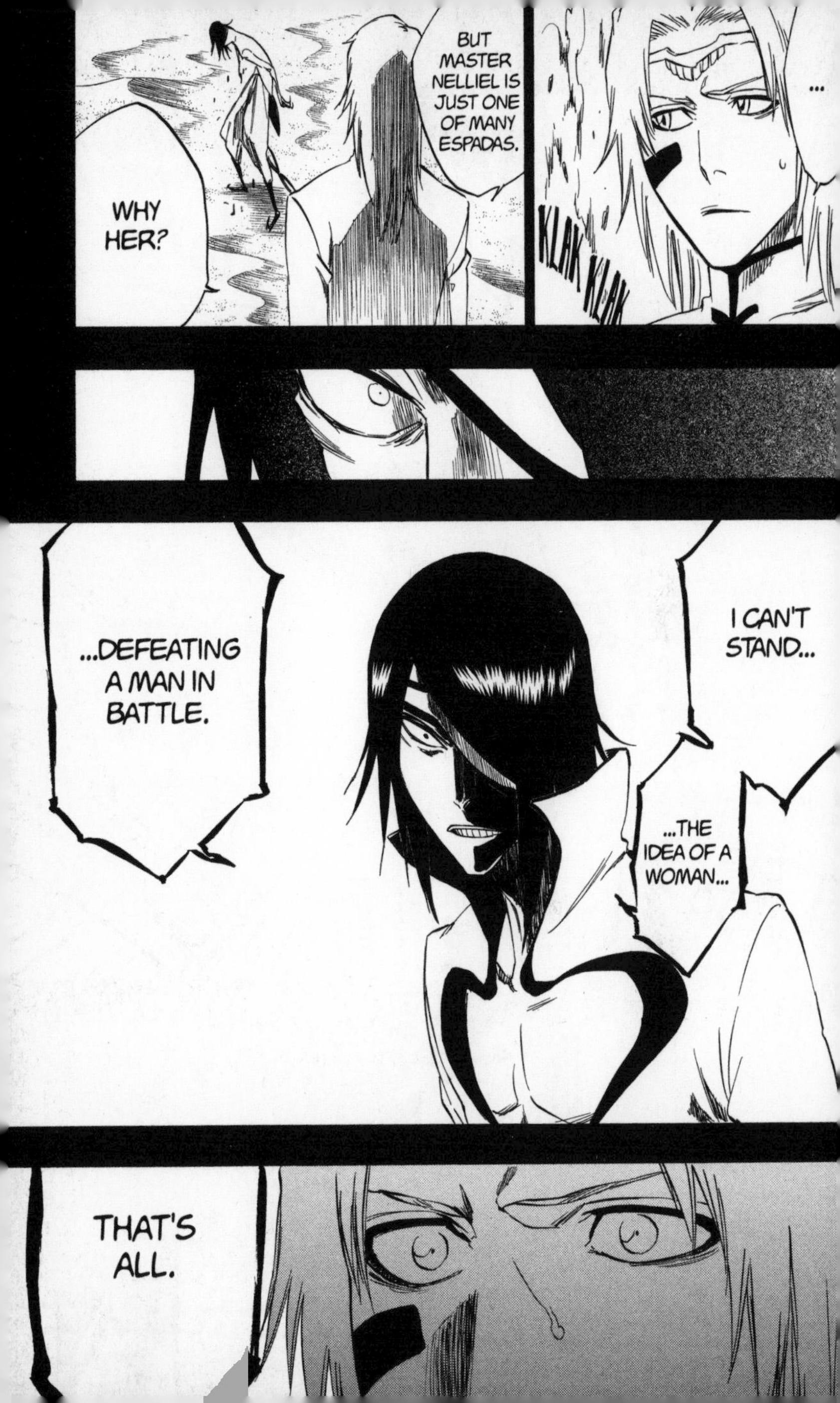
...
KLAK KLAK KLAK
BUT MASTER NELLIEL IS JUST ONE OF MANY ESPADAS.
WHY HER?
I CAN'T STAND...
...THE IDEA OF A WOMAN...
...DEFEATING A MAN IN BATTLE.
THAT'S ALL.

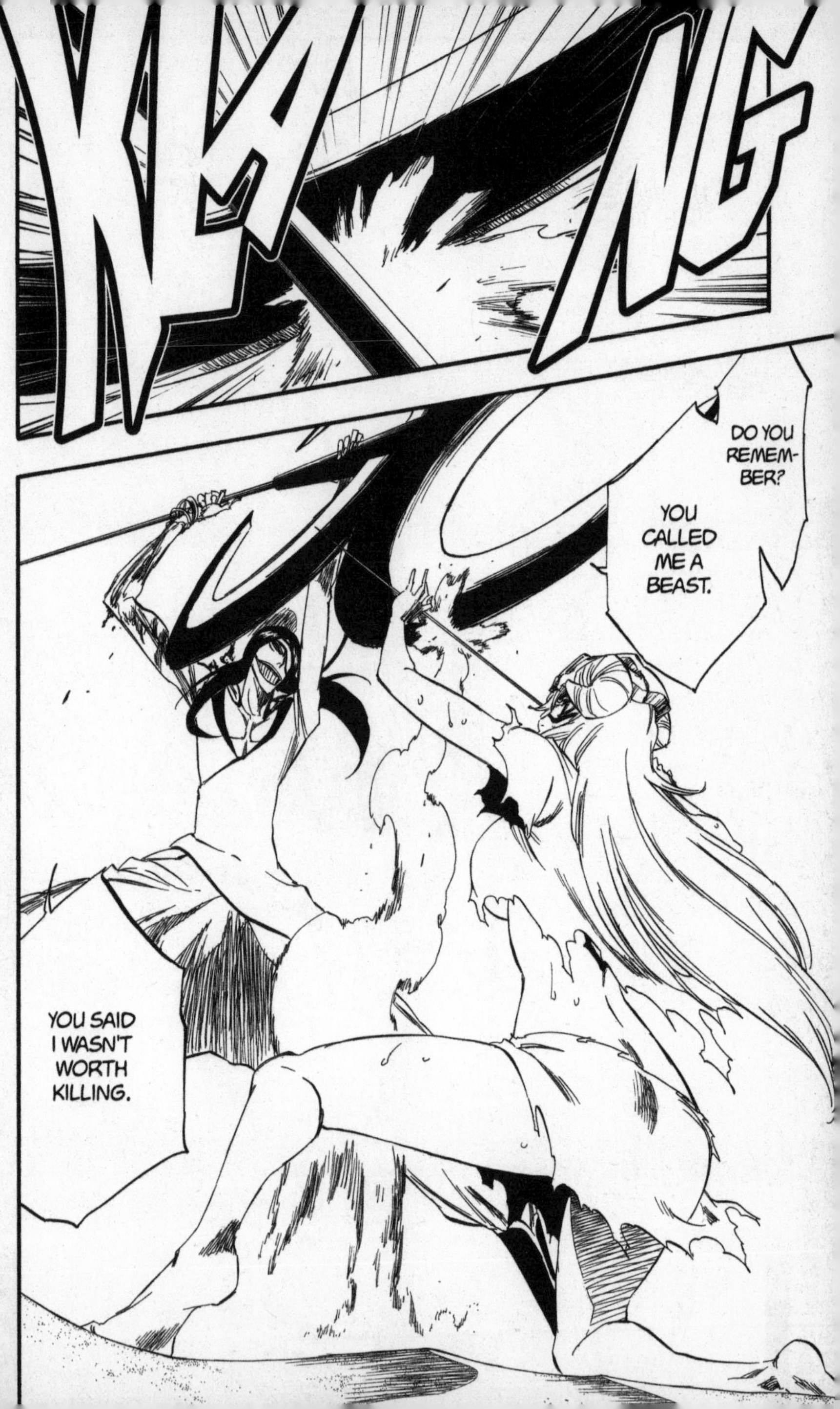
KA-NG
DO YOU REMEMBER?
YOU CALLED ME A BEAST.
YOU SAID I WASN'T WORTH KILLING.

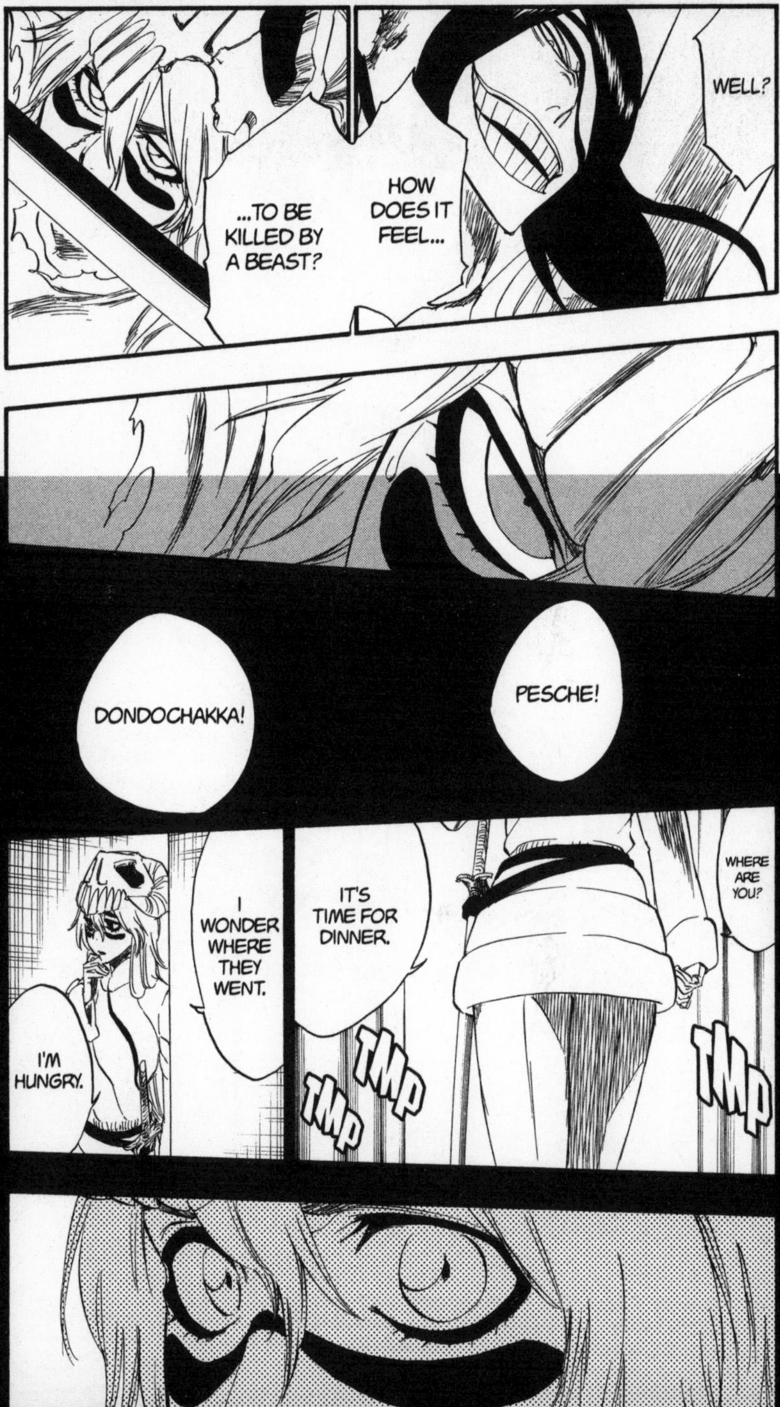
WELL?
HOW DOES IT FEEL...
...TO BE KILLED BY A BEAST?
PESCHE!
DONDOCHAKKA!
WHERE ARE YOU?
IT'S TIME FOR DINNER.
TMP
TMP
TMP
I WONDER WHERE THEY WENT.
I'M HUNGRY.

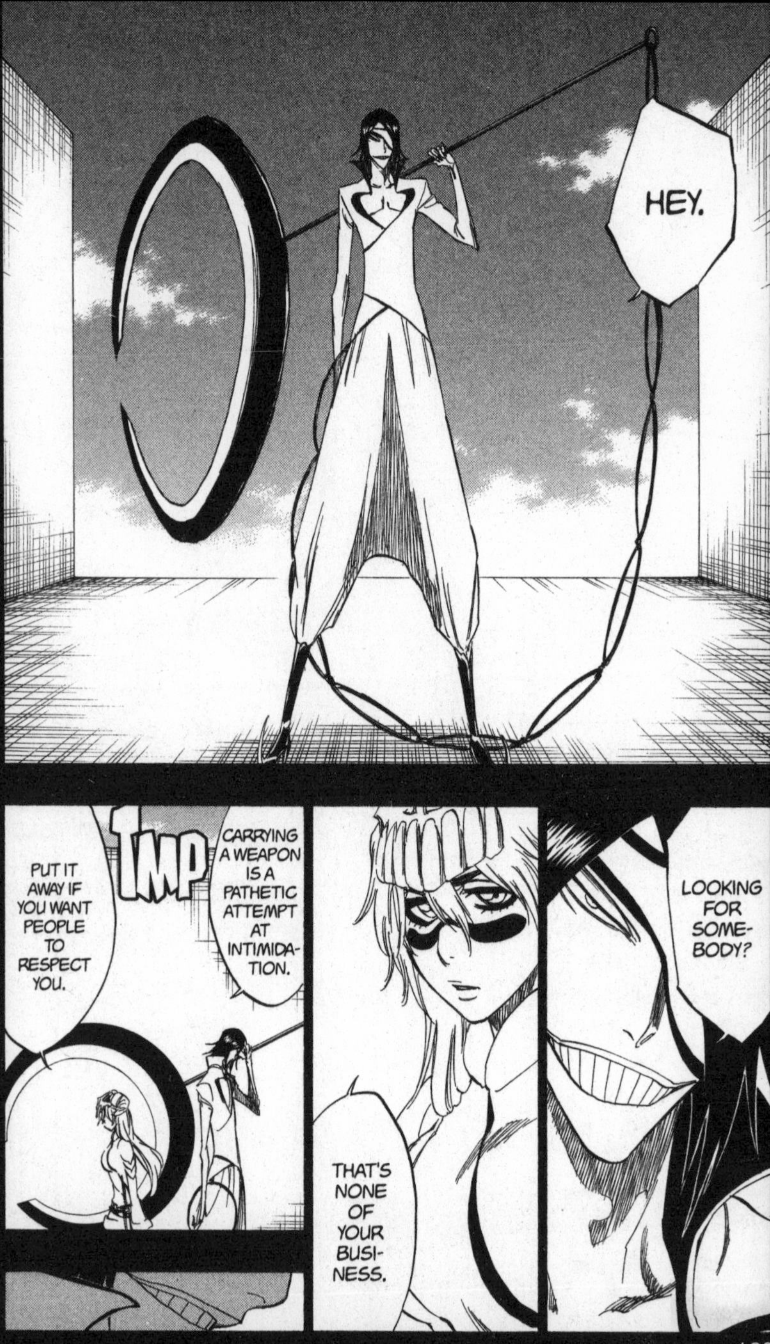
HEY.
LOOKING FOR SOME-BODY?
THAT'S NONE OF YOUR BUSI-NESS.
CARRYING A WEAPON IS A PATHETIC ATTEMPT AT INTIMIDA-TION.
TMP
PUT IT AWAY IF YOU WANT PEOPLE TO RESPECT YOU.

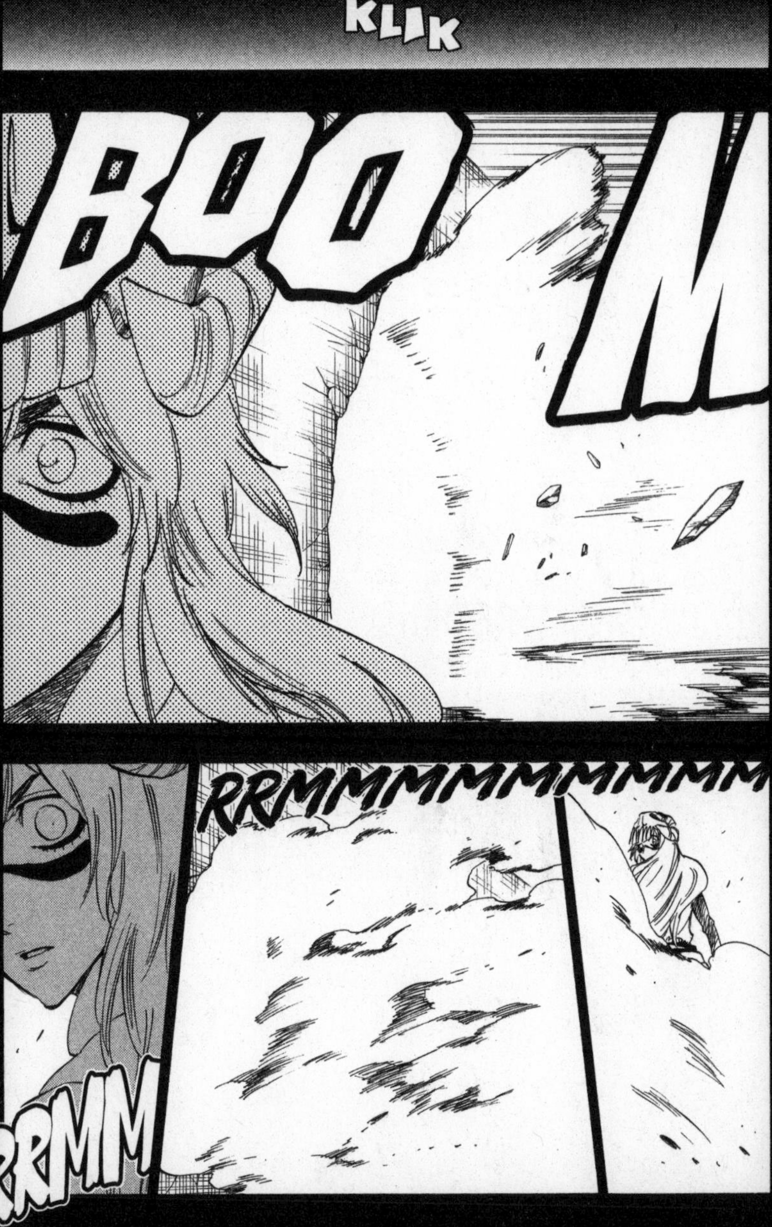
KLIK
BOOM
RRMMMMMMMMMMMM
RRMM

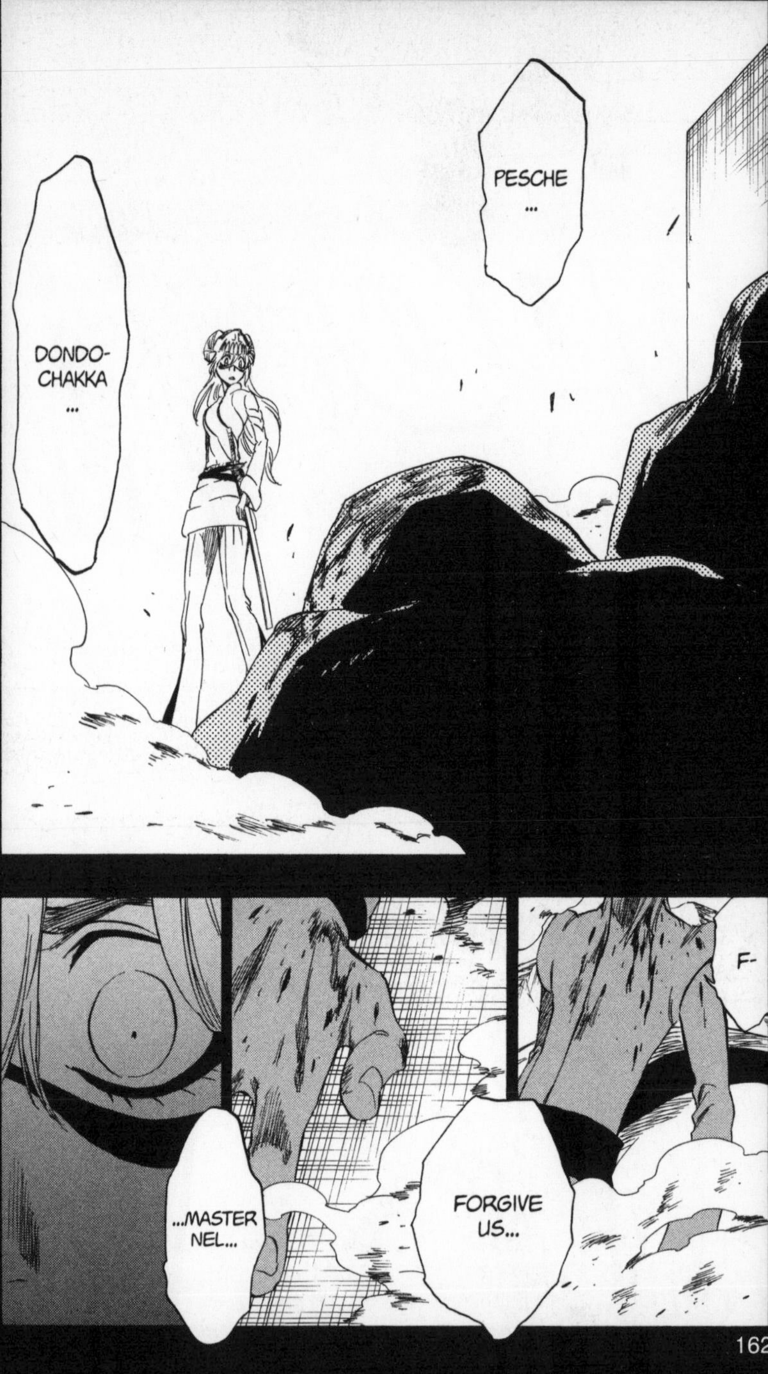
PESCHE ...
DONDO-CHAKKA ...
F-
FORGIVE US...
...MASTER NEL...

READ THIS WAY

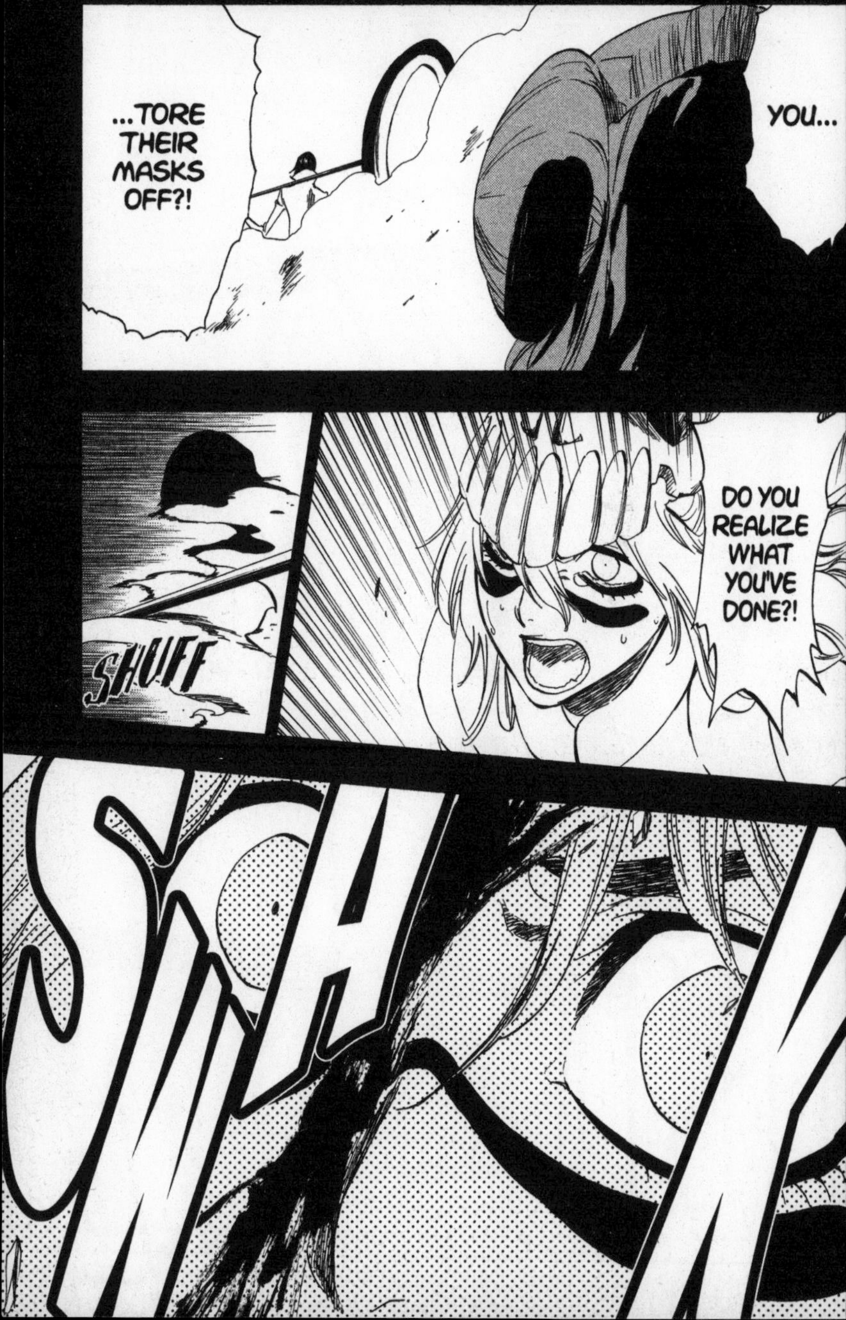
YOU...
...TORE THEIR MASKS OFF?!
DO YOU REALIZE WHAT YOU'VE DONE?!
SHUFF

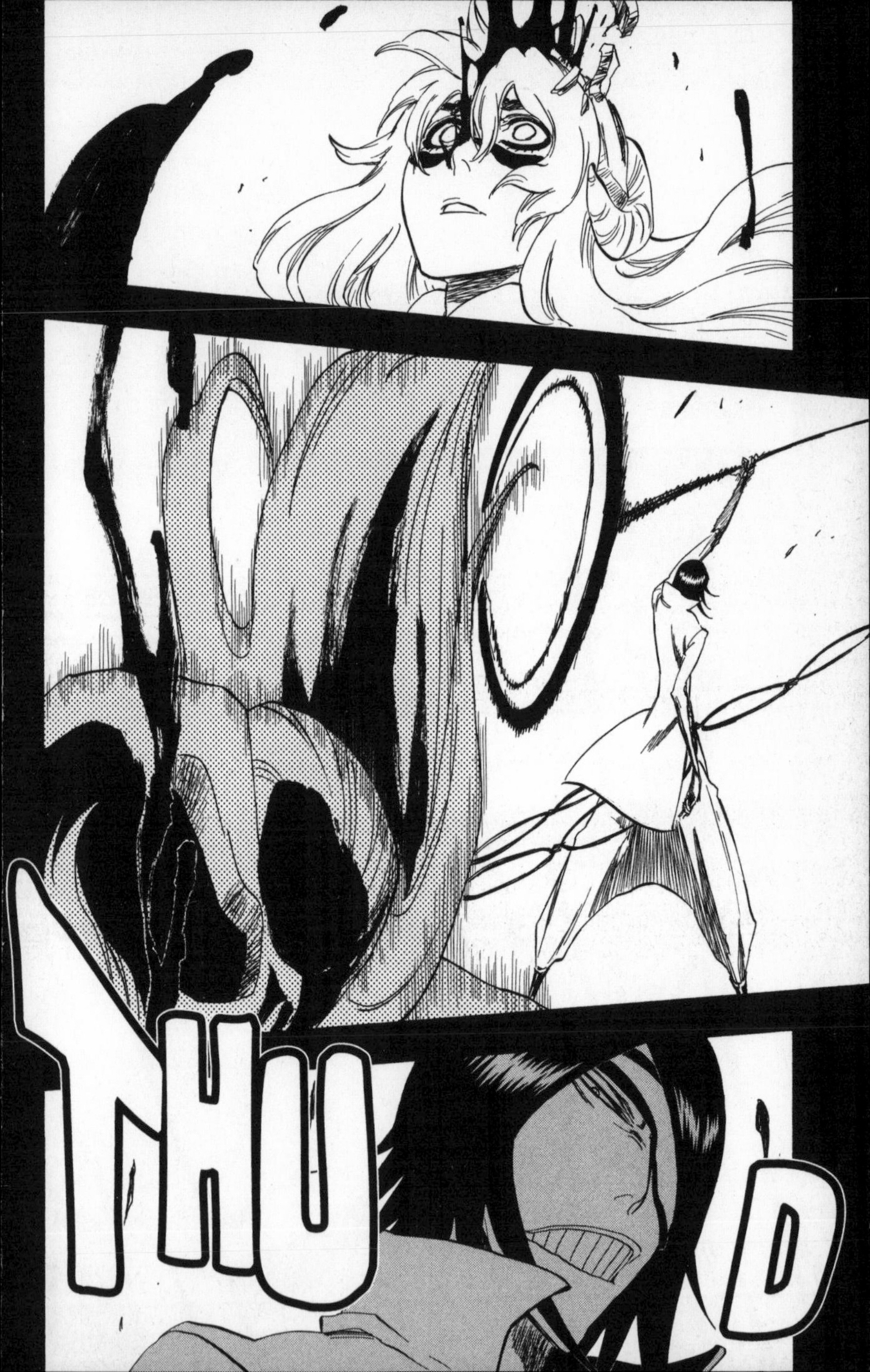
THUD

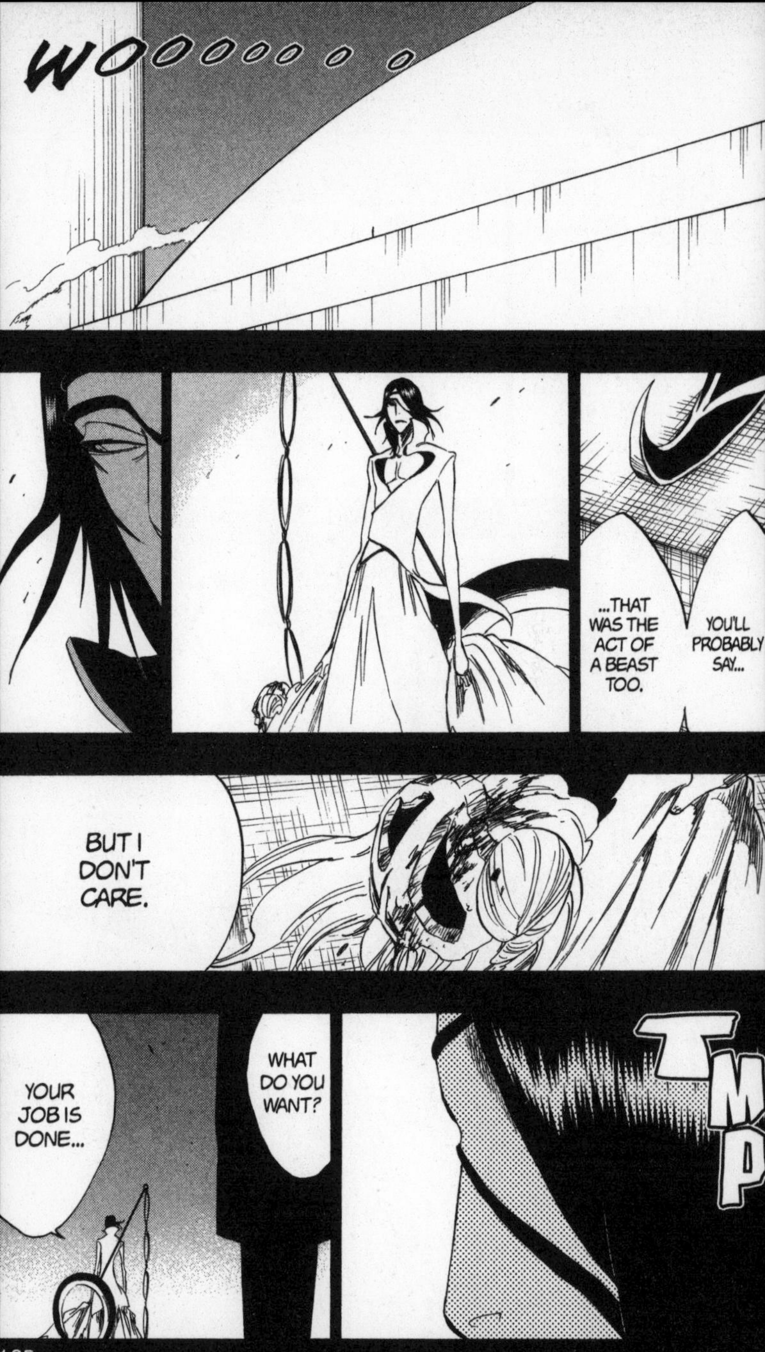
WOOOOOO O O
YOU'LL PROBABLY SAY...
...THAT WAS THE ACT OF A BEAST TOO.
BUT I DON'T CARE.
TMP
WHAT DO YOU WANT?
YOUR JOB IS DONE...

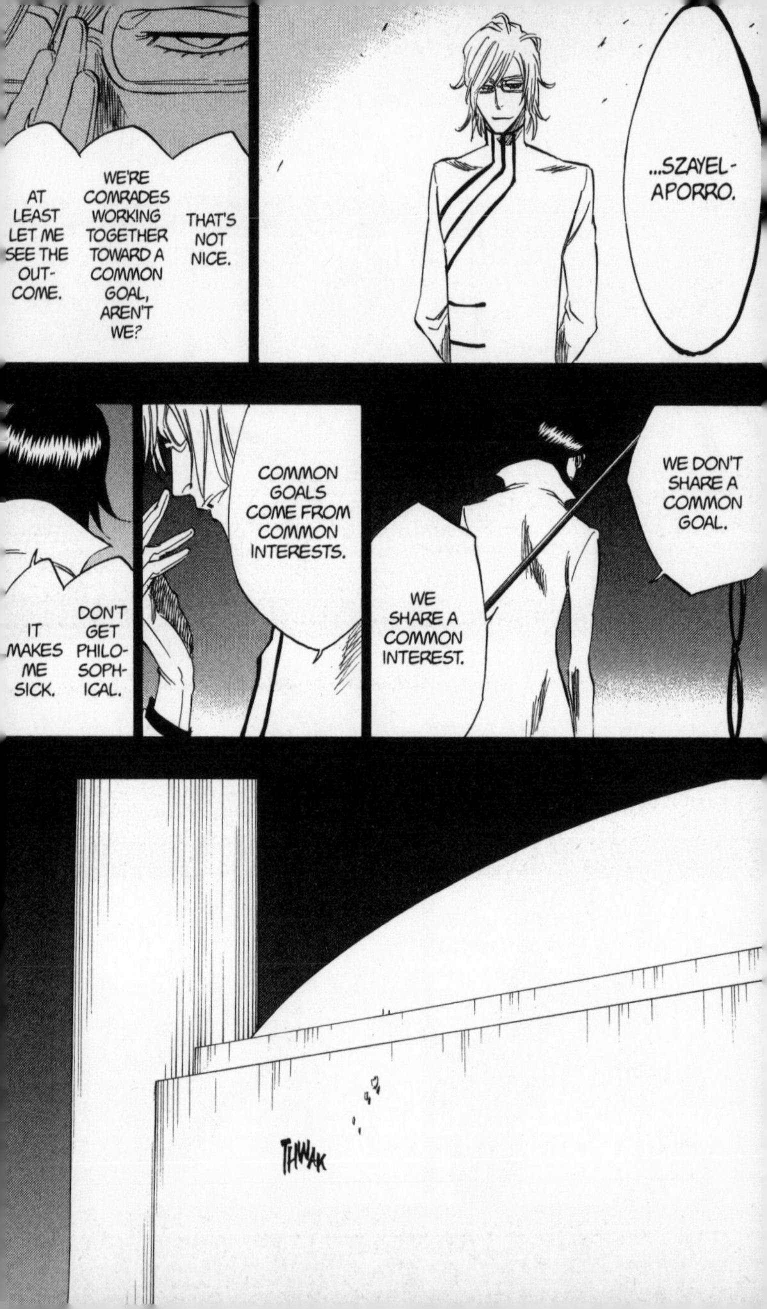
...SZAYEL-APORRO.
THAT'S NOT NICE.
WE'RE COMRADES WORKING TOGETHER TOWARD A COMMON GOAL, AREN'T WE?
AT LEAST LET ME SEE THE OUT-COME.
WE DON'T SHARE A COMMON GOAL.
WE SHARE A COMMON INTEREST.
COMMON GOALS COME FROM COMMON INTERESTS.
DON'T GET PHILO-SOPH-ICAL.
IT MAKES ME SICK.
THWAK

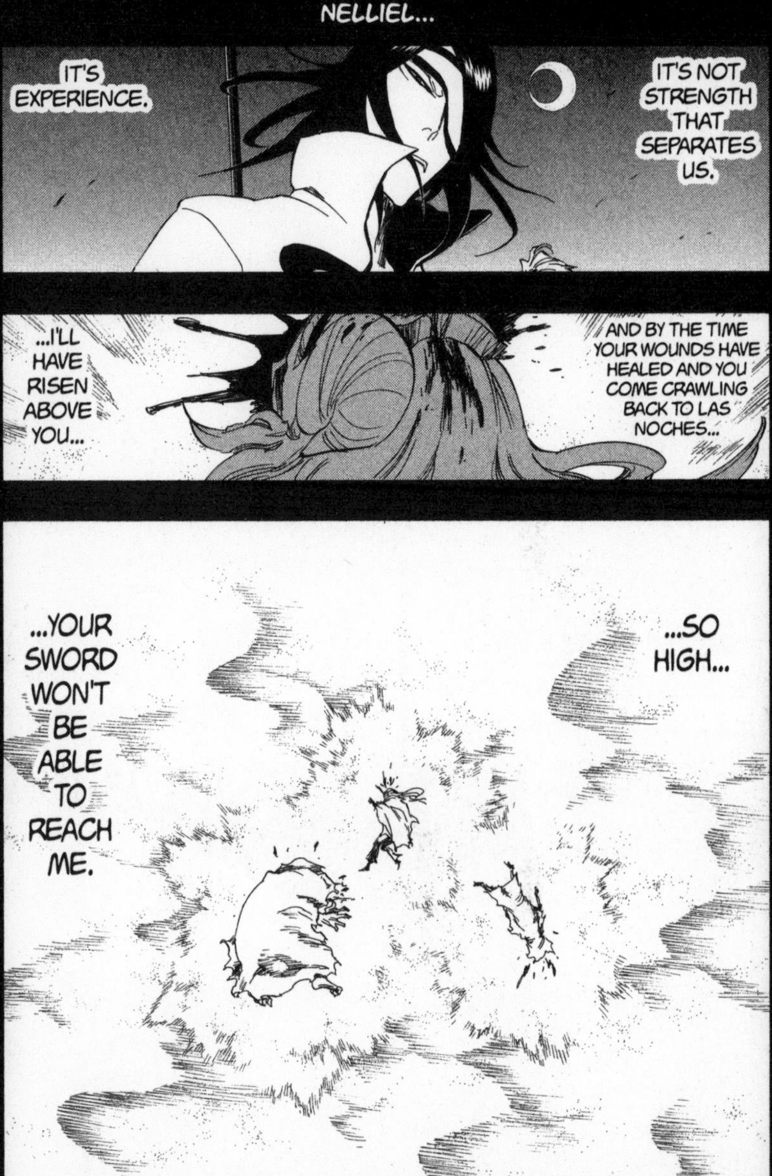
NELLIEL...
IT'S NOT STRENGTH THAT SEPARATES US.
IT'S EXPERIENCE.
AND BY THE TIME YOUR WOUNDS HAVE HEALED AND YOU COME CRAWLING BACK TO LAS NOCHES...
...I'LL HAVE RISEN ABOVE YOU...
...SO HIGH...
...YOUR SWORD WON'T BE ABLE TO REACH ME.

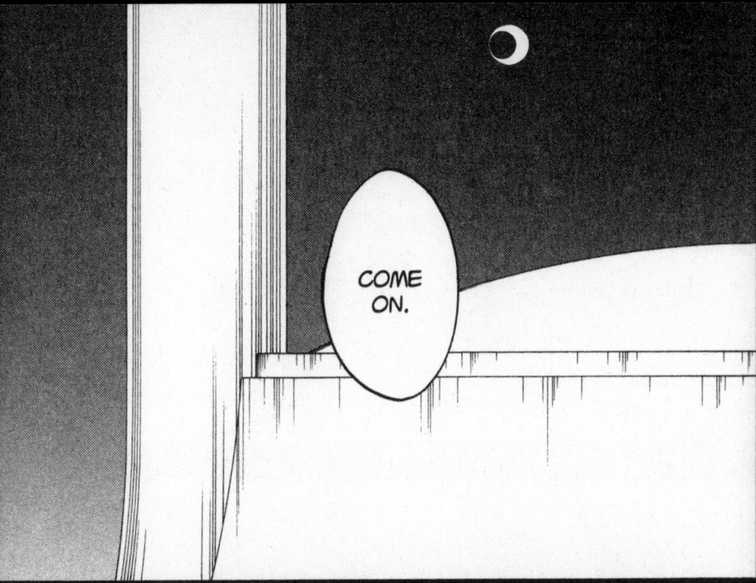
COME ON.

295. The Last Mission

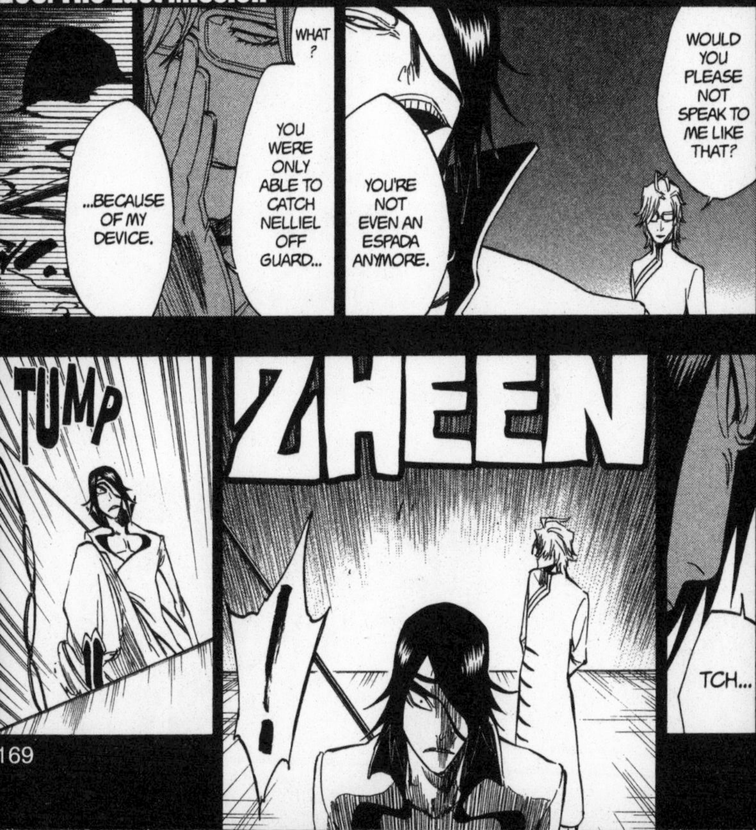
WOULD YOU PLEASE NOT SPEAK TO ME LIKE THAT?
YOU'RE NOT EVEN AN ESPADA ANYMORE.
WHAT?
YOU WERE ONLY ABLE TO CATCH NELLIEL OFF GUARD...
...BECAUSE OF MY DEVICE.
TCH...
ZHEEN
TUMP

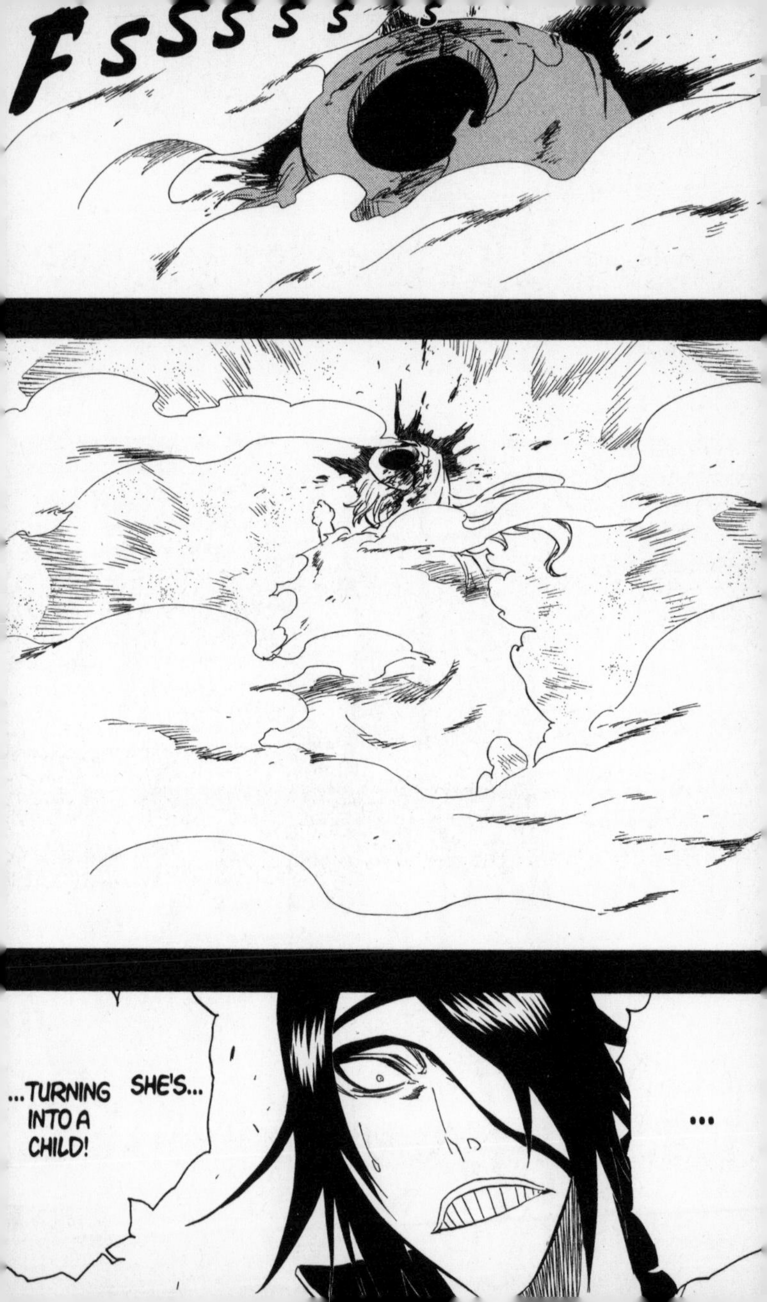
FSSSSSSS
...
SHE'S...
...TURNING INTO A CHILD!

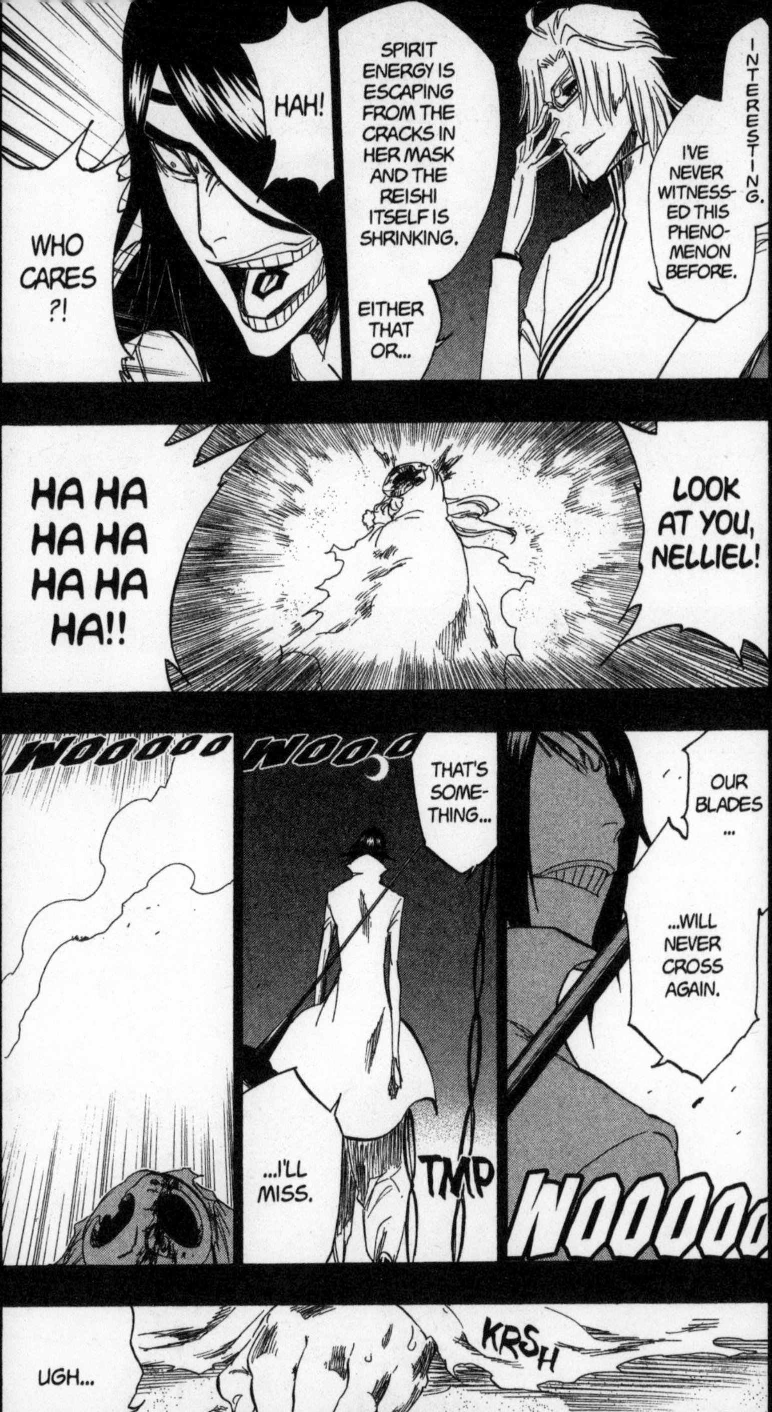
INTERESTING.
I'VE NEVER WITNESSED THIS PHENOMENON BEFORE.
SPIRIT ENERGY IS ESCAPING FROM THE CRACKS IN HER MASK AND THE REISHI ITSELF IS SHRINKING.
EITHER THAT OR...
HAH!
WHO CARES?!
LOOK AT YOU, NELLIEL!
HA HA HA HA HA HA HA!!
OUR BLADES...
...WILL NEVER CROSS AGAIN.
WOOOOO
THAT'S SOMETHING...
...I'LL MISS.
TMP
WOOOO
WOOOOOO
KRSH
UGH...

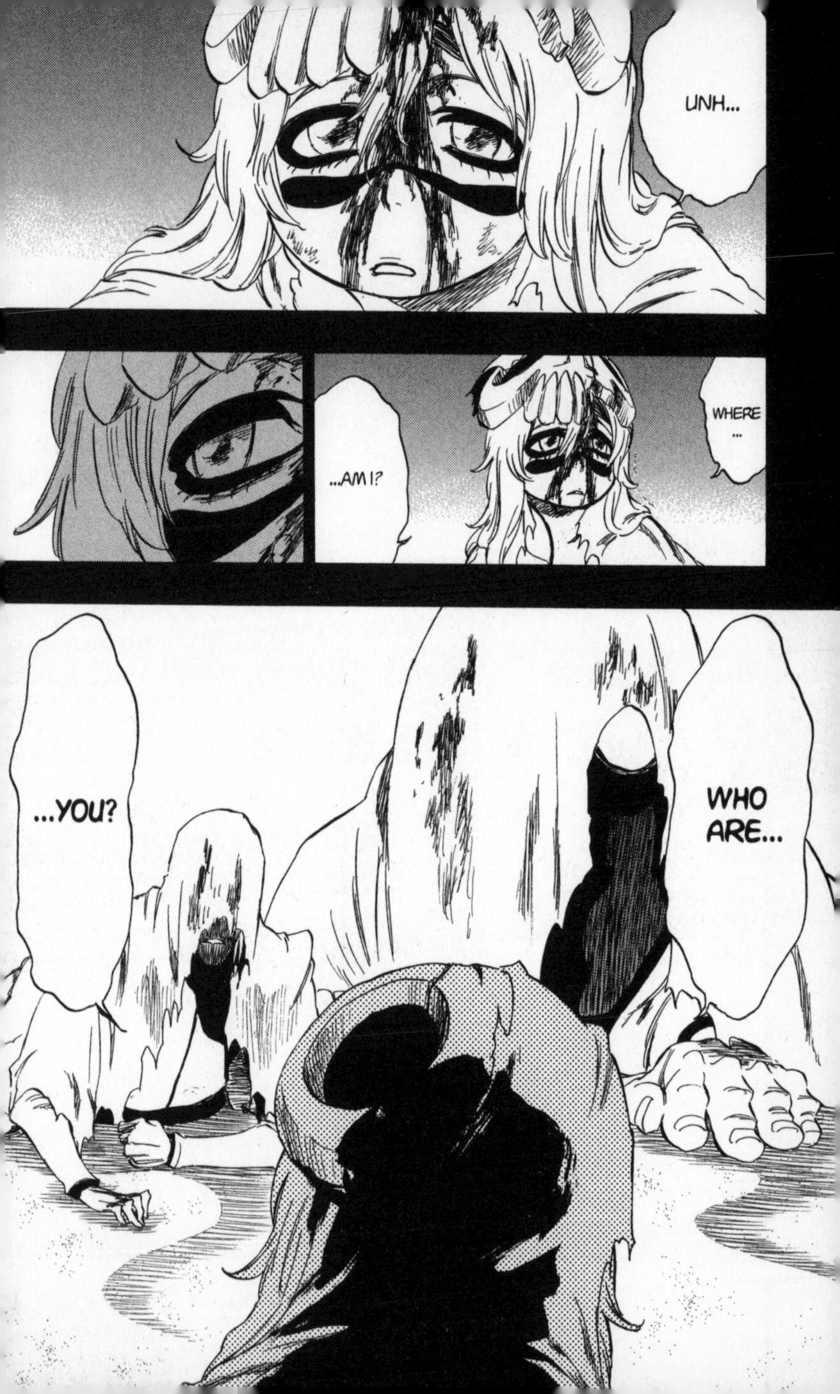
UNH...
WHERE ...
...AM I?
WHO ARE...
...YOU?

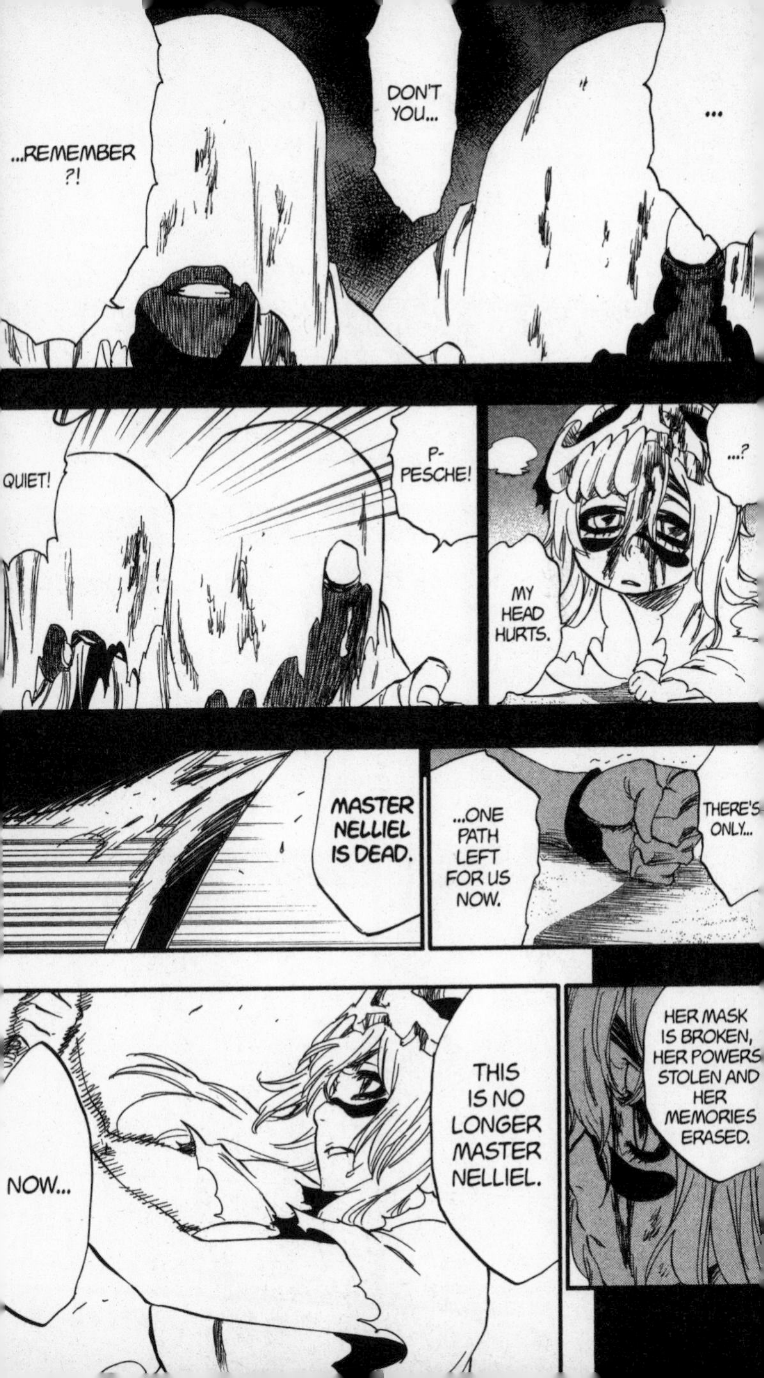
...
DON'T YOU...
...REMEMBER ?!
...?
MY HEAD HURTS.
P-PESCHE!
QUIET!
THERE'S ONLY...
...ONE PATH LEFT FOR US NOW.
MASTER NELLIEL IS DEAD.
HER MASK IS BROKEN, HER POWERS STOLEN AND HER MEMORIES ERASED.
THIS IS NO LONGER MASTER NELLIEL.
NOW...

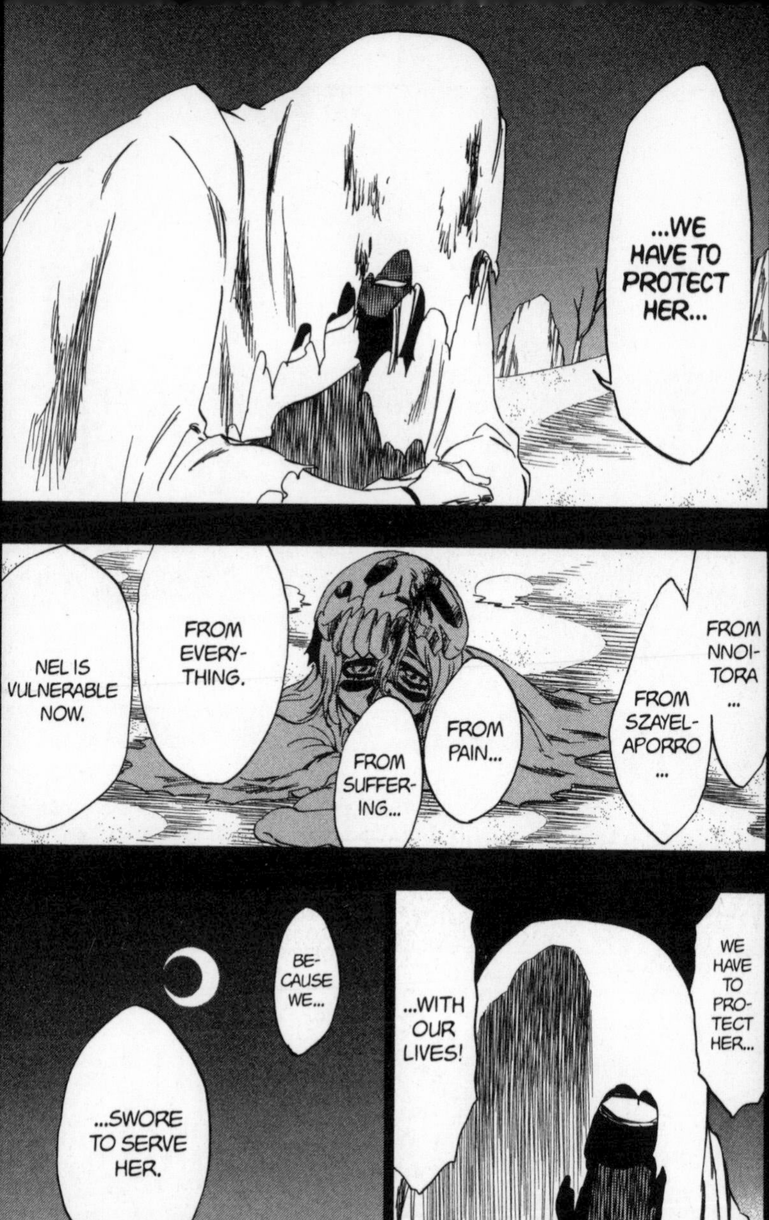
...WE HAVE TO PROTECT HER...
FROM NNOITORA...
FROM SZAYEL-APORRO...
FROM PAIN...
FROM SUFFER-ING...
FROM EVERY-THING.
NEL IS VULNERABLE NOW.
WE HAVE TO PRO-TECT HER...
...WITH OUR LIVES!
BE-CAUSE WE...
...SWORE TO SERVE HER.

...WE HAVE NOW.

THAT'S THE ONLY DUTY...

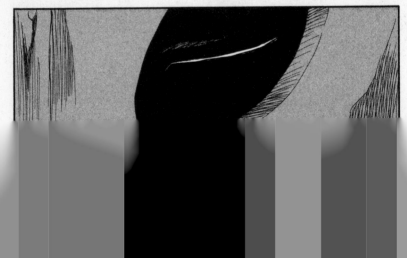

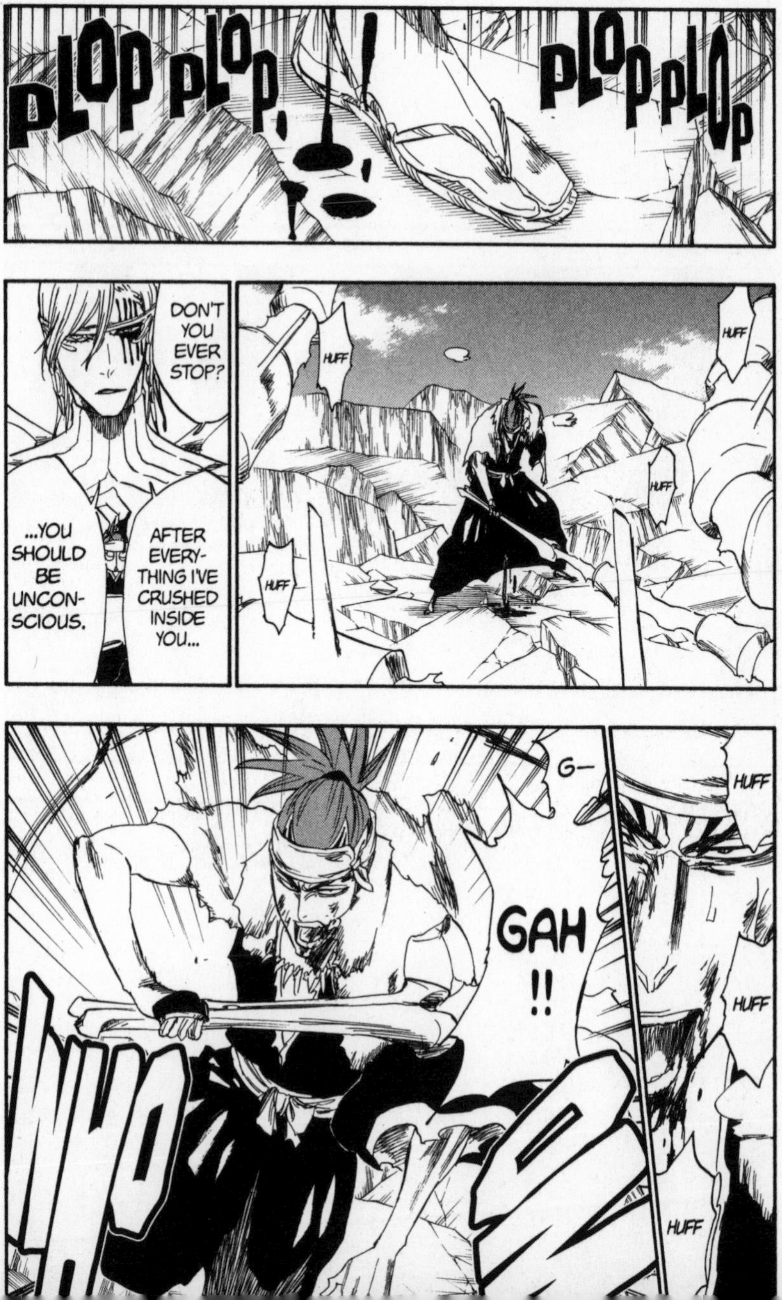
PLOP PLOP
PLOP PLOP
HUFF
HUFF
HUFF
HUFF
DON'T YOU EVER STOP?
AFTER EVERYTHING I'VE CRUSHED INSIDE YOU...
...YOU SHOULD BE UNCONSCIOUS.
HUFF
HUFF
HUFF
G—
GAH!!

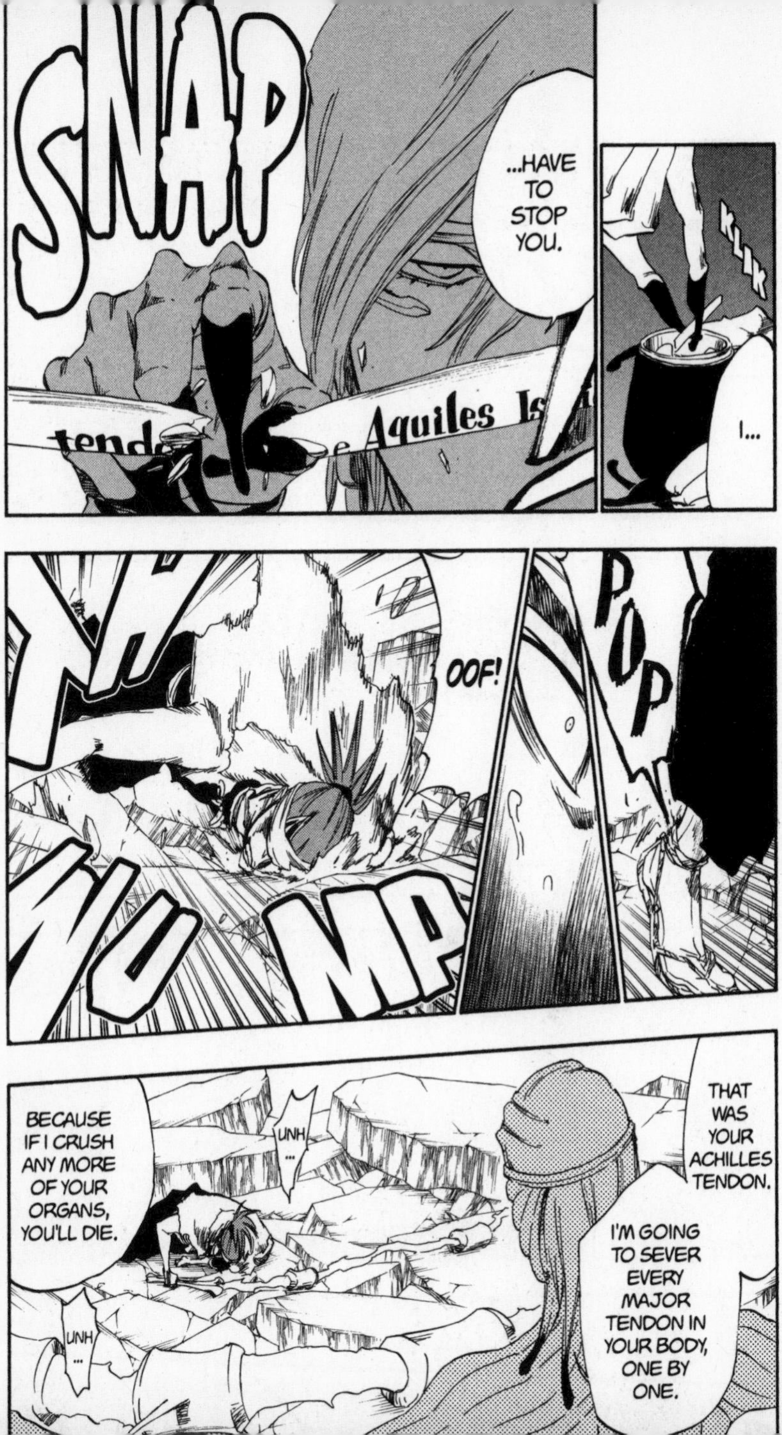
KLIK
I...
...HAVE TO STOP YOU.
SNAP
Aquiles
POP
POP
OOF!
WU MP
THAT WAS YOUR ACHILLES TENDON.
I'M GOING TO SEVER EVERY MAJOR TENDON IN YOUR BODY, ONE BY ONE.
UNH...
BECAUSE IF I CRUSH ANY MORE OF YOUR ORGANS, YOU'LL DIE.
UNH...

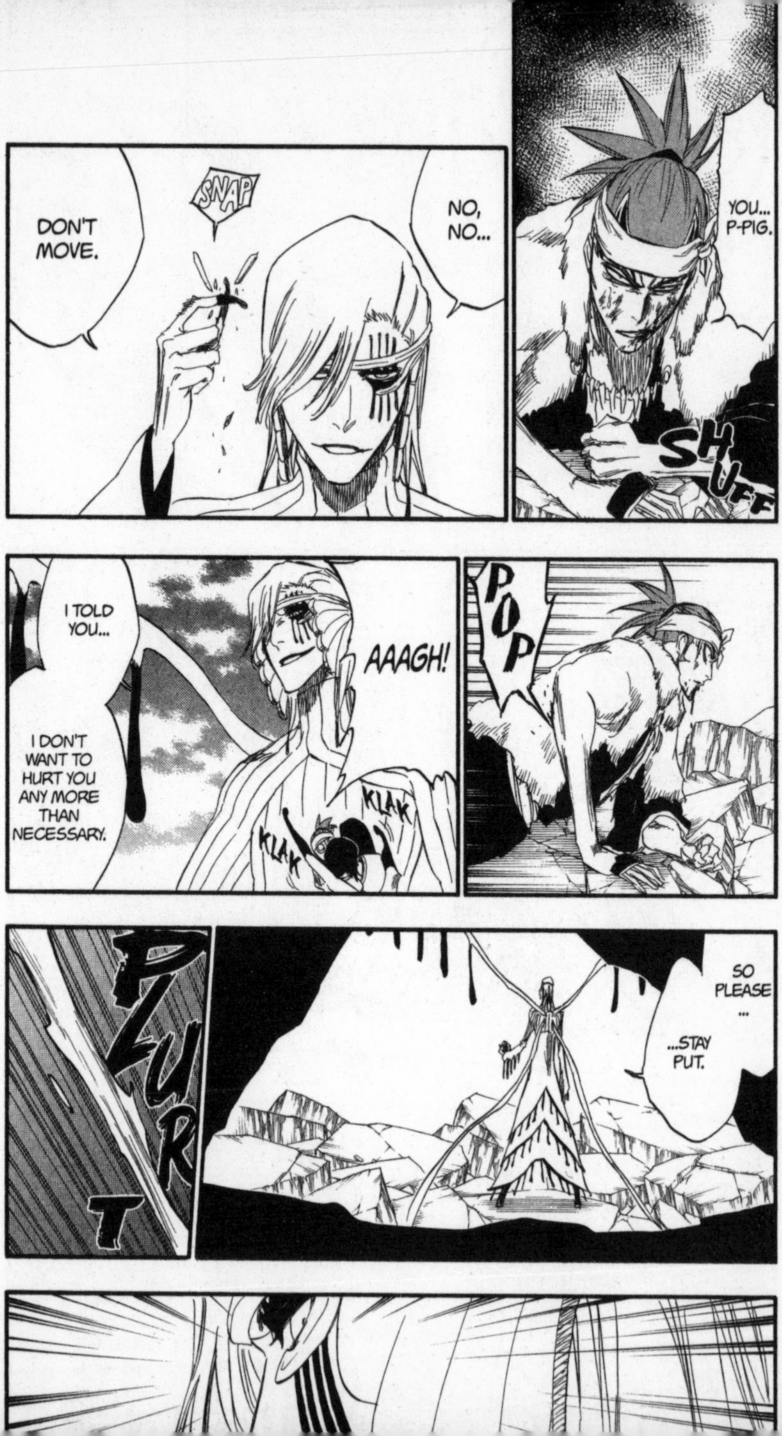
YOU... P-PIG.
SHUFF
NO, NO...
SNAP
DON'T MOVE.
POP
AAAGH!
I TOLD YOU...
I DON'T WANT TO HURT YOU ANY MORE THAN NECESSARY.
KLAK
KLAK
SO PLEASE ...
...STAY PUT.
PLURT

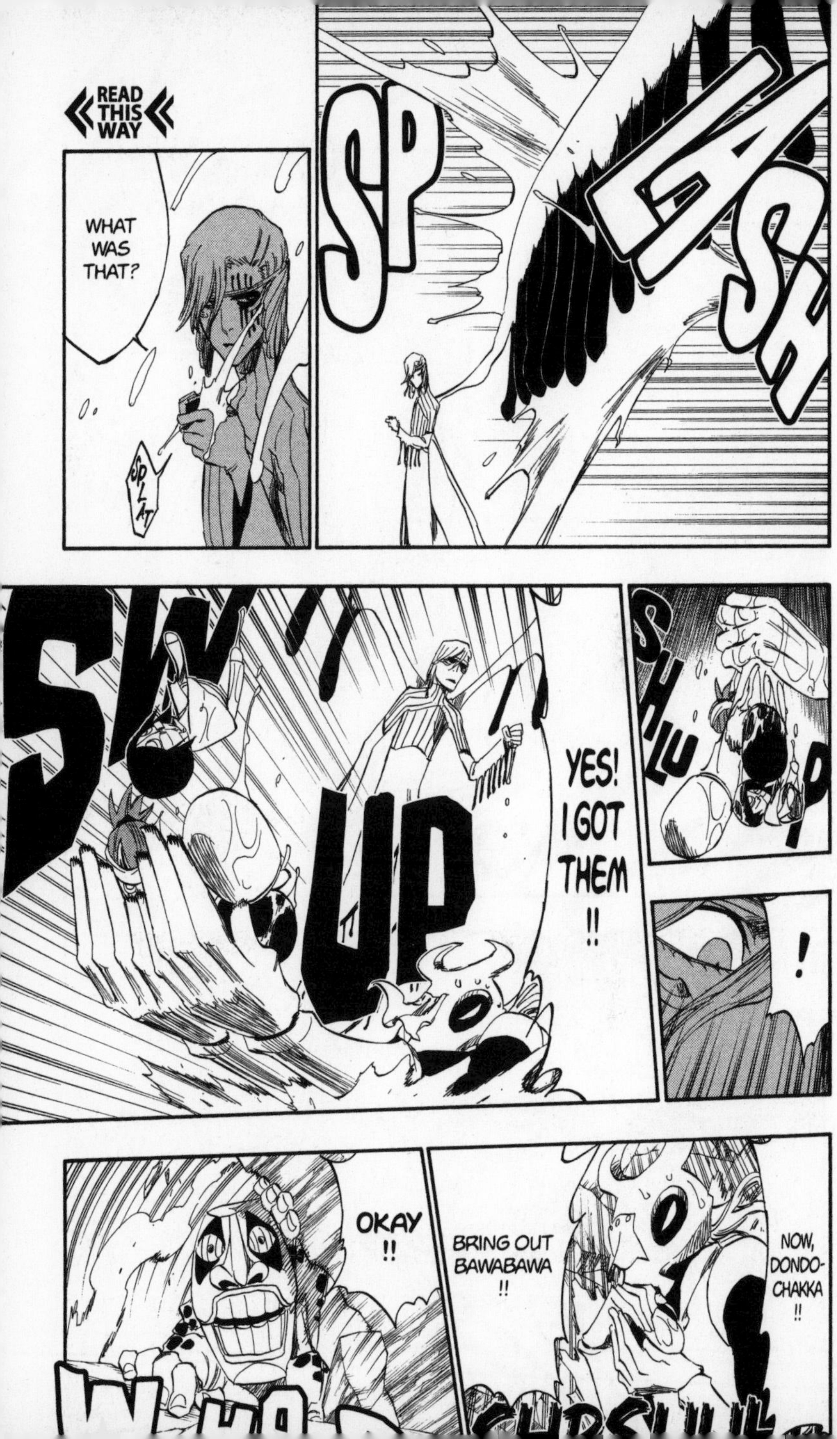
READ THIS WAY
SPLASH
WHAT WAS THAT?
SPLAT
!
YES! I GOT THEM !!
NOW, DONDO-CHAKKA !!
BRING OUT BAWABAWA !!
OKAY !!

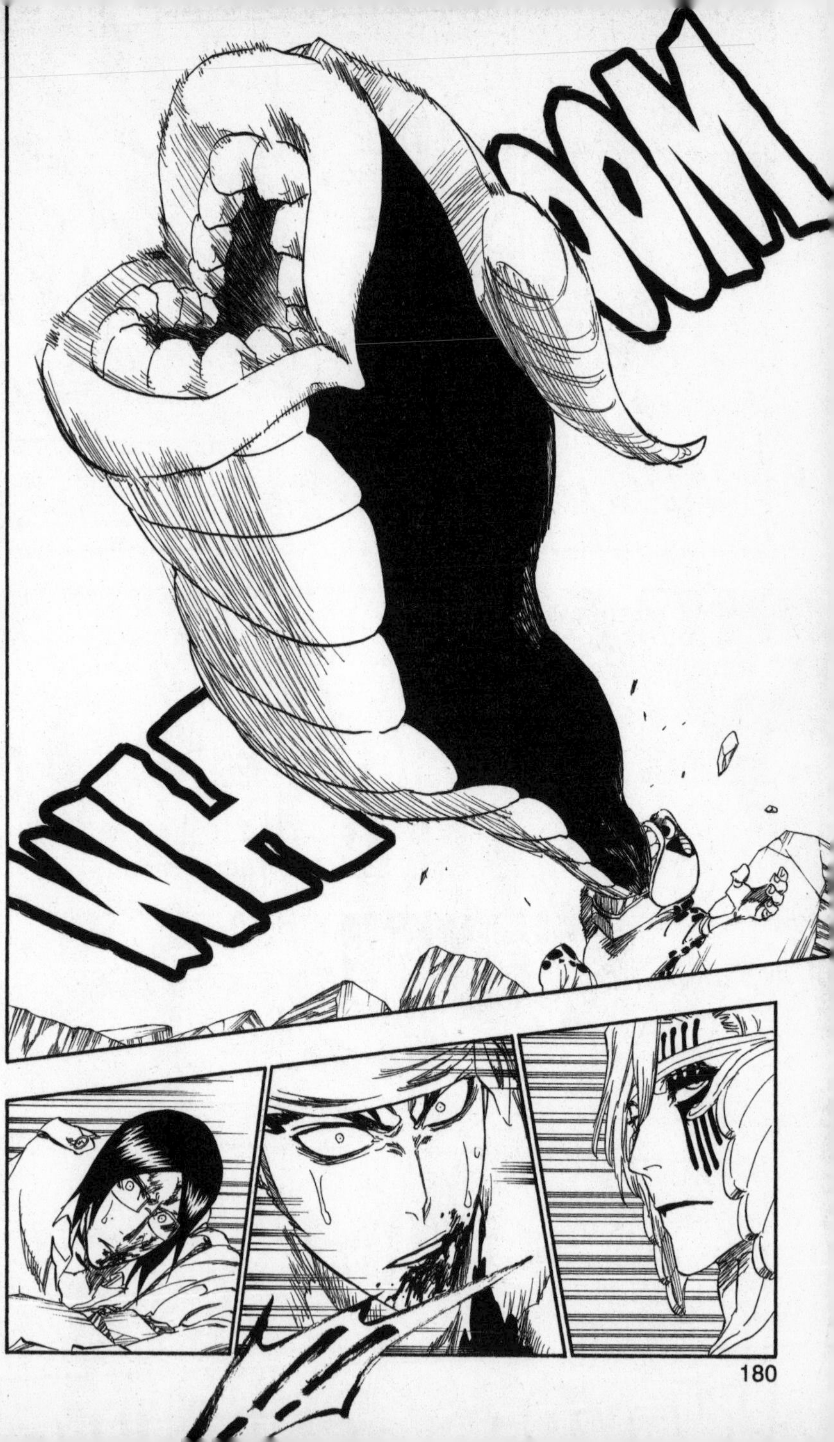
WH-OOM

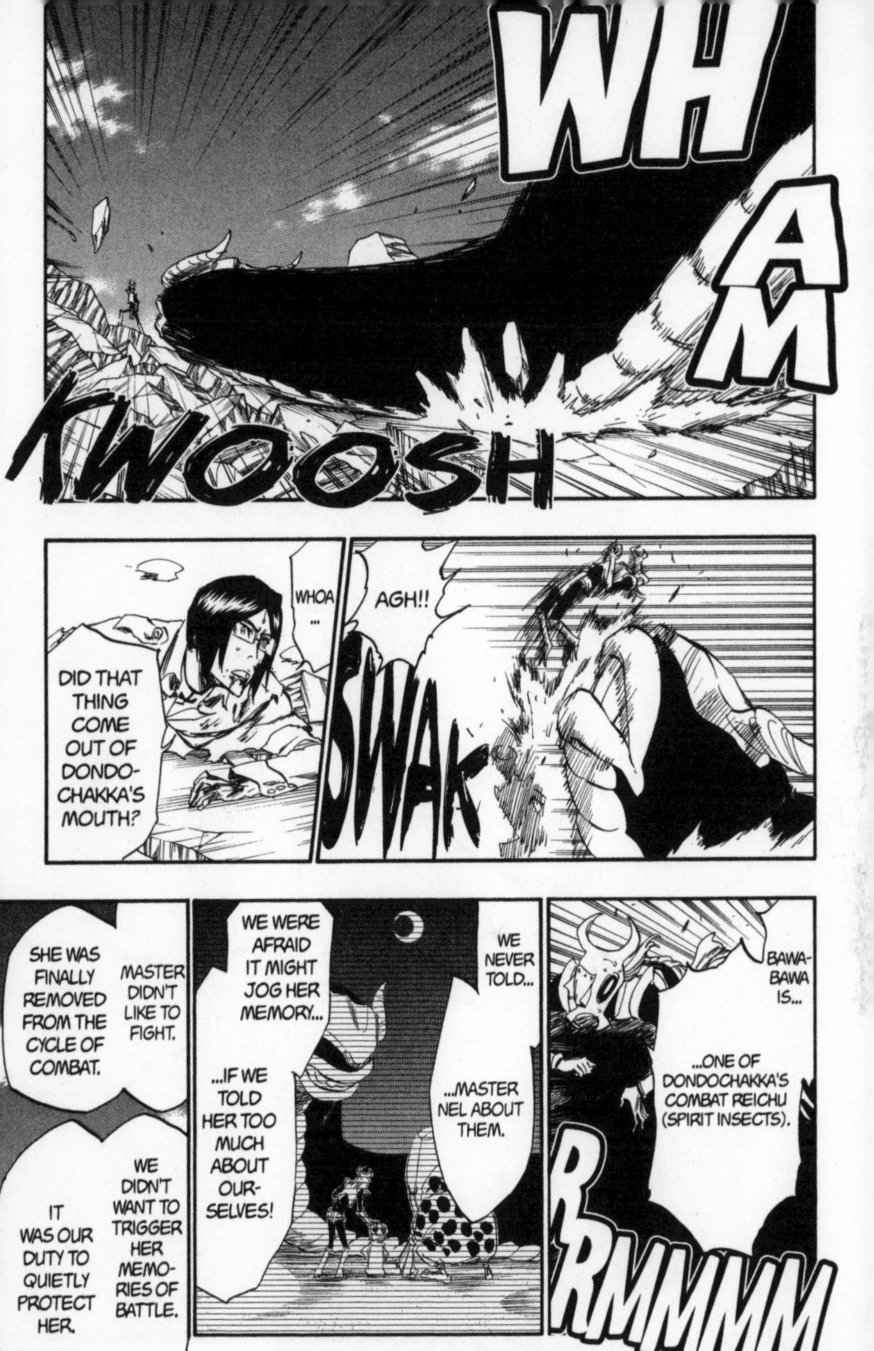
WHAM
KWOOSH
AGH!!
SWAK
WHOA...
DID THAT THING COME OUT OF DONDO-CHAKKA'S MOUTH?
BAWA-BAWA IS...
...ONE OF DONDOCHAKKA'S COMBAT REICHU (SPIRIT INSECTS).
RRMMMMM
WE NEVER TOLD...
...MASTER NEL ABOUT THEM.
WE WERE AFRAID IT MIGHT JOG HER MEMORY...
...IF WE TOLD HER TOO MUCH ABOUT OUR-SELVES!
MASTER DIDN'T LIKE TO FIGHT.
SHE WAS FINALLY REMOVED FROM THE CYCLE OF COMBAT.
WE DIDN'T WANT TO TRIGGER HER MEMO-RIES OF BATTLE.
IT WAS OUR DUTY TO QUIETLY PROTECT HER.

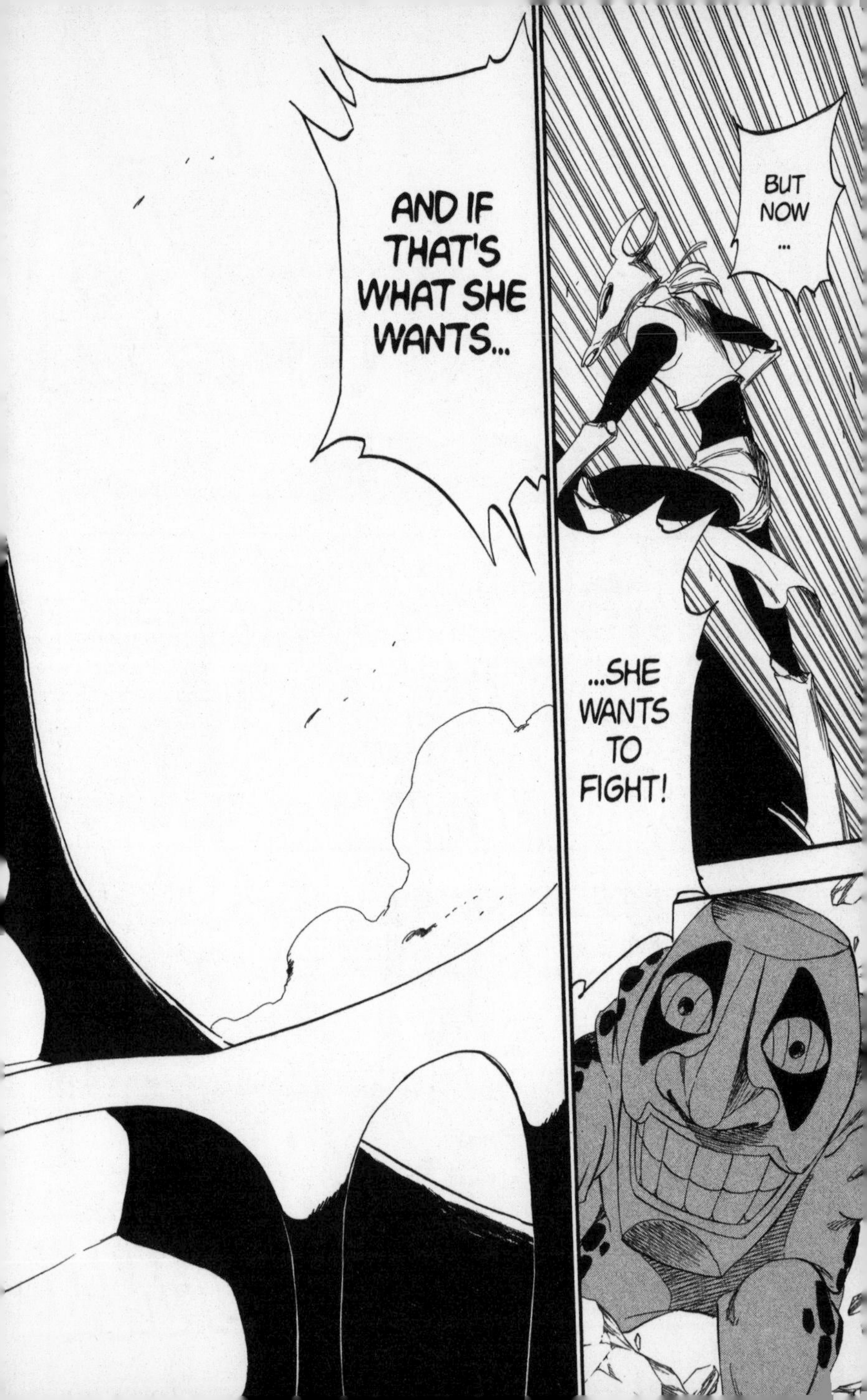
BUT NOW ...
...SHE WANTS TO FIGHT!
AND IF THAT'S WHAT SHE WANTS...

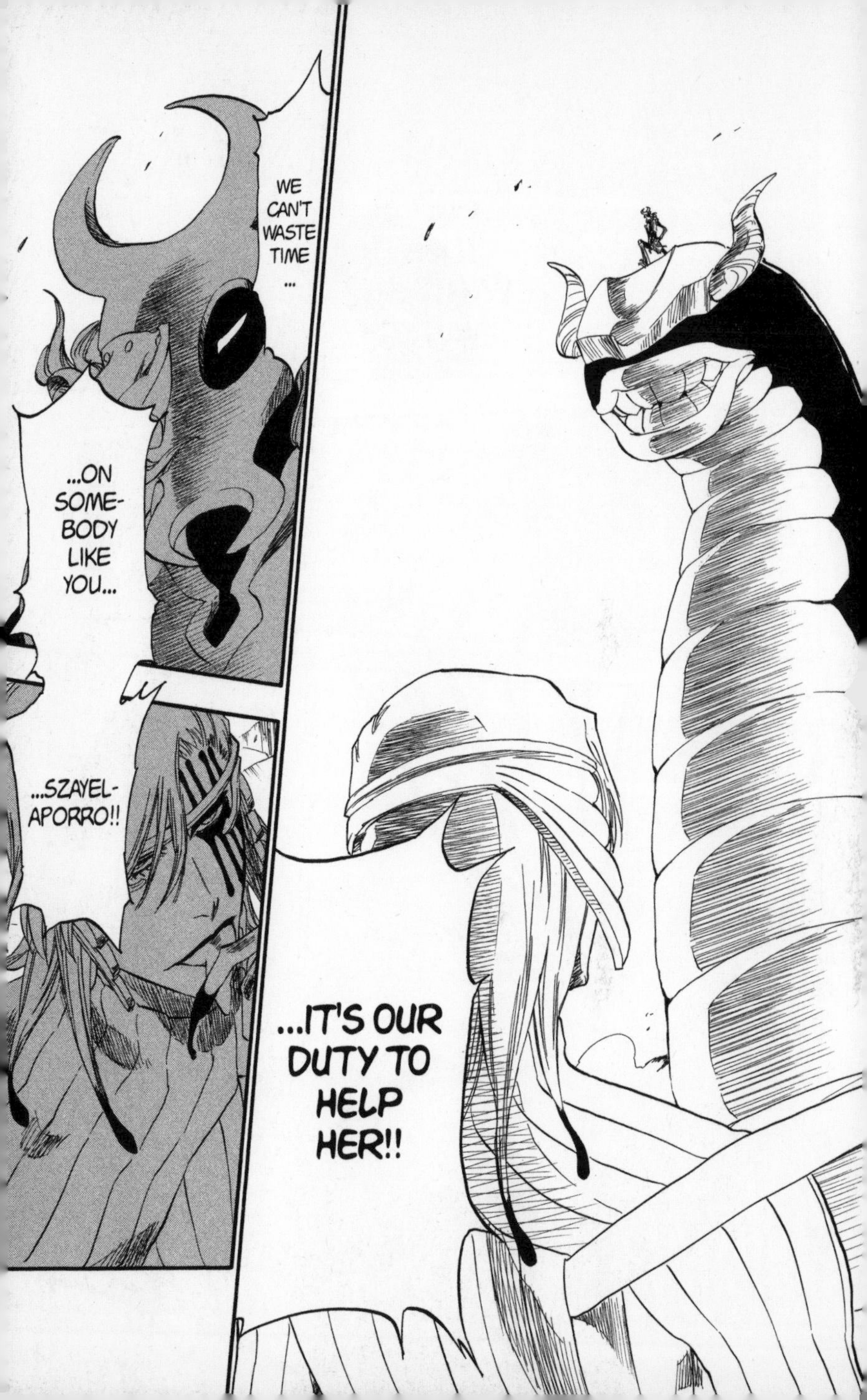
...IT'S OUR DUTY TO HELP HER!!
WE CAN'T WASTE TIME ...
...ON SOMEBODY LIKE YOU...
...SZAYEL-APORRO!!

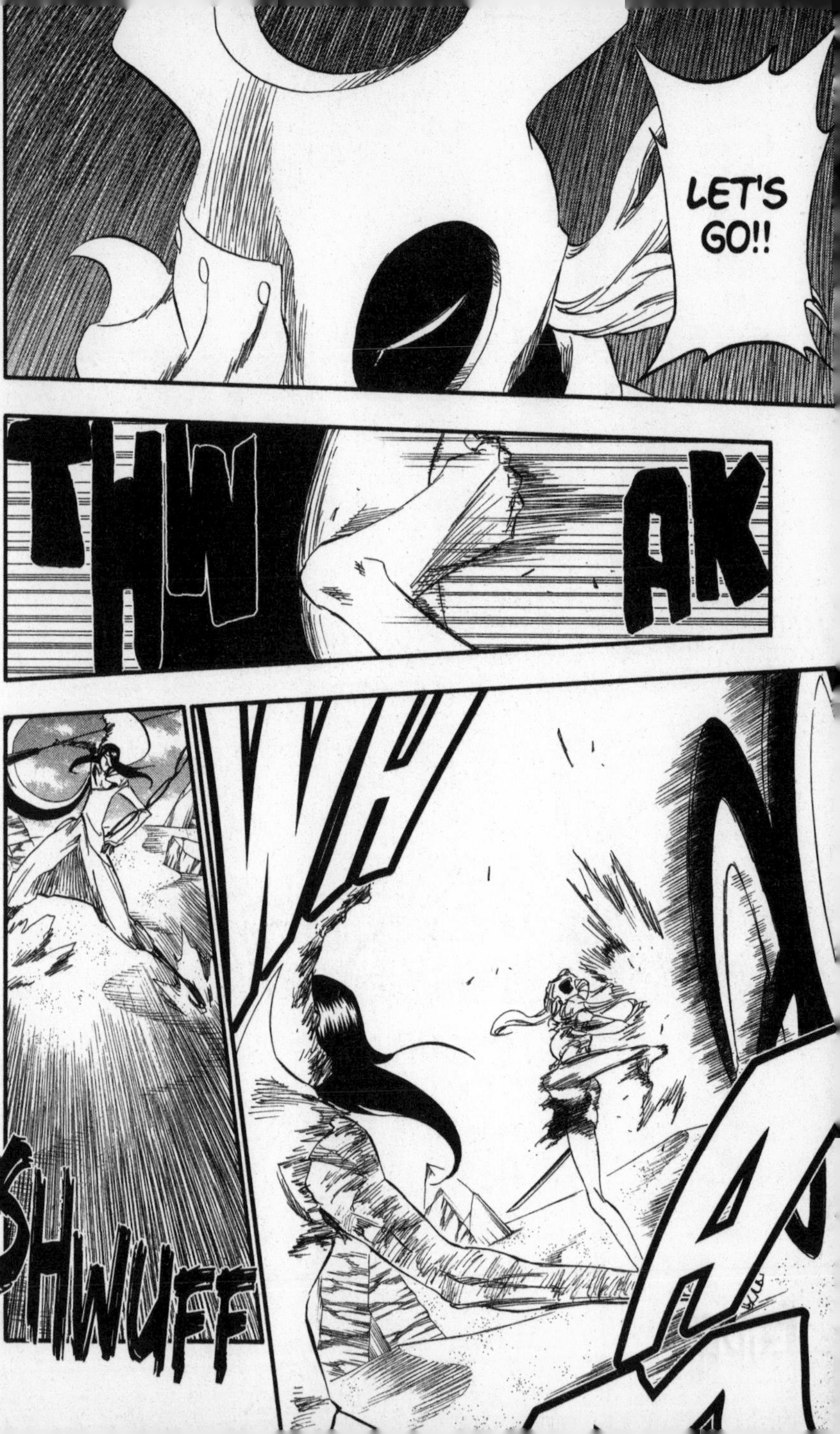
LET'S GO!!
THWAK
SHWUFF

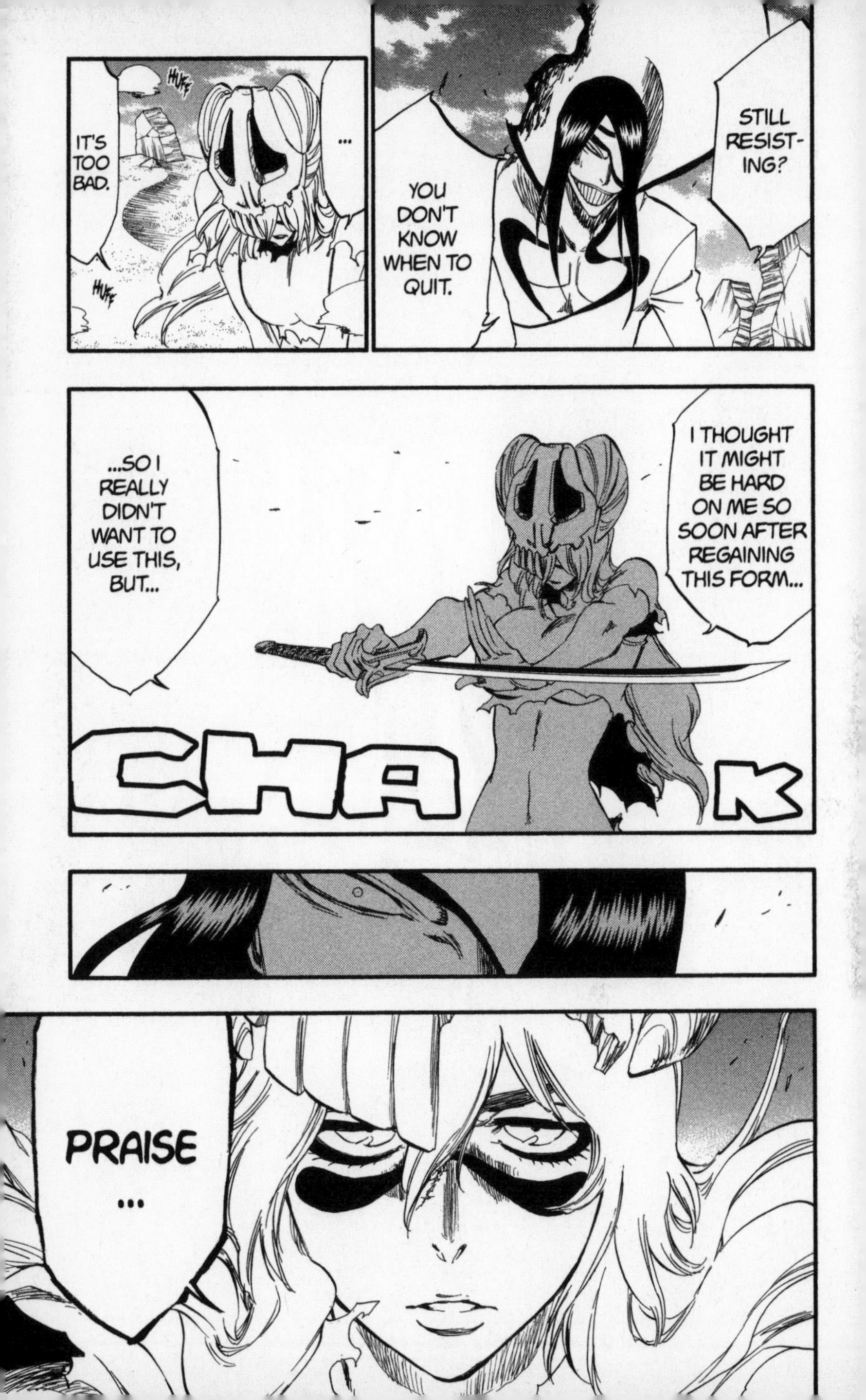
STILL RESIST- ING?
YOU DON'T KNOW WHEN TO QUIT.
...
HUFF
IT'S TOO BAD.
HUFF
I THOUGHT IT MIGHT BE HARD ON ME SO SOON AFTER REGAINING THIS FORM...
...SO I REALLY DIDN'T WANT TO USE THIS, BUT...
CHAK
PRAISE ...

CONTI
NUED
IN
BLEACH
34

MODEL SHEET FOR THE BLEACH TV SHOW 2 "THE BRAND-NEW COMMANDER"

THIS IS THE CHARACTER DESIGN
CHART FOR THE ORIGINAL STORY
"NEW CAPTAIN SHUSUKE AMAGAI"
IN THE TV ANIME VERSION OF *BLEACH*.
I WAS FORTUNATE ENOUGH TO BE INVOLVED
IN THE EARLY DEVELOPMENT OF THIS SERIES,
THOUGH NOT AS MUCH AS WITH THE MOVIE.
IT WAS A VERY VALUABLE EXPERIENCE.
THE SCRIPT IS STILL BEING CHECKED
AS I WRITE THIS, BUT I THINK
IT'S GOING TO BE GREAT.
I'M AS EAGER TO SEE IT AS ANYONE.

RURICHIYO KASUMIÔJI

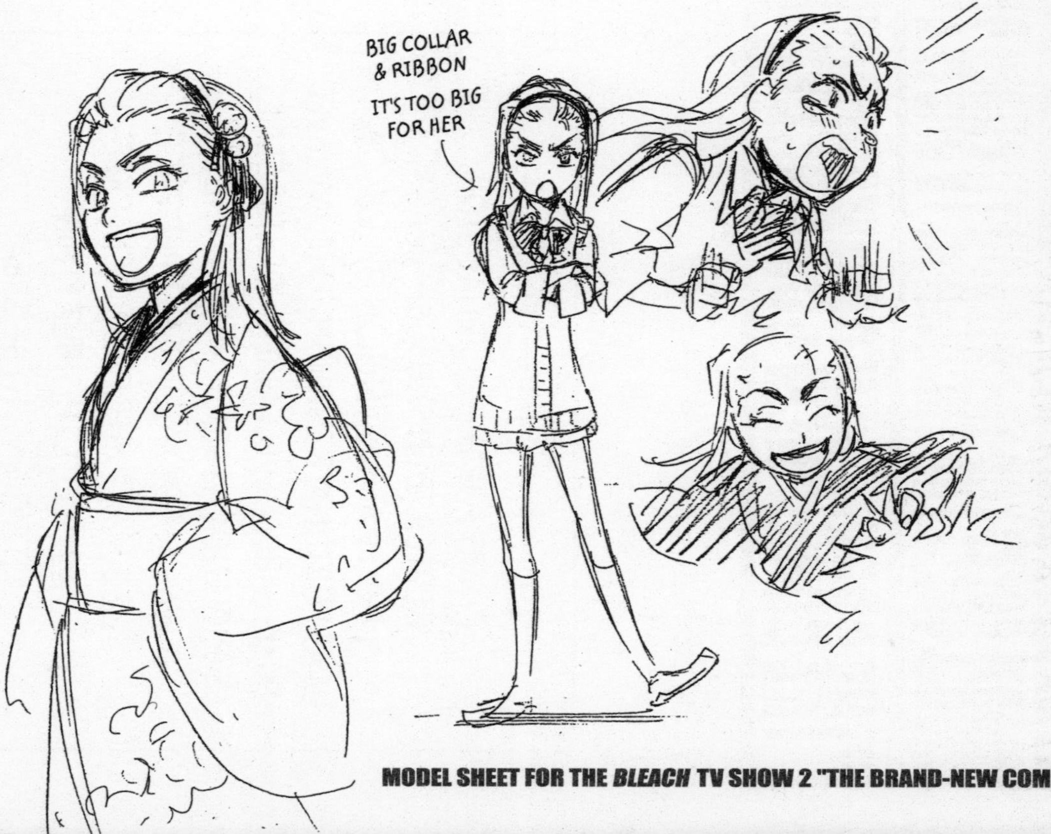
BIG COLLAR & RIBBON
IT'S TOO BIG FOR HER

MODEL SHEET FOR THE *BLEACH* TV SHOW 2 "THE BRAND-NEW COMMANDER"

KENRYÛ (RYÛSEI KENZAKI)

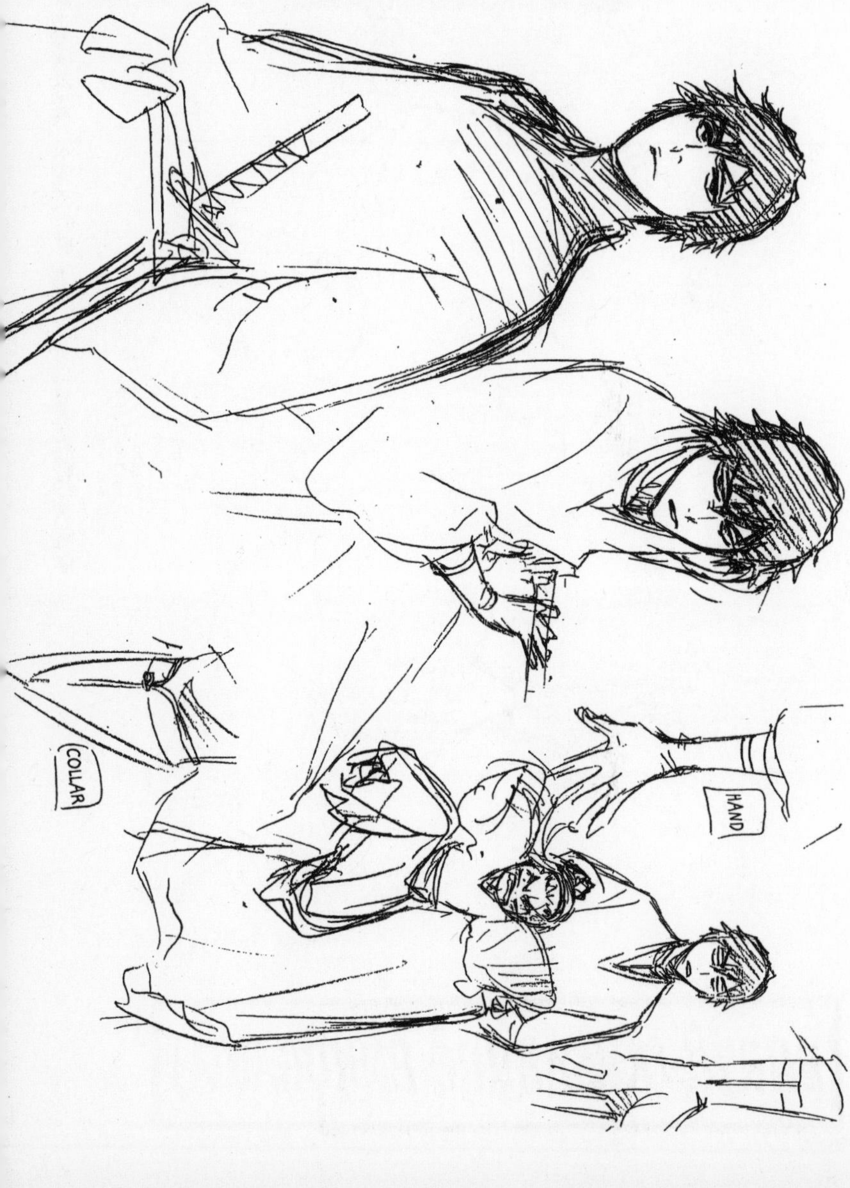
COLLAR
HAND

ENRYÛ (RUSABURÔ ENKÔGAWA)

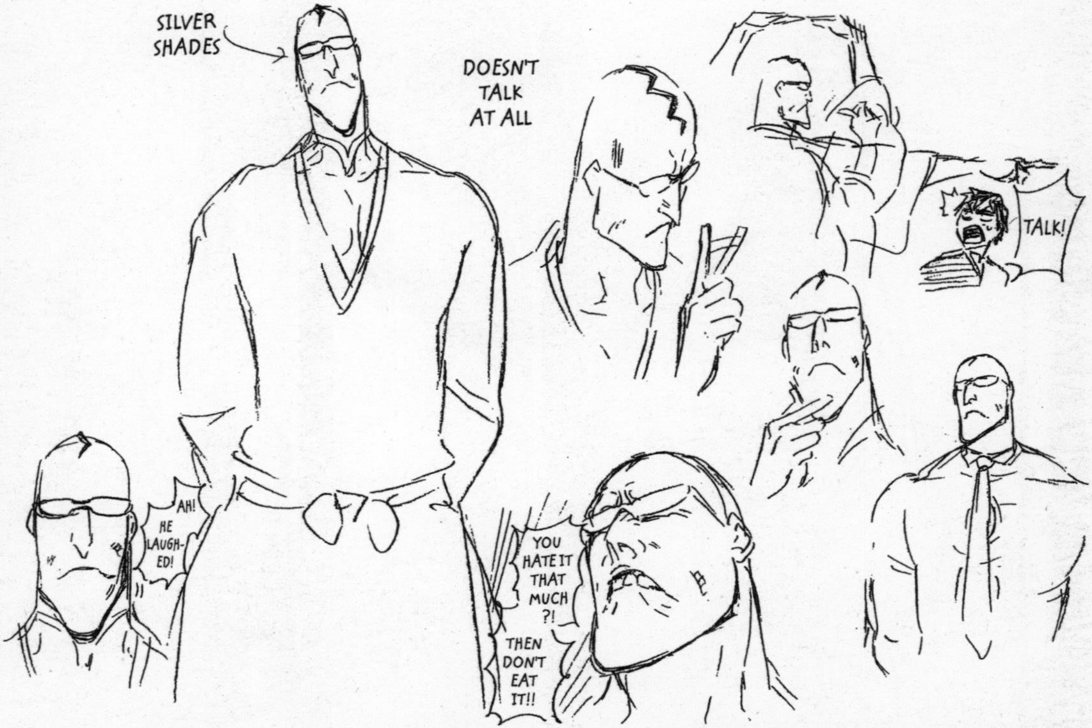
TALK!
DOESN'T TALK AT ALL
SILVER SHADES
YOU HATE IT THAT MUCH ?!
THEN DON'T EAT IT!!
AH! HE LAUGHED!

MODEL SHEET FOR THE *BLEACH* TV SHOW 2 "THE BRAND-NEW COMMANDER"

Next Volume Preview

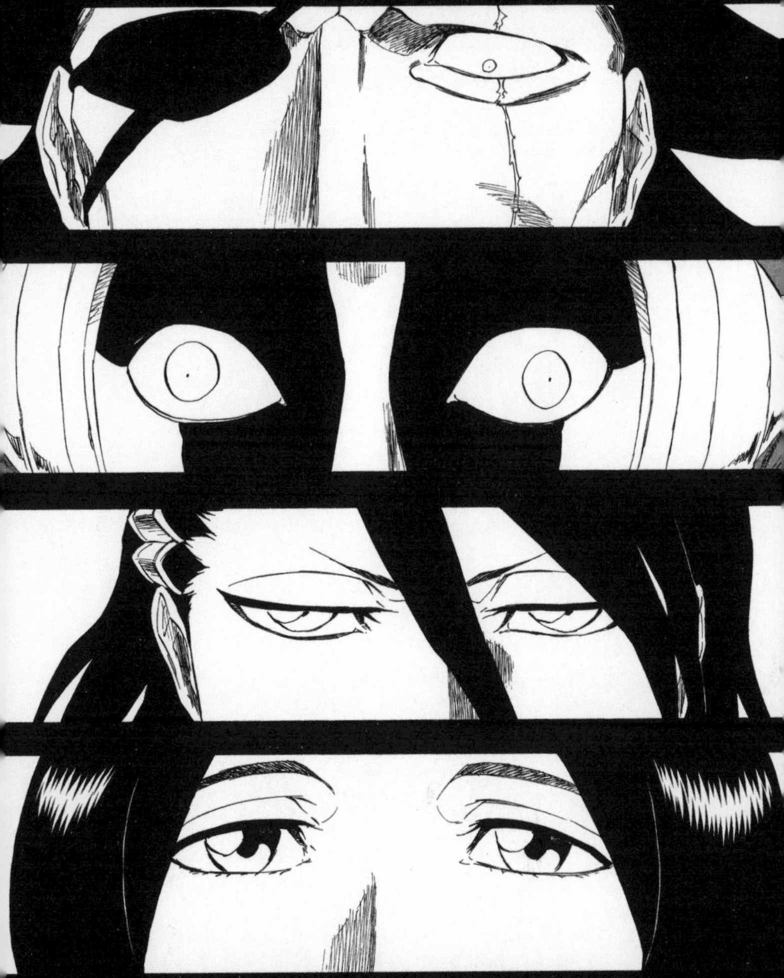

As the battle between Nel and Nnoitora quickly escalates, the Arrancars suddenly gain the upper hand. Just when the situation appears hopeless, help comes from an unexpected source.

Read it first in SHONEN JUMP magazine!

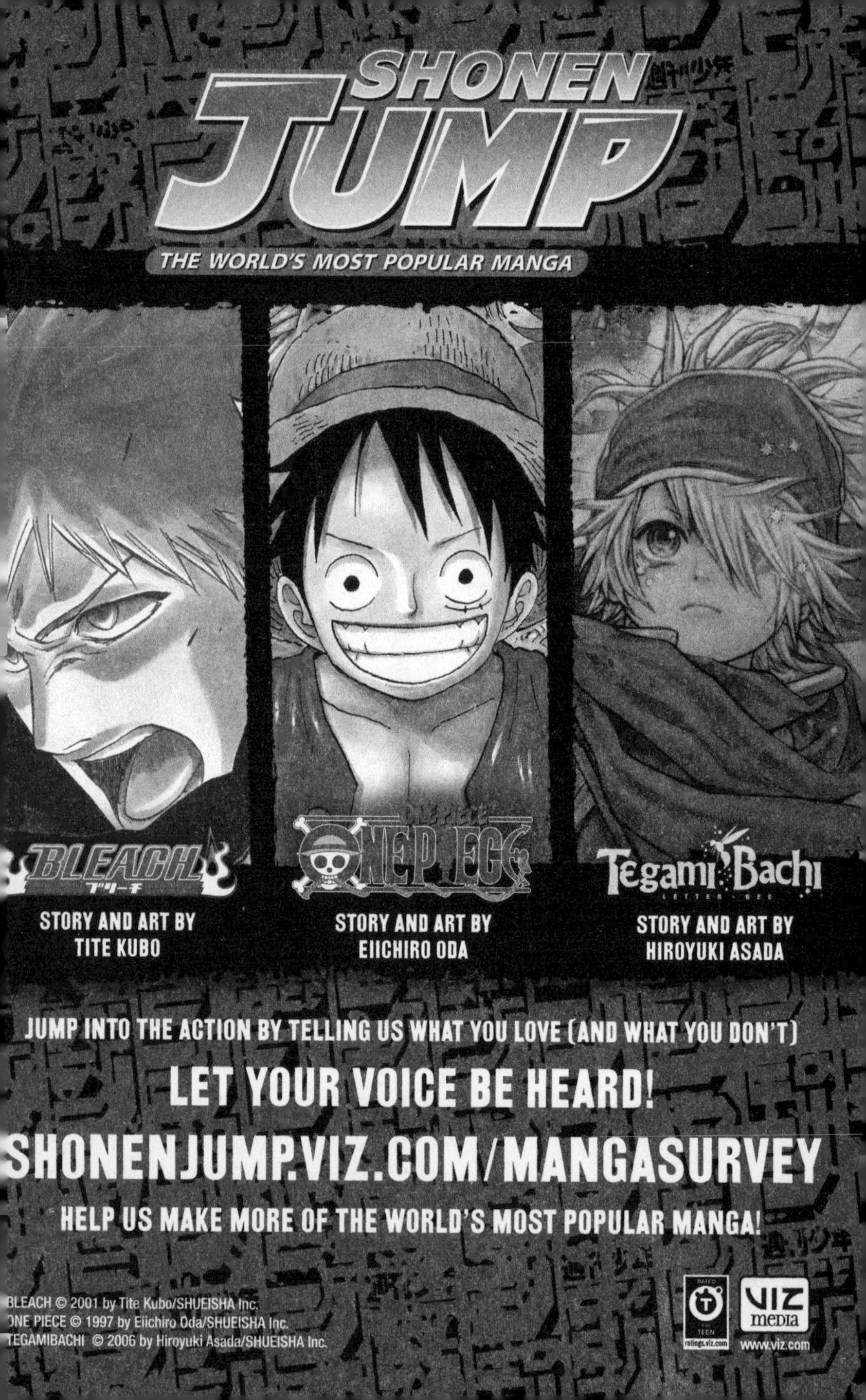

SHONEN JUMP

THE WORLD'S MOST POPULAR MANGA

BLEACH

STORY AND ART BY
TITE KUBO

ONE PIECE

STORY AND ART BY
EIICHIRO ODA

Tegami Bachi
LETTER BEE

STORY AND ART BY
HIROYUKI ASADA

JUMP INTO THE ACTION BY TELLING US WHAT YOU LOVE (AND WHAT YOU DON'T)

LET YOUR VOICE BE HEARD!

SHONENJUMP.VIZ.COM/MANGASURVEY

HELP US MAKE MORE OF THE WORLD'S MOST POPULAR MANGA!